D1535889

PREPARED UNDER THE DIRECTION
OF
PIERRE TISNÉ AND LAURENT TISNÉ
BY
FRANÇOISE OLIVIER-MICHEL
AND
CLAUDE GISLER

Translated by
Raymond Rudorff

First published in the U.S.A. 1966 by E.P. Dutton & Co., Inc.
English translation copyright, ©, 1966 by Editions Pierre Tisné.
Copyright, ©, 1964 by Editions Pierre Tisné.

First published in France 1964 by Editions Pierre Tisné, Paris,
under the title *Guide Artistique de la France.*
Reproduction rights reserved by S.P.A.D.E.M. and A.D.A.G.P.

Printed in France

GUIDE
TO THE
ART TREASURES
OF FRANCE

NEW YORK : E. P. DUTTON & CO., INC.

708.4
G946

THIS BOOK HAS BEEN PLANNED AS A GUIDE TO THE ARTS IN FRANCE. An ambitious aim perhaps - but a worth-while one.

The subject is immense, ranging as it does from some of the world's greatest masterpieces to countless minor but no less fascinating works. Faced by the diversity of an art ranging through time and space, from the Stone Age to the present day, from the prehistoric menhirs of Carnac to the great portals of Chartres cathedral and the terraces of Versailles, from the painted bulls of Lascaux to the paintings of Cézanne and Matisse, the publishers have had to contend with the almost insoluble problem of selection.

Some sacrifices were unfortunately inevitable. We have had to offer a choice of our own making to the reader — a thousand sites and three thousand pictures. But limited as it necessarily must be, such a selection is still enough to permit the reader and the traveller to make those comparisons which lead us to understand the unique spirit of a work, of a style. "... Every comparison of a great number of works in the same style creates the masterpieces of this style because it forces us to understand its particular meaning." (André Malraux, Voices of Silence).

Nothing essential has been omitted. Certain details have been mentioned to re-awake the interest of even the most blasé tourist in the best-known monuments and sites. We have made especial mention of museums and the finest treasures they contain. We have also mentioned other, humbler works and curiosities — an old wind-mill, popular images, a quaint wooden statue or an old pigeon-house — any of which may well tempt the more enterprising tourist to make a diversion from the beaten track.

The authors have remembered Henry Miller, that great friend of France, who said: "The sensitive observer, as he takes his daily stroll, will see these things not only with his own eyes, but with the eyes of those who went before, they will become a thousand times more precious, more meaningful to him, knowing how intently how lovingly and discerningly, other painters looked at them" (Remember to remember).

In this way we shall see Douai and Honfleur through the eyes of a Corot, Rouen as Monet saw it, the Aix of Cézanne and the Saint-Remy of Van Gogh's last paintings.

This guide is devoted to only man-made works and has avoided offering any purely "touristic information". You will find the painted bisons of Niaux in it but not the caves of Padirac, for example. The information we have given is intended to stimulate curiosity, to help the reader to discover and remember. The plan of the book is strictly geographical throughout: the only headings used are the names of provinces and towns. And yet... may we hope that the reader will find this book more than a mere illustrated atlas, but, in its way, a history in itself of those arts which are the glory of France?

Pierre Tisné

3053   THE ARKANSAS ARTS CENTER
MacArthur Park
Little Rock, Arkansas

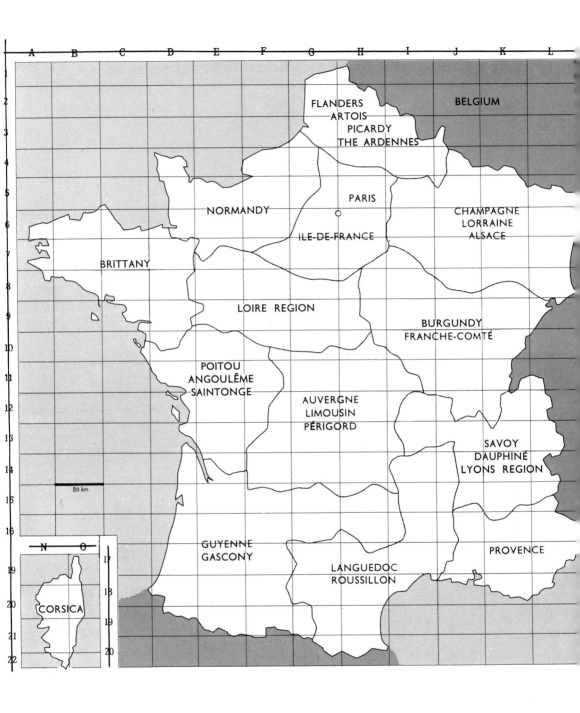

The book is divided into fourteen chapters which deal with Paris and thirteen regions of France, beginning with Flanders, Artois, Picardy and the Ardennes in the north and finishing with Provence and Corsica in the south.

In each chapter the towns are listed alphabetically and a reference is given to the map of the region at the beginning of the chapter.

CONTENTS

I

FLANDRE - ARTOIS - PICARDIE - ARDENNE

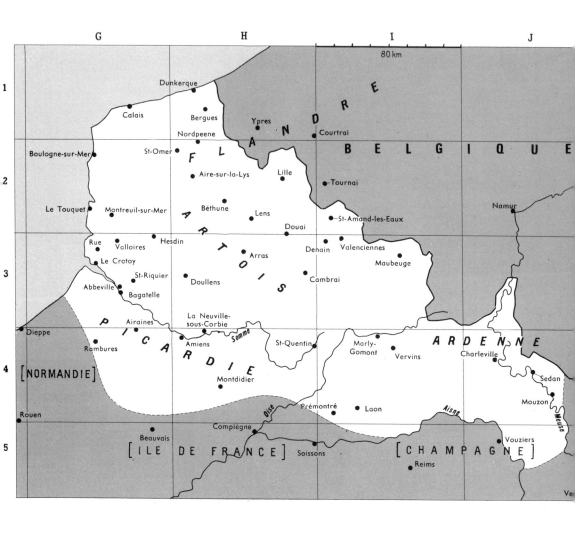

G   H   I   J

80 km

1

Dunkerque

Calais   Bergues   Ypres   F L A N D R E
         Nordpeene   Courtrai

Boulogne-sur-Mer   St-Omer   B E L G I Q U E

2   Aire-sur-la-Lys   Lille

Le Touquet   Tournai   Namur
        Montreuil-sur-Mer   Béthune   Lens   St-Amand-les-Eaux
                               Douai

Rue   Valloires Hesdin   Denain Valenciennes
Le Crotoy   Arras   Maubeuge
3 St-Riquier   Doullens   A R T O I S Cambrai
Abbeville Bagatelle

       Airaines   La Neuville-
               sous-Corbie
Dieppe   P I C A R D I E   Somme   A R D E N N E
  Rambures   Amiens   St-Quentin   Marly-
4 [NORMANDIE]   Gomont Vervins   Charleville
                Montdidier   Sedan
Rouen   Prémontré Laon   Mouzon
                Oise   Aisne   Meuse
      Beauvais   Compiègne   Vouziers
5 [ILE DE FRANCE] Soissons   [CHAMPAGNE]
                          Reims
                                      Ve

A French province in the reign of Philip Augustus, when the cathedral of Amiens was raised, then Burgundian territory until 1477 when it was restored to France in the reign of Louis XI. It is interesting to remember that Arras, only 120 miles from Paris, was only freed from Spanish domination in the mid-17th century and that Lille was only confirmed as a French possession in the early 18th century.

The varied history of the northern provinces of France has left its imprint on art and architecture where Flemish and French culture met, and Burgundian and Spanish styles mingled in the houses, belfries, public squares and town halls to give the region its rich and individual flavour.

Sancta mar-ia uirgo   robertus abbas
uirtutum r-egina   de claro mar-isco.

MAURICE QUENTIN DE LA TOUR (1704-1788) - SELF-PORTRAIT -
MUSÉE DE PICARDIE, AMIENS *(Giraudon)*

PAGE FROM THE MANUSCRIPT OF ROBERT DE BÉTHUNE - FRENCH
ART, 14TH CENTURY - BIBLIOTHÈQUE MUNICIPALE, SAINT-OMER
(Giraudon)

AIRAINES 2

AIRE-SUR-LA-LYS 3

ABBEVILLE 1

ABBEVILLE *Somme.* G 3.

Three portals with pointed gables are the main surviving
features of the early 16th-century collegiate church of Saint-
Vulfran which was badly damaged during the last war. The
church is a beautiful example of the Flamboyant Gothic style.
Other sights in the town include a few ancient houses, somewhat
lost among dull modern buildings, a respectable museum (portraits
by Largillière and Nattier) and a fine manuscript library.

1 Portals of the collegiate church of Saint-Vulfran, 1539.

AIRAINES *Somme.* G 4.

The baptismal font of the church of Notre-Dame (13th century)
is carved in the form of a sarcophagus, in a summary Romanesque
style. It is decorated with reliefs depicting sinners saved from
damnation by baptismal water.

2 Baptismal font of the church of Notre-Dame, 11th century.

AIRE-SUR-LA-LYS 4

AIRE-SUR-LA-LYS *Pas-de-Calais.* H 2.

The former collegiate church of Saint-Pierre is a fine example of
Renaissance Flamboyant art but the most charming monument
in the town is the Bailliage, a beautiful square stone and brick
house of the Renaissance period, with groin-vaulted arcades. The
façade is distinguished by a small bay-window, and the edifice
is crowned by a very elegant frieze with reliefs of reclining
female figures.

3 Tower of the collegiate church of Saint-Pierre, 175 feet in
height, 16th-18th centuries. 4 Le Bailliage, 1603, restored.

11

9

10

AMIENS *Somme.* H 4.

The cathedral of Amiens is one of the most beautiful in France. It was built over a relic of Saint-John the Baptist which had been brought to France from Constantinople in 1206. Although the edifice has miraculously escaped destruction in two world wars, the original design was somewhat altered by the 19th-century architect-restorer Viollet-le-Duc who filled the gap between the two towers with a Gothic-style ornamental arcade, known as the "Bell-ringers' Gallery". But his intervention should not be condemned too severely, for the original façade was somewhat unbalanced as a whole, the towers being disproportionately heavy and the gable over the centre portal lacking sufficient upward thrust. Despite all its faults, some of the greatest achievements of Gothic sculpture are to be seen on the façade, such as the famous quatrefoil frieze with its detailed images depicting scenes of 13th-century daily life, the Kings' Gallery (restored in the 19th century), and the lovely image of the "Beau Dieu" with its serene, peaceful expression. Although the "Golden Virgin" in the south portal is deservedly famous for its mischievous smile and coquettish attitude, it unfortunately became the prototype for countless uninspired imitations.

The cathedral interior is a miracle of clarity and architectural technique. The nave rises to a breath-taking height of 140 feet. The ground plan, with its main nave, two aisles, choir, ambulatory and seven side-chapels became the model for many later cathedrals. Of the rich interior decoration, we only have space to mention the remarkable choir with its hundred wooden stalls, all carved with representations of some four thousand different personages. Quite unique of its kind, this work was due to the generosity of a 15th-century patron of the arts, Adrien de Hérencourt. The most important building in Amiens apart from the cathedral is the Perret "tower" — a useless building which is only to be deplored since it spoils the silhouette of the cathedral and the city skyline when seen from the north. By contrast, the important Musée de Picardie has one of the richest collections of paintings in the whole of France, including a curious series of pictures of the Confraternity of the City, fine Spanish and Flemish paintings, and an important collection of French 18th-century paintings including the remarkable series of "Hunting scenes in nine foreign countries" painted for Versailles by Pater, Lancret, etc. The Museum also contains some important modern works and is decorated by a series of frescoes by Puvis de Chavannes.

1 Cathedral façade, 13th c. 2 Aerial view of the cathedral. 3 Kings' Gallery and the frieze. 4 The Beau Dieu. 5 The nave, looking towards the great rose-window. 6 The Golden Virgin, 14th c. 7 Choir-stalls, 16th c. 8 The month of March, detail from the base of the façade, 13th c.

MUSÉE DE PICARDIE

9 El Greco (1541-1624): Portrait of a man. 10 Mathieu Prieur (born c. 1552): Group-portrait of the Confraternity of Puy-Notre-Dame, 1603. 11 Maurice Quentin de la Tour (1704-1788): Self-portrait, pastel. 12 Fragonard (1732-1806): Washerwomen.

12

4

1

3

2

5

6

8

7

ARRAS 5

ARRAS 4

ARRAS *Pas-de-Calais.* H 3.

The imposing Town Hall with its belfry in the Grand-Place was rebuilt in the 20th century, but in the purest style of the Flemish Renaissance. It was built with the old bricks with such fidelity to the original design that it is hard to believe that it is in fact a reconstruction, and it is the finest example of Flemish architecture to be found in France. The palace of Saint-Vaast is a major example of monastic architecture in the 18th century and the pilastered portal is crowned by a beautiful armorial fronton flanked by two statues by Duthoit. The Palace is now the home of the museum which was installed in the rooms around the lovely cloisters and the courtyard with its well, and its treasures include the famous mask of a woman with a veiled chin, a funerary sculpture of the 14th century, the gold medal of the Beaurains Treasure (296 A.D.) and the reclining effigy of Gilles Lefrançois (15th c.) as well as fine French paintings of the 17th and 19th centuries.

1 Town hall and belfry, reconstructed in the 20th c. 2 Grand-Place, 17th c., restored. 3 Monumental portal of the Palais Saint-Vaast, 18th c.

PALAIS SAINT-VAAST

4 Anonymous portrait of Hieronymus Bosch, Codex of the Library. 5 Funerary mask, 14th c. 6 Claude Vignon (1593-1760): The Martyrdom of Saint Matthew.

BAGATELLE-EN-PICARDIE (1 mile from Abbeville) *Somme.* G 3.

The little château of Bagatelle-en-Picardie, built in white stone and brick, has survived intact, together with its furnishings, its interior decoration, and its gardens. It has been attributed to the architect Gabriel and was the "folly" of a rich carpet and textile manufacturer, but only in the sense of being built for recreation and rest in the country. The charming oval-shaped summer salon contains paintings attributed to Perronneau.

7 The château, attributed to Gabriel, 1754. 8 The Salon d'Été, 18th c.

BERGUES *Nord.* H 1.

The "Gendarmerie" or former Mont-de-Piété, was built by the engineer Cobergher in about 1629 as an imitation of the Italian palatial Renaissance style, and now contains a picture gallery.

9 The "Gendarmerie", c. 1629.

BOULOGNE-SUR-MER *Pas-de-Calais.* G 2.

The sea port was badly damaged during the last war and has been rebuilt. But the belfry, the ancient keep of the palace, and the Upper City with its thick walls, where the palace of the Counts of Boulogne once stood, have survived as witnesses to the city's dramatic history. Built in 1886, the basilica of Notre-Dame dominates the city and is crowned by a nobly-designed cupola. The gateway at the Porte Gayolle is part of the former fortified enceinte which surrounded the city on four sides, each side measuring more than 400 yards in length (13th century). The city's main pride is its invaluable collection of manuscripts and incunabula in its library, and the collection of Greek vases (the most important in France after that of the Louvre) in the city museum.

10 Belfry, lower storey, 13th c., upper storey 17th c.

MUNICIPAL LIBRARY

11 Page from the Psalter of Saint-Bertin, the Nativity, 11th c.

MUNICIPAL MUSEUM

12 Attic vase, 5th c. B.C. 13 Guérin (1774-1833): Portrait of the artist's daughter.

BOULOGNE 12

ARRAS 1

ARRAS 2

ARRAS 3

ARRAS 6

BAGATELLE 8

BERGUES 9

BAGATELLE 7

BOULOGNE 10

BOULOGNE 11

BOULOGNE 13

3053

THE ARKANSAS ARTS CENTER
MacArthur Park
Little Rock, Arkansas

CALAIS *Pas-de-Calais.* G 1.

The most famous monument in the city of Calais is the sculpture group of the Burghers who wished to give up their own lives in order to save the city from massacre after it had been captured in 1347 by Edward III of England. Sculpted by Rodin in 1895, the work is overwhelmingly realistic and is carved in a strictly sober style. The attitude of the figure of Eustache de Saint-Pierre, with his neck thrust forward, is typical of Rodin's style. The old watch tower is certainly the only remaining vestige of the old city and still towers above the modern harbour.

I Watch tower, 13th-19th c. 2 Auguste Rodin (1840-1917): Monument to the Burghers of Calais, 1895.

CAMBRAI *Nord.* H 3.

Most of the city's monuments have still survived. The most interesting for the visitor are the beautiful old house with its 16th-century wooden beams in the main square, and opposite, the lovely chapel of the Great Seminary, a former Jesuit church with a façade completed in 1695 and similar style to the Gesu in Rome. Its exuberant ornamentation is almost excessive but perfectly Italianate. The gateway of Notre-Dame was built in the early 18th century and is still Renaissance in spirit. Diamond-moulded façade is rhythmed by pilasters, Tuscan for the first storey, Doric for the upper storey.

3 Porte Notre-Dame, c. 1622. 4 Spanish house, 1595. 5 Façade of the chapel of the Great Seminary, 1695.

CHARLEVILLE *Ardennes.* J 4.

Arthur Rimbaud was born in Charleville at 14, rue Thiers, in 1854 and a room in the municipal museum is devoted to the memory of the "poète maudit". The Place Ducale is an admirable square built in stone and rose-coloured brick and is similar in style to its contemporary, the Place des Vosges, in Paris.

6 Place Ducale, 17th c. 7 Fantin-Latour (1836-1902): Portrait of Arthur Rimbaud, detail from the "Table corner", Louvre Museum.

CHARLEVILLE 7

DOUAI 10

DOUAI *Nord.* H 2.

Fought over by the French, the Flemish and the Spanish, Douai was the main university city of the north of France from the 16th century onwards until it was superseded by Lille in the 19th century. As in every town in the north of France, its lovely belfry was a symbol of communal liberty, and was built between 1386 and 1410. It rises above a town hall which is only partially historic (15th c.). The Charterhouse of Douai is a group of 17th-century buildings and contains the municipal museum. The most important works in the collections are: A *tripod of Bacchus*, engraved bronze of the Gallo-Roman period, *Polyptych of the Trinity*, painted by Jean Bellegambe for the Abbey of Anchin in about 1510, the *Portrait of a Venetian Woman* by Veronese, an *Apostle's Head* by Jordaens, and a *Forest Scene* by Ruysdaël.

8 J.-B.-C. Corot (1796-1875): the Belfry of Douai, Musée du Louvre, Paris.

MUSÉE MUNICIPAL

9 Jean Bellegambe (1470-1534): Polyptych of the Trinity, c. 1510. 10 Jordaens (1593-1678): Apostle's head. 11 Jean de Boulogne (1524-1608): Samson.

CALAIS 1

CALAIS 2

CAMBRAI 3

CAMBRAI 4

CAMBRAI 5

CHARLEVILLE 6

DOUAI 11

DOUAI 8

DOUAI 9

19

HESDIN *Pas-de-Calais.* G 3.

The little town of Hesdin was founded by Charles V in 1554 and two monuments of this age have still survived: the stone brattice of the town hall, richly sculpted, and the brick-built church with a porch decorated in a highly profane style.

1 Brattice of the Town Hall, 16th c. 2 Portal of the church, 1582.

LAON 9

LAON *Aisne.* I 4.

The cathedral of Laon was the first great French cathedral to be built (it was almost completed by the end of the 12th century). During the building, when a carriage was unable to ride up a steep slope, the driver was suddenly helped by a mysterious ox which disappeared as suddenly as it had come. The architect of the cathedral placed sixteen sculpted figures of oxen at the corners of the towers in order to depict the miracle and also, it would seem, to symbolise the restraint, order, and strength of the overall design of the cathedral. No other French cathedral has such a sober façade and such noble lofty towers. The nave rises in three storeys, two of them being Romanesque. Sculpted ornament is rare and almost exclusively vegetal in theme. The choir is nearly as long as the nave and originally seated eighty canons and is now partitioned-off by a sumptuous Louis XIV railing. The former bishop's palace which now contains the Law Court, dates from the 13th century and shelters the little two-storey chapel of Saint-Nicolas with its spiral staircase. The octagonal chapel of the Templars also dates from the 12th century; it is now an important museum of Graeco-Roman antiquities thanks to the La Charlonie collection, as well as being a museum of painting, in which works by the brothers Le Nain, who were born in Laon, are of particular interest. Other interesting parts of the city include the Ardon gateway (13th c.), the ramparts, the church of Saint-Martin (12th c.) and lastly the library which is one of the richest in the province, containing printed books, manuscripts, incunabula and an amusing Gallo-Roman mosaic showing Orpheus dressed in a Phrygian cap charming various animals.

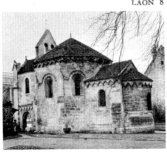

LAON 8

3 Façade of the cathedral of Notre-Dame, 12th c. 4 Detail of one of the towers, carved oxen, 12th c. 5 Elevation of the nave, 12th c. 6 Choir and great rose-window, 12th c. 7 Ancient episcopal palace, 13th c. 8 Templars' chapel, 12th c.

MUNICIPAL LIBRARY

9 Gallo-Roman mosaic: Orpheus charming animals. Found at Blanzy-les-Fismes.

HESDIN 1

HESDIN 2

LAON 3

LAON 4

LAON 5

LAON 6

LAON 7

LILLE *Nord.* H 2.

The famous two Goyas in the museum at Lille are enough in themselves to attract the art-lover to the former capital of Flanders, but the Palais des Beaux-Arts has many other treasures and probably the richest collection outside Paris. Apart from its great collection of Flemish masters — as would only be expected — 15th-century works, paintings by Rubens, Jordaens, and Dutch masters such as De Witte and Frans Hals, it contains representatives of the Italian school (Veronese), some German primitives, and finally, examples of the French school ranging from Poussin's *Moses saved from the waters* to Vieira da Silva. In addition, the Wicar collection, comprises some three thousand drawings, mostly of the Italian school. The city of Lille itself is almost entirely modern, with a high and noble belfry (a combined clock-tower and lighthouse) as befits a capital city. The noblest relic of past splendours is the old Stock Exchange (Bourse) built in brick and stone by Julien Destré in 1652. The Paris and Roubaix gateways, the citadel designed by Vauban, the chapel of the Rihour Palace, the Hospice Comtesse and finally the church of Saint-Maurice are all only of secondary interest.

I Courtyard of the old Bourse, 17th c.

PALAIS DES BEAUX-ARTS

2 Lille censer, gilded copper, 13th c. 3 Thierry Bouts (c. 1415-1475): Fountain of youth. 4 Petrus Christus (died 1472): Portrait of Philip the Good. 5 El Greco (1541-1624): The Agony in the Garden. 6 Rubens (1577-1640): Descent from the Cross. 7 Frans Hals (1580-1666): The Witch of Harlem, Hille Bobbe. 8 Van Dyck (1599-1641): Crucifixion. 9 Goya (1746-1828): The young women. 10 Goya: The old women. 11 Delacroix (1798-1863): Medea.

2

I

MARLY-GOMONT 12

MARLY-GOMONT *Aisne.* I 4.

The valley of the Oise lay in the path of invaders throughout the Middle Ages and is full of little fortified churches in which the population would take refuge in times of war. The churches of the Thiérarche are well known to archaeologists and because of their defensive towers have been compared to fortresses. Apart from the fortified church of Marly, those of Wimy, Prisces, Braye and Origny are also worth visiting.

12 The church of Marly, 15th c.

3

4

5

7

8

6

9

10

11

MONTREUIL-SUR-MER I

MONTREUIL-SUR-MER *Pas-de-Calais.* G 2.

The charm of this little town is due to its protective brick ramparts of the 13th, 16th and 17th centuries. The church of Saint-Saulve has kept its elegant 15th century portal (tower of the 12th c., lantern of the 18th c.).

1 Portal of the church of Saint-Saulve, 15th c.

MOUZON *Ardennes.* J 4.

The ancient Benedictine abbey church of Mouzon is almost entirely Gothic and the loveliest church in the Ardennes. In style it ressembles the cathedrals of Laon and Notre-Dame of Paris. The main portal is consecrated to the Virgin Mary and has a very beautiful tympanum divided in three registers.

2 Main portal of the abbey church of Notre-Dame, 13th c.

LA NEUVILLE-SOUS-CORBIE *Somme.* H 4.

The church of Notre-Dame de l'Assomption has a magnificent tympanum above the main portal with a high relief depicting Christ's entry into Jerusalem on Palm Sunday. This precious work is one of the few left in this part of France, so often ravaged by war.

3 Portal of the church of Notre-Dame de l'Assomption, 15th c.

NORDPEENE *Nord.* H 2.

The square monolithic basin and the pedestal of the baptismal font of the church at Nordpeene are sculpted in blue stone from Tournai. They are carved with low-relief sculptures depicting monsters and human-headed animals symbolising sins, washed away by baptism. This type of Romanesque baptismal font is frequently to be found in the north of France.

4 Baptismal font, stone (3 feet wide), 11th-12th c.

PRÉMONTRÉ *Aisne.* I 4.

The former abbey of the Premonstratensian Order is now a psychiatric hospital and comprises three main buildings. Each building has a rounded façade designed in the form of a mitre. The purity of the lines and the sobriety of the decoration make it a delight to the eye. The left wing has an imposing stone staircase.

5 Façade of the centre building of the former abbey 18th c.

RUE 9

RAMBURES (near Oisemont) *Somme.* G 4.

The tricolour château of Rambures, with its red brick foundations, its white curtains and grey slate roofs, is an impregnable fortress formed of four main towers connected by half-towers. The main edifice dates from the 15th century but the castle has been frequently restored by the descendants of the original occupants.

6 Château of Rambures, 15th c.

RUE *Somme.* G 3.

The chapel of the Saint-Esprit (Holy Ghost) is decorated in a Flamboyant Gothic style throughout and even the buttresses are covered with a profusion of decorative carving and clusters of statues which have unfortunately suffered from mutilation. The interior of the chapel has finely decorated vaults with elaborate pendants, delicately carved vestibule partitions and a beautiful stone retable. The whole structure dates from the 15th century as does the massive, square belfry of the Town Hall, crowned with four small corner towers added in the 19th century.

7 Façade of the chapel of the Holy Ghost, 15th c. 8 Portals of the chapel, 15th c. 9 Pendant knob-bosses, 15th c.

MOUZON 2

NORDPEENE 4

LA NEUVILLE-SOUS-CORBIE 3

RAMBURES 6

PRÉMONTRÉ 5

RUE 8

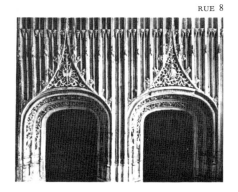

RUE 7

25

ST-AMAND-LES-EAUX I

SAINT-AMAND-LES-EAUX *Nord.* I 2.

All that remains of the ancient Benedictine abbey of Saint-Amand-les-Eaux which was destroyed in the Revolution is the tower. It is one of the architectural curiosities of the region and by its design and decoration might almost be part of an Indian temple. On closer inspection, it is seen to be composed of five storeys, in which the five orders — Tuscan, Doric, Ionic, Corinthian and Composite — have been superimposed in the manner of Vignola or Palladio. The sheriff's house in the town was built by the same architect, the abbot Nicolas du Bois.

I Tower of the old abbey, built by Nicolas du Bois, c. 1650.

SAINT-OMER *Pas-de-Calais.* H 2.

The abbey of Saint-Bertin was an ambitious construction which has been allowed to fall into ruin through neglect and downright stupidity. In 1947 its magnificent tower collapsed, as was only to be expected, and only a few ruins now survive. The main remaining glories of Saint-Omer are the cathedral Notre-Dame with its tower (15th century) and fine Renaissance tombs and the church of Saint-Denis, with its tower decorated with blind arcades. To-day, the town's main source of interest is the Sandelin museum, an old mansion containing four thousand ceramics, some fine paintings of the 18th century French school and a unique treasure: the *Foot of the Cross of Godefroy de Clair*, the sole surviving relic of the abbey of Saint-Bertin. The library is very rich in manuscripts and incunabula.

2 Ruins of the tower of Saint-Bertin, 15th c.

MUSÉE-HOTEL SANDELIN

3 Boilly (1761-1845): The jealous old man. 4 Pedestal of the cross from the abbey of Saint-Bertin, 12th c.

SAINT-QUENTIN *Aisne.* H 4.

It is in his "preparations", as the Goncourts called them, that the art of the painter Maurice Quentin de la Tour best expressed itself. The museum in his native town which is devoted to his work has a collection of ninety of his pastels, among which the most outstanding are *The abbé Hubert seated at his table*, *Mme de Pompadour*, *Mme de la Poupelinière*, *M. de Julienne* and *Mlle Marie Fel*.

The collegiate church has suffered greatly but has been restored. It is a beautiful structure, 400 feet in length, mostly dating from the 13th century and almost certainly designed by the famous Villard de Honnecourt. The bold elevation of the choir closely resembles that of Rheims cathedral. Double transept. The charming Town Hall in the Flamboyant Gothic style, completed in 1509, has a seven bay portico like that of Arras Town Hall.

ST-RIQUIER 8

5 Town Hall, 1509, restored in the 19th c. 6 Interior of the collegiate church, 14th c.

MUSÉE ANTOINE LÉCUYER

7 Maurice Quentin de la Tour (1704-1788): Mlle Marie Fel.

SAINT-RIQUIER *Somme.* G 3.

The Benedictine basilica of Saint-Riquier belongs to the second rank as regards size, for it is some 300 feet long (Amiens cathedral is 450 feet long). Part of the transept dates from the 13th century but the main structure dates from the 15th-16th c. and is built in the finest Flamboyant Gothic style. The church has an unusual front tower and a vast Lady Chapel. The portal is overburdened with finely carved sculptures which lack any logical arrangement. The Treasury of the town has a fine vaulted hall with remnants of paintings dating from 1528, illustrating the legend of the Three Dead Men and the Three Living Men.

8 The belfry, 13th-16th c. 9 West front of the abbey church, 15th-16th c. 10 The Tree of Jesse, tympanum of the portal of Saint-Riquier, 16th c.

ST-OMER 2

ST-OMER 3

ST-OMER 4

ST-QUENTIN 5

ST-RIQUIER 10

ST-QUENTIN 7

ST-QUENTIN 6

ST-RIQUIER 9

27

VALENCIENNES 1

VALENCIENNES 2

VALENCIENNES *Nord.* I 3.

The museum at Valenciennes contains the works of three artists born in the town: Pater, Watteau and Carpeaux. The Musée des Beaux-Arts also has a very fine collection of 18th-century drawings of the French school and almost three thousand of Carpeaux's drawings. Of monuments, the fine old Louis XV houses of the Place d'Armes and the so-called "Spanish" houses have all been destroyed. The church of Saint-Géry also suffered greatly: it is part 13th-century, part modern, but greatly damaged by a fire in 1958, in which it lost its famous carvings in the choir. They were a series of fifty-four oak panels carved with scenes from the life of Saint-Norbert (13th c.). Of the church of Saint-Nicolas, only the white marble Renaissance rood-screen has survived.

MUSÉE DES BEAUX-ARTS

1 Antoine Watteau (1684-1721): Portrait of Pater. 2 J.-B. Pater (1695-1736): Country amusements.

VALLOIRES *Somme.* G 3.

The former Cistercian abbey of Valloires was reconstructed in the 18th century and is now a preventorium. The chapel contains wood carvings in the German Baroque style carved by the famous Austrian sculptor Pfaffenhoffen. The choir railings are of remarkable workmanship and were the work of Jean Veyren. Also to be seen: the funerary effigies of the Count and Countess of Ponthieu, who founded the abbey in the 13th century.

3 Detail of the funerary effigy of the Count of Ponthieu, 13th c.

VOUZIERS *Ardennes.* J 5.

The portal of the church of Saint-Maurille was executed in 1534 by the fine Champenois sculptor Jehan Laruens: the design is sober and comprises three semi-circular portals separated by life-size statues of saints.

4 Façade of the church of Saint-Morille, by Jehan Laruens, 16th c.

VOUZIERS 4 VALLOIRES 3

II

NORMANDIE

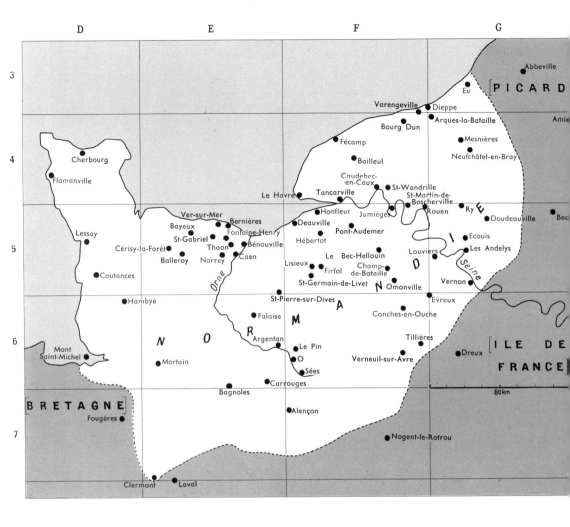

HIC:NVNTIATVM:EST: HIC: DOMVS:IN

WILLELM° DE:HAROLD: CEN:DITVR:

JUG IN ROUEN FAIENCE, 17TH C., MUSÉE DU LOUVRE, PARIS
(*Connaissance des Arts - Ionesco*)

BAYEUX EMBROIDERY, DETAIL, 11TH C., MUSÉE DE LA REINE
MATHILDE, BAYEUX (*Hélène Jeanbrau*)

Invaders from the sea came to fight for the fertile fields of Normandy against local lords in their massive fortresses. The monasteries of Jumièges, Lessay, Saint-Wandrille are among the most impressive examples of Cistercian art in France and cities such as Caen and Rouen are among the most glorious centres of Norman Gothic art. It is also a province of rich rolling fields, countless country houses, châteaux and manors. The cloudy landscapes attracted painters through the ages, especially the Impressionists who made it their chosen domain.

ALENÇON 2

ARGENTAN 5

ALENÇON *Orne.* F 7.

A lace factory was founded at Alençon in 1665, to imitate and compete with the Venetian lace industry. Alençon lace is characterised by a light background, geometrical motifs, and light flower and bouquet patterns. The church of Notre-Dame has a curious three-sided Flamboyant Gothic porch, with abundant decoration, gables and bell-turrets in the upper storeys. The stained-glass windows in the nave (1530) are of exceptional quality.

1 Church of Notre-Dame, Jean Lemoine, 1506. 2 Alençon point-lace, 17th c., Musée de peinture.

LES ANDELYS *Eure.* G 5.

Standing on the steep chalk cliffs overlooking the meandering Seine at Les Andelys are the ruins of the most imposing of all fortresses built in France in the late 12th century. Built in 1196, the fortress of Château-Gaillard kept the armies of Philip Augustus at bay in 1204. A little distance away from the fortress, the village of Grand-Andely, with a lovely 15th-century church, completed in the 16th c., further embellished in the 17th c., and offering a striking contrast between the Flamboyant Gothic and the Renaissance styles. Very fine stained-glass windows and a Renaissance organ-case. The church of Saint-Sauveur in Petit-Andely dates from the 12th century.

3 Chateau-Gaillard, late 12th c. 4 Church of Notre-Dame, Grand-Andely, 15th-17th c.

ARGENTAN *Orne.* E 6.

The town of Argentan was very badly damaged during the last war but its two churches of Saint-Germain and Saint-Martin have been largely restored. The first, built between the 15th and 17th c. has the peculiarity of having transepts which end in apses. The façade on the rue Saint-Germain is a fine example of the Flamboyant Gothic style.

5 The church of Saint-Germain, 15th c.

ARQUES-LA-BATAILLE *Seine-Maritime.* G 4.

The church of Notre-Dame was completed in 1515 during the reign of Henri III, and further embellished during the 17th century by the addition of a fine rood-screen in stone with fluted columns. The name of the village is derived from the battle fought by Henri IV against the Duke of Mayenne in 1589.

6 Rood-screen, church of Notre-Dame, 17th c.

BAILLEUL (near Angerville) *Seine-Maritime.* F 4.

The early Renaissance château of Bailleul is particularly interesting because of its two nearly blind side wings, and its other façades which are richly decorated with three superimposed orders. The building is crowned with high pyramidal roofs and imposing chimney stacks. It is one of the most attractive châteaux in Normandy.

7 Wing of the château, 16th c. 8 Main front.

BALLEROY *Calvados.* E 5.

At the end of the imposing main street in the village rise the high slate roofs of the château of Balleroy. Built in a severely restrained style of violet schist and white stone; independent roofs, all different in height. The architecture is attributed to François Mansart, and the château is decorated with painted ceilings by Lemoyne and paintings by Mignard. Sumptuous decoration; beautiful trimmed box-trees in the gardens facing the façade.

9 Façade of the château, seen from the main courtyard, 1636. 10 Drawing room, 17th c.

ALENÇON 1

LES ANDELYS 3

LES ANDELYS 4

ARQUES-LA-BATAILLE 6

BAILLEUL 7

BALLEROY 9

BALLEROY 10

BAILLEUL 8

BAYEUX 7

LE BEC-HELLOUIN 8

BERNIÈRES 11

BAYEUX *Calvados*. E 5.

The famous Bayeux 'tapestry', embroidered in wool on linen, and some 215 feet long, is known in French by the traditional but inaccurate name of 'Queen Mathilde's Tapestry'. It can be seen in the museum of Bayeux. Quite unique of its kind, this Romanesque embroidery is a kind of cartoon-strip with captions and relates the story of the Conquest of England by William the Conqueror, depicting the costumes, weapons, and ships of the 11th century in remarkable detail. Although Mathilde was the wife of William the Conqueror there is no basis whatsoever for believing that it was by her hand, and it is generally believed to have been commissioned in England as an ornament for the apse of Bayeux cathedral. The cathedral itself is distinguished by the one-piece roof covering the ambulatory and side chapels, the lantern-tower of the 15th century (unfortunately crowned in the 19th c.) and above all by the great bays running down the nave, decorated in typical Norman Romanesque style (finely sculpted corner-stones and ornamental arcades) and the Gothic aisles. Despite the importance of the tapestry and the cathedral, mention must be made of the old mansions and houses of this attractive town: many still have wooden beams and sculpted pillars; several mansions in the classical style.

1 Cathedral of Notre-Dame, 13th c. 2 Romanesque nave of the cathedral, 12th and 13th c. 3 The apse of the cathedral 13th c. 4 The crypt, 11th c. 5 Detail of the great bays in the nave, 12th c. 6 15th-c. house, corner of rue Saint-Martin and rue des Cuisiniers. 7 Bayeux 'Tapestry', known as Queen Mathilde's Tapestry (250 feet × 20 inches), detail, late 11th c., Bayeux Museum.

LE BEC-HELLOUIN *Eure*. F 5.

The old abbey of Le Bec-Hellouin has recently been restored to the Benedictine order and is now used for worship again. The bell-tower (now without its spire), the vaulted refectory and the monastery buildings of the 17th and 18th centuries are all that remain of the old abbey.

8 Tour Saint-Nicolas, 1467.

BÉNOUVILLE *Calvados*. E 5.

The château of Bénouville is one of the few surviving creations of Ledoux, the architect of Salines de Chaux (q.v. Arc-et-Senans) and is a fine example of his audacious style tempered by Louis XVI classicism.

9 The château, by C.-N. Ledoux (1736-1806), 18th c. 10 Main staircase.

BERNIÈRES-SUR-MER *Calvados*. E 5.

The churches of Bernières and Langrune are flanked with superb spires with bell-turrets in a sober Norman Gothic style, modelled upon the towers of the church of Saint-Étienne at Caen and that of Coutances (q.v.).

11 Spire of the church at Bernières, 210 feet high, 13th c.

BAYEUX I

BAYEUX 2

BAYEUX 3

BAYEUX 4

BAYEUX 5

BAYEUX 6

BÉNOUVILLE 10

BÉNOUVILLE 9

BOURG-DUN I

BOURG-DUN *Seine-Maritime*. F 4.

The church is built in a very composite style for although begun in the 11th c. it was only completed in the 16th c. Its square tower is Gothic, the south arm of the transept is Flamboyant (vaults with pendant knob-bosses) and the baptismal font is Renaissance.

1 Bas-relief, detail of baptismal font, 16th c.

CAEN *Calvados*. E 5.

Although terribly damaged during the war, Caen has managed to keep its churches intact. Thanks to well thought-out rebuilding of the residential quarters, the churches (restored and lovelier than ever) can now be seen to their best advantage. Standing in the very heart of the university city, the castle-citadel built by William the Conqueror in the 11th century has been disengaged from the ruins that surrounded it at the end of the war when many of the city's inhabitants probably saw it for the first time. In order to expiate their sins, William and his wife Mathilde founded two abbeys at Caen. The Abbaye aux Hommes with its enormous church of Saint-Étienne (350 feet long) is built in the Romanesque and Gothic styles. The façade with twin towers is an example of Norman architecture at its finest. The Abbaye aux Dames has a church dedicated to the Holy Trinity; entirely Romanesque in period except for the crowning of the two massive towers which was completed in the 17th century. Other churches which should be visited include the Vieux Saint-Nicolas, a now unused Romanesque edifice with a charming cemetery, the 15th-century Vieux Saint-Étienne, the Gothic and Renaissance Saint-Sauveur, and finally the lovely church of Saint-Pierre with a perfectly restored, truncated, white tower and an outstanding Renaissance apse. Although the war spared all these churches, it was disastrous for other old buildings, for only the Hôtel de Valois d'Escoville, completed in 1540, is now worth mentioning.

2 Abbaye aux Hommes, church of Saint-Étienne, 12th-13th c. 3 Abbaye aux Dames, church of the Trinity, 12th c. 4 Nave of the Abbaye aux Dames. 5 Church of Saint-Pierre, 14th-16th c. 6 Choir of the church of Saint-Pierre. 7 Church of Vieux Saint-Nicolas, 12th c. 8 Hôtel de Valois d'Escoville, 1540. 9 Tower of the Gens d'Armes, 14th-15th c.

CARROUGES 10

CARROUGES *Orne*. E 6.

The château of Carrouges is peculiar in having a lower storey reserved for commoners, and a richly furnished upper storey for noble occupants. The various buildings which date from the Middle Ages to the 17th century were all added by successive generations of the same family. The elegant 16th-century lodge by the entrance is in contrast with the thickset mass of the château itself. Particularly worth noting is the fine stone balustrade running around the dry moats.

10 The château, 15th-17th c.

CAUDEBEC-EN-CAUX II

CAUDEBEC-EN-CAUX *Seine-Maritime*. F 4.

When bombs fell around the church of Notre-Dame at Caudebec in June 1940, the heat from the fires was so great that the bells began to melt and started pealing by themselves. The whole of the church is in the Flamboyant Gothic style and has always attracted connoisseurs. Some old houses have still survived (in one, now destroyed, a river used to flow through the kitchen) along the narrow little streets by the Seine, near Villequier where Victor Hugo's daughter was drowned.

11 Façade of the church of Notre-Dame, 14th-16th c.

CAEN 3

CAEN 2

CAEN 4

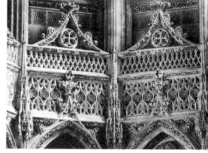

CAEN 6

CAEN 7

CAEN 5

CAEN 8

CAEN 9

CÉRISY-LA-FORÊT *Manche.* E 5.

The most beautiful Romanesque abbey church in Normandy has survived with only three of its original eight bays, which give it a particularly massive appearance. Its noble three-storeyed elevation is majestic. Inside, early 15th-century choir-stalls.

1 Abbey church, 11th-12th c., altered in the 18th c.

CHAMP-DE-BATAILLE (near Sainte-Opportune-du-Bosc) *Eure.* F 5.

We can no longer say for certain to just which battle between a Norman baron and his vassals the château owes its name. We should first admire its broken pediment portico, surmounted with statues like some triumphal arch. The château was completed in 1701 by Alexandre de Créqui and consists of two wings, facing each other, each 250 feet in length. One wing was reserved for common tenants, the other for nobles. Space and sweeping horizontal lines are the main features of the design of this admirable château which was built in brick despite all its Louis XIV aspect.

2 South portico with broken pediment, 1701. 3 View from the courtyard.

CLERMONT (near Laval) *Mayenne.* E 7.

Clermont was one of the great Cistercian abbeys and sister to that at Clairvaux. It was founded by Saint-Bernard with the aid of the Counts of Laval whose tomb has been discovered, and once counted two hundred monks as its tenants. It was condemned to be destroyed and then became used as farm stables and fell into great neglect, but was saved in 1935 when two artists acquired the property. Part of the roof has been restored by the École des Beaux-Arts in Paris, and restoration is being continued by a team of young artists, mostly volunteers. The Romanesque portal is one of the purest stylistically in the whole province.

CLERMONT 4

4 Romanesque portal of the abbey, 12th c.

CONCHES-EN-OUCHE *Eure.* F 6.

Related by its name and its relics to the church of Sainte-Foy de Conques (q.v.), the church of Sainte-Foy de Conches is lit inside by splendid Renaissance stained-glass windows inspired by Dürer's works. An alabaster trytych of the 15th century of English origin depicts scenes from the Passion in minute detail.

5 Choir and stained-glass windows of the church of Sainte-Foy, 15th-16th c. 6 Alabaster tryptych, 15th c., English art.

COUTANCES *Manche.* D 5.

The cathedral of Notre-Dame at Coutances is a fine example of Gothic style at its purest characterised by certain Norman elements. Its front towers, its superb lantern-tower and apse with flying buttresses in tiers make it one of the greatest masterpieces of Norman art. The cathedral was built in the 13th century over an earlier Romanesque structure. The vertical lines of the façade are repeated in the interior by the vast nave with its hundred clusters of colonnettes. The Renaissance period church of Saint-Pierre also possesses a fine lantern-tower. The town was rebuilt after the war by Arretche, the architect of Saint-Malo.

DIEPPE 10

7 Façade of the cathedral of Notre-Dame, 13th c. 8 The apse. 9 The nave.

DIEPPE *Seine-Maritime.* G 3.

Ship-owners, sailors and ivory-carvers have contributed to the fame of the town which also became renowned as a sea-side resort after first being made fashionable by the Duchess of Berry. The church of Saint-Jacques in a pure Flamboyant style, the 17th-century church of Saint-Rémy and the museum of ivory are the main witnesses to the city's past.

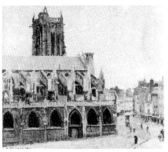

10 Pissarro (1830-1903): Church of Saint-Jacques, Louvre Museum.

CÉRISY-LA-FORÊT 1

CHAMP-DE-BATAILLE 2

CHAMP-DE-BATAILLE 3

CONCHES-EN-OUCHE 5

COUTANCES 7

CONCHES-EN-OUCHE 6

COUTANCES 9

COUTANCES 8

DOUDEAUVILLE (near Étrepagny) *Seine-Maritime.* G 5.

The wooden vaulting of some of the churches in the region seems to have been built by boat-builders since it resembles the hull of a boat. The crossing over the choir is a very fine example of this art.

1 Timber-vaulting in the church of Doudeauville, 16th c.

ÉCOUIS *Eure.* G 5.

Although the Gothic church of Écouis is of negligeable importance it was transformed into a treasure house by Enguerrand de Marigny, Superintendant of Finances during the reign of Philip the Handsome, for he embellished it with a number of beautiful 14th-century statues.

2 Saint Mary the Egyptian, church of Notre-Dame, early 14th c.
3 Saint Anne.

EU *Seine-Maritime.* G 3.

Normandy is so rich in Gothic churches that for once we may neglect the typically Norman Gothic church of Saint-Laurent, lovely as it is, and restored by Viollet-le-Duc, in favour of the richer and more interesting college. It was founded by Catherine of Clèves in 1532 and contains a lovely chapel with a majestic doorway in Louis XIII style. Inside the chapel, the marble tombs of the Duke and Duchess of Guise are particularly worth noting. They were carved in the 17th century and have sometimes been attributed to Italian artists, sometimes to Germain Pilon or Simon Guillain.

4 Doorway of the college chapel, 1624. 5 Tomb of the Duke of Guise, Henri le Balafré, 17th c. 6 Tomb of the Duchess of Guise, Catherine of Clèves, 17th c.

ÉVREUX 9

ÉVREUX *Eure.* G 6.

The architecture of Évreux cathedral has undergone many stylistic changes (from the 13th to 17th c.) and suffered from many wars. Its 14th and 15th-century stained glass is particularly worth noting, especially in the Lady Chapel. The ambulatory is curtained-off by carved wooden screens of the Renaissance period, which show a particularly high degree of inspiration. The clock-tower of the abbey church of Saint-Taurin has still survived: it is a 15th-century belfry. Inside the church, a 13th-century reliquary (gilt, silver, and enamels) offered by Saint-Louis: it is certainly one of the finest specimens of the Gothic silversmith's art in France.

7 Reliquary of Saint-Taurin, 13th c., church of Saint-Taurin.
8 Pierre d'Évreux presented to the Virgin, stained-glass window of the cathedral, 14th c. 9 Belfry, 15th c. 10 Screen of the cathedral ambulatory, 16th c.

FALAISE 11

FALAISE *Calvados.* E 6.

It was at Falaise that William the Conqueror was born in 1027, the son of Robert le Diable and a tanner's daughter. The high rectangular keep with its Romanesque windows and the Talbot tower with its twelve-feet-thick walls were built after his lifetime. In the town, the beautiful Renaissance church of the Trinity should be seen.

11 Keep and Talbot tower, 12th and 15th c.

DOUDEAUVILLE 1

ÉCOUIS 3

ÉCOUIS 2

EU 5

EU 6

EU 4

ÉVREUX 10

ÉVREUX 7

ÉVREUX 8

43

FÉCAMP *Seine-Maritime*. F 4.

The church of the Trinity at Fécamp formerly belonged to an abbey. With its lantern-tower nearly as high as that of Notre-Dame in Paris, and equally long nave, it is one of the largest Gothic churches in the whole of France. The exterior was built during different periods but has kept a unity of style. The immense interior which is largely lit by the lantern-tower (square in design like that at Langrune) contains several important works, including the *Dormition of the Virgin* in the right arm of the transept, a fine late 15th-c. group sculpture, and a stone Renaissance-style screen dating from about 1510.

1 Lantern-tower of the church of the Trinity, 13th c.

FIRFOL *Calvados*. F 5.

Old manor-houses, cottages and picturesque farms lie among the lush fields and apple orchards of Normandy. The thatched roofs and oak-beamed buildings of the village of Firfol are part of the Norman landscape and have equal charm.

2 The manor house, 16th c.

FIRFOL 2

FLAMANVILLE *Manche*. D 4.

The château of Flamanville is built with granite from the nearby cliffs overlooking the sea. The château is composed of a series of buildings grouped around a fine courtyard, and is built in classical Louis XIV style. The entrance is surmounted by a curving pediment with a bell-turret with a clock.

3 The château of Flamanville, 1658.

FONTAINE-HENRY *Calvados*. E 5.

The château of Fontaine-Henry stands in the midst of a great, leafy park. Its most striking characteristic is its immense roof which is higher than the actual building it covers. The building was first built in the Gothic style then decorated in early and classical Renaissance styles. The building was continued by several generations of the Harcourt family in the 15th and 16th centuries and still belongs to their descendants.

4 The château of Fontaine-Henry, 15th-16th c. 5 Courtyard and well, Renaissance period.

HAMBYE *Manche*. D 6.

The highly picturesque and photogenic ruins of the former abbey of Hambye mainly consist of the church with its Romanesque nave (early 13th c.) and the Gothic choir (late 13th c.) lit by a majestic lantern-tower.

6 Ruins of the abbey church of Hamby, 13th c.

HAMBYE 6

LE HAVRE *Seine-Maritime*. F 4.

The great port of Le Havre is entirely modern in its architecture and was greatly rebuilt after the last war. Its fine museum is built in the same modern spirit as the port. A monumental sculpture by Adam stands outside it on the terrace. Inside, one of the chief attractions is the large collection of works by Eugène Boudin who was born at Honfleur, and which includes 140 sketches and 8 paintings. The modern church of Saint-Joseph has been built in reinforced concrete, on a design by Joseph Perret, and its tower soars to a height of 330 feet.

7 The Musée des Beaux-Arts, by Lagneau, Audiguier and Jankovic, 1961, sculpture by Adam. 8 A room in the museum. 9 Eugène Boudin (1824-1898): the Seine at Caudebec-en-Caux, Musée des Beaux-Arts. 10 Interior of the tower of the church of Saint-Joseph, by Perret and Audiguier.

FÉCAMP I

FLAMANVILLE 3

FONTAINE-HENRY 4

FONTAINE-HENRY 5

LE HAVRE IO

LE HAVRE 9

LE HAVRE 7

LE HAVRE 8

45

HÉBERTOT I

HÉBERTOT (near St-André-d'Hébertot) *Calvados*. F 5.
The château of Hébertot used to belong to the d'Aguesseau family. Looking from left to right, the façade can be seen to consist of a 17th-century corbelled tower, a beautiful classical-style façade of the Regency period and a little, early 19th-century lodge. The château is surrounded by a beautiful park.
I Façade of the château of Hébertot, 17th-19th c.

HONFLEUR *Calvados*. F 5.
The little port of Honfleur was a favourite resort of artists in the early 19th century. Eugène Isabey had come there in 1824 and Corot in 1830, but it was from 1860 onwards that Honfleur and the Saint-Siméon farmhouse became famous for it was painted by Jongkind in 1863, by Boudin who was born in the area, and by Manet and Bazille in 1864. Most of the painters who visited Honfleur returned year after year and the Saint-Siméon farm gave its name to a kind of pre-Impressionist school of painting.
The late 15th-century church of Sainte-Catherine is unique of its kind: it is built in the Flamboyant Gothic style and has a curious free-standing tower. It was built by shipwrights, entirely of wood in the shape of a ship's hull, and contains a rich collection of ex-votos. The Vieux Bassin and the Lieutenance (remains of an early 16th-century castle) have survived intact. Together with the Chapelle de Grâce they inspired paintings by Corot. Eugène Boudin painted numerous pictures of the harbour and the Seine estuary in which he captured the atmosphere of his native town.
2 The church of Sainte-Catherine, 15th c. 3 Notre-Dame de Grâce, interior. 4 La Lieutenance, 16th c. 5 Chapelle de Grâce, 17th c. 6 Eugène Boudin (1824-1898): The beach at Trouville, c. 1865, Musée Eugène Boudin. 7 Boudin: Entrance to the port of Honfleur, 1857.

JUMIÈGES *Seine-Maritime*. F 5.
The ruins at Jumièges are so beautiful that when we see them we are likely to forget that they are all that remain of the three churches that once were the glory of the abbey in the 10th and 11th centuries. Of one church, nothing has survived, two bays remain of the second (church of Saint-Pierre), and of the third, that of Notre-Dame, we may still see a lovely stone shell, and a front with two octagonal towers and a façade decorated with arcades. Time and 19th-century demolitions have destroyed the Romanesque structure and the Gothic choir as well as the other buildings of the abbey.
8 Façade of the church of Notre-Dame, 11th c. 9 The nave, looking towards the choir, 11th c. 10 The nave, looking towards the façade, 11th c.

LISIEUX 12

LESSAY *Manche*. D 5.
Thanks to remarkable restoration, the great church of Lessay has regained its former splendour. It is a Benedictine abbey church built in the Romanesque style, with some groin-vaulting. A beautiful inner gallery runs around the interior of the building.
11 Square tower of the abbey church of Lessay, 11th-12th c., restored.

LISIEUX *Calvados*. F 5.
Although the war omitted to destroy the pastry-cook style basilica of Sainte-Thérèse of the Infant Jesus, it happily spared the 11th-12th-century cathedral of Saint-Pierre. Although often transformed, the church still has a fine Norman Gothic façade (except for the south tower, rebuilt in the Romanesque style in the 16th c.), a nave which recalls the style of the Ile-de-France, and a Flamboyant axial chapel of Notre-Dame containing the remains of Joan of Arc's prosecutor, Bishop Cauchon. In the Law Courts, built in the 17th century, the so-called "Golden chamber" has preserved its fine coffered ceiling.
12 Façade of the cathedral of Saint-Pierre, 13th c., altered. 13 The ambulatory.

LISIEUX 13

HONFLEUR 2

HONFLEUR 3

HONFLEUR 4

HONFLEUR 7

HONFLEUR 6

HONFLEUR 5

JUMIÈGES 10

JUMIÈGES 8

LESSAY 11

JUMIÈGES 9

LOUVIERS 1

LOUVIERS *Eure.* G 5.

The church of Notre-Dame shows the Flamboyant Gothic style at its climax on the exterior, particularly in the south front and the portal where the decoration seems to have been chased rather than sculpted.

1 South side of the church of Notre-Dame, 15th c.

MESNIÈRES-EN-BRAY *Seine-Maritime.* G 4.

The château was built in the Renaissance style in six years. It consists of three main buildings around a central courtyard which formerly had a draw-bridge opening on the fourth side, until it was replaced in the 17th century by a staircase rising over a stone bridge. The chapel has a steep-sloping roof and contains Renaissance stained-glass windows. Inside the château, a gallery of sculpted deer wearing real horns.

2 The château of Mesnières-en-Bray, 1546.

MESNIÈRES-EN-BRAY 2

MONT-ST-MICHEL 3

MONT-ST-MICHEL 4

MONT-SAINT-MICHEL *Manche.* D 6.

Not even the commercialism which has disfigured its main street can affect the singular beauty of Mont-Saint-Michel. On this isolated rock, more than a mile from the mainland, an oratory was founded in 709. It was replaced in the 10th century by a Carolingian church which gave way to a Romanesque basilica. Built between 1022 and 1135, it was burnt in 1203 by Philip Augustus during his war against the Duke of Normandy, reconstructed at his own expense and fortified in the 13th century.

The church is the oldest building on the rock. It has a fine Romanesque nave and, in contrast, a choir (1450-1521) which is a fine example of the Flamboyant Gothic style. The surrounding buildings which huddle against the steep slopes of the rock form an imposing architectural complex, dating from 1203 to 1228. The building on the west slope is known as "La Merveille": it is built in several storeys, beginning with the cellar and pillared crypt, rising up to the guests' chamber (sober pillars and a monumental chimney), the refectory (a curious feature is the lighting: the light source is invisible to anyone in it) and finally to the cloister, now happily restored. Unlike most 13th-century buildings there is no sculpture. Besides its artistic qualities, the play of light on the surrounding sands at low tide, and the dash of the waves against the foot of the ramparts (14th and 15th c.) add to the picturesque appeal of the Mount. The best view of the Mont-Saint-Michel is that from the Park at Avranches on the mainland.

3 Overall view of the Mount. 4 La Merveille. 5 Crypt of the Aquilon, 11th c. 6 Promenade of the Monks, 11th c. 7 Hall of the knights, 12th c. 8 Monks' refectory, 13th c. 9 Cloister, 13th c. 10 Nave of the church, 12th c. 11 Choir, 13th c. 12 Relief, detail of the choir, 13th c.

MONT-ST-MICHEL 6

MONT-ST-MICHEL 5

MONT-ST-MICHEL 7

MONT-ST-MICHEL 10

MONT-ST-MICHEL 11

MONT-ST-MICHEL 12

MONT-ST-MICHEL 8

MONT-ST-MICHEL 9

49

MORTAIN *Manche.* E 6.

Situated in the very heart of "Norman Switzerland", the little town of Mortain has been skilfully rebuilt. Its Gothic church of Saint-Évroult, built in granite, has all the severity of style of the Breton churches. The Abbaye Blanche which was inhabited by cloistered nuns from the 12th to the 18th centuries, consists of a church and a partly Romanesque, partly Gothic cloister, which has been well restored.

1 Cloister of the Abbaye Blanche, 12th-13th c.

NEUFCHATEL-EN-BRAY 2

NEUFCHATEL-EN-BRAY *Seine-Maritime.* G 4.

The little town of Neufchatel-en-Bray was tragically destroyed in 1940. Now entirely rebuilt, it possesses a modern theatre and law court, built by the architect Paul Auzelle. The church of Notre-Dame contains a handsome 15th-century *Entombment of Christ.*

2 Theatre, by Auzelle.

NORREY *Calvados.* E 5.

The Gothic church of Norrey was almost entirely destroyed but is now a fine example of radical restoration, begun in 1944.

3 Church of Norrey, 13th c., restored.

Ô (at Mortrée) *Orne.* F 6.

The château of Ô is a rather fanciful combination of three main structures, all built at different periods, united by steep, sharp-pointed slate roofs. The east side of the château is built in late 15th-century Flamboyant style, the south is early Renaissance, and the west is 18th-century. The whole building is built on pilework in marshy ground.

4 The château of Ô, south wing, 16th c.

OMONVILLE (at Tremblay) *Eure.* F 5.

The centre of the façade of the château of Omonville is decorated with a canted forepart designed by Chartier, an architect from Conches. Fine outbuildings and a terrace with clipped box-bushes.

5 Façade of the château, by Chartier, 1754.

LE PIN (or Pin-au-Haras) *Orne.* F 6.

The château was built for the director of a stock-breeding farm founded by Colbert, and was designed by Jules Hardouin-Mansart. It has changed neither its appearance nor its original purpose for some two hundred stallions of different pedigrees are still raised there.

6 Façade of the château, by J. Hardouin-Mansart, 1728.

PONT-AUDEMER *Eure.* F 5.

The church of Saint-Ouen at Pont-Audemer has fine Norman-Romanesque period arcades in the nave decorated in a Flamboyant Gothic style, with fine carving and richly patterned corner-stones. Beautiful Renaissance stained-glass windows.

7 Nave of the church of Saint-Ouen, decoration of the 15th c.
8 Unfinished façade, late 15th c.

NORREY 3

MORTAIN I

OMONVILLE 5

Ô 4

LE PIN 6

PONT-AUDEMER 8

PONT-AUDEMER 7

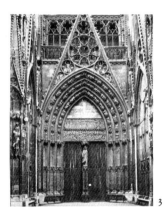

ROUEN *Seine-Maritime*. F 5.

The "museum-city" of Rouen, capital of Normandy, cruelly suffered during the last war. Although its great river port is as busy as ever (the modern cranes painted blue, red and yellow standing out against the misty background) the quaysides along the Seine have been rebuilt and raised and have lost all their old character. But despite some damage, the great monuments of the past have been preserved. The cathedral of Notre-Dame, begun in 1201 and only completed in 1530, offers examples of every variation of the Gothic style. No important building any longer stands between it and the river, from where its wonderfully graceful silhouette can be admired at leisure. This was the cathedral that Claude Monet studied at various times of day in order to catch every subtle variation in the play of the light on its façade (*See* PARIS - Musée du Jeu de Paume).

The old quarter around the cathedral has still survived, many of its old timbered houses now transformed into antique shops.

The church of Saint-Maclou was begun in 1437 and with its unusual five-bay porch is a fine specimen of the Flamboyant Gothic style. The nearby cloister or Aître Saint-Maclou is the last remaining example of a medieval charnel-house. The church of Saint-Ouen was built between 1318 and the beginning of the 16th-century and is a shining example of Gothic style, its tower topped by a curious kind of crown of sharp pinnacles whence its name of 'crowned tower'. The churches of Saint-Godard and Saint-Patrice are famous for their Renaissance stained-glass windows.

Cathedral of Notre-Dame, 13th-16th c. 1 Claude Monet (1840-1926): Rouen Cathedral, 1894, Musée du Jeu de Paume, Paris. 2 Façade. 3 Portal of the Booksellers (Portail des Libraires), 14th c. 4 Nave. 5 South aisle. 6 Portal of Saint-John the Baptist: detail. 7 Staircase of the Library, 15th c. 8 Tomb of the Sénéchal de Brézé, 1544, attributed to Jean Goujon. 9 Tombs of the Cardinals of Amboise, 16th c., by Roland Le Roux. 10 Façade of the church of Saint-Maclou, 15th c. 11 Cloister of Saint-Maclou, 15th c. 12 Church of Saint-Ouen, 14th c.

12

10

7

5

4

9

8

11

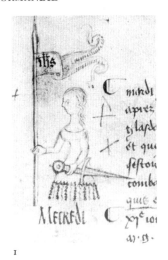

1

The whole city is rich in civil architecture of the 15th and 16th centuries: the Great Clock Tower (1527), a lodge spanning the street called La Grosse Horloge in the heart of the shopping quarter; the Law Courts (16th c.), although now without their fine ceilings, burned in 1944, and still showing signs of war damage on the exterior. Unfortunately a great number of old houses with carved beams were destroyed in the war. It was in the Place du Vieux Marché that Joan of Arc was burned at the stake on May 30, 1431. Nearby, the statues of Pierre Corneille and Gustave Flaubert.

The Musée des Beaux-Arts is very rich in French works of the 17th, 18th and 19th centuries and also has examples of the Spanish, Flemish and Dutch schools, and a fine collection of Rouen faïence. The church of Saint-Laurent (15th c.) has been transformed into a museum of iron-work around the nucleus of the important Le Secq des Tournelles collection and should not be missed.

1 Joan of Arc, eye-witness sketch. 2 The Great Clock Tower, 1527. 3 Hôtel de Bourgthéroulde, 16th c. 4 Logis Saint-Romain, 16th c. 5 Great courtyard of the Law Courts, 16th c.

MUSÉE DES BEAUX-ARTS

6 Gérard David (c. 1450-1525): Virgin with Child surrounded by Saints. 7 Delacroix (1798-1863): The judgment of Trajan. 8 Sisley (1839-1899): Inundation. 9 Monet (1840-1926): La rue Montorgueil à Paris, July 14th. 10 Faïence plate from Rouen, with radial decoration. 11 Iron door-knocker, 15th c., Musée Le Secq des Tournelles.

11

10

2

3

4

5

7

9

6

8

RY I

ST-PIERRE-SUR-DIVES 8

RY *Seine-Maritime.* G 5.

Ry was the model for Flaubert's town of Yonville-l'Abbaye where Emma Bovary dragged out her sad existence. It is also famous for the finely-sculpted wooden porch of its church.

I Sculpted wood porch of the church of Ry, 16th c.

SAINT-GABRIEL (Priory of) *Calvados.* E 5.

The priory was founded in the 11th century and is now a school of horticulture. It consists of several buildings dating from the 13th and 15th centuries grouped around a beautiful courtyard with a monumental gateway. In the neighbourhood, the castle of Brécy, with its equally fine gateway of the 17th century, should be seen.

2 Courtyard of the priory, 13th-14th c.

SAINT-GERMAIN-DE-LIVET *Calvados.* F 5.

A fairy-tale Norman manor, beautifully built in white stone and green and red varnished bricks: it stands on an isle surrounded by the waters of La Touques. At the back of its courtyard, the wooden wing of a 15th-century manor.

3 Entrance to the château, 1584.

SAINT-MARTIN-DE-BOSCHERVILLE *Seine-Maritime.* F 5.

The abbey church of Saint-Georges has survived practically untouched and in its original state. Designed on nearly the same lines as that of Saint-Nicolas at Caen, it has a fine Romanesque nave, with 13th-century groin-vaulting, with some very fine capitals with relief sculpture which show the influence of the school of Chartres, and some lovely corbels in the cornices. All that has survived of the abbey buildings is the chapter house dating from 1170.

4 Church of Saint-Georges, 11th c. 5 The nave, 11th-13th c. 6 Capital, 11th c. 7 Corner stone: detail of the arcades in the nave.

SAINT-PIERRE-SUR-DIVES *Calvados.* E 5.

The Benedictine order was so active in Normandy that a great many of their monasteries have still remained, some in ruins, some in a good state of preservation. That of Saint-Pierre was built between the 12th and 14th centuries. It consists of a fine church in the classical Norman style, and a beautiful chapter house paved with glazed bricks. In the town, the great Gothic market hall with its three aisles should be visited.

8 Chapter house of the abbey, 13th c.

SAINT-WANDRILLE *Seine-Maritime.* F 4.

The abbey of Saint-Wandrille was founded by its namesake in the 7th century. Since that date, it was constantly a prey to destructions and reconstructions until the 19th century. The most interesting part of the abbey is the ruins of the Gothic abbey church, of which the springing of the transept remains, supported by its powerful clusters of columns, then the cloister of the 14th-15th centuries, and along the north side of the cloister, the charming wash-basin with six taps, built into the wall to the right of the refectory, in a half-Gothic, half-Renaissance style. The buildings became a Benedictine abbey in the 10th century and were given back to the order in 1931. The monks now live in buildings of various dates which were added in the course of the centuries.

9 Ruins of the transept of the abbey church, late 13th c. 10 Gallery of the cloister, 14th c. 11 Door of the refectory and wash-basin, 15th c.

ST-GABRIEL **2**

ST-GERMAIN-DE-LIVET **3**

ST-MARTIN-DE-BOSCHERVILLE **4**

ST-MARTIN-DE-BOSCHERVILLE **7**

ST-MARTIN-DE-BOSCHERVILLE **5**

ST-MARTIN-DE-BOSCHERVILLE **6**

ST-WANDRILLE **9**

ST-WANDRILLE **11**

ST-WANDRILLE **10**

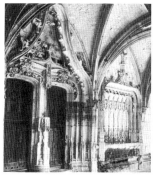

57

SÉES *Orne.* F 6.

The stone armature of this Gothic cathedral was considered insufficient to support the structure, and since the 16th century, buttresses were added both in the interior and on the exterior to prevent collapse. The magnificent choir is a masterpiece of lace-work in stone, enclosing beautiful Gothic stained-glass windows. Particularly fine are the graceful piers running up each column to meet the rib-vaulting. The altar is a fine example of Louis XVI style (bronze and marble sculpted by Brousseau in 1786). In the church of Notre-Dame de la Place (16th c.) fine polychrome wooden bas-reliefs.

1 Choir of the cathedral of Notre-Dame, 16th c. 2 Rose-window in the west front, 14th c.

TANCARVILLE *Seine-Maritime.* F 4.

The suspension bridge of Tancarville is a magnificent and elegant example of modern bridge building and a technical triumph. Its single span some 610 yards long rises 50 yards above the Seine some 20 miles from Le Havre.

At the château of Tancarville, some remains of the 10th century castle; most of the building is either 13th or 16th century. It stands on a remarkable site, on a chalk promontory 150 feet high.

3 Suspension bridge, 1959.

THAON *Calvados.* E 5.

The lovely Romanesque church of Thaon is prettily situated in the midst of a wooded grove and has a curious square bell-tower with unusual arcading. A festooned cornice runs right round the building under the roof, with corbels and blind arcading. In the nave, wooden capitals and beams.

4 The church of Thaon, 11th-12th c.

VARENGEVILLE 8

TILLIÈRES-SUR-AVRE *Eure.* F 6.

The originality and richness of the ceiling of the choir in the church make the building an artistic achievement of the first order. Each rib in the ceiling is supported by a spandrel and ends in a pendant knob-boss, sculpted in the Italian style like the rest of the decoration. The work was commissioned in 1535 by the Bishop of Lisieux.

5 Detail of the ceiling, choir of the church, 1546.

VARENGEVILLE-SUR-MER *Seine-Maritime.* F 4.

A pretty sea-side resort. The visitor will first come upon the chapel of Saint-Dominique with stained-glass windows by Braque, and then the manor of Ango, built in the 16th century by a rich ship-owner from Dieppe who was banker to François I. From the tower at the corner of his manor house he could watch the movements of his caravels in the port of Dieppe. The massive round-tower with its patterns of stone and red and black brick symbolised his lordly power. The old fortified manor has still kept its charm and former shape. At the end of a path leading onto a cliff, with a church and a cemetery overlooking the sea, one of the finest views of the Norman coast can be obtained.

6 Courtyard of the manor of Ango and Italianate loggia, 1532. 7 The round-tower. 8 Braque (1882-1963): Stained-glass window in the chapel of Saint-Dominique, 1955, executed by Paul Bony.

SÉES 1

SÉES 2

TANCARVILLE 3

TILLIÈRES-SUR-AVRE 5

THAON 4

VARENGEVILLE 7

VARENGEVILLE 6

VERNEUIL-SUR-AVRE 1

VERNEUIL-SUR-AVRE 2

VERNEUIL-SUR-AVRE *Eure*. F 6.

The crowned tower of the church of Sainte-Madeleine resembles the Beurre Tower of Rouen cathedral but surpasses it by the quality of its sculpture (16th c.). The church of Notre-Dame is equally rich in Renaissance statues. Numerous Norman houses in the town.

1 Tower of Sainte-Madeleine, 190 feet high, c. 1520. 2 Old manor house with turret, 16th c.

VERNON *Eure*. G 5.

The church of Vernon was begun in the 12th and completed in the 14th century. On the façade, a beautiful rose-window between two graceful soaring pinions.

3 Façade of the church of Notre-Dame, 14th c.

VER-SUR-MER *Calvados*. E 5.

The church is flanked by a fine Romanesque tower which has survived intact since the 11th century. It consists of four successive, receding storeys with bays and below the first storey a door above ground level which was reached by ladder, the tower providing a refuge in case of attack.

4 Church and 11th-century bell-tower.

VERNON 3

VER-SUR-MER 4

III

ILE-DE-FRANCE

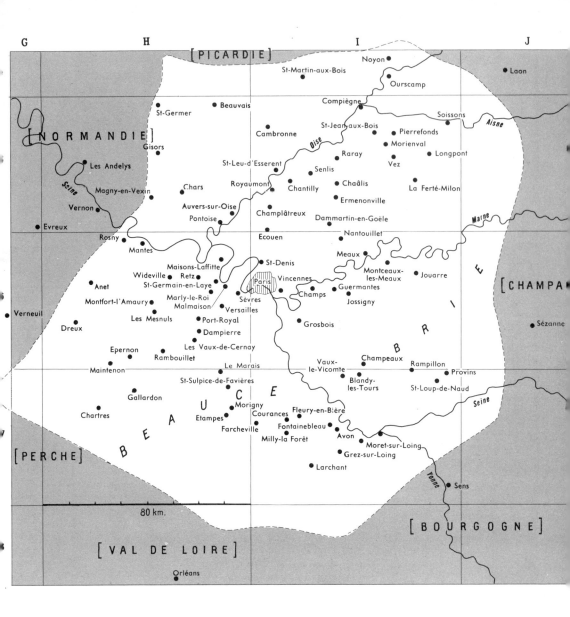

G   H   I   J

[PICARDIE]

Noyon

St-Martin-aux-Bois

Laon

Ourscamp

Compiègne

Beauvais

St-Germer

Soissons

Aisne

[NORMANDIE]

Cambronne

St-Jean-aux-Bois

Pierrefonds

Oise

Morienval

Gisors

Raray

Vez

Longpont

Les Andelys

St-Leu-d'Esserent

Senlis

Magny-en-Vexin

Chars

Royaumont

Chantilly

Chaâlis

La Ferté-Milon

Seine

Auvers-sur-Oise

Ermenonville

Vernon

Pontoise

Champlâtreux

Dammartin-en-Goële

Marne

Evreux

Ecouen

Nantouillet

Rosny

Meaux

Mantes

Maisons-Laffitte

St-Denis

Vincennes

Montceaux-les-Meaux

Jouarre

[CHAMPA

Wideville

Retz

Paris

Champs

Guermantes

Anet

St-Germain-en-Laye

Sèvres

Jossigny

B R I E

Montfort-l'Amaury

Marly-le-Roi

Malmaison

Versailles

Sézanne

Dreux

Les Mesnuls

Port-Royal

Grosbois

Verneuil

Dampierre

Epernon

Les Vaux-de-Cernay

Rambouillet

Champeaux

Rampillon

Maintenon

Le Marais

Vaux-le-Vicomte

Provins

St-Sulpice-de-Favières

Blandy-les-Tours

St-Loup-de-Naud

Gallardon

Morigny

B E A U C E

Seine

Chartres

Etampes

Courances

Fleury-en-Bière

Farcheville

Fontainebleau

Milly-la-Forêt

Avon

Moret-sur-Loing

Grez-sur-Loing

Yonne

Larchant

Sens

80 km.

[BOURGOGNE]

[PERCHE]

[VAL DE LOIRE]

Orléans

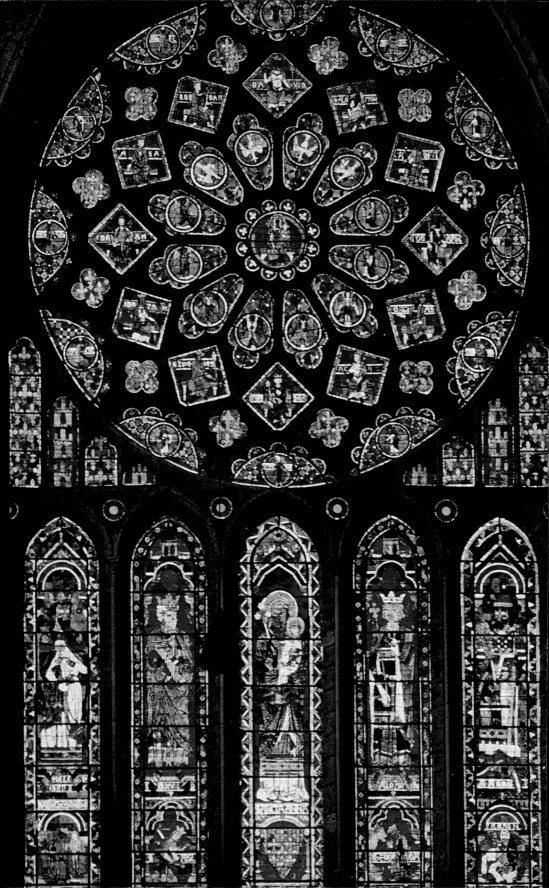

MINIATURE FROM THE TRÈS RICHES HEURES DU DUC DE BERRY,
DETAIL, 15TH C., MUSÉE CONDÉ, CHANTILLY *(Giraudon)*

NORTH ROSE-WINDOW OF CHARTRES CATHEDRAL, C. 1230 *(Fronval)*

Country of God from Chartres to Senlis, domain of kings from Versailles to Compiègne and Fontainebleau, favoured region of landscape painters who like Corot and Sisley, delighted in painting its grey cloudy skies or brilliant pale blue skies. According to Balzac, the Ile-de-France was "of all the places I have seen, the nearest to Paradise".

ANET *Eure-et-Loir.* H 6.

The château of Anet was built in 1548 by Philibert de l'Orme for Henri II and is still filled with the memories of Diane de Poitiers, the king's favourite. Always clothed in black-and-white, in elegant mourning dress for her husband Louis de Brézé, Diane was a great inspiration to artists and directed their work with the same skill with which she directed the education of royal children. The remains of the château include the main façade, the left wing of the main courtyard, the chapel and some buildings added in the 17th century by the Duke of Vendôme, grandson of King Henri IV. The old monumental portal has now been removed to the courtyard of the École des Beaux-Arts in Paris where it may still be seen, and Goujon's Fountain of Diana is now in the Louvre. Part of the interior decoration has been kept in its original state: it includes Fontainebleau tapestries, furniture and stained-glass windows.

1 Main doorway of the château; in the tympanum, a cast of Diana as Huntress by B. Cellini (original in the Louvre), 1552. 2 The chapel, 1552. 3 Jean Goujon (1515-1567): Diana, Musée du Louvre, from the park of the château.

AUVERS-SUR-OISE *Seine-et-Oise.* H 5.

It was at Auvers that Van Gogh committed suicide on July 27th 1890. He now lies beside his brother Théo in the cemetery of the little village where he had been looked after by Doctor Gachet. The church and the town hall of Auvers have remained as much as they were when painted by Van Gogh shortly before his death. The main part of the Gachet collection — outstanding for its paintings by Van Gogh — was bequeathed to the Louvre in 1954 by the doctor's son.

4 Church of Notre-Dame, 12th c. 5 Van Gogh (1853-1890): The church at Auvers, 1890, Musée du Louvre. 6 Tombs of Vincent and Théo Van Gogh in the cemetery.

AVON *Seine-et-Marne.* I 7.

Although very close to Fontainebleau, Avon never shared in its splendour and remained a country village even though its church was the parish church of the château until the Revolution. The nave dates from before the 12th century and the 18th-century wooden portal and porch are in a remarkably simple style.

7 Porch of the church, 18th c.

BEAUVAIS *Oise.* H 5.

Founded in 1247, Beauvais cathedral is the highest in the whole of Christendom, measuring some 210 feet from the ground to the roof. Work on it was often interrupted, it partly collapsed and was restored and is still incomplete. It simply consists of a choir and transept as work on the nave was abandoned. The interior is lit by 16th-century and modern stained-glass windows. Time is given by an astronomic clock copied after that at Strasbourg, and its tapestries are a reminder that the Tapestry Manufactory of Beauvais was established by Colbert in 1662, before later being removed to the Gobelins in Paris. The church of Saint-Étienne has a nave in the Romanesque style and a Flamboyant Gothic choir. In the nave, a wooden statue of Saint Wilgeforte, a young virgin whose prayers enabled her to grow a beard in order to discourage the advances of a pagan suitor.

8 View of the cathedral of Saint-Pierre, 13th c. 9 Choir of the cathedral, 145 feet in height. 10 Church of Saint-Étienne, stained-glass window: The Tree of Jesse, by Engrand le Prince, 16th c. 11 Cloister and chapter house, 14th-16th c. 12 Law courts, 14th c. 13 Head of Christ, stone carving, 13th c., Departmental Museum of Oise.

ANET 1

ANET 2

AUVERS 4

AUVERS 5

AUVERS 6

BEAUVAIS 8

BEAUVAIS 9

BEAUVAIS 12

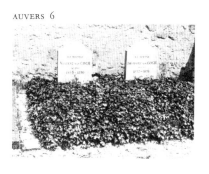

BEAUVAIS 11

BEAUVAIS 10

67

CHAALIS 5

CHAALIS 4

CHAMPLATREUX 9

BLANDY-LES-TOURS *Seine-et-Marne*. I 7.

The château of Blandy was designed on a hexagonal ground-plan. All that now remains of its enceinte are five towers built in the 15th century for the viscounts of Melun.

I Aerial view of the castle, 14th c.

CAMBRONNE-LÈS-CLERMONT *Oise*. I 5.

Standing on a hill, the church of Cambronne dominates the neighbourhood with its fine octagonal Romanesque tower. The nave is supported by columns with capitals sculpted in a naive style.

2 Nave of the church, 12th-13th c. 3 Capitals in the nave, details of the columns.

CHAALIS *Oise*. I 5.

Of the first Cistercian abbey that was built in the 13th century and then destroyed by time, and the second that had been begun by Jean Aubert in 1736, partly destroyed in the Revolution, never completed, all that remain are some picturesque ruins, where the poet Gérard de Nerval used to wander as a child. An elegant 18th-century house built by Jean Aubert houses part of the collection of the Musée Jacquemart-André at Paris.

4 Ruins of the abbey church, 13th c. 5 Musée Jacquemart-André, School of Giotto (c. 1266-1337): Saint John the Baptist.

CHAMPEAUX *Seine-et-Marne*. I 6.

In the days of its splendour, forty-two canons and chaplains used to sit in the superb sculpted choir-stalls of the collegiate church of Saint-Martin at Champeaux; the immense nave of 1220 is flooded with light.

6 Nave of the church, 1220. 7-8 Choir-stalls: sculpted misericords by Richard Falaise, 1522.

CHAMPLATREUX *Seine-et-Oise*. I 5.

The magnificent Louis XV château, built for the Président Molé, has two façades with contrary rhythms, and corner lodges respectively crowned by a arched and a triangular pediment. The same alternating theme recurs in the central lodges which are very typical examples of the early classical style which had already begun to make its appearance.

9 The château, by Jean-Michel Chevotet, 1757.

CHAMPS *Seine-et-Marne*. I 6.

During the reign of Louis XV, comfort became highly fashionable and châteaux were transformed to make them more agreeable for everyday life. In the château at Champs, built by J.-B. Bullet, the rooms were converted so that bath-rooms and what must have been one of the first dining-rooms could be installed. Madame de Pompadour must have been attracted by so much comfort for she was one of the château's tenants. It now is used as a residence for guests of the President of the French Republic.

10 The château and the flower-beds, 18th c. 11 Chinese salon, by Christophe Huet, c. 1755.

BLANDY-LES-TOURS 1

CAMBRONNE 2

CHAMPEAUX 7

CAMBRONNE 3

CHAMPEAUX 6

CHAMPEAUX 8

CHAMPS 11

CHAMPS 10

69

CHANTILLY *Oise.* I 5.

Four successive châteaux have been built on the rocky isle in the midst of the marshes which was the original site of Chantilly. But the great castle built by Pierre de Chambiges in 1528 and the little château built by Jean Bullant in about 1560 are mainly famous through their connection with the great family of Montmorency and in particular Anne of Montmorency who was a courtier to six kings of France. The great château was razed to the ground in the Revolution and reconstructed in the late 19th century when the Prince Henri of Orléans, Duke of Aumale, godson and heir of the last Duke of Condé, acquired it. The successive embellishments made by generations of the Montmorency family, the gardens designed by Le Nôtre, the terrace and the rich interior decoration made Chantilly rival the splendour of the greatest royal châteaux. In 1769 the Duke of Enghien built a third château which looks over the pond, and the poetic Maison de Sylvie. The Duke of Aumale formed the great art collections which provided the basis for the present Musée Condé. They include more than 600 paintings, ranging from the Italian primitives to Delacroix, including such masterpieces as a *Virgin* by Raphaël. The *Mystical Marriage of Saint Francis* by Sassetta, Piero di Cosimo's *Simonetta*, etc. Christophe Huet painted a series of very strange ornamental grotesques for the château. The 690 16th-century drawings, mostly by Jean Clouet (1485-1540) and his son François (1520-1572) make a collection quite unique of its kind. Equally priceless are some of the illuminated mss. in the library *(Ingeburge Psalter,* c. 1200; *Très Riches Heures du Duc de Berry,* by the Brothers Limbourg, 1409-1416; *Book of Hours of Étienne Chevalier,* by Jean Fouquet, c. 1450-1455).

1 Aerial view of the château. 2 The Great Stables by Jean Aubert, 1735.

MUSÉE CONDÉ

3 Pol, Hermant and Hennequin de Limbourg: Departure for the Hunt, miniature painting from the *Très Riches Heures du Duc de Berry,* c. 1409-1416. 4 Jean Fouquet (c. 1415-1477): page from the Book of Hours of Étienne Chevalier, c. 1455. 5 Filippino Lippi (1457-1504): Esther and Ehasuerus, detail. 6 F. Clouet (c. 1520-1572): Portrait of the Queen Jeanne of Navarre as a child, drawing. 7 François Clouet: Portrait of Charles IX. 8 Enguerrand Quarton and Pierre Villate: The Virgin of Mercy, 1452. 9 Nicolas Poussin (1594-1665): The childhood of Bacchus.

CHANTILLY 6

CHANTILLY 8

CHARS *Seine-et-Oise.* H 5.

Despite the small dimensions of the church at Chars, the choir appears vaster than it really is thanks to its five radiating chapels and the fine harmony of the semi-circular bays in the gallery and the storey of rose-windows — rather unusual in the Ile-de-France.

10 Choir of the church, 12th-13th c.

CHANTILLY 1

CHANTILLY 2

CHANTILLY 7

CHANTILLY 4

CHANTILLY 3

CHARS 10

CHANTILLY 9

CHANTILLY 5

71

1

CHARTRES *Eure-et-Loir*. H 7.

Whether first seen in the distance, rising over the wheat fields of the Beauce, as Peguy first saw it ("the hardest ear of corn that ever rose upwards"), whether we admire the marvellous figures of the columnar statues in its portals with their majestic vertical lines and the sweeping folds of their draperies, whether we see it soaring above the roofs of the little houses along the river Eure as it was painted by the artist Bombois, or whether we fly over it, the cathedral of Notre-Dame de Chartres deserves all its fame. It was built in a great burst of fervour between 1194 and 1225 and has remained practically intact in its original state despite three fires and some partial reconstruction. The south tower (height 320 feet) is a marvel of architecture even in its very simplicity. The great pillars which support the nave (115 feet high) have a purposeful lightness which was often taken as a perfect example. The rose-window in the west front has an unequalled beauty which no photograph can ever capture. The stained-glass windows with their religious scenes are masterly examples of the art and craftsmanship of the time. The sculpture is infinitely rich: apart from the statues in the portals, particular note should be taken of a donkey playing the hurdy-gurdy placed high up on the south side — a surprising subject in a surprising place! (see NANTES). Among so many fine sculptures, Chartres features a theme which is almost unique in the history of art: The image of Adam in God's mind, a tiny and yet monumental figure standing in the curve of an arch in the north portal where the entire cycle of Creation is represented in stone. The glory of the cathedral makes it all too easy to forget that Chartres is an exceptionally rich town in lovely old buildings and houses. The church of Saint-Pierre was built over a period of five centuries: it was begun by a Benedictine abbey in the 10th and 11th centuries, was later transformed, and given a choir of great elegance which was completed in the 14th century. The city museum has been installed in the ancient Bishop's palace (17th-18th c.) and contains various collections of which the most important are its tapestries and enamel work (The Twelve Apostles, by Leonard Limosin, 1545, made for François I). An excellent series of prints proves that the popular imagery of Chartres can rival with the later productions of Épinal, Rennes and Strasbourg.

1 The cathedral of Chartres, seen from the plain. 2 Columnar statue in the Royal Portal: the Queen of Sheba, 12th c. 3 Chartres pillars: diagrammatical section, 12th c. 4 Rose-window in the Royal Portal, 13th c. 5 Bombois (born 1883): le Vieux Chartres, Musée National d'Art Moderne, Paris. 6 Aerial view of the cathedral, 1194-1225. 7 Adam in the mind of God. 8 North portal, 13th c. 9 Stained-glass window: Saint Eustache at the Hunt, 13th c. 10 Columnar statues in the Royal Portal, 12th c. 11 Aristotle, detail from the Royal Portal, 12th c. 12 Angel with a sun-dial, 12th c. 13 Adoration of the Shepherds, detail from the Royal Portal, 12th c.

2

6

5

9

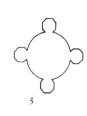

3

8

4

12

13

7

10

11

73

COMPIÈGNE *Oise*. I 5.

After Versailles and Fontainebleau, Compiègne is the third most important royal and imperial palace in France. Its severe and almost monotonous main façade is 600 feet long, and the entire palace covers a triangular area of about 4 acres. It was built by the Gabriel brothers for Louis XV in 1738 on the site of a previous château which had been built for Charles V. It was there that Louis XVI met his bride-to-be, Marie-Antoinette, in 1770, and they were both to take an active interest in the interior decoration of the palace, although they never had the time to benefit from it.

Napoleon III and the Empress Eugénie were very fond of the palace and received famous guests there. It was there, to amuse his hosts, that the writer Mérimée composed his famous dictation, in the course of which the Empress made the record number of 62 mistakes. The architecture is only of secondary interest but the interior decoration of the palace illustrates the entire history of style from Louis XV to Napoleon III, amid tapestries of hunting scenes by Oudry and superb furniture. The former apartments of the Marshals of France have been converted into the Museum of the Second Empire, and the old kitchen courtyard now houses the Musée de la Voiture et du Tourisme with its collection of old carriages and vehicles.

The beautiful Town Hall, built by Louis XII in the 16th century in the Gothic style, has a collection of 85 000 historic figurines, and in the Directory-style Hôtel de Songeons, a private collector, M. Vivenel, has gathered the finest collection of Greek vases in France outside the Louvre. The façade of the meat market was built by the architect Ledoux.

1 Château façade, by Ange Gabriel, 1738. 2 Winterhalter (1806-1873): The Empress Eugénie and her ladies-in-waiting, Musée du Second Empire. 3 Town Hall, 16th c. 4 Crater from Apulia, 4th c. B. C., Musée Vivenel. 5 F. Desportes (1661-1743): Landscape, Museum of the Palace.

COMPIÈGNE 4

COURANCES *Seine-et-Oise*. I 7.

A long drive leads from the main road to the château of Courances, built in brick and stonework, with typical Louis XIII-style pointed towers. It was built for Cosme Clausse, like that of Fleury-en-Bière, now belongs to the Marquis of Ganay and is famous for its gardens, designed by Le Nôtre. The horseshoe staircase on the main façade is a copy of that at Fontainebleau and dates from the 19th century.

6 Façade and gardens of the château, 1550.

DAMMARTIN-EN-GOELE *Seine-et-Marne*. I 5.

Apart from the works of famous great artists, France is rich in many anonymous masterpieces which show the blossoming of some unknown local talent. In the collegiate church of Notre-Dame, a very fine wrought-iron railing, attributed to a certain Coquet. The fine portal dates from 1482 and is dedicated to Saint John the Baptist.

7 Collegiate church of Notre-Dame, wrought-iron railings, Louis XV period.

DAMPIERRE 8

DAMPIERRE *Seine-et-Oise*. H 6.

The château of Dampierre lies somewhat below the road but is worth seeking out because of its great charm and beauty. It was built by Jules Hardouin-Mansart between 1675 and 1683 for the Duke of Luynes whose descendant is the present proprietor. Park designed by Le Nôtre. The little Louis XIII château at La Cour-Senlisse is the annex to the main château.

8 Façade of the château looking over park and outbuildings, 17th c.

COMPIÈGNE 1

COMPIÈGNE 3

COMPIÈGNE 2

COMPIÈGNE 5

DAMMARTIN-EN-GOELE 7

COURANCES 6

75

DREUX 2

DREUX *Eure-et-Loir.* H 6.

The glory of Dreux is its architecture, largely due to the dynasty of the Métezeau architects who were born in the city. One of them built the Saint-Gervais church in Paris. The church of Saint-Pierre was reconstructed in the Flamboyant style in the 15th century and has fine portals, stained-glass windows of the 15th and 16th centuries, and a superb organ case of 1614 made after a design by Clément Métezeau. Beside the church, a lovely 16th-c. belfry: first storey, Flamboyant in style, second, Renaissance, campanile dating from the 17th c. The Musée d'Art et d'Histoire is housed in a secularized chapel and contains two lovely Louis XV consoles from Madame de Pompadour's château at Crécy, and very beautiful Romanesque capitals from the church of Saint-Étienne.

1 Church of Saint-Pierre, 15th c. 2 Belfry, 1512-1531. 3-4 Romanesque capitals from the church of Saint-Étienne, Musée d'Art et d'Histoire, 12th c.

ÉCOUEN *Seine-et-Oise.* I 5.

Although the identity of the architect of the château of Écouen is still a subject for controversy, we do know that it was completed by Jean Bullant, and that he was responsible for much of the decoration and the finishing (1556). Thanks to this collaboration, the château of Écouen, built by Anne de Montmorency, the owner of Chantilly, is the most beautiful Renaissance château near Paris, built at a time when the Italianate influence was waning. It is also by far the best preserved château of its time, thanks to its high-quality stonework and the absence of fragile superstructures. Inside, all that remain of the original decoration are eleven monumental fire places, in polychrome marble, like that of the main reception room, or else simply painted in fresco, grisaille or natural colours. The château has now been given back the role that Napoleon I assigned to it in 1807: a school for the Légion d'Honneur. In 1544 Anne of Montmorency also built a church, with very fine stained-glass windows, at Écouen.

5 Façade of the château, looking onto the gardens, 1556. 6 Fireplace in the main reception room, statue of Renown by Jean Goujon, 1551. 7 Portico in the courtyard, north wing, 16th c.

ÉPERNON *Eure-et-Loir.* H 6.

Interesting civic architecture at Épernon: wood-beamed houses in the Rue Druet, houses with wooden pillars (16th c.) in the Place du Change, and especially the Pressoirs, a former cellar now below ground, with three rib-vaulted aisles, and pillars with finely carved capitals.

8 Les Pressoirs, cellar, 13th c.

ERMENONVILLE 9

ERMENONVILLE *Oise.* I 5.

The park at Ermenonville which surrounds an old château of Gabrielle d'Estrées was entirely the creation of the Marquis of Girardin who began it in 1763, to apply his theory of "the composition of landscapes and means of embellishing nature". The park includes lakes, grottos, waterfalls, a hamlet (ten years earlier than that of Versailles) fake ruins of the temple of philosophy, and various "works". Jean-Jacques Rousseau, who was a friend of the Marquis, died at Ermenonville in 1778 and was buried on the isle of the poplars, before being later removed to the Panthéon in Paris.

9 Tomb of J.-J. Rousseau, project attributed to Hubert Robert, bas-relief by J.-P. Lesueur, 1778. 10 Temple of philosophy, late 18th c.

DREUX 1

DREUX 3

ÉCOUEN 7

DREUX 4

ÉCOUEN 5

ERMENONVILLE 10

ÉCOUEN 6

ÉPERNON 8

77

FARCHEVILLE 3

LA FERTÉ-MILON 4

ÉTAMPES *Seine-et-Oise.* H 7.

The Tour Guinette, a superb rough stone tower built on a quatrefoil ground plan is all that remains of the ancient royal castle, of the 12th century. Dating from the same period is the church of Notre-Dame du Fort with its beautiful Romanesque tower. Although the south portal is badly damaged it has still kept some statues which may be compared with those in the Royal Portal at Chartres. Many ancient houses are worth visiting: for example, the town house of Diane de Poitiers in the Rue Sainte-Croix, which was built by Jean Goujon in 1554; that of Anne de Pisseleu, 1538, and lastly, the Town Hall which has been over-restored but contains a museum with some interesting antiquities.

1 Portal of the church of Notre-Dame-du-Fort, 12th c. **2** Railing from the abbey of Morigny, 12th c., municipal museum.

FARCHEVILLE *Seine-et-Marne.* I 7.

A feudal fortress with unusual pointed-arch machicolation, in a style more usually found in Provence. The framework structure of the seignorial dwelling, the tithe barn, the chapel and the cellars date from the first years of the building, due to Hugues de Banville, chamberlain of Philip the Handsome.

3 Fortified walls of the fortress, late 13th c.

LA FERTÉ-MILON *Aisne.* I 5.

Rising in the middle of an open field, are the astonishing remains of the important fortress of La Ferté-Milon which was dismantled by king Henri IV. In the town, the church of Notre-Dame has an unusually wide choir.

4 Castle walls, 13th c.

FLEURY-EN-BIÈRE *Seine-et-Marne.* I 7.

Farm buildings of rare quality, three centuries old, characterise this old, vast château with its immense courtyard. A double C brick pattern in the walls indicates that the château was built for Cosme Clausse, who was also the owner of the château of Courances, built by Pierre Lescot.

5 Façade of the château, 16th-17th c. **6** Out-buildings of the château.

FONTAINEBLEAU *Seine-et-Marne.* I 7.

Fontainebleau is one of the three great palaces of France. It was begun by Philip Augustus and Saint Louis and owes most of its decoration to François I who made it his favourite residence. The king entrusted the work of decoration to two skilful Italian artists, Rosso and Primaticcio, who worked there from 1528 to 1547. Henri II, Henri IV, Louis XIV, Louis XV, Napoleon I and Louis-Philippe all altered, destroyed and rebuilt parts of the palace, and the result is a splendid medley of styles. The Cour des Adieux, built in 1529, is famous for its magnificent horse-shoe stair-case. Other fine features of the palace include the Cour de la Fontaine (Fountain courtyard) by the Carp Pond, the Porte Dorée (Golden Gate) of 1528, and the Cour Ovale (Oval Courtyard) which is even more beautiful when seen from the windows of the Ball-room. The immense but varied interior contains wall-paintings and stuccoes in the Italian style in the gallery of François I and the Ball-room, the most beautiful room in the entire palace. The refurnished royal and imperial apartments are of great interest. Behind the palace, the Place d'Armes can be seen, together with a magnificent view onto the great canal.

7 Napoleon's farewell to his soldiers in the courtyard of the Cheval Blanc, April 20 1814, Épinal print. **8** The horseshoe staircase, Jean Du Cerceau, 1634. **9** The Oval Courtyard, 16th c. **10** Ball-room, Gilles le Bretonet and Philibert de l'Orme, 16th c. **11** Galerie François I, stucco decoration by Primaticcio, 16th c. **12** Council room in the Grands Appartements, decorated 1753.

FONTAINEBLEAU 7

LES ADIEUX DE FONTAINEBLEAU.

ÉTAMPES 1   FLEURY 6   FLEURY 5

FONTAINEBLEAU 8

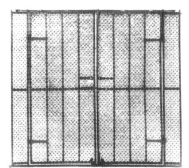

ÉTAMPES 2

FONTAINEBLEAU 9   FONTAINEBLEAU 11

FONTAINEBLEAU 12   FONTAINEBLEAU 10

79

GALLARDON *Eure-et-Loir.* H 7.

Like most religious monuments in France, the church of Gallardon contains a medley of Romanesque, Gothic and Renaissance styles. Fine apse and choir. The town itself has the prettiest old house in France and is dominated by the curiously shaped tower of its old fortress.

1 Apse of the church, Romanesque and Gothic styles. 2 Wooden bowl-vaulted ceiling of the church, Gothic beams, 17th c. paintings. 3 The Wooden House (Maison de Bois), c. 1500, Rue Porte-Mouton.

GISORS *Eure.* H 5.

The beautiful Renaissance church of Saint-Gervais-Saint-Protais has suffered both the ravages of time and the damage of the last war. Now restored, it was originally built by the Grappin brothers, the architects of the château of Ambleville. In the town: remains of a very fine fortress of the 11th and 12th c., with groin-vaulted towers of three storeys.

4 Fortress, 11th-12th c. 5 Aisle of the church of Saint-Gervais-Saint-Protais, 16th c. 6 Pillar of the Merchants (Pilier des Marchands), 16th c.

GUERMANTES 10

GREZ-SUR-LOING *Seine-et-Marne.* I 7.

The church of this delightful village has a Romanesque portal protected by a fine 13th-c. porch-tower, strengthened by thick buttresses. The numerous painters who frequented the village must also have been impressed by the curious Romanesque capitals in the nave and the 12th-century Tour de Ganne.

7 Porch tower of the church, 13th c.

GROSBOIS (near Boissy-Saint-Léger) *Seine-et-Oise.* I 6.

The château of Grosbois was completed during the reign of Louis XIII and was first lived in by the Duke of Valois. Later inhabitants included the Count of Provence, the future Louis XVIII, Barras, General Moreau, and, in the reign of Napoleon, Marshal Berthier, who rested there between campaigns and had it decorated by fine Empire style furnishings. In the dining room: paintings by Abraham Bosse, and a wonderful collection of Empire furniture as souvenirs of the "reign" of Berthier.

8 The château, 17th c. 9 Dining room, paintings by Abraham Bosse, 17th c.

GUERMANTES 11

GUERMANTES (2 miles from Lagny-sur-Marne) *Seine-et-Marne.* I 6.

The superb 90 feet-long gallery with its eighteen windows opening onto the park of the château of Guermantes is known as the "Belle Inutile". It was decorated by Merelle with copies of the most famous paintings by Rubens, Raphaël, Veronese, Van Dyck, etc. Proust was enchanted by the name of Guermantes but described a quite different château in his books.

10 Aerial view of the château, 18th c. 11 The great Gallery of the château, Robert de Cotte, c. 1709.

JOSSIGNY *Seine-et-Marne.* I 6.

Standing in the midst of a garden overgrown with weeds is the delightful little Louis XV château of Jossigny, its interior decoration still intact. The roofs were given the shape of Chinese pagodas by the Lord of Graviers, Claude-François Le Conte, who began work on the château in 1743.

12 Main façade of the château, 1743.

GALLARDON 2

GALLARDON I

GALLARDON 3

GISORS 5

GISORS 6

GISORS 4

GREZ-SUR-LOING 7

GROSBOIS 8

JOSSIGNY 12

GROSBOIS 9

LARCHANT 2

LARCHANT 3

MAGNY-EN-VEXIN 6

JOUARRE *Seine-et-Marne*. I 6.

The crypt of the abbey of Jouarre is 13 centuries old and certainly one of the oldest religious monuments in the whole of France. It contains the only surviving example of a Merovingian wall.

1 Abbey crypt, 7th c.

LARCHANT *Seine-et-Marne*. I 7.

The importance of the church at Larchant is due to the story of its patron, Saint Mathurin, who cured the daughter of the Roman emperor Maximian among other miracles. The chapter of Notre-Dame of Paris generously donated the costs of the building of this admirable church which is still visited by pilgrims. Only the choir and the transept have survived the buffetings of three storms and the ravages of the wars of religion, but the half-ruined tower is still extremely impressive.

2 Tower of the church of Saint-Mathurin, 13th c. **3** Portal of the church of Saint-Mathurin, 14th c.

LONGPONT *Aisne*. I 5.

Only a few beautiful vestiges remain of the enormous abbey church whose nave once measured more than three hundred feet in length. It was consecrated by Saint Louis in 1227. The monastery buildings were restored in the 18th century, and their iron-work balconies are worthy of note.

4 Ruins of the abbey church, 13th c. **5** Monastic building of the abbey, 18th c.

MAGNY-EN-VEXIN *Seine-et-Oise*. H 5.

The church is an example of the transition between the Gothic and Renaissance styles. In the interior, a very fine baptismal font, sculpted ceiling, various statuettes and the tomb of the Duke of Villeroy, Lord of Magny.

6 Tomb of the Duke of Villeroy, church of Magny-en-Vexin, 16th c.

MAINTENON *Eure-et-Loir*. H 6.

The château of Maintenon was Louis XIV's wedding gift to his bride, Madame de Maintenon, the governess of his children. The building bears witness to the four different periods in which it was built: a large 13th-century tower, three 14th-century round-towers, a magnificent main building of the 16th century, and finally Madame de Maintenon's own additions. The aqueduct is a reminder of Louis XIV's project for diverting the waters of the Eure river to Versailles: because of an outbreak of marsh-fever, the work was never completed.

7 Façade of the château seen from the park, 15th c. **8** Unfinished aqueduct, 17th c.

MAISONS-LAFFITTE *Seine-et-Oise*. H 6.

To-day, unfortunately, it is no longer possible to see the château of Maisons as it was when François Mansart built it. All that remains of his masterpiece is the main building which was only just saved from demolition by being bought by the state. It was built in white stone from Chantilly for the President of Longueil in the 17th century. The main building combines the Doric, Ionic and Corinthian orders superimposed and the same motif is repeated throughout the entire building. The steep-sloped roof is still in the Louis XIII style. The railings of the great vestibule are now in the Galerie d'Apollon in the Musée du Louvre.

9 The château, façade from the main courtyard, François Mansart (1642-1651). **10** Great vestibule, sculptures by J. Sarrasin, 17th c.

LONGPONT 5   LONGPONT 4   JOUARRE 1

MAINTENON 8

MAINTENON 7

MAISONS-LAFFITTE 10

MAISONS-LAFFITTE 9

MANTES 6

MALMAISON *Seine-et-Oise*. H 6.

The house at Malmaison where Josephine Bonaparte lived is so filled with historic and romantic memories of the Napoleonic era that it might be expected to be a Directory-style or at least late 18th-century building but, in fact, it was built early in the 17th century (1620-1622). This simple but enchanting dwelling was once surrounded by a splendid park when Josephine bought it in 1799, three years after her marriage. It was there that she retired after her divorce in 1809 and died in 1814. She had virtually bankrupted herself with the cost of various embellishments to the house, but now most of the furniture and Percier's and Fontaine's interior decoration has been restored and Malmaison has become a Napoleonic museum rich in sentimental memories.

1 Main façade of the château, 18th c. **2** Study of the emperor Napoleon, 19th c. **3** Baron Gérard (1770-1837): The Empress Josephine at Malmaison, Château de Malmaison.

MANTES *Seine-et-Oise*. H 6.

Mantes suffered some thirty bombardments during the last war but managed to preserve her collegiate church intact. Like Notre-Dame of Paris it is an important example of the Gothic style of architecture in the Ile-de-France. The chapel was added in the 14th century and the old stained-glass windows have now been replaced by fine modern windows by Grüber. In the town, the Porte au Prêtre (Priest's Door) — the doorway of an old timbered house — and a handsome Renaissance fountain with its various basins, have still survived as reminders of the charming old town that was destroyed during the war.

4 View of the cathedral, 13th c. **5** South portal of the cathedral, 14th c. **6** Chapel of Navarre, c. 1325, stained-glass window by Grüber, 20th-c.

LE MARAIS *Seine-et-Oise*. H 7.

The elegant château of Le Marais faces an ornamental pond. Its superb portico contains a double flight staircase which leads to the apartments of the ground floor, situated above ground level.

7 Façade of the château facing the main courtyard, 1770.

MARLY-LE-ROI *Seine-et-Oise*. H 6.

Of the castle built for Louis XIV by Mansart in 1679, on a more modest scale than that of Versailles, and of the elegant noblemen's lodges flanking it, little remains but traces of the foundations, for they were allowed to fall into decay, were gradually pillaged and sold, stone by stone, during the 19th century. Nonetheless the site has remained as it was, and the line of trees uniting the park with the forest has survived. Another survival is the handsome horse-trough which was once decorated by the winged horses sculpted by Coysevox, and then the more majestic horses by Coustou (both sets now removed to the entry of the Champs-Élysées in Paris). The church where Louis XIV and Madame de Maintenon used to pray was built by Mansart (1688-90) and replaced an earlier building of the 13th century. It contains a painting of the Descent from the Cross of the French school, dating from 1516.

8 Horse-pond, 17th c. **9** The château, engraving by Perelle, 17th c.

MALMAISON 2

MALMAISON I

MALMAISON 3

MANTES 4

MANTES 5

LE MARAIS 7

MARLY-LE-ROI 8

MARLY-LE-ROI 9

85

MEAUX 4

MEAUX 3

MEAUX *Seine-et-Marne.* I 6.

The Gothic cathedral of Meaux is filled with memories of Bossuet, who became Bishop of Meaux in 1682 and was buried there under a simple, black marble tombstone. Also connected with the famous orator is the old Bishopric where he composed some of his most famous sermons. The Bishop's palace contains two fine vaulted rooms of the 12th century, and, on the façade, the sloping ramp leading to the first storey, built by Briçonnet, the gouty bishop of the 16th century, who was unable to walk up stairs. The Bossuet museum has been installed in the palace and contains various interesting souvenirs of the bishop and an important sculpture collection.

1 Cathedral of Saint-Étienne, Flamboyant Gothic porch, 14th c. 2 Old Bishop's Palace, 12th and 17th c. 3 Head of Ogier the Dane, Romanesque period, Musée Bossuet. 4 Portrait of Bossuet, engraving, 17th c.

LES MESNULS *Seine-et-Oise.* H 6.

The château of Mesnuls can be seen from the road, lined by magnificent linden-trees. It was built in brick and stone in the late Renaissance, was restored by Marshal de Villars in the 18th century, and is now a re-education centre. In the interior, staircase and paintings in grisaille after Oudry.

5 Façade of the château, 1530 and 17th c.

MILLY-LA-FORÊT *Seine-et-Oise.* I 7.

The two towers which are all that remain of the former castle are a reminder that Milly is a very ancient town and was once the property of King Dagobert I. The covered market, made of chestnut wood, and the Gothic tower of the church should be seen at Milly before visiting Saint-Blaise-des-Simples, a tiny 12th-century chapel dedicated to the patron saint of medicinal plants (or simples), with interior decorations by Jean Cocteau.

6 Market place, 1479. 7 Near Milly: chapel of Saint-Blaise-des-Simples, fresco by Jean Cocteau, 1959.

MONTCEAUX-LES-MEAUX *Seine-et-Marne.* I 6.

The memories of two famous women are evoked by the ruins of the château of Montceaux: Catherine de Medicis and Gabrielle d'Estrées who received the château as a gift from Henri IV. The remains of the doorways and the chapel are flanked by fine fluted Corinthian columns. The main body of the château was destroyed after the Revolution.

8 Square lodge of the château, Philibert de l'Orme, 16th c. 9 Chapelle des Orgeries, 16th c.

MONTFORT-L'AMAURY *Seine-et-Oise.* H 6.

The town owes its name to the Montfort family whose most illustrious member, Simon de Montfort, led the ruthless crusade against the Albigensians in the 13th century. The late 15th-century church is in the centre of a picturesque quarter of ancient houses, and has fine Renaissance stained-glass windows. A beautiful Flamboyant Gothic doorway leads to the old charnel-house with its beamed roof. Victor Hugo lived in the 16th-century house at 9, rue de la Treille, which may be seen in the old district with steep sloping streets, around the church.

10 Doorway of the old charnel-house, 15th c. 11 Charnel-house cloister, 15th c.

MEAUX 1

MEAUX 2

LES MESNULS 5

MILLY-LA-FORÊT 6

MONTCEAUX-LES-MEAUX 8   MONTCEAUX-LES-MEAUX 9

MONTFORT-L'AMAURY 10

MONTFORT-L'AMAURY 11

87

MORET-SUR-LOING 3

MORET-SUR-LOING *Seine-et-Marne*. I 7.

The little town of Moret is situated on the old road to Burgundy and is still protected by two old 14th-century gate-towers. Parisians may be surprised to find the porch of the house of François I beside the town-hall: it was re-sited there in 1957 after having been removed to the Cours Albert I for 36 years through a whim of the actress Mlle Mars. From the old bridge, reconstructed after the war, the visitor may recognise the views of the town that were so often painted by Sisley, who spent the last twenty years of his life at Moret.

I Sisley (1839-1899): View of Moret. **2** House of François I (so-called), 1572. **3** Porte de Samois, 14th c.

MORIENVAL *Oise*. I 5.

The church at Morienval is one of the finest Romanesque monuments in France and is practically a history lesson in itself. The bell-towers, pillars of the nave and the vault of the ambulatory are the first examples of the Gothic style in the Ile-de-France since the last is rib-vaulted and dates from 1125. Renan was an enthusiastic admirer of the church and the first work of reconstruction was due to his efforts.

4 Church of Notre-Dame, 12th c. **5** The choir, 12th c. **6** Capital, 12th c.

MORIGNY 7

MORIGNY *Seine-et-Oise*. H 7.

The old Benedictine abbey of Morigny has suffered the ravages of time and has been reduced to a number of separate ruins. It was founded in the 11th century and is now in part a parish church, in part a private residence. The modern village square was built on the site of the nave of the church.

7 Square tower, 13th c., and staircase-turret, 16th c. **8** Tombstone (reverse of the church façade), 1359.

NANTOUILLET *Seine-et-Marne*. I 6.

Before the Renaissance style was assimilated by French art, it remained wholly Italian in spirit. The château of Nantouillet is far more Italianate in style than the later châteaux of Chantilly and Écouen. The doorway of the 13th-century church is also of the Renaissance. Both the château and the doorway are the work of Cardinal Duprat who was Chancellor to François I.

9 Main building of the château, 1521.

NOYON *Aisne*. I 4.

The cathedral where Charlemagne was crowned King of Neustria and Hugh Capet king of France is a magnificent example of the early Gothic style and combines the severity of Romanesque architecture with the fine carving of the Gothic master-craftsmen. The choir dates from 1150, the façade from 1290, the south tower from 1220 and the north tower from the 14th century. The vast interior is without stained-glass windows which gives it an austere aspect as if to remind one that Calvin was born in Noyon in 1509. At the side of the church, the chapter library (known as the "Ancienne Librairie") has a collection of nearly 4 000 ancient books including the 9th-century Morienval Evangeliary.

10 Cathedral towers, 12th and 14th c. **II** Nave and aisle, 13th c. **12** Chapter house, 13th c. **13** Wood façade of the Ancienne Librairie, 16th c.

NOYON 10

MORET-SUR-LOING 2

MORET-SUR-LOING 1

MORIENVAL 4

MORIENVAL 6

MORIENVAL 5

MORIGNY 8

NANTOUILLET 9

NOYON 13

NOYON 11

NOYON 12

89

OURSCAMP *Oise.* I 4.

A Cistercian abbey was established at Ourscamp in 1129 and numerous buildings were added in the 18th century but the buildings are now in ruins owing to extensive war damage. The Gothic infirmary is the only one of its kind to survive intact in the whole of France.

1 Infirmary, 1240. 2 Ruins of the church, 13th c.

PIERREFONDS *Oise.* I 5.

The ancient fortress of Pierrefonds had a long history and was dismantled, burnt and pillaged before being entirely rebuilt by Napoleon III for the amusement of his court. What we now see is a model fortress as seen by Viollet-le-Duc who decorated and reconstructed the original structure with, perhaps, excessive perfection.

3 The fortress, Viollet-le-Duc, 1857.

PONTOISE *Seine-et-Oise.* H 5.

Nothing now remains of the medieval castle of Pontoise in which Saint-Louis fell ill and made a vow to seek the Holy Cross. The church of Saint-Maclou is partly 12th-century and partly 15th-16th-century and shows the best styles of both periods. The magnificent choir is very early Gothic and the Flamboyant portal is richly sculpted. The church is richly furnished: statues, wooden stalls and 17th-century pulpit, 18th-century organ and, in the chapel of the Passion, a stone Entombment of 1550. The 15th-century Hôtel d'Estouteville has been transformed by the municipality into the Musée Tavet-Delacour and contains a fine collection of "toiles de Jouy".

4 Life-size group sculpture, 1550. 5-6 Renaissance capitals.

PORT-ROYAL 8

PORT-ROYAL *Seine-et-Oise.* H 6.

It is difficult to explain the hostility shown towards Port-Royal for more than sixty years, from the time of Richelieu to Louis XIV. The persecution of the Jansenist order and their headquarters at Port-Royal ended with the total destruction of the abbey. The most famous figures in the history of Port-Royal, the "Solitaires", such as Arnauld, Nicole, and Lemaistre de Sacy all died before the close of the 17th century; Mother Angélique, the guiding spirit in the convent had died in 1661, and Pascal, the friend of the Jansenist, in 1662. But it was only in 1709 that the community of Port-Royal, then reduced to a few obscure but still obstinate nuns, was dispersed by the police and the buildings razed to the ground. All that may now be seen are a wall of the cloister of the 15th century, the 16th-century pigeon-house, and the foundations of the church, which was the last to be destroyed in 1712. But the Maison des Granges (1652) on a little hill, where Racine learned Greek and Latin, is still intact and has been transformed into a museum with a collection of relics and documents of the period.

7 The pigeon-house, 16th c. 8 Death mask of Pascal (1623-1662). 9 La Maison des Granges, 17th c.

OURSCAMP 1

PIERREFONDS 3

OURSCAMP 2

PONTOISE 5

PONTOISE 6

PONTOISE 4

PORT-ROYAL 9

PORT-ROYAL 7

91

PROVINS 2

PROVINS 3

PROVINS *Seine-et-Marne.* I 7.

Provins was a very important market-town in the Champagne region during the whole of the Middle Ages and both the upper part of the town, the more commercial quarter, and the lower, more monastic part, have kept many signs of its former prosperity. The most important remains of the medieval town are the ramparts of the upper town which are still flanked with gateways (St-Jean) and towers like that of the keep or Caesar's Tower (Tour de César) with two rooms on two storeys, one square, the other octagonal, as well as several dungeon cells; it is crowned by a fine 16th-century beamed roof. Next in importance, the "Grange aux Dîmes", a former military edifice which became a market and then, in the 14th century, a barn where the tithes from the harvests were stored. Now a museum of sculpture and local art, the "Grange" has preserved its magnificent cellars with rib-vaulting and two Gothic storeys. In the church of Saint-Ayoul, alabaster carvings of the Virgin and the Angel Musicians, both dating from the 16th century. Fine remains of civic architecture include two 13th-century houses in the Rue des Capucins, the Maison du Bourreau (Executioner's House), the Hôtel-Dieu with its fine 13th-century portal, and especially, the 15th-century cloister of the general hospital.

I The ramparts, 12th and 13th c. 2 La Tour de César, 12th and 16th c. 3 La Grange aux Dîmes (Tithe Barn), 12th c. 4 Portal of the church of Sainte-Croix, 16th c. 5 Church of Saint-Quiriace, the Evangelists, stucco decoration on the pendentives of the dome.

RAMBOUILLET *Seine-et-Oise.* H 6.

The quadrangular design of the château was already laid down in 1375 by Jean Bernier but building continued until the 19th century. The château is now a summer residence of the President of the Republic. The wainscoting is only surpassed by that in the château of Versailles. Very beautiful parterres and a great water-garden with ponds and canals. The park contains several charming little lodges, like Marie-Antoinette's dairy, decorated by Sauvage, and the lodge with shell-work decoration, built by the Duke of Penthièvre in 1778, in the English garden.

6 The château. 7 Small salon in the Pavillon des Coquillages, 1778. 8 Interior of Marie-Antoinette's dairy, statue of the Goat-girl by Pierre Julien, 1776.

RAMPILLON 11

RAMPILLON *Seine-et-Marne.* I 6.

The church of Rampillon dominates the little village around it and has beautifully sculpted doorways in striking contrast to the total bareness of the soaring nave, only ornamented by its triforiums. The church's only rich treasure is to be found at the end of the south aisle: a large wooden sculpted retable of the 16th-century, with a 14th-century Virgin.

9 Porch of the church of Saint-Eliphe, 13th c. 10 Lintel of the main portal, the Last Judgment. 11 Frieze carving on the main portal, the Seasons. 12 Sculpted wood retable from the church of Saint-Eliphe, 16th c.

PROVINS I

PROVINS 4

PROVINS 5

RAMBOUILLET 6

RAMBOUILLET 7

RAMBOUILLET 8

RAMPILLON 12

RAMPILLON 9

RAMPILLON 10

RARAY *Oise.* I 5.

A highly original sculpted alley leads to the Louis XIII château of Raray: on one side of the alley a deer hunt, on the other side, a boar hunt have been carved along arcaded walls, with the lively sculptures of thirty-eight hunting dogs. Jean Cocteau was charmed by the château and used it as the setting for his film "La Belle et la Bête".

I Sculpted hunting scene, central alley of the château, 17th c.

RETZ (désert de) *Seine-et-Oise.* H 6.

The "follies" in the highly original garden at Retz, dating from the reign of Louis XVI, are slowly decaying from abandon and the encroachment of vegetation: a house in the form of a truncated, fluted column, and a pagoda are the sole survivors of the various buildings which once graced the park. The site has neither been restored nor opened to the public and is in danger of disappearing completely.

2 House in form of a fluted truncated column, late 18th c. credited to Boullée. 3 Chinese pavilion, late 18th c.

ROSNY 4

ROSNY *Seine-et-Oise.* H 6.

The façade of the château may be seen from the main road: it was built for Sully, a minister of Henry IV, in the pure, rather massive style to which the king gave his name. The Duchess of Berry lived there from 1820 to 1830, and Corot often painted in its grounds in about 1840 when he was the guest of his friends, the Osmond family, who were then the tenants of the château.

4 J.-B.-C. Corot (1796-1875): The château of Rosny, 1840, Musée du Louvre.

ROYAUMONT *Seine-et-Oise.* I 5.

Thanks to the Centre Culturel, the former abbey of Royaumont has taken on a new lease of life. It was originally a Cistercian abbey built in 1228 by Saint Louis, and its admirable series of monastic buildings have still survived to-day. The cloister, the superb Gothic refectory where Saint Louis served the monks, and the old kitchens, which were simply and tastefully furnished by the last proprietors, should all be visited as well as the abbey palace which was built by Le Masson in 1785 after the style of Ledoux.

5 Abbey cloister, 13th c. 6 The refectory of the abbey, 13th c. 7 The abbey palace, 18th c.

RARAY 1

RETZ 2

RETZ 3

ROYAUMONT 6

ROYAUMONT 7

ROYAUMONT 5

3

SAINT-DENIS *Seine.* I 6.

The royal basilica of Saint-Denis is unrivalled for its long and eventful history. It was dedicated originally to Saint Denis who was the first Bishop of Paris and martyred in about 250, and who is represented with his head held in his hands. Nothing has remained of the first church which was built at the instigation of Saint Genevieve in about 475, and then transformed and enlarged under the Merovingians by Dagobert in about 630. It was again rebuilt by the abbé Fulrad in 775 during the reign of Pepin the Short, the first of the Carolingian kings. Then, in the 12th century, the most famous of all the abbey's abbots, Suger, added a choir, an imposing narthex and a bell-tower to the nave and the Romanesque crypt, in about 1130-1144. Finally, in about 1231, Saint Louis widened the choir, rebuilt the nave and transformed the building into a masterpiece of the Gothic style with the aid of Pierre de Montreuil, the greatest architect of the Middle Ages. The masonry of Saint-Denis was so perfect that it was taken as an ideal example for medieval builders. The church was restored in the 19th century and almost entirely rebuilt by Viollet-le-Duc who showed conscientious respect for the original design.

In the course of the Middle Ages and the Renaissance, the great basilica became the last resting place for the kings of France, their families and their greatest servants. The tombs were all emptied during the Revolution but recent excavations have brought up a great number of ancient sarcophagi from the ground under the 8th-century crypt. One of the remains which was identified was that of Queen Arnegonde, one of the wives of Clotaire III, who died in about 680. Fragments of her robe, and splendid jewels were brought to light, as precious evidence for the history of Merovingian civilisation (fine breast-plate, 11 inches long, in cloisonné enamel). To visit Saint-Denis is a lesson in French history and also in funerary sculpture, for the basilica contains examples ranging from recumbent effigies on ornamented tombs to life-size kneeling monumental effigies of the sovereigns. Under a mausoleum flanked by the figures of the four virtues, the recumbent effigy of Louis XII and his wife Anne de Bretagne: with her head flung back, her flowing hair and one knee raised to lift the shroud, the sculpture has a strongly Romantic flavour. The monument of François I is the most important work by reason of its architecture, for apart from the expressiveness of its fine recumbent effigies, it is noteworthy for the richness of its decoration, and its marble statues and bas-reliefs. Those of the stylobate, by Pierre Bontemps (died 1570) trace the whole history of the reign and the most remarkable relief, showing the Battle of Marignan, seems, by its mass of pikes, to be a reminder of Paolo Uccello's battle paintings.

I Façade of the basilica of Saint-Denis, 12th c. 2 Crossing. 3 Transverse section of a pillar. 4 View of the crypt, 12th c. 5 Virgin and Child, polychrome wood, 12th c. 6 Chancel: tomb of Dagobert I, 13th c. 7 South arm of the transept, detail of recumbent effigy of Louis de Sancerre, 15th c. 8 North arm of the transept, tomb of Louis XII, Jean Juste. 9 Detail of recumbent effigy of Anne de Bretagne, 1532. 10 Right-hand aisle, Pierre Bontemps: the Battle of Marignan, detail from the tomb of François I, 16th c.

10

1

2

5

4

6

8

7

9

ST-GERMAIN-EN-LAYE 3

ST-JEAN-AUX-BOIS 6

ST-LOUP-DE-NAUD 11

SAINT-GERMAIN-EN-LAYE *Seine-et-Oise*. H 6.

Several successive châteaux have been built on the site chosen by Louis le Gros in about 1122, and only the Sainte-Chapelle, built by Saint-Louis in 1238, has survived all the vicissitudes of the château's history. Many architects worked at Saint-Germain under the orders of their king: Pierre de Chambiges for François I, Philibert de l'Orme for Henri II, Guillaume Marchant for Henri IV, and Le Vau and J. Hardouin-Mansart for Louis XIV. The terrace which dominates the valley of the Seine and looks towards Paris was one of Le Nôtre's masterpieces (1669-1673): 2,500 yards long it gives the gardens their majestic character. Lastly, in the 19th century, Napoleon III had the château restored to its original aspect as it was under François I, and in 1862 installed a museum of antiquities dating from the prehistoric to the Merovingian periods and which has just been beautifully reorganised. The kings of France were very fond of the château of Saint-Germain which explains the number of fine old mansions in the town.

1 Inner courtyard of the château, 16th c. 2 Sainte-Chapelle, 1238. 3 Sword handles, bronze age, Musée des Antiquités Nationales. 4 Hieronymus Bosch (c. 1450-1516): the Conjurer, Musée Municipal, place Maurice-Berteaux.

SAINT-GERMER-DE-FLY *Oise*. H 5.

Two remarkable examples of the Gothic style can be seen side by side at Saint-Germer. The church is an example of the very best primitive Gothic and the Sainte-Chapelle, modelled after its namesake at Paris, is in a more measured style, with high gabled windows.

5 Apse of the church, 1175, and Sainte-Chapelle, by Pierre de Wesencourt, 1366.

SAINT-JEAN-AUX-BOIS *Oise*. I 5.

This pretty village still lives up to its name since the little late 12th-century church, the stone 18th-century bridge and the 16th-century gateway are still surrounded by woods. Next to the church, a fine 12th-century chapter house.

6 Church, late 12th c., single-columned aisle.

SAINT-LEU-D'ESSERENT *Oise*. I 5.

The beautiful church of Saint-Leu, with its single nave and no transept, was greatly admired by Renan for the unity of its style, which is entirely of the 12th century. It is one of the most beautiful churches in the Ile-de-France, its charm also being due to the quality of the stone from nearby quarries which is the same as that used for the building of Chartres, Sens and Versailles.

7 The church and narthex, 12th c. 8 Vaulting of the nave. 9 Keystone of the vault with four kings, narthex.

SAINT-LOUP-DE-NAUD *Seine-et-Marne*. I 7.

What could be more surprising than to find a country church with a portal rivalling the Royal Portal of Chartres cathedral in interest? Such is the great attraction of the church at Saint-Loup. The columnar statues are of an equal quality and have survived in a perfect state. The interior is late Romanesque-early Gothic; unfortunately the quite exceptional Romanesque frescoes were repainted at the end of the 19th century.

10 Portal of the church, about 1170. 11 Columnar statue in the porch, 12th c.

ST-GERMAIN-EN-LAYE 1

ST-GERMAIN-EN-LAYE 2

ST-GERMAIN-EN-LAYE 4

ST-LOUP-DE-NAUD 10

ST-GERMER-DE-FLY 5

ST-LEU-D'ESSERENT 7

ST-LEU-D'ESSERENT 9

ST-LEU-D'ESSERENT 8

99

ST-MARTIN-AUX-BOIS 1

ST-SULPICE-DE-FAVIÈRES 2

SENLIS 7

SÈVRES 14

SAINT-MARTIN-AUX-BOIS *Oise.* I 4.

The former Augustine abbey of Saint-Martin was transformed into farm-buildings, and its fortified gateway protected access to a 13th-century church in which the beauty of the choir fully rivals that of Beauvais. Stalls of the 16th century, sculpted with humorous figures, some 14th-century statues of the Virgin, and a fine Pietà of the 16th century in the sacristy.

I Interior of the church, 13th c.

SAINT-SULPICE-DE-FAVIÈRES *Seine-et-Oise.* H 7.

The large church of Saint-Sulpice was originally built because of the pilgrimage to Saint-Sulpice, bishop of Bourges, in 647. The three tiers of windows in the apse are superb and should be admired both from the exterior and interior. The main impression given by the church is one of lightness and majesty.

2 Interior of the church, 13th c.

SENLIS *Oise.* I 5.

Hunting has always been one of the principal attractions of the region of Senlis and the first French kings had already built a castle at Senlis, where Louis V died as the result of a hunting accident. The great cathedral of Senlis emphasises the importance of the region. It was begun in 1153, and has a severely plain Romanesque façade flanked by two towers, one of which is crowned by a famous 13th-century spire. The great portal and especially the sculpted lintel inspired the later portals of Chartres, Notre-Dame at Paris, Amiens and Reims. Work on the cathedral was continued throughout the centuries, and the Flamboyant portal of the south arm of the transept was carved in the 16th century by Pierre de Chambiges, the architect of the nearby château of Chantilly. The 220 feet-long nave is ornamented with fine galleries which allow one to obtain a fine and rare view of the whole of the church. The façade of the church of Saint-Pierre which was transformed into a market hall, is a very good example of Flamboyant architecture, between the Romanesque tower with its Gothic spire and the Renaissance tower.

The Haubergier archaeological museum has been installed in a 16th-century mansion, of which there are several in Senlis, notably that in the Place Lanavit. Hunting has finally resumed its rights by installing itself in the priory of the château (18th c.) where there is a museum quite unique of its kind in the whole of Europe, illustrating the art of hunting with hounds.

3 Tympanum of the west portal of the cathedral: the Coronation of the Virgin, 13th c. 4 Façade of the south transept of the cathedral, Pierre de Chambiges, 16th c. 5 Galleries in the cathedral. 6 Façade of the former church of Saint-Pierre, 15th c. 7 Oudry (1686-1755): Dog with a bowl, chimney screen, Musée de la Vènerie.

SÈVRES *Seine-et-Oise.* H 6.

There is no type of ceramic, whatever its origin or its date, which is not represented in the museum at Sèvres. The museum was specially built for this purpose in 1876, next to the National Manufactory of Sèvres which was established in 1756 under the patronage of Madame de Pompadour. Visitors are also admitted to the workshops in the porcelain factory.

8 Faïence from Rhodes (or Iznik), bottle, 16th c. 9 Faïence from Delft, decorative panel, 17th c. 10 Faïence from Rouen (blue pattern), vase, 17th c. 11 Faïence from Moustiers (pattern by Bérain), serving dish, 18th c. 12 Soft porcelain from Vincennes, watering-jug, 1755. 13 Sèvres porcelain, coffee cup from a set belonging to Napoleon, early 19th c. 14 Unglazed Sèvres porcelain, Danse champêtre, 19th c.

SENLIS 5

SENLIS 6

SENLIS 4

SENLIS 3

SÈVRES 9

SÈVRES 12

SÈVRES 10

SÈVRES 11

SÈVRES 13

SÈVRES 8

SOISSONS *Aisne*. I 5.

Soissons deserves to be famous for its churches rather than for the quite confused story of the "Vase" which every French school-child knows. The cathedral of Saint-Gervais-Saint-Protais has had a long and eventful history but despite its restorations has kept its robust design, free from any superfluous ornamentation. The south portal, which was the first part of the church to be built, and the light, airy nave are particularly worthy of notice, and the choir is a fine example of Lanceolate Gothic. In the north arm of the transept, an *Adoration of the Shepherds* which Rubens painted as a gift for the Franciscan Friars who had cured him of an illness.

Like the cathedral, the ancient abbey of Saint-Jean-des-Vignes suffered from many wars and restorations. Wide 14th-century cloister, 13th-century church façade and cellars of the abbey. The municipal museum has been installed in the last of Soissons' important churches, where the white stone choir of the old church, with its entirely 13th-century design should be admired, besides certain of the exhibits such as the great gallo-Roman silver dish, the head of a negress by Houdon, and two very fine paintings by Boudin.

I South transept of the cathedral of Saint-Gervais-Saint-Protais, 13th c. 2 Façade of the abbey church of Saint-Jean-des-Vignes, 13th c. 3 Choir of the church of Saint-Léger, 13th c.

LES VAUX-DE-CERNAY *Seine-et-Oise*. H 6.

The abbey was begun by the Benedictines and continued by the Cistercians in the course of its construction in 1147. The façade of the abbey church and its pointed-arch portal have survived almost intact, as well as the greater part of the monks' refectory which was more than a hundred yards long when built.

4 Ruins of the abbey church: rose window in the façade, 12th c. 5 Monks' refectory.

VAUX-LE-VICOMTE *Seine-et-Marne*. I 7.

Work on the château of Vaux-le-Vicomte was begun in 1656 on the orders of the Superintendent Nicolas Fouquet (1615-1680). Thousands of workmen took part in the building, transforming the landscape and even razing villages to the ground. For its inauguration in 1661, Fouquet gave a feast of almost unbelievable magnificence in honour of the young king Louis XIV but several weeks later he was arrested, to die in prison nineteen years later. The château was built by Le Vau in freestone (a revolutionary procedure in comparison with the brick building of the châteaux of Louis XIII), and was decorated by Le Brun, its gardens being designed by Le Nôtre. The same artists later all worked at Versailles for the same royal master. The château has now been skilfully restored, as have the French formal gardens with their ponds and fountains, so that we may now see Vaux-le-Vicomte as La Fontaine, Fouquet's guest, once described it in his verse.

6 Main façade, Le Vau (1656-1661). 7 Façade facing the gardens, by Le Vau, parterres by Le Nôtre. 8 The great oval salon, by Le Brun. 9 Portrait of Fouquet, engraving, 17th c.

VAUX-LE-VICOMTE 9

VAUX-LE-VICOMTE 7

SOISSONS 2

SOISSONS 1

SOISSONS 3

LES VAUX-DE-CERNAY 5

LES VAUX-DE-CERNAY 4

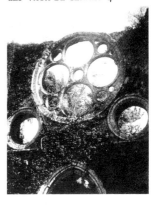

VAUX-LE-VICOMTE 8

VAUX-LE-VICOMTE 6

1

VERSAILLES *Seine-et-Oise.* H 6.

It was at Versailles that the French monarchs built the greatest architectural monument to European civilisation. The guiding spirit in its construction was Louis XIV and the Sun-King has become identified completely with the palace.

In order to carry out this tremendous undertaking, Louis XIV was able to rely on the services of artists of the very first rank, such as the architect Jules Hardouin-Mansart (1646-1708), Le Nôtre (1613-1700) who created the most beautiful park in the world, and Charles Le Brun (1619-1690), who was grand-master of the buildings, and who directed all the work of decoration, surrounded by a galaxy of artists.

Louis XIII had owned a hunting lodge at Versailles, built by Philibert Le Roy. In 1668, filled by a desire for grandeur and dissatisfied with the still unfinished Louvre, Louis XIV ordered his architect Le Vau to transform the little Louis XIII château, and had Mansart continue the work after 1678, despite the opposition of Colbert who disapproved of such sumptuous extravagance. Louis XIV overcame all obstacles: the terrain too narrow and surrounded by marshes, was without trees and water, but hills were levelled, the soil was drained, forests were planted and water brought from Marly. The king visited the site every day and conferred with the builders and after fifty years of work the 1,800 feet long palace was at last ready to receive the thousand courtiers and four thousand servants who were to live there according to the rigid etiquette that Saint-Simon has described for posterity.

After the splendour of the Sun-King's reign, Louis XV attempted to return to a more intimate atmosphere when he moved to Versailles in 1738. Louis XVI was to follow suit and Marie-Antoinette built her miniature farm to play in, and it was at Versailles that absolute monarchy came to its end on October 6, 1789. Everything that could be carried was pillaged, destroyed, sold or transferred to the Louvre and it was even believed for a time that Versailles would be demolished. Louis-Philippe prevented the disaster by offering his own savings as a first contribution towards the rescue of the palace.

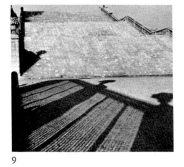

9

1 Aerial view of the château and the gardens. 2 Marble courtyard, 17th c. 3 Façade of the château facing the gardens, by Le Vau, F. d'Orbay and J. Hardouin-Mansart, 1708. 4 Pool of Apollo by Tuby, 1670. 5 Nymphs bathing, bas-relief by Girardon, 1675. 6 Grandes Baigneuses by Renoir, 1885, Coll. Carroll S. Tyson, Philadelphia, U. S. A. 7 Apollo served by Nymphs, Girardon and Regnaudin, 1675. 8 Tritons grooming Apollo's horses, by G. and B. Massy, 1675. 9 The Hundred Stairs, by Mansart, 1688.

3

2

4

7

8

5

6

The approach to the palace is by the majestic avenue, past the Grandes Écuries (which held 2,500 horses), and the magnificent gilded railings into the immense front courtyard dominated by a statue of Louis XIV. At the end of the little marble courtyard (Cour de Marbre) which was once paved with black and white stones, the red-brick façade of Louis XIII's château stands in contrast to the monumental wings in white stone (already used by Le Vau at Vaux-le-Vicomte). A side door gives access to the interior of the palace. The great apartments of Louis XIV are resplendent with marble and gold and the Hall of Mirrors (Galerie des Glaces) (1678-1684) overlooks the terrace that Le Vau had built above the gardens; in the great hall, each window faces a mirror, the largest of their time to be made in a single piece. The small apartments of Louis XV and Louis XVI show the evolution of royal taste and the transition from courtly splendour to a taste for comfort and intimacy. An important part of the palace has been transformed into a museum of the Glories of France, with a rich collection of historical paintings and portraits. The Opera has been entirely restored, with its decorations of painted wood-panels by Pajou in the 18th century. The park, with the Grand Canal at its centre, is filled with statues, fountains, lodges and leads to the two Trianons and the cottages of the Queen (Hameau de la Reine) where Marie-Antoinette used to hold court with her ladies-in-waiting, dressed as shepherdesses. Girardon's bas-reliefs, the *Bathing Nymphs* inspired Renoir's masterpiece the *Grandes Baigneuses* in 1885.

The town of Versailles is a fine example of 17th-18th century town-planning; no house was allowed (or is allowed even now) to rise higher than the palace. The streets are lined with *hôtels* and the visitor can easily lose himself in the past as he walks the streets of a town that was entirely consecrated to the glory of the king and his court for a century and a half.

9

1 The Grand Trianon, by J. Hardouin-Mansart, 1687. 2 The Petit Trianon, by Gabriel, 1768. 3 The Cottage of Marie-Antoinette, by Mique, 1778. 4 The Galerie des Glaces, by Mansart and Le Brun, 1684. 5 Ceiling of the Salon of Hercules by Lemoyne, 1736. 6 Corner cabinet of Louis XV and King's Study, by Oeben and Riesener, 1769. 7 The chapel of the palace, by J. Hardouin-Mansart and R. de Cotte, 1707. 8 The Opéra, by J.-A. Gabriel, 1770. 9 Portrait of Claude d'Annebault, Marshal of France, 16th c. 10 Mignard (1610-1695): The Duchess of Maine as a child, with parrot. 11 Nattier (1685-1766): Madame Adelaïde de France, dressed as Diana. 12 Baron Gros (1771-1835): the Battle of Aboukir.

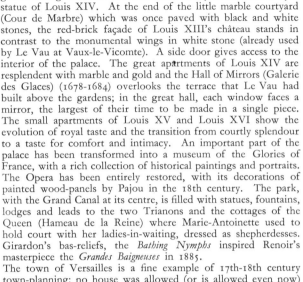

10

11

12

1

2

3

4

8

5

7

6

VEZ 1

VEZ *Aisne.* I 5.

The Musée du Valois has been installed in the chapel of the medieval castle of Vez which was rebuilt in the 14th century, and is dominated by a superb keep.

1 Keep of the castle, 14th c.

VINCENNES *Seine.* I 6.

Standing in the outskirts of the city of Paris, Vincennes is the only surviving royal residence of the Middle Ages. Nothing remains of the castle built by Philip Augustus and Saint-Louis. It was reconstructed and enlarged in the 14th century by Philip VI, John the Good and Charles V, abandoned, then altered to fit the taste of the time for Mazarin by Le Vau in about 1652, but Louis XIV preferred the palace of Versailles, and Napoleon turned the castle into an arsenal.

Despite all these vicissitudes, the castle has retained its original appearence: the 14th-century keep has been disengaged, the chapel has had its 16th-century stained-glass windows restored, the 17th-century portico has been repaired and the Pavillon du Roi is now completely restored.

2 View of the castle, keep 14th c., Sainte-Chapelle 16th c., Pavillon du Roi 17th c. 3 The keep, 14th c.

WIDEVILLE *Seine-et-Oise.* H 6.

This charming Louis XIII château has kept its original period interior decoration with paintings by Simon Vouet. In the park, the grotto or "nympheum" of the 17th century is a rare surviving example of the rustic follies of the period (q. v. La Bastie d'Urfé).

4 Nympheum of the château, 17th c.

VINCENNES 2

VINCENNES 3

WIDEVILLE 4

IV

MIRROR OF MARIE DE MÉDICIS, 16TH C., GALERIE D'APOLLON,
MUSÉE DU LOUVRE, PARIS *(Bulloz)*

AUGUSTE RENOIR (1841-1920), MOULIN DE LA GALETTE, DETAIL,
MUSÉE DU JEU DE PAUME, PARIS

PARIS

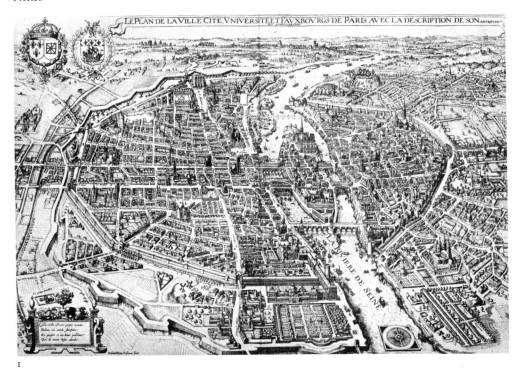

I

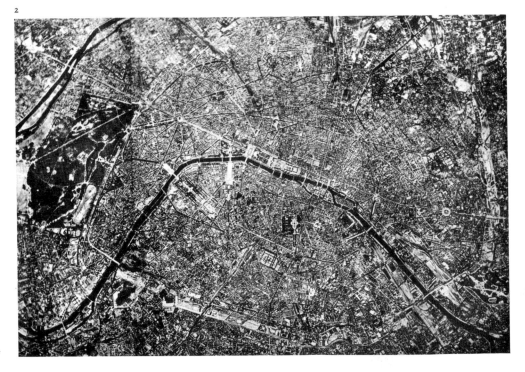

2

As Michelet said of France, Paris is a human being.

By a sort of sentimental tradition, the older generation of Parisians still think of Paris being a city contained within the old line of its fortifications, with the bends of the Seine determining the city's shape, the islands constituting its heart, and the twenty bridges giving rhythm to the flow of the river. But the modern city and the suburbs have spread far beyond the old city bounds, and have doubled the area and the population of Paris, which now counts nearly nine million inhabitants.

But the fact remains that it is only within the ancient enceinte that the remains of the two thousand years of the city's history are to be found. Some relics are only of interest for the historian such as the arena of Lutetia, the thermae of the emperor Julian (4th c.) or the remains of Philip Augustus' wall (12th c.). If we look at the plan of Paris as drawn by Mérion in 1615, we will see how the city had grown during the reign of Louis XIII, when some twenty windmills could be counted by the gates of Paris.

To know what sort of city Paris is, we should approach it from the east, as Attila had wished to do in the 5th century. Admittedly, the approach via the eastern suburbs is not very inviting, but it will soon lead to the apse of Notre-Dame, the old houses of the Ile Saint-Louis and the Ile de la Cité, the historic district of the Place des Vosges and the old *hôtels* of the Marais, the church of Saint-Eustache, the parish church of the Halles, and from there, to the Palace of the Louvre, often transformed in the course of its history, and always growing richer in treasures. From there, we shall come to the Place de la Concorde, that great square which reaches out towards the Palais Bourbon and the Madeleine, and opening from the Tuileries onto the noble Champs-Élysées which, in turn, will take us to the majestic Arch of Triumph and past it into the most modern Paris of all — the Palais de la Défense. Or else you might prefer to follow the river itself through the city, coming out of the city again after passing by the recently built Palais de Chaillot on its hill, and the famous Eiffel Tower, soaring anachronistically above the École Militaire and the Invalides, and for which the Parisians have shown such curious affection. The inquisitive tourist might also care to visit some other famous monument such as the Opéra or the pseudo-Byzantine basilica of the Sacré-Cœur in Montmartre, among the famous night-clubs and cafés on the "Butte".

Let us follow the history of Paris through its many monuments. To describe them, the following order has been adopted: first, the bridges on the Seine, then the buildings, both great and small, that give Paris its character, religious monuments (the oldest of which date from the 12th century), such civil monuments as palaces and *hôtels*, and lastly, the fountains and statues which decorate the squares and streets of Paris.

There are more than thirty museums in Paris and some are renowned throughout the world but they cannot possibly be described in a few lines and a few pictures. All we can do in this guide is to give a brief but representative idea of their richness through a few, well-chosen examples.

I

2

3

4

If we approach Paris from the east, as suggested, by following the Seine, we shall first come to Bercy and Charenton which are still suburbs for the city only really begins at the Pont d'Austerlitz or, even better, the Pont Sully (1878), which crosses the Ile Saint-Louis at the eastern extremity of the island.

It is at the *Pont de la Tournelle* (1) that we shall catch our first real glimpse of Paris. It was first a wooden bridge (1369) connecting the left bank to the Ile de la Cité and it has been rebuilt several times, the last being in 1928; the statue of Saint Geneviève protecting the city is by Landowski, but is not particularly successful.

The Ile Saint-Louis was a creation of Louis XIII, for when it was linked to the right bank by the *Pont Marie* (2) by the engineer Marie (1618-1635), the islet was completely bare. The houses were all built in the space of a few years whence the unity of style of its buildings. Downstream, at the far tip of the Ile de la Cité, the *Pont-Neuf* (3) is the oldest bridge of all: a double bridge, it was begun by Henry III (1578). Its statue of Henry IV (who was assassinated nearby in the Rue de la Ferronerie) by Lemot (1818) is still a popular meeting place. No less popular with Parisians is the *Pont des Arts* (4) which was built in the Second Empire, to connect the Louvre with the Collège Mazarin. The *Pont-Royal* (5), built by Louis XIV (1689) which ends at

5

7

8

6

9

the Pavillon de Flore, at the extreme end of the Louvre, is one of the finest examples of monumental bridge building.

The more modern bridges, towards the west of the city, are not without a charm and a history of their own (*The Pont de la Concorde* is an integral part of the great square; illustration on the following page).

The *Pont Alexandre III* (6), decorated with lamp holders in the *art-nouveau* style of 1900, is a witness to the famous Franco-Russian alliance of the time. The *Zouave* (7) of the *Pont de l'Alma* (1856) is a well-known Parisian character and serves as a gauge in times of flood. The *Pont d'Iéna* (8) was nobly transformed for the Exhibition of 1937 and serves as a hyphen between the Eiffel Tower and the Palais de Chaillot.

The Pont de Grenelle, built in 1875, is decorated with a small-scale replica of Bartholdi's famous *Statue of Liberty* (9) at the entrance to New York harbour.

Recently, the last of the bridges of Paris was the arched viaduct of Point-du-Jour at Auteuil but it has now been entirely transformed by the work in progress for a new highway.

We should not forget that the bridges of Paris are constantly changing. It was only in 1786 that the artist Hubert Robert painted the *Demolition of the houses on the Pont Notre-Dame* (10), for, in older times, all the bridges were covered with houses and stalls.

10

3

2

1

4

The *Pont de la Concorde* (1) was built in 1790 and then impressively and successfully widened in 1930, and is now an integral part of the great square which is one of the most striking examples of monumental architecture in the world. Gabriel's palaces, the fountains, the horses from Marly by Coustou and Coyscvox, the surprising obelisk, and the radiating avenues which give on one side onto the Tuileries, on the other, to the *Champs-Élysées* (2) and the Arc de Triomphe, and the north-south avenues running from the Madeleine to the Palais Bourbon all contribute to give the square its world-wide renown. Originally the Place Louis XV, it was named the Place de la Revolution before finally becoming the Place de la Concorde. Its present enchanting aspect was the result of gradual changes: the palaces and the design of the square date from 1775; the bridge from 1790; the horses of Marly, 1795; the transformation of the Palais Bourbon by the addition of the colonnade, 1807; the Madeleine which completes the balance of the design was finished between 1828 and 1842, after many difficulties; the Arc de Triomphe, 1836; the obelisk was raised by Louis-Philippe in 1836 and the two *fountains* were built between 1836 and 1846 (3).

The gardens of the Tuileries which adjoin the square contain one of the most striking monuments of the 19th century: the *Arc de Triomphe du Carrousel* (4), built by Denon (1808) which was formerly a gateway to the Tuileries, and since the burning of the Palace in 1871, forming an axis with the *Arc de Triomphe* (9) (1836) or *Arc de l'Étoile*, of which it seems to be a smaller-scale replica, at the other end of the Champs-Élysées.

By following the Seine through Paris it has not been possible to visit the great squares which are the glory of the "right bank". The ancient *Place Royale*, now the *Place des Vosges* (5) was built by Henry IV in 1605 and was the first attempt at opening out a wide space in the heart of the chaotic old city. The square has kept its unity of style, with its red-brick buildings and sloping slate roofs. The square of the *Théâtre Français* (6), just outside the Palais-Royal has kept its pleasing, old-fashioned Second Empire aspect. The magnificently designed *Place Vendôme* (7) is one of the most elegant squares in the whole of Paris and was laid out between 1687-1720. The imperial column was set up in 1810 to replace a statue of Louis XIV, and was pulled down by the Communards in 1871, when, it may be remembered, the unfortunate artist Courbet was accused of complicity and had to flee from France. The *Place de l'Opéra* (8) was originally the centre of Paris but, with the expansion of the city, it is now rather to the west of centre. The Opéra itself was built by Charles Garnier in 1875 in a sumptuous, rather heavy, composite style, and is a masterpiece of Second Empire architecture. The piercing of the *Avenue de l'Opéra* towards the Louvre was one of the greatest revolutions in town planning accomplished by the Baron Haussmann.

5

6

7

8

9

117

More outlying great squares such as the *Places de la Nation, République* and *Italie* together with the monuments in their centre are of little artistic merit. But the Place de la Bastille is worth visiting for the great column in its centre and the inlaid paving stones in the square which show the outlines of the 14th-century fortress whose destruction in 1789 was the symbol of the French Revolution: a large *faïence stove* in the shape of the Bastille may be seen in the Musée Carnavalet (1) and the popular celebrations in Paris on the 14th of July commemorate its storming by the people. Other squares which evoke the true spirit of old Paris include the little *Place Furstenberg* (2) right behind Saint-Germain-des-Prés, where Delacroix's studio (now a small museum) may be seen; at the other end of Paris, in Montmartre, the Théâtre de l'Atelier in the *Place Dancourt* (3) continues the adventurous traditions of the old Théâtre-Libre, but the nearby *Place du Tertre* (4) adjoining the basilica of the Sacré-Cœur has now been transformed into a tourist-attraction with its cafés and bars and is only a caricature of what it had been during the heroic period of the Butte, when Renoir could be seen carrying his great painting (now in the Jeu de Paume) from his studio in the Rue Cortot to the Moulin de la Galette in 1876. This was the time when such artists as Van Gogh, Toulouse-Lautrec and Utrillo, the author of the famous *"Rue Saint-Rustique"* (5) (now in the Roudinesco Collection) among so many others, all lived and worked in Montmartre.

Paris had broken out of its old bounds during the reign of François I to take the shape we may see in Mérion's view of the city as it was under Louis XIII (1615), and walls, fortifications and gateways were built around it as late as 1915. The *Porte Saint-Denis* by Blondel (6), 1671, and the *Porte Saint-Martin* (7) by Pierre Bullet, 1674, at the beginning of what are still called the Grands Boulevards, are relics of the old walled city.

In 1785, an architectural genius, Claude-Nicolas Ledoux, began to build a series of gateways and toll-houses around the new enceinte which were never completed, but we may still see the *Rotonde de la Villette* (8), 1789.

1

2

5

4

3

6

8

7

4

2

In order to see monumental Paris properly we should follow the course of time and no longer that of the Seine.

Most of the buildings of Paris, religious or secular, which were built before the 19th century are to be found within a restricted area, within the city limits as shown in Merion's plan. This area can be roughly defined as that lying between the Panthéon, the Salpetrière Hospital and the Luxembourg Palace on the left bank, in the south, and between the Bastille, Place des Vosges and the Marais district on the right bank to the north and east; from the Louvre and the Concorde on the right bank to the west, and over the river to the south from Saint-Germain-des-Prés as far as the Invalides.

ECCLESIASTICAL ARCHITECTURE

Even though *Notre-Dame* (1) is not the most ancient Parisian monument (the apse of *Saint-Martin-des-Champs* (2) dates from 1140) it is the pride of the city. It was built before the cathedral of Chartres, being begun in 1163 on the site of an ancient temple on ground which had become a marsh, and work was continued during the whole of the 12th and 13th centuries. Notre-Dame is built in a very pure radiant Gothic style, and is the prototype of the cathedral with one great *main nave and double aisles with high galleries* (3) (height of the vault 110 feet, length of the nave 400 feet). During the reign of Saint Louis (1265), the architect Pierre de Montereau added an off-set transept with a sumptuous *Rose window* in the Flamboyant Gothic style (4). The restoration of the cathedral, begun in 1844 by Viollet-le-Duc was certainly necessary but even though he showed great respect for the original fabric much of the sculpture was completely restored, such as the famous *Galerie des Rois* and the gargoyles: nevertheless, the *Virgin Portal* on the left (5) and the *choir-screen* (6), decorated on the exterior with polychrome bas-reliefs (14th c.) have survived in their original state. One of the most genuine of the French naïve painters, *Louis Vivin* (1861-1936), has painted a very expressive view of Notre-Dame, showing both the façade and the south front side-by-side in a style close to that of the analytical cubists (7).

3

I

6

5

VIVIN 7

1

2

3

Saint-Pierre-de-Montmartre (1), adjoining the basilica of the Sacré-Cœur, is one of the earliest Romanesque buildings in Paris (1147), together with the churches of *Saint-Julien-le-Pauvre* (2), second half of the 12th century, and *Saint-Germain-de-Charonne* (3) which is partly 12th-century and has a 13th-century tower. The intrinsic beauty of the latter church is heightened by its situation in a picturesque little country cemetery which has survived. Despite alterations, the tower and the nave of *Saint-Germain-des-Prés* (4) are good examples of the Romanesque style, and the quarter surrounding the church is famous for its youth and gaiety. The *Sainte-Chapelle* (5) is a superb example of the Gothic style at its finest: it was built by Saint Louis in 1248, in the enceinte of the ancient palace, to contain a reliquary with a fragment of the True Cross. The magnificent ribbed vaulting is a triumph of Gothic architecture, and the walls seem to be little more than a framework for the soaring *stained-glass windows* (6).
The Hundred Years War held up the development of architecture in Paris, but when peace returned, the Flamboyant style, the last manifestation of the Gothic spirit, took hold of architecture in the mid-15th century. The *Tour Saint-Jacques* (7) was built in 1522 and flanked the south portal of the church of Saint-Jacques de la Boucherie which was the Paris shrine for pilgrims on their way to Saint James of Compostella. *Saint-Séverin* is a magnificent example of Flamboyant Gothic style and was praised by J.-K. Huysmans who drew attention to the *columns* of *the ambulatory* (8) which fan out at the top like palm-trees, dating from 1494. The porch of *Saint-Germain-l'Auxerrois* (9), dating from 1439, is another magnificent example of the Flamboyant style (the centre portal dates from the 13th century).
With its façade, and three superimposed pediments, the late 15th-16th-century church of *Saint-Étienne-du-Mont* (10) shows a progressive change in styles; the interior contains the only *rood-screen* in Paris (11).

4

5

6

7

8

9

11

10

123

1

3

2

4

5

124

The church of *Saint-Eustache* (1), a vast edifice in the very heart of the Halles district, was begun in 1532 and only finished in the mid-17th century, but it still adheres to the Gothic tradition with its main nave and two double-aisles. It was in the reign of Louis XIII that the first Italian-style domed churches made their appearance in Paris, the first being the *Chapelle des Carmes* (2), built in 1620. The foundation-stone was laid by the queen Marie de Médicis as a nostalgic souvenir of the domes of Florence. Many other domes can be seen against the Paris skyline, such as that of the *Sorbonne* (3); only the chapel is ancient (1635), with its tomb of Richelieu by Girardon (1694) for the rest of the building was built in 1884. The *Val-de-Grâce* was created by Queen Anne of Austria who had an elegant lodge built in the gardens as her personal residence; the chapel (4) was designed by François Mansart and was completed in 1665. It was part of a Benedictine convent; the altar (5) has rich Baroque decoration inspired by that at Saint Peter's in Rome by Bernini.

The chapel of the *Salpêtrière* (6) was the work of Libéral Bruant (1676); a hospital had been founded in 1656 by Louis XIV on the site of an arsenal of the reign of Louis XIII (the name is derived from the salt-petre with which gun-powder was made). Three domed edifices which no longer serve their original religious purpose and which will be described later are: the Palace of the Institute with its cupola, now the home of the Académie Française and originally the chapel of the Collège des Quatre Nations created by Mazarin in 1661 and completed in 1688; and lastly, the two most important and also most recent domes: that of the Invalides, built by J. Hardouin-Mansart in 1706, and the highest of all (250 feet), that of the Panthéon, which Soufflot built in 1780, and which was destined to be a church dedicated to Saint Geneviève.

The church of *Saint-Gervais-et-Saint-Protais* (7) is very ancient (6th c.) but it was rebuilt in the 14th century and it was only in 1621 that it was given its Italian Jesuit-style portal which has nothing in common with the Gothic interior.

The church of Notre-Dame-des-Victoires was commissioned by Louis XIII to commemorate the taking of La Rochelle and was begun in 1629 by Le Muet in a Baroque Jesuit style but was only completed in 1731 when the porch was built.

Saint-Roch was built between 1633 and 1740; its staircase is part of history for it was from there that the young Bonaparte fired upon the royalist rebels who were threatening the Convention on the 13 Vendémiaire, Year IV of the Republic (1795). *Saint-Sulpice* (8) was begun in 1665 after a design by Le Vau but was only finished in 1745 by Servandoni who built the façade, and the south tower has remained unfinished. Delacroix was commissioned to decorate the chapel of the *Saints-Anges* in 1849 and worked in the church from 1853 until his death in 1863; the two main paintings in the chapel: *Heliodorus expelled from the Temple* and *Jacob wrestling with the Angel* (9) are among his masterpieces. After Soufflot's Panthéon, the greatest religious structure of the 19th century was the *Madeleine* (10). The work began in 1764: it was to have been a church dedicated to Saint-Madeleine, designed as a classical temple with a peristyle of fifty-two columns. Work was interrupted by the Revolution, continued by Napoleon who wanted to transform the building into a Temple of Glory, interrupted again, and then continued under the Restoration and only completed in 1842. The basilica of the *Sacré-Cœur* (11) at Montmartre, which dominates the whole of Paris, was built by national subscription by Abadie from 1873 onwards, in a neo-Romanesque-Byzantine style and was only completed some fifty years later.

A number of modern churches have been built in Paris since the beginning of the century. *Notre-Dame-du-Raincy* (12) in the neighbouring suburbs is a successful example of concrete architecture and was built by Perret in 1922. The church of the Saint-Esprit in the Avenue Daumesnil dates from 1935 and its novelty mainly lies in its lighting and painted wall decoration, Desvallières' Stations of the Cross running around the entire building, the large panel of the Pentecost by Maurice Denis, etc.

The architects who were commissioned to rebuild Saint-Pierre-de-Chaillot were more traditional for they adopted a style which was Romanesque-Byzantine in inspiration (1937).

6

7

9

10

8

12

11

2

3

SECULAR ARCHITECTURE

The towers of the *Conciergerie* (1), the oldest secular building in Paris, have survived as reminders of the enceinte of the first royal palace that was enlarged by Philip the Handsome at the end of the 13th century. The Clock-Tower (Tour de l'Horloge) was also built during Philip's reign but the clock itself dates from 1334. The Sainte-Chapelle is now enclosed within the circuit of the modern buildings of the Palais de Justice (Law Courts). The vaulted chambers of the Conciergerie are as majestic as any in Mont-Saint-Michel or the Pope's Palace at Avignon.

At the end of the 14th century, Philip the Handsome's successors abandoned the palace on the Ile de la Cité for that of the Louvre. Of all the most ancient buildings in Paris, it is the *Louvre* (2) that is the richest in historical memories. As we may see from a page from the *Très Riches Heures du duc de Berry*, 1415 (3), the palace was built in the style of a fortress by Philip Augustus, and was begun in 1204. It became the favourite residence of the monarchy from the reign of Charles V (1364-1380) onwards. In 1527, François I pulled down the great tower and began work on a new palace. In 1563 Catherine de Medicis began yet another palace which was later joined by two wings, the Petite Galerie and the *Grande Galerie* (4) running alongside the Seine (late 16th — early 17th c.). After the Revolution the Court settled permanently in the Tuileries, leaving the Louvre as a museum. The triumphal arch of the Carrousel, built in the classical style to commemorate Napoleon's victories, was used from 1806 onwards as a monumental entrance into the gardens of the palace. The Tuileries and the left wing of the Louvre were burnt in the Commune rising in 1871. The Louvre wing was rebuilt by Lefuel (1875-1878) and the extremity of its façade overlooking the Seine was decorated with Carpeaux's famous group sculpture representing the *Triumph of Flora* (5).

The most important parts of the palace include: the *Cour carrée* (6), with its south façade by Pierre Lescot; it was begun under François I and finished under Henri II. It is the very heart of the old buildings, together with the Pavillon de l'Horloge (1625) which is decorated with caryatids after designs by the sculptor Sarrazin; the Pavillon Sully, contained in Pierre Lescot's façade (7) faces the great courtyard (1554); *Perrault's colonnade* (8) which terminates the palace was designed by a doctor-architect, the brother of the author of the fairy tales, in 1670.

Inside the palace, two of the main features of interest, among so many others, are: the *Salle des Cariatides* (9) by Jean Goujon (1550), and the ceiling of the *Galerie d'Apollon* (10) which was reconstructed after a fire during the reign of Louis XIV by Lebrun. The decoration of the centre of the vault was completed by Delacroix with his painting of "Apollo defeating the serpent Python". Finally, it would be difficult to imagine the great staircase without the glorious *Winged Victory* (11) which was discovered on the isle of Samothrace in 1863 and brought to the Louvre in 1866.

1

5

4

7

8

10

6

9

11

1

2

The Conciergerie has been mentioned as one of the most ancient vestiges of medieval Paris. Only the turrets now remain of the *hôtel des Abbés de Fécamp*, in the Rue Hautefeuille (13th c.) and the *hôtel de Clisson* (c. 1300). The *hôtel de Cluny* (1) is set amid the ruins of the Baths of Julian, and its oldest part dates from the 15th century. Its chapel, the former oratory of the Benedictine abbey, has a single central pillar which supports vaulting of incomparable elegance.

The hôtel Lamoignon (24, Rue Pavée) was built in 1580 for Diane de France, the daughter of Henri II.

The 17th century was a very important period for civic architecture in Paris. Little now remains of the Louis XIII style, in brick and stone: the finest surviving example is the lovely Place des Vosges in the heart of the district of the Marais, which was then an elegant residential quarter.

The *hôtel Carnavalet* (3), 23, Rue de Sévigné, dates in part from before the 17th century for it was begun by J. Bullant in 1544, but it was given its present appearance by Du Cerceau, and then Mansart who completed it (1655-1661). Madame de Sévigné lived there from 1677 until the year of her death in 1696.

The façade facing the courtyard of the *hôtel de Sully* (4), 62, rue Saint-Antoine (1624), by Jean Androuet Du Cerceau, is ornamented with fine figures representing the Seasons.

The hôtel de Juigné, 5, rue de Thorigny, was built in 1656 by Jean Bouiller for a salt-tax-gatherer, whence its nick-name of hôtel Salé. Its staircase is justly renowned for the purity of its lines.

The *hôtel de Beauvais* (5), 68, rue François-Miron (1655) was built by the architect Antoine Le Pautre who was able to avoid the monotony of the usual square courtyard by giving it the form of an elegant oval, which was very suitable in view of the restricted space he had at his disposal.

Many of the *hôtels* of the Marais are no longer used as residences; one of the exceptions is that of the Ambassadors of Holland at 67, rue Vieille-du-Temple, built in 1655. The Medusa's head over the *doorway* (6) is a particularly fine piece of decoration.

At about the same time, two splendid private dwellings were raised on the Ile Saint-Louis. One, the hôtel Lambert, is still inhabited, like the hôtel of the Ambassadors of Holland; it was built in 1640 by Le Vau for the President Lambert, and contains splendid decorations by Le Brun, especially in the *Galerie d'Hercule* (7). Only a few steps away, on the same quayside, the *hôtel de Lauzun* (8), 17, quai d'Anjou, built in 1658. It was once famous for its literary gatherings attended by such writers as Gauthier and Baudelaire, etc. The interior is sumptuously decorated.

In the Val-de-Grâce, the small *Pavillon d'Anne d'Autriche* (9) completes one of the finest 17th-century architectural groups in Paris. If the 17th century left such beautiful private dwellings for us to admire, we may imagine the splendour of the palaces and larger buildings.

The palace of the *Luxembourg* (10) was begun in 1615 by Salomon de Brosse for Marie de Medicis. The great series of paintings by Rubens (1621-1625) in honour of the Queen has been removed to the Louvre. Delacroix painted the decorations for the Library in 1847. The south façade giving onto the gardens was pushed forward during the 19th century.

The *Palais-Royal* (11) was first called the Palais-Cardinal; it was built by Lemercier for Richelieu in 1639 and became the Palais-Royal after his death; at the end of the century it became the property of the Duc d'Orléans, the Regent, who entirely transformed it. With its elegant, regular succession of arcades and its garden it became a fashionable meeting place and a centre for gaming and pleasure. It was there that Camille Desmoulins urged the Parisians to revolt in 1789. The *Galerie des Proues*, which has been preserved, is a reminder of Richelieu's interest in the navy. The *Palais Mazarin* (12), the Collège des Quatre Nations, was commissioned by Cardinal Mazarin only a few days before his death in 1661 and work began in 1665 after designs by Le Vau.

9

3

5

4

7

6

8

12

10

11

129

1

2

The magnificent façade of the *hôtel des Invalides* (1) by Libéral Bruant, dates from 1671-1676 and avoids any suggestion of monotony by the discreet and successful use of ornamental trophies. The *dome* (2) was raised by J. Hardouin-Mansart between 1679 and 1706 when the Chapelle Saint-Louis appeared to be too small. The façade derives from the Gesu in Rome and the dome, covered with gilded lead, is the finest religious monument to have been built in France since the Renaissance. A number of important buildings, follies and princely lodges date from the 18th century. The National Archives occupy two of the most magnificent *hôtels* in all of Paris: the *hôtel de Rohan* (3), built by Delamair in 1705, with its luxurious decoration extending even to the outbuildings, with the *Chevaux du Soleil* (4) over the stables; the *hôtel de Soubise* (5), 1705-1709, with its superbly harmonious horse-shoe courtyard with fifty-six columns.

The Élysée Palace, the dwelling of the Presidents of the Republic, the former hôtel d'Évreux (1718, by Mollet) has the vastest private gardens in the whole of Paris. The *hôtel Matignon* (6), 1718, is also by Mollet. The *hôtel Biron* (7), 1728, by Aubert and Gabriel, was lived in by Rodin from 1904 and is a rare example of the Regency style. The *Palais de la Légion d'Honneur* (8), the hôtel de Salm, dates from 1782. The *Palais-Bourbon* was built in 1728 for the dowager duchess of Bourbon, daughter of Madame de Montespan, and originally had a façade of gardens and terraces overlooking the Seine but it was altered in 1762, and in 1804 it was given its present pillared façade to make it conform to the style of the Place de la Concorde; the *inner courtyard* has remained unchanged (9). The palace has become the Chamber of Deputies and its library was completely decorated by Delacroix (1838-1847) with themes from classical legends. The buildings of the *École Militaire* (10) date from 1751 and were completed in 1771 after designs by Gabriel.

The tiny *Palais de Bagatelle* (11) was built in sixty days in 1775 as the result of a wager between the Comte d'Artois and his sister-in-law the Queen Marie-Antoinette.

Many other less important but no less charming buildings have survived from the 18th century: the *château des Ternes*, the lodge of the Princes of Lamballe at Passy, the prince's lodge now part of the Hospice Debrousse, the hôtel de Massa (1784) which was dismantled and removed, brick by brick, to its present home behind the Observatory, and the Pavillon Favart in the heart of the present popular quarter of Menilmontant, etc.

The most monumental, massive architectural creation of the 18th century in Paris was Soufflot's *Panthéon* (12) (1757-1780). It was first a church dedicated to Saint Geneviève, then transformed in 1791 into a temple to the glory of great men. Its frescoes by Puvis de Chavannes are a reminder of its original purpose for they represent scenes from the life of the saint.

In 1803, Eugène de Beauharnais acquired the *hôtel* (78, rue de Lille) that the architect Boffrand had built for himself in 1714, and transformed it, by adding the graceful *peristyle* in the "Egyptian" style (13); this splendid *hôtel* has preserved its original interior decoration.

13

4

3

5

7

6

II

8

9

12

10

4

3

The Emperor Napoleon had little time to build but the Arc de Triomphe was his great inspiration. It was commissioned in 1806, and was begun after a design by Chalgrin but only completed in 1836. A *child's drawing* (1) shows it in all its glory; the columns are decorated with large sculpted reliefs of which the finest is Rude's *Marseillaise* (2).

Charles Garnier's *Opéra* (begun in 1862 but only inaugurated in 1875) is the most important monument left by the Second Empire. Its style is confused, but its vast proportions and its great *staircase* (3) are highly impressive and its interior design makes it the most beautiful theatre in Paris. Carpeaux's *Danse* (4) which completed the decoration in 1869 caused a scandal at the time.

The Hôtel de Ville (Town Hall) was destroyed by ·fire in 1871 and was faithfully reconstructed in 1888; the 16th-and 17th-century design is inspired by the Renaissance but was transformed in the 19th century.

The world-famous *Eiffel Tower* (5) was built by the engineer Eiffel for the exhibition of 1889 and when it was built it was the highest structure in the world (900 feet) and has remained as an outstanding example of iron construction, in the age which preceded architecture in cement. From the same period date several blocks of flats such as that at *29, avenue Rapp* (6) which is a fine example of *art nouveau* architecture. The Theatre des Champs-Élysées with its sober lines was a bold architectural achievement (A. and G. Perret, 1913) and its decoration with frescoes by Maurice Denis and bas-reliefs by Bourdelle marks a date in the history of architecture. In a few years there was a complete change in building styles and techniques. The *Palais de Chaillot* (7) with its immense curving wings and the immense Palais des Musées on the Quai de New York which extends as far as the Avenue Wilson 12 yards higher up a slope, were both completed for the 1937 Paris Exhibition. Among the most recent spectacular achievements of Paris architecture we may mention those that have transformed the skyline of the capital: the *UNESCO building* (8), place Fontenoy, by Breuer, Nervi and Zehrfuss, 1958, with decorations including a *mosaic wall by Miró* (9), a Calder mobile, a sculpture by Moore, and frescoes by Picasso; the *C. N. I. T.* (10) at the Rond-Point de la Defense, by Zehrfuss in 1961, and the most recent, the *Palais de la Radio* (11), quai de Passy, with its strictly geometric masses, by H. Bernard in 1962.

I

2

5

6

7

8

9

10

11

I

FOUNTAINS

Paris has always been short of water. Now only a matter of pipes and taps, it was formerly a pretext for the building of durable monuments in the form of fountains, however insufficient they might be. The oldest of these works of art is certainly that hidden at the back of a courtyard at 160, rue de Belleville: the *Regard* (1), a small stone dome crowned with a lantern which dates from the 16th century. This modest and forgotten relic was the precursor of the ancient water towers of the city.

Standing in another quarter which is now bereft of its former splendour, the *Fontaine des Innocents* (2) (square des Innocents) may be seen to be a masterpiece of the Renaissance (1549); designed by Lescot, its water nymphs are the work of Jean Goujon.

The grotto with stalactites of the *Fontaine Médicis* (3) was by Salomon de Brosse (1624) who built it after completing the Palais du Luxembourg. It was entirely transformed in 1863 and completed by a group sculpture representing Acis and Galatea surprised by the jealous Polyphemus.

The 18th century gave Paris the elegant Fontaine des Quatre-Saisons in the rue de Grenelle; its *bas-reliefs* (4) by Bouchardon (1745) are its greatest merit for the central part is rather too heavy and massive in proportion to the narrowness of the street.

The Parc Monceau was once a highly elegant meeting place: its *Naumachia* (5) with its columns and ruins that came from a rotonda of Catherine de Medicis are souvenirs of the 18th century for the design was by Carmontelle in 1785.

In the 19th century Paris was enriched by the addition of several important fountains. Two fountains in the purest Empire style date from 1806: the *Fontaine de la Paix* (6) by Voimer which finally found a permanent home in the allée du Séminaire (rue Bonaparte) after it was cleared of buildings. The fountain was first sited in the centre of the Place Saint-Sulpice where it must have been rather lost and was then for a time banished to the market at Saint-Germain. The academic but nonetheless charming ornamental motifs on the fountain represent Commerce, Industry, Agriculture and the Arts. The Fontaine de la Paix has a twin in the Fontaine de Mars by Bralle in the rue Saint-Dominique; the latter was lucky in always remaining on its original site, facing the military hospital which has since disappeared. The Fontaine des Orateurs Sacrés in the place Saint-Sulpice is infinitely better adapted to the vast dimensions of the square. Built to replace the little Fontaine de la Paix, it has sculptures representing Bossuet, Fénelon, Massillon, and Fléchier (by Visconti, 1844). The great naturalist Cuvier would suffer if he could now see the fountain that Vigoureux dedicated to him in 1840, at one of the corners of the Jardin des Plantes, for it features a crocodile with its head turned in an anatomically impossible position.

The *Fontaine Molière* (7) at the corner of the rue Richelieu and the rue Molière is Visconti's masterpiece (1844). It was set up in memory of the great dramatist who died nearby.

The *Fontaine du Palmier* (8) with the column which gave it its name dates from 1808 but its enlarged basin and the sphinxes decorating it date from the rearrangement of the square of the Châtelet in 1858. The *Fontaine Saint-Michel* (9). built by Davioud in 1860, is part of the same scheme.

The *Fontaine de l'Observatoire* (10), equally by Davioud (1875) is a happy exception to the numerous pompous and banal fountains that were built during the Third Republic. It is famous for Carpeaux's statues of the four continents of the world (he left out Oceania); the horses are by Frémiet.

The great London art-patron, Richard Wallace, a collector of French art, was very fond of Paris and sorry for its thirsty *clochards* (tramps). He was responsible for the building of a hundred "*Wallace Fountains*" (11) throughout the city; only a few are still left, especially that of the Place Saint-Sulpice which is still running and still has its cup.

II

2

3

7

5

4

9

6

8

10

135

7

8

STATUES

To mention the statues of Paris is a difficult task and any choice must be an arbitrary one for there are several hundred in the capital, not to mention a good number of empty pedestals, whose statues had been taken by the Germans and melted down during the Occupation — not necessarily a loss to art in every case! Of the most famous statues still standing, we may mention: *Henri IV* (1), perfectly sited in the middle of the Pont-Neuf, Paris' oldest bridge. The first statue was by Jean de Bologne but it was destroyed on August 13th, 1792 and replaced by Lemot's statue in 1818. The little square of the Vert Galant, in commemoration of the gallant king, marks the extreme end of the Ile de la Cité. The equestrian statue of *Louis XIV* (2) which is so perfectly set off by the Place des Victoires around it (opened up in 1684 by the Maréchal de la Feuillade in order to flatter the king) is not particularly old (Bosio, 1822) but it is in perfect harmony with the houses designed by J. Hardouin-Mansart. The centre of the square was originally occupied by a monumental standing statue of Louis XIV in his coronation robes, by Desjardins, but it disappeared during the Revolution.

It is to Colbert and Louis XIV that the Parisians owe their most beautiful gardens, the Tuileries, designed by Le Nôtre in 1664. The statues of the *Fleuves* (Rivers) (3) gracefully ornament the ends of the alleys leading to the terrace. On the terrace and near to the great museums of the Jeu de Paume and the Orangerie lies a large *Reclining nude* by Maillol (4).

Coysevox's statues of Mercury and *Renown* (Renommée) (6) were banished from Marly to make room for Coustou's *Horses* (5) and were resited in 1719 at the doorway to the gardens of the Tuileries; in 1795 they were joined by Coustou's *Horses* who were set facing them as rivals, occupying a lordly position at the entrance to the Champs-Élysées, giving a majestic final touch to the avenue.

Rude (1784-1855) owed his fame in Paris to his figures of the Departure or Marseillaise, as it is known, on the Arc de Triomphe. But another of his statues still stands in the avenue de l'Observatoire, happily spared by the war: that of *Marshal Ney* (7) (1853) which is equally full of passionate movement. It was at this very site that Ney, Duke of Elchingen and Prince of Moskova, was shot on December 7th 1815.

Rodin's *Balzac* (8) should also be mentioned. It was built after a subscription had been easily collected but it was not until 1939 that it found a highly suitable site after a great deal of controversy and the heated opposition of the whole of officialdom, in the very heart of Montparnasse on the Boulevard Raspail.

Many statues do not deserve a mention. They are of every variety from the queens lining the terrace of the Luxembourg gardens whose value is purely sentimental since they have looked down on generations of young lovers, to the three statues of Joan of Arc, which, on foot or on horseback, are all equally lacking in life and spirit. More than a hundred others might be mentioned, all of philosophers, writers, rulers, soldiers, etc. Some are so well known that the Parisians now feel a certain affection for them, such as *Clemenceau* (9) on his rock in the forest of Fontainebleau (by Cognié, 1932) standing a little way back from the Champs-Élysées or the *Levassor* (10) by the Porte Maillot which is by Camille Lefèvre, an extraordinary evocation of the early age of the motor car and rather touching in its naivety. It is also worth looking up at the green copper horses at the corners of the roof of the Grand-Palais: the colossal *Quadriga* (11) by Recipon are a miracle of technique and elegance even if the building below them is of rather questionable taste.

1

2

6

5

4

3

9

II

10

I

MUSÉE DU LOUVRE

Although the Palace of the Louvre was first built in 1204, the history of the museum only covers two centuries. The first collections date from the reign of François I and were enriched by his successors; the collection of paintings was increased from two hundred to two thousand by Louis XIV and Colbert alone. In 1746 it was first suggested that the masterpieces of the royal collection should be grouped together and exhibited. Most of the works were then in the apartments of the Superintendance of the Buildings at Versailles; part of the collection was then transferred to the Luxembourg Palace. The matter was taken up again in 1768 but first the Grande Galerie by the water's edge had to be altered (and first of all, its tenants had to be evacuated for more than thirty lodgings had been installed, where artists and simple courtiers were living) and then the lighting had to be transformed. Plans were drawn up for the work by Soufflot and Hubert Robert. In 1793 a decree of the Convention created a Central Museum of the Arts in the Louvre. In 1794, after David's intervention, the museum was declared open to all citizens.

The victorious peace treaties of 1794, 1796 and 1797 and Napoleon's victories greatly enriched the collections in the museum which, as a result of a proposal by Cambacérès, was baptised the Musée Napoléon in 1805. A highly expert keeper, the Baron Denon, collected a great number of works in Italy in 1811. But after the downfall of the Empire the question of the recent acquisitions was brought into the courts and Denon had to return a great number of works. Nevertheless he was both skilful and lucky enough to keep the works of Italian primitives, Cimabue, Giotto, Fra Angelico, etc. for they were then esteemed of little value by the Italian authorities, as well as the Wedding at Cana by Veronese because of the difficulties of transporting such a huge canvas. The museum continued to make acquisitions and in 1821 the Venus of Milo was offered to Louis XVIII by the Marquis de Rivière, Ambassador of France at Constantinople. The Louvre has continued to benefit from important bequests and donations such as the magnificent Lacaze Collection (which included Rembrandt's *Bathsheba*, and paintings by Hals, Ribera and Fragonard, etc.) in 1869, the Moreau-Nélaton, Camondo, Caillebotte, Chocquet and Chauchard collections and more recently, the Carlos de Beistegui, Doctor Paul Gachet and Paul Guillaume collections. It is now one of the world's most complete museums with over two hundred thousand works of art.

The collections are divided in six departments: 1. Greek and Roman Antiquities. 2. Oriental Antiquities. 3. Egyptian Antiquities. 4. Sculpture of the Middle Ages, the Renaissance and Modern Times. 5. Painting and Drawings (The Cabinet des Dessins is a particularly important part of this department). 6. Works of art (this department is also responsible for the Musée de Cluny).

ANCIENT SCULPTURE

1 Sumerian art (3200-2700 B.C.): Archaic statuette. 2 Chaldaean art (2450 B.C.): Seated statue of Gudea. 3 Aegean pre-hellenic art (3000-2400 B.C.): Idol from Paros. 4 Persian Achaemenid art (early 5th c. B.C.): Frieze of archers. 5 Egyptian art, El Amarna period (1375-1350 B.C.): Head from a harp. 6 Egyptian art, Old Kingdom (2800-2300 B.C.): The Seated Scribe. 7 Egyptian art, New Kingdom (1580-1090 B.C.): The Lady Tui. 8 Archaic Greek art (7th-6th c. B.C.): Hera of Samos. 9 Archaic Greek art (7th-6th c. B.C.): The "Cavalier Rampin", head of a horseman. 10 Hellenistic Greek art (1st c. B.C.): Venus of Milo. 11 Etruscan art (c. 500 B.C.): Sarcophagus of Cerveteri. 12 Roman art (2nd c.): The Emperor Augustus.

2

3

4

5

6

7

8

9

10

11

12

3

2

4

6

12TH TO 19TH CENTURY SCULPTURE

1 French art (12th c.): The Queen of Sheba. 2 Donatello (1386-1466): Saint John the Baptist. 3 Italian art (16th c.): Young Florentine, polychrome bust. 4 German art (16th c.): Saint Mary Aegyptiaca. 5 Michelangelo (1475-1564): Slave, c. 1515. 6 Burgundian art (late 15th c.): Tomb of Philippe Pot, polychrome stone, height 6 feet. 7 Michel Colombe (died 1512): Saint George and the Dragon. 8 Germain Pilon (c. 1536-1590): Tomb of Valeriane Balbiani, c. 1572, detail. 9 Puget (1620-1694): Milo of Croton, marble, height 8 feet 5 inches, 1682. 10 Coysevox (1640-1720): Le Grand Condé, 1688. 11 Pigalle (1714-1785): Mercury fastening his winged scandals, marble, height 24 inches, 1744. 12 Barye (1796-1875): Lapith and Centaur, bronze, 1850.

1

5

7

8

10

9

11

12

I

PAINTING

ITALY, TRECENTO AND QUATTROCENTO

1 Giotto (c. 1266-1337): Saint Francis receiving the stigmata, 1312. **2** Fra Angelico (1387-1455): Martyrdom of Saints Cosmos and Damian. **3** Paolo Uccello (c. 1400-1475): Battle of San Romano. **4** Pisanello (c. 1395-1455): Portrait of a Princess of the House of Este. **5** Ghirlandaio (1449-1494): Portrait of an old man and his son. **6** Botticelli (1444-1510): The Virgin and Child and Saint John, 1496. **7** Mantegna (1451-1506): Parnassus. **8** Giovanni Bellini (1430-1516): Christ giving blessing.

2

3

4

5

6

7

8

9

10

FRANCE, 15TH CENTURY

9 School of Avignon (15th c.): Pietà of Villeneuve-lès-Avignon.
10 Fouquet (c. 1415-1477): Portrait of Charles VII, c. 1444.

11

12

13   14

FLANDERS, 15TH CENTURY

11 Rogier Van der Weyden (1400-1464): Braque Triptych.
12 Jean Van Eyck (c. 1380-1440): The Virgin of Autun.
13 Hans Memling (c. 1433-1494): The Virgin of Jacques Floreins.
14 Brueghel (c. 1525-1569): The Beggars.

ITALY, 15TH CENTURY

The Louvre has the privilege of possessing seven of Leonardo da
Vinci's (1452-1519) few works: The Mona Lisa, Saint Anne,
the Virgin and Child, Saint John the Baptist, The Virgin of the
Rocks (15), the early Annunciation, Bacchus, and the Portrait of
Lucrezia Crivelli.

15

143

1

2

ITALY, 16TH CENTURY

1 Giorgione (1478-1511): Concert champêtre. **2** Titian (1477?-1576): Jupiter and Antiope. **3** Raphaël (1483-1520): Portrait of Balthasar Castiglione.

3

4

5

6

7

FRANCE, 16TH CENTURY

4 School of Fontainebleau (16th c.): Diane Chasseresse. **5** Jean Clouet (c. 1485-1541): Portrait of François I. **6** Jean Cousin the Elder (died 1560): Eva Prima Pandora, c. 1548. **7** French school (16th c.): Allegorical portrait of the Duchess Gabrielle d'Estrées and the Marquise de Villars.

8

9

8 Tintoretto (1518-1594): Susannah and the Elders **9** Paolo Veronese (1528-1588): The Wedding at Cana. **10** Caravaggio (1573-1610): The Fortune teller.

10

11

12

13

11 Holbein (1498-1543): Portrait of Nicolas Kratzer. **12** Albrecht Dürer (1471-1528): Self-portrait. **13** Lucas Cranach the Elder (1472-1553): Venus in a landscape.

14 El Greco (1541-1614): Crucifixion.

14

1

2

3

4

5

6

7

FRANCE, 17TH CENTURY

1 Georges de La Tour (1593-1652): The Magdalene.
2 Louis Le Nain (1593-1648): Return from hay-making.
3 Philippe de Champaigne (1602-1674): The Miracle of the
Holy Thorn, 1662. 4 Nicolas Poussin (1594-1665): Ruth and Booz.
5 Claude Gellée, *called* Le Lorrain (1600-1682): Ulysses returning
Chryseis to her father. 6 Baugin (c. 1630): The Five Senses.
7 Rigaud (1659-1690): Louis XIV in Coronation robes.
8 Le Brun (1619-1690): Entry of Cardinal Séguier into Rouen.

8
146

9

10

11

FLANDERS, 17TH CENTURY

An entire room is devoted to the twenty five paintings that
Rubens executed for the Luxembourg for Marie de Medicis,
whose life they depicted (1625). The Naïads of the Landing of
Marie de Medicis and especially the sheen of water on their bodies
were greatly admired by Delacroix.
9 P.-P. Rubens (1577-1640): Kermess. **10** Jordaens (1593-1678):
The Four Evangelists. **11** Van Dyck (1599-1641): Portrait of
Charles I.

12

13

14

15

SPAIN, 17TH CENTURY

12 Zurbaran (1598-1664): The Funeral of Saint Bonaventura.
13 Velazquez (1599-1660): The Infanta Maria-Teresa. **14** Murillo
(1617-1660): Kitchen of the Angels. **15** Ribera (1591-1652): The
club-footed boy.

147

1

2

3

4

HOLLAND, 17TH CENTURY

1 Rembrandt (1606-1669): Bathsheba. 2 Frans Hals (1580-1666): The Gipsy. 3 Ruysdaël (1629-1682): A Storm at Sea. 4 Vermeer of Delft (1632-1675): The Lace-maker.

5

ENGLAND, 18TH CENTURY

5 Reynolds (1723-1792): Master Hare, portrait of a child.

SPAIN, 18TH CENTURY

6 Goya (1746-1828): The Countess Carpio (Beistegui Collection).

6

7

8

9

10

11

12

FRANCE, 18TH CENTURY

7 J.-B. Chardin (1699-1779): Still life. **8** Antoine Watteau (1684-1721): Embarkation for Cythera. **9** Joseph Vernet (1714-1789): The Ponte Rotto at Rome. **10** Maurice Quentin de La Tour (1704-1788): The Marquise de Pompadour, pastel (Cabinet des Dessins). **11** François Boucher (1703-1770): Diana at her toilet. **12** Jean-Honoré Fragonard (1732-1806): Sleeping Bacchante.

ITALY, 18TH CENTURY

13 Francesco Guardi (1712-1793): Departure of the Bucentaur.

13

149

1

2

3

4

5

6

7

FRANCE, 19TH CENTURY

1 Jacques-Louis David (1748-1825): The oath of the Horatii (1785).
2 Ingres (1780-1867): The Turkish Bath. 3 David: Marie-Antoinette
on her way to the scaffold, drawing (Rothschild Collection).
4 Géricault (1791-1824): The Raft of the Medusa. 5 Delacroix
(1798-1863): Massacre at Chios. 6 Courbet (1819-1877): The Artist's
Studio. 7 Corot (1796-1875): Narni, the bridge of Augustus on
the Nera, sketch.

OBJETS D'ART

The Department of Objets d'Art in the Louvre is responsible for works dating from after the Carolingian period but for greater convenience, objects which are administratively classed as "Antiquities" in the museum are also illustrated here. Among the "objets d'art" we must mention the magnificent jewellery collection in the Galerie d'Apollon, with its ceiling painted by Delacroix, and especially the *Régent*, a 137-carat royal diamond.

8

9

10

13

11

12

8 Mesopotamian art (c. 1365 B.C.): Ras Shamra patera. 9 Greek art (second half 5th c. B.C.): White Attic jug: Charon's boat. 10 Etruscan art (5th-2nd c. B.C.): Engraved mirror. 11 French art (18th c.): Ciborium of Alpais, champlevé Limoges enamel. 12 French art (12th c.): Eagle of Süger, porphyry and gilded silver, height 17 inches. 13 Italian art (16th c.): Mirror of Marie de Medicis, enamelled gold, rock crystal and precious stones, height 18 inches. 14 French art (18th c.): Incense-burner, mount in gilded bronze and China porcelain.

14

MUSÉE DU JEU DE PAUME

The museum dates from the time of the Caillebotte bequest (1894). Caillebotte was a friend and emulator of the Impressionists: the acceptance by the State of his collection and their entry into the Louvre in 1897 caused a storm of controversy. The Jeu de Paume was arranged in 1920 and modernised in 1947. No other museum has such a representative collection of Impressionist masterpieces. First, are represented the precursors of the movement: Boudin, Jongkind, Lépine and Manet, whose *Olympia* marked a decisive step forward in modern art when it was exhibited in the 1865 Salon. Monet, Pissarro and Sisley were all pure Impressionists. The transformation of Monet's art can be followed from his *Women in a garden* to his great series of 1890-1900 (*Meules, Rouen,* and *Nympheas* in the neighbouring Orangerie). For Renoir, Impressionism was only a phase in his art and we may see the beginning and the end of his Impressionist experiment in the *Bal du Moulin de la Galette* and the two enormous nudes in *Après le bain*. Although Degas and Toulouse-Lautrec joined the school for a while they were never really a part of the movement. Cézanne and Van Gogh represent the reaction to Impressionism after they had both been tempted by it at first. The neo-Impressionism of Seurat and Signac which transformed what was an instinctive way of painting into a rigid system marked the final failure of the movement, and while Monet returned to his original style, the Symbolist paintings of Gauguin and Redon were a clear breakaway from the movement. Douanier Rousseau, the great master of Primitive painting, is also represented in the museum, side-by-side with the Impressionist masters.

1 Edouard Manet (1832-1883): Olympia, 1863. 2 Claude Monet (1840-1926): Women in a garden. 3 Alfred Sisley (1859-1899): Inundation at Port-Marly, 1876. 4 Auguste Renoir (1841-1919): The Moulin de la Galette, 1876. 5 Camille Pissarro (1830-1903): The Stagecoach at Louveciennes. 6 Vincent Van Gogh (1853-1890): Self-portrait, 1890. 7 Edgar Degas (1834-1917): The Tub, pastel, 1886. 8 Degas: La Danseuse de quatorze ans, wax and cloth, height 38 1/2 inches. 9 Paul Cézanne (1839-1906): The bridge at Mennecy, 1879. 10 Toulouse-Lautrec (1864-1901): Jane Avril dancing. 11 Paul Gauguin (1845-1903): The White horse, 1893. 12 Henri Rousseau (1844-1910): The Snake Charmer. 13 Georges Seurat (1859-1891): Poseuse de face (The Painter's Model).

1

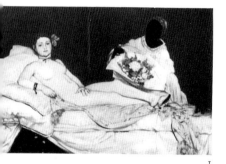

2

4

3

5

6

7

8

9

10

11

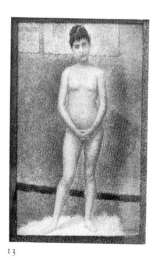

12

13

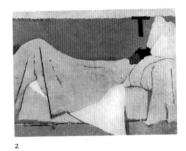

1

2

3

4

5

6
154

MUSÉE NATIONAL D'ART MODERNE
(NATIONAL MUSEUM OF MODERN ART)

The museum was founded in 1937 for the Paris Exhibition and contains examples of all the various movements and aspects of modern art (from the Impressionist and Post-Impressionist periods onwards).

The painters of the school of Paris, both living and dead, who worked from the '20s onwards are largely represented and the greatest have a room of their own in which their evolution may be studied (e.g. Braque, Matisse and Picasso).

The history of French painting from 1890 to the present day can be followed in the museum which has examples of such various schools and movements as the Nabis, the Fauves, Cubism, Surrealism, Naive painting, neo-realism, and abstraction.

I Pierre Bonnard (1867-1947): The Toilet. 2 Edmond Vuillard (1868-1940): In bed. 3 Henri Matisse (1869-1954): Le Luxe. 4 Maurice de Vlaminck (1876-1958): Street at Marly. 5 Raoul Dufy (1877-1953): The Paddock at Deauville. 6 Albert Marquet (1875-1947): Blond woman. 7 Amedeo Modigliani (1884-1920): Nude. 8 Georges Rouault (1871-1958): Christian nocturne, 1952. 9 Maurice Utrillo (1883-1955): La Rue du Mont-Cenis. 10 Georges Braque (1882-1963): Composition. II Robert Delaunay (1885-1941): La Ville de Paris, 1910-1912. 12 Fernand Léger (1881-1955): Woman in green. 13 Pablo Picasso (born 1881): The Muse, 1935. 14 Salvador Dali (born 1904): Composition. 15 Seraphine Louis (1884-1934): The Tree of Paradise. 16 Nicolas de Staël (1914-1955): The Roofs.

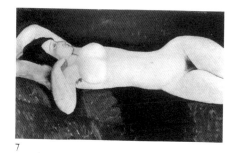

7

8

9

10

11

12

13

14

15

16

MUSÉE MUNICIPAL D'ART MODERNE
(MUNICIPAL MUSEUM OF MODERN ART)

Facing the Musée National and installed in the same building, the Musée Municipal — now being completed — has inherited the collections from the Petit-Palais, acquring all the works dating after the Fauves and, in particular, the Girardin collection. It is continually being enriched by purchases and donations.
1 Maria Blanchard (1881-1932): Boy with a straw hat. 2 Marc Chagall (born 1887): The Street. 3 Georges Rouault (1871-1958): The Drunken Woman. 4 Henri Matisse (1869-1954): The Dance, 1932. 5 Marcel Gromaire (born 1892): San Francisco. 6 Bernard Buffet (born 1928): Naked woman on a sofa, 1949.

MUSÉE DU PETIT-PALAIS

The Petit-Palais (its official title is: Musée des Beaux-Arts de la Ville de Paris) is an eclectic museum and owes most of its riches to private donations. It is well represented in 19th-century painting with works by Courbet, Daumier, Manet *(Portrait of Duret)* and has a unique collection of paintings by the sculptor Carpeaux, and water-colours by Constantin Guys. It also has a noteworthy collection of *objets d'art* ranging from Greek vases to African sculpture, by way of the Italian Renaissance.
7 Rembrandt (1606-1669): Sick woman, drawing. 8 Carpeaux (1827-1875): Ball during the Second Empire, sketch. 9 Daumier (1808-1879): The organ-grinder, drawing. 10 Courbet (1819-1877): Young ladies on the banks of the Seine. 11 J.-B. Corot (1796-1875): Marietta.

7

12

MUSÉE MARMOTTAN

The Musée Marmottan was formed as a hobby by a rich factory owner who was a born collector and has retained its original aspect (furniture, fine 16th-century portraits, etc.). One of the most famous paintings that can be seen there is Monet's *Impression, sun rising* (exhibited in 1874) which is supposed to have given the Impressionist movement its name.
12 Claude Monet (1840-1926): Impression, sun rising.

MUSÉE GUSTAVE MOREAU

The museum was created by the artist himself in his own house (1898). Moreau was greatly admired by Huysmans and inspired his pupils (Desvallières, Marquet, Matisse and Rouault) but his highly literary art (Oedipus and the Sphinx, Salome, Orpheus) may seem rather too theatrical to some eyes; he may also be considered as the precursor of the "informel" artists.
13 Gustave Moreau (1826-1898): The Apparition.

13

156

1

2

3

4

5

6

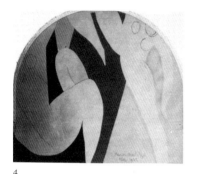

8

9

10

11

157

2

1

3

4

MUSÉE BOURDELLE

The museum was bequeathed to the city of Paris by Bourdelle's widow and contains the artist's studio with various finished and unfinished works, his tools and familiar objects.

1 Antoine Bourdelle (1861-1929): View of a room in the museum.

MUSÉE RODIN

Almost all of Rodin's work is displayed in a worthy setting — that of the hôtel Biron where he lived and worked from 1904 onwards. Apart from fine paintings by Van Gogh, Renoir, Carrière, etc., Rodin's splendid wash-drawings may be seen on the walls. In the garden: the great model for the *Porte de l'Enfer* which was never completed in its entirety, but of which some fragments may be seen, each being a masterpiece in its own right; the monument was to have been crowned by the *Three Shadows*.

2 Auguste Rodin (1840-1917): Drawing. 3 The Shadow.

MUSÉE DES MONUMENTS FRANÇAIS

Unlike the fine museum at Barcelona to which frescoes were transferred from the lovely old churches of Catalonia, the Musée des Monuments Français in the Palais de Chaillot only exhibits fine quality plaster-casts and copies of Romanesque, Gothic and Renaissance sculptures and frescoes which can be studied by the visitor at his ease.

MUSÉE POSTAL

Part of the attraction of philately is the artistic skill shown in engraving vignettes on such a small scale. The Postal Museum is installed in the hôtel de Choiseul-Praslin (1732) and contains a unique collection of rare stamps and exhibits illustrating the history of postal services throughout the ages.

MUSÉE DE L'ARMÉE

The Musée de l'Armée in the Invalides has a large collection of weapons, uniforms, and battle paintings. Some of the exhibits are works of art in their own right, such as the gold-inlaid silver coat of armour of François I. Near the tomb of Napoleon (under the dome) which attracts millions of visitors each year, the museum has a moving collection of Napoleonic relics (his small hat, the grey riding coat, the bed from Saint Helena).

4 Italian art (16th c.): Iron helmet with *repoussé* decoration.

MUSÉE DE LA MARINE

The naval museum in the handsome galleries of the Palais de Chaillot contains maps, ship-models and uniforms and, the main attraction, a life size model of the forward cabin of the galley La Réale and sculptures by Puget.

MUSÉE DE L'HOMME (ETHNOGRAPHICAL MUSEUM)

The Musée de l'Homme represents all branches of ethnography and anthropology and the exhibits are displayed as much for instructional purposes as for their aesthetic qualities. The collection of primitive art is one of the richest in the world, and covers European and African pre-history, African ethnography, arctic cultures, and the civilisations of Russia and Asia, Oceania and the American continents.

5 Baoule mask, Ivory Coast. 6 Venus de Lespugne, height 6 inches. 7 Stone head from Easter Island. 8 Death's head, Mexico, rock-crystal. 9 Bark painting or *tapa*, New Guinea.

5

6

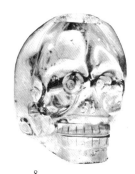

7

8

9

MUSÉE DES ARTS ET TRADITIONS POPULAIRES (MUSEUM OF POPULAR ARTS AND TRADITIONS)

Also in the Palais de Chaillot, the Museum was separated from the Musée de l'Homme in 1937 and covers every aspect of French folk art and tradition: costumes and dwellings, tools and crafts, music and dance, literature and iconography (more than eighty thousand pictures and popular images).

MUSÉE DE L'ASSISTANCE PUBLIQUE (MUSEUM OF SOCIAL WELFARE)

This original but largely unknown museum, installed in the 17th-century hôtel de Miramion which has been attributed to Mansart, illustrates the history of hospital services and has a fine collection of costumes, ustensils, historical documents and especially a unique collection of pharmaceutical jugs.

10 Pharmaceutical faïence jug from Rouen, 17th c.

10

159

1

2

MUSÉE DE CLUNY

The Musée de Cluny is set in ancient monastic buildings that were transformed in the late 15th century. It now houses a collection of objects dating from the Carolingian period to the 16th century: furniture, tapestries, ivories, sculptures, metal work, enamels, miniatures, etc. Its most famous exhibits include the wonderful set of the six tapestries of the "Lady and the Unicorn" which were discovered in the château of Boussac in the Creuse department by George Sand and Prosper Mérimée, and the Basle altar-piece which the Emperor Henri II had offered to the cathedral (1002-1024).

1 French art (16th c.): Sight, one of the six tapestries of the "Lady and the Unicorn". 2 German art (11th c.): Gold altar decoration, known as the Basle altar-piece.

3

5

4

MUSÉE CARNAVALET

The whole history of Paris, both intimate and great, is brought to life again in the Carnavalet museum which is housed in a noble *hôtel* in the Marais district. Particularly interesting is the series of remarkably reconstructed small salons with their walls covered with fine panelling saved from the old *hôtels* that have been demolished. The rich library may also be visited. The memory of Madame de Sévigné has been kept alive in several rooms which have been furnished with her personal belongings.

3 Robert Nanteuil (1623-1678): Portrait of Mme de Sévigné. 4 The Gardens of Tivoli, c. 1830, colour print. 5 Sign of the lock-smith "Filliol".

MUSÉE JACQUEMART-ANDRÉ

The museum is a handsome late 19th-century building which was the private residence of M. and Mme Jacquemart-André, and it contains their admirable collection of French 18th-century art and Italian art: furniture, paintings, sculpture, terracottas, etc. ranging from large frescoes by Tiepolo to snuff-box lids. The abbey of Chaâlis in the Oise is an annex to the museum.

6 Rembrandt (1606-1669): Christ at Emmaus, c. 1630.

6

MUSÉE DES ARTS DÉCORATIFS
(MUSEUM OF DECORATIVE ART)

The museum contains more than examples of the applied arts for a large number of fine sculptures, paintings and drawings are also on display. But the main attraction of the museum is its outstanding variety of furniture, hangings and tapestries, vases and ornaments. Although medieval furniture can also be seen in the Cluny Museum, masterpieces of the cabinet-maker's art at the Camondo, Marmottan and Cognacq-Jay museums, and fine bronzes by Caffieri at the Louvre, the Musée des Arts Decoratifs is the only museum where we may study *Art Nouveau* which has now been re-evaluated after a long period of neglect. Although all the furniture rooms are in course of restoration, that of the 19th century is now completed.

7 Walnut cupboard, in the style of J.-A. Du Cerceau (late 16th c.).
8 Couch of the Louis XIV period (late 17th c.), carved wood and gilt. 9 Louis XV secretaire, by J.-F. Leleu (18th c.), marquetry and Japanese lacquer panels, with chiselled bronze-gilt decorations.
10 Gold pendant, gems, rubies, agate, enamel, height 4 1/2 inches, by Vever, 1900.

7

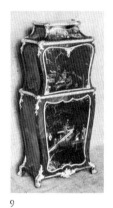

8

9

10

MUSÉE COGNACQ-JAY

The museum was the personal foundation of M. Ernest Cognacq and reflects the taste of this great collector for the 18th century: furniture, *objets d'art*, and paintings of the period (mostly by French artists, but some fine works by Guardi and the Italian and English schools).

MUSÉE NISSIM DE CAMONDO

The museum is named after a flyer who was killed in the 1914-1918 war. His father was a great art patron and personally reconstructed the interior of an art lover's house of the late 18th century: particularly fine furniture, paintings, extremely rare carpets, bronzes and fine Chinese vases.

11 *Petit bureau:* 18th-c. furniture, decoration and *objets d'art*, Aubusson carpet in Savonnerie stitch-work (c. 1790).

11

1

MUSÉE VICTOR HUGO

The house in the Place des Vosges where Victor Hugo lived has been transformed into a museum containing souvenirs and portraits of the writer and especially a collection of his fine pen and wash drawings.

1 Victor Hugo (1802-1885): The Three Trees, pen-and-ink drawing.

2

BIBLIOTHÈQUE DE L'OPÉRA
(LIBRARY-MUSEUM OF THE OPÉRA)

The library-museum of the Paris Opéra is mostly devoted to music and ballet. It contains many precious souvenirs, models for décor, costumes, statues and portraits connected with the Opéra.

2 Auguste Renoir (1841-1919): Portrait of Richard Wagner.

FOYER DU THÉÂTRE FRANÇAIS

The Foyer des Artistes has a collection of portraits of actors and dramatists and works of the finest 18th and 19th-century sculptors

3 Houdon (1741-1828): Seated statue of Voltaire, 1781.

3

4   5   6   7

MUSÉE GUIMET

The Musée Guimet was founded by an art-lover in Lyons and
was removed to Paris in 1888. In 1945 it inherited the collections
of Asian art from the Louvre and is now the greatest museum
in France for art of the Far-East. It contains magnificent examples
of sculpture, ceramics, painting and miniatures from India,
Indo-China, Indonesia and Malaya, Central Asia, Tibet, China
and Japan.
4 South Indian art (12th c.): Dancing female figure, bronze.
5 Khmer art (late 12th c. Female divinity from Angkor, Bayon
style. **6** Khmer art (13th c.): Buddha. **7** Chinese art (615-907):
Tang figure of a dancer. **8** Indian art (18th c.): Seated couple
in a garden, miniature painting.

8

9

MUSÉE CERNUSCHI

The main collections of the Musée Cernuschi consist of works
dating from the great periods of Chinese and Japanese art.
Extremely elegant display and temporary exhibitions.
9 Chinese art (8th-10th c.): Horses and grooms, from Touen-Hang,
painting on silk. **10** Chinese art (Shang period, 14th-11th c. B.C.):
Square T'ing, ritual vase for food offerings, bronze, height
8 1/2 inches.

MUSÉE D'ENNERY

The enormous success won by the playwright Ennery, author of
the play "Les Deux Orphelines", at the end of the last century
allowed him to accumulate an important collection of very small
Chinese and Japanese objects, including two thousand *netsuké*,
which may now be seen in the Museum.

10

BIBLIOTHÈQUE NATIONALE

The library of the Bibliothèque Nationale contains nearly five million volumes and is completed by the more specialised libraries such as the Doucet Library for the arts (administered by the Sorbonne), the Arts Décoratifs, Forney and Guimet libraries (the last for the Far-East). Although it has necessarily been enlarged and altered at various times its oldest buildings are works of art in themselves. The Galerie Mazarine (where important exhibitions are held every year) has remained intact, as a reminder that Cardinal Mazarin acquired the hôtel du President Tubeuf in 1644 and had it transformed by François Mansart in 1645.

CABINET DES MANUSCRITS

The Cabinet des Manuscrits has a collection of more than a hundred thousand manuscripts of which more than ten thousand contain miniatures. The greatest of these treasures have been displayed to the public in three successive exhibitions.

1

1 Franco-Spanish school (12th c.): The Apocalypse of Saint-Sever: Fall of the bad angels.

CABINET DES ESTAMPES

The Print Collection is universal in its scope and contains the finest examples of the engraver's art, often in their rarest "states", as well as a large variety of Japanese prints and popular imagery.
2 Albrecht Dürer (1471-1528): The Rhinoceros, engraving.
3 Edgar Degas (1834-1917): Page from a sketch-book, study of the Bellelli family.

CABINET DES MÉDAILLES ET ANTIQUES

For the coin-collector, the collections of the Cabinet des Médailles are an inexhaustible treasure-house. Coins of every age, medals and intaglios, cameos (four hundred) are displayed together with many precious pieces of sculpture and gold- and silver-work.
4 Glorification of Germanicus, so-called Cameo of the Sainte-Chapelle.

2

3

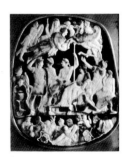

4

MUSÉE MONÉTAIRE

The hôtel des Monnaies was the first edifice to be built in the Louis XVI style, by J.-D. Antoine, in 1777. It was used as a mint from the very beginning and the Monetary Museum which Charles X founded in 1827 contains fine and very varied collections of coins and medals of every period. The central chamber is built in a very pure Louis XVI monumental style, with twenty Corinthian columns supporting balconies running round an octagonal gallery.
5 Gallic coin.

5

V

CHAMPAGNE - ALSACE - LORRAINE

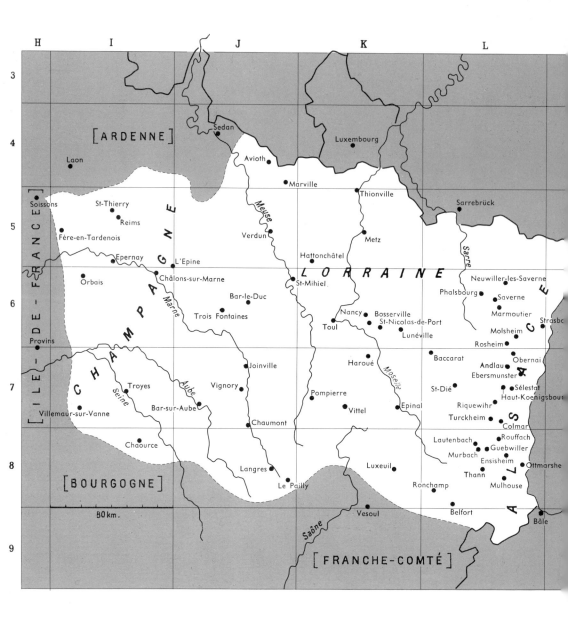

ENTOMBMENT, POLYCHROME STONE, 1478, CHURCH OF SAINT-
PIERRE-SAINT-PAUL, NEUWILLER *(Fronval)*

MATHIAS GRUNEWALD (1455?-1528), ISSENHEIM ALTARPIECE,
DETAIL, 15TH C., UNTERLINDEN MUSEUM, COLMAR *(Giraudon)*

*For centuries, while the kings of France were being crowned in
the great cathedral of Reims in Champagne, the neighbouring
province of Lorraine kept its independence as a duchy while
remaining part of the Empire, like Alsace. The culture of
Alsace is Germanic in tradition but it has a personal style
like that of Colmar which gave its name to an independent
school of painting in the 15th century, distinguished by the
names of Schongauer and Grünewald.*

*Lorraine differed by following the French tradition — more
than ever under its last prince, the Polish Stanislas, who transformed the capital, Nancy, in the 18th century. We only have
to name Georges de La Tour, Claude Gellée (Le Lorrain)
and the sculptor Ligier Richier to show how great was the
liberty of expression of Lorraine artists. Some were equally
independent of character like Jacques Callot, the official painter
of sieges, who defied Louis XIV by refusing to paint the siege
of Nancy, his native town.*

ANDLAU 2

ANDLAU 1

ANDLAU *Bas-Rhin.* L 7.

In the 9th century, the rejected wife of Charles the Fat, Saint Richarde, founded a monastery near Andlau in a spot which she had been shown by a she-bear. A stone carving of the bear may still be seen to-day in the crypt of the 12th-century Romanesque church, which was completed and decorated in the interior in the 17th century. The church is famous for its fine portal with a lintel carved with a scene from the Creation, and especially its frieze (façade and north side of the church). The frieze is sculpted in a bold and somewhat naive style and depicts epic deeds and scenes from legends which now seem strange to us as they have long been forgotten.

1 Detail from the portal of the church, 12th c. 2 Detail from the sculpted frieze on the façade, woman riding a fish, symbol of the sea, and knights in combat.

AVIOTH *Meuse.* J 4.

The great pilgrims' church at Avioth is a blend of the pure Gothic and Flamboyant styles for it was built during the 14th and 15th centuries. Its sculpture is remarkable in style and of a very high quality. The furnishings in the interior, which includes an ambulatory (unusual for the region), have remained intact. At the entrance to the cemetery stands a kind of hexagonal lantern which seems to have been used for receiving the offerings of the pilgrims, whence its name of "Recevresse" but it might also have served simply as a *lanterne des morts* (graveyard turret or "dead men's lantern" which contained a lighted lantern to indicate a cemetery).

3 The "Recevresse" and the doorway of the cemetery, 15th c.

BACCARAT *Meurthe-et-Moselle.* L 7.

Beside the famous crystal works founded during the reign of Louis XVI, a modern church of concrete covered with tiles and copper, girdled by a continuous band of Baccarat crystal windows inlaid in concrete motifs.

4 Façade of the church and bell-tower, by Nicolas Kasis, 1957. 5 Window of the church, Baccarat crystal and concrete, 1957.

BAR-LE-DUC *Meuse.* J 6.

The high, calm and solitary town of Bar-le-Duc has great style: interesting Renaissance houses, remains of the château of the Dukes of Bar, beautiful courtyard of the college founded by Gilles de Trèves in 1571, flanked on both sides by a gallery with balconies and finally the late 15th-century Gothic church of Saint-Pierre or Saint-Étienne with its remarkable monument by Ligier Richier for the heart of René de Chalon: according to the dead man's wish, the sculpture shows his skeleton as it was supposed to appear three years after his death, holding his heart in its out-stretched hand.

6 Façade of the church of Saint-Pierre, 15th c. 7 Ligier Richier (1500-1567): the skeleton of René de Chalon. 8 Courtyard of the college, 1571.

BACCARAT 4

BACCARAT 5

AVIOTH 3

BAR-LE-DUC 7

BAR-LE-DUC 6

BAR-LE-DUC 8

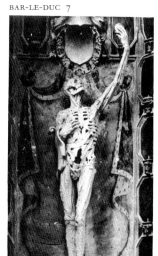

171

BAR-SUR-AUBE *Aube.* J 7.

The church of Saint-Pierre consists of a Gothic structure (in the early Burgundian style) surrounded by a Renaissance wooden gallery, and a domed tower built in 1722 and later restored.

1 Church of Saint-Pierre, 12th-15th-18th c.

BOSSERVILLE 2

BOSSERVILLE (Charterhouse of) *Meurthe-et-Moselle.* K 6.

The Charterhouse of Bosserville was built by an Italian architect, Giovanni Betto, who was very active in Lorraine in the 17th century. Despite its regrettable state of decay the building is a very fine example of Classical architecture in the Italianate style.

2 The great staircase of the Charterhouse, 17th c.

CHALONS-SUR-MARNE *Marne.* I 6.

Several partly Romanesque churches await the visitor at Chalons: Saint-Alpin, Saint-Loup, Notre-Dame-en-Vaux and the cathedral of Saint-Étienne. The cathedral was begun in the Romanesque period but was continued until the 18th century, and its fine tower by the porch of the north transept dates from its earliest period. Like many others in the region, the church of Notre-Dame-en-Vaux has a Romanesque structure covered with later Gothic decoration.

3 North side of the cathedral of Saint-Étienne, 12th-15th c.
4 Apse of the cathedral, 12th c.

CHAOURCE *Aube.* I 8.

The church of Saint-Jean-Baptiste, built in a part-Gothic, part-Renaissance style, has been eclipsed by the magnificent sculptures of the *Entombment of Christ* in a side chapel.
The tomb containing the remains of Nicolas de Monstier was dedicated by him to his wife in 1515, according to the inscription on it. A second inscription on the tunic of one of the soldiers of the guard states "Mathieu du Tronchay" but it is unlikely that this is the name of the sculptor; it has been attributed instead to a local workshop, whose masterpiece it was (q.v. *Entombment* at Chatillon). The sorrow, tenderness and dignity of the expressions, the composition, and the masterly but sober style make it a deeply moving work of a high artistic order.

5 The Entombment of Christ, 1515. 6 Detail of the Holy Women.

CHAUMONT *Haute-Marne.* J 7.

In the highly elegant church of Saint-Jean-Baptiste, the 13th-century Gothic style has blended harmoniously with the refined style of the Renaissance. Particularly noteworthy are the south portal, the transept, the choir, and some statues by Bouchardon.

7 South portal of the church of Saint-Jean-Baptiste, 14th c.

BAR-SUR-AUBE 1

CHALONS-SUR-MARNE 4

CHALONS-SUR-MARNE 3

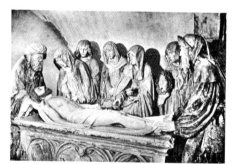

CHAOURCE 5

CHAOURCE 6

CHAUMONT 7

I

2

COLMAR *Haut-Rhin*. L 7.

Colmar is a traditional Alsatian town with narrrow winding streets bordered with sculpted and decorated old houses such as the Pfister house, La Maison des Têtes and the Old Customs House (Ancienne Douane), but first and foremost it is the home of one of the most important museums in France. The museum is most famous for its collection of primitive Alsatian masters, the School of Colmar, and Matthias Grünewald's Issenheim altarpiece which is one of the great paintings of the world. To come upon the immense painted wings of this altarpiece after having crossed the cloister of Unterlinden (so named because of its linden trees), in the ancient 13th-century Dominican convent now transformed into the museum, is a breathtaking revelation. The wings of the altar are now opened up but formerly they were only displayed on special feast-days. Its many panels include the Calvary in the centre, the Entombed Christ below, the Joys of the Virgin, the Annunciation, the Virgin Mother, the Angels in Glory, the Temptation of Saint Anthony, etc. It can only be appreciated fully at leisure for each subject is treated in a different style, ranging from the naturalistic to the fantastic, always with an unrivalled virtuosity. Apart from Grünewald's masterpiece, the museum also includes Martin Schongauer's *Passion* and *Annunciation* (The more important *Virgin of the Rose-bush* is in the church of Saint-Martin), and Gaspard Isenmann's *Lamentation of Christ* and *Flagellation*. To sum up, Colmar is a town to which the visitor will come with curiosity and return with passion.

1 Cathedral of Saint-Martin, 13th-14th c. 2 Martin Schongauer (c. 1445-c. 1491): The Virgin of the Rose-bush, 1473.

MUSÉE D'UNTERLINDEN
3 The cloister, 13th c. 4-5-6-7-8 Mathias Grünewald (died 1523): The Issenheim altarpiece. 9 Gaspard Isenmann (died 1492): The Flagellation. 10 Old Customs House, 15th-16th c. 11 Pfister House, 1537. 12 Maison des Têtes, 1609.

9

10

11

12   3

4

5

6

7

8

ENSISHEIM 2

EBERSMUNSTER *Bas-Rhin.* L 7.

The abbey church of Ebersmunster is an excellent example of early Austrian and German Baroque. By its bulbous towers, its pastel-coloured nave with lavish gold decorations it expresses the Baroque attempt to unite architecture, sculpture and painting in a single art.

1 Interior of the abbey church, 1722.

ENSISHEIM *Haut-Rhin.* L 8.

The former place of the Austrian regent in Alsace (now the Town Hall) is built in a strikingly sober style. The ground floor with its arcades has fine star-vaulted ceilings; the Council Chamber, now restored, is richly decorated in the Renaissance style. The town contains several other fine houses of the same period.

2 Town Hall, by Stephan Gadinner, 1547.

ÉPINAL *Vosges,* K 7.

The name of this small town in the Vosges is famous through France and even abroad for its brightly coloured, naively drawn popular images. Playing cards were already being made at Épinal in the 16th century, and in the 17th century a manufacturer launched a series of religious prints to ward off evils. In the 18th century the Pellerins became famous for their prints and later in the century Georgin and Reveille became the best known artists working for this firm. Their images of soldiers, famous men, scenes from fairy tales and historic events in French history were sold all over France. The prints were made with coloured wood-blocks on fine, laid paper, and were underlined by captions which were often naive and sometimes ironical. In the Museum of the image factory at Épinal we may see a collection of images from many foreign countries as well as the treasures of the local production. The museum also contains an important selection of Gallo-Roman sculpture the works of the "Leuques" who lived in the Vosges in the early years of the Christian era. The collection of paintings includes works of Georges de La Tour who was rediscovered after the last war after a long period of neglect. He had been honoured in his lifetime by Louis XIII who had commissioned him to paint a prophylactic image of Saint Sebastian fo protect the king from an outbreak of plague during his visit to Lorraine.

MUSÉE DÉPARTEMENTAL DES VOSGES

3-4-5 Épinal imagery, 19th c. 6 Gallo-Roman stele, Woman in a shop. 7 Rembrandt (1606-1669): Portrait of a woman, 1661. 8 Georges de La Tour (1593-1652): Woman visiting a prisoner.

NOTRE-DAME-DE-L'ÉPINE (or L'ÉPINE) *Marne.* I 5.

The Renaissance style only made its way slowly and discreetly into the architecture of the churches of Champagne and the mid 15th-century cathedral-like pilgrims' basilica of l'Épine is entirely Flamboyant in style. The nave is even archaic in style and shows affinities with that of Reims cathedral; it is separated from the choir by a stone rood-screen (15th c.).

9 Façade of the church of Notre-Dame de l'Épine, 15th c., altered.

FÈRE-EN-TARDENOIS 10

FÈRE-EN-TARDENOIS *Aisne.* I 5.

In the village, market-hall (1552) with handsome stone pillars. Two miles away an enormous bridge built for Anne de Montmorency leads to the château which she had received as a gift from François I. The bridge now only leads to eight ruined but still impressive towers.

10 Château de Fère, monumental bridge by Jean Bullant, 17th c.

EBERSMUNSTER I

ÉPINAL 6

ÉPINAL 3

S.' BLAISE, S.' GUÉRIN,
PRIEZ POUR LA CONSERVATION DE NOS BESTIAUX.

A ÉPINAL, chez PELLERIN, Imprimeur-Libraire.

ÉPINAL 4

BATAILLE DES PYRAMIDES.

ÉPINAL 5

LE CHEMIN DE FER.

ÉPINAL 8

NOTRE-DAME-DE-L'ÉPINE 9

ÉPINAL 7

HATTONCHATEL 4

HAUT-KŒNIGSBOURG 5

GUEBWILLER *Haut-Rhin*. L 8.

Throughout the centuries many great Alsatian artists worked in the church of Notre-Dame which is the most interesting monument in the town for it is an example of the final, successful achievement of a balance between German stylistic influences and the purely French style. It was built on a design by Beuque, the architect of Besançon, by G.I. Ritter and decorated with sculptures by Fidelès Sporrer. The late Baroque Louis XVI nave is intersected by a monumental entablature supported by Corinthian columns with gilded capitals. With the churches of Colmar, Ebersmunster and Molsheim, the church is one of the finest examples of Alsatian Baroque. The church of Saint-Léger which is Romanesque on the exterior and Gothic in the interior has affinities with Sainte-Foy de Sélestat but has been excessively restored. In the church of the Dominicans, some interesting 14th-century mural paintings on the rood-screen.

1 Church of Saint-Léger, 12th, 14th c., restored 19th c. 2 Interior of the church of Notre-Dame, by G.I.Ritter, 1779.

HAROUÉ *Meurthe-et-Moselle*. K 7.

The Parisian architect Boffrand was brought to Lorraine by the Duke Leopold and built the château of Beauvau-Craon between 1720 and 1731. The greatest artists of the time worked with him: Jean Lamour for the railings, Guibal for the statues, Pillement and Hubert Robert for the decorative paintings, and Le Brun for the designs of the tapestries.

3 Château façade, by Boffrand, 1731.

HATTONCHATEL *Meuse*. K 5.

The great polychrome stone altarpiece in the 14th-century church (15th-c. cloister, restored) has been readily attributed to Ligier Richier. The theatrical composition, movement and tragic expressions of the figures are all in the style of the great Lorraine sculptor.

4 Detail from the altarpiece, attributed to Ligier Richier, 1523.

HAUT-KOENIGSBOURG (near Kintzheim) *Bas-Rhin*. L 7.

The fortress of Haut-Koenigsbourg is surrounded by red sandstone walls. It was built in 1479 by Oswald of Thierstein and was restored as a residence for the German Emperor, William II, in 1908.

5 View of the fortress, 15th c., restored.

JOINVILLE *Haute-Marne*. J 7.

To earn forgiveness for his wild behaviour, the Duke of Lorraine offered his wife, Antoinette de Bourbon, a very pretty manor house at Joinville with a single raised storey reminiscent of the château at Écouen. A high roof pierced with dormer-windows crowns the building which stands in the middle of extensive gardens which have now become a public park.

6 The château du Grand Jardin, 1546.

LANGRES *Haute-Marne*. J 8.

Langres is one of those unjustly neglected towns which are considered drab and uninteresting without being really known. But it has important ramparts in a nearly perfect state, punctuated with fortified gateways (Tour de Navarre) and a cathedral with a Graeco-Roman façade (Daviller, 1768) with a superb early Gothic nave in true Burgundian style. Langres also deserves to be visited for its fine Renaissance *hôtels*.

7 Nave of the cathedral of Saint-Mammes, late 12th c. 8 Porte des Moulins, by Camus, 1647. 9 Hôtel de Diane de Poitiers, façade facing the courtyard, 16th c.

GUEBWILLER 2

GUEBWILLER 1

HAROUÉ 3

JOINVILLE 6

LANGRES 7

LANGRES 8

LANGRES 9

LAUTENBACH I

MARMOUTIER 8

MARMOUTIER 9

LAUTENBACH *Haut-Rhin*. L 8.

The only part of the church of Saint-Jean-Baptiste which has not suffered from unfortunate restoration is the twin-bay porch which is a highly original example of Alsatian Romanesque architecture; it has a façade of three Romanesque arches and Gothic vaulting under the porch in yellow and red brick.

I The romanesque arches of the porch, 1150.

LUNÉVILLE *Meurthe-et-Moselle*. K 6.

The court of Leopold, Duke of Lorraine, spent many happy years at the château of Lunéville, an admirable achievement by Boffrand modelled upon Versailles and completed in 1706. The Parc des Bosquets was created by Héré who collaborated with Boffrand to build the Baroque church of Saint-Jacques. The church is boldly designed and has fine Regency interior decoration.

2 Front courtyard of the château, by Boffrand, 1706. 3 Interior of the church of Saint-Jacques, by Boffrand et Héré, 1747.

LUXEUIL *Haute-Saône*. K 8.

The curative powers of the warm thermal springs in the region had been discovered by the Gauls and the Romans had built thermal baths which were renowned for three centuries. The town then became famous when the Irish monk Saint Columba founded a monastery at Luxeuil in the 11th century. The abbey church was built in the 14th century in a pure Gothic style despite its late date and is adjoined by a gallery which is all that remains of a beautiful 13th-century cloister.

The charm of the old town is due to its many fine Renaissance houses which were the dwellings of such important personages as Perrin Jouffroy (Maison Carrée) the father of Louis XI's favourite cardinal who lived in the building opposite (Maison du Cardinal Jouffroy); a little distance away may be seen the house of François I which is that of an abbot of the monastery.

4 Cloister of the basilica of Saint-Pierre, 13th c. 5 Maison Carrée, 1440. 6 Maison du Cardinal Jouffroy, 1460. 7 Maison de François Ier de la Palud, 16th c.

MARMOUTIER *Bas-Rhin*. L 6.

With its massive red and white sandstone masonry, the façade of the abbey church of Marmoutier is one of the most famous sights in Alsace. But one should not forget the importance of this example of Rhenish architecture which still shows a completely Carolingian spirit although belonging to the Romanesque period, with its Lombard fascia, frontons and towers. Not many people know that the nave, which was built in a pure Gothic style in the 13th century, was completed with extreme taste by a groin-vaulted choir in the mid 18th century. In the choir, the Louis XV stalls dating from around the year 1770 are the most beautiful in the whole of Alsace together with those at Neubourg.

8 Façade of the abbey church, c. 1140. 9 Detail of a choir-stall, c. 1770.

MARVILLE *Meuse*. J 4.

If it were not for their bad state of preservation, the town would offer an astonishing array of Renaissance style houses dating from the 15th-16th and 17th centuries (time of the Spanish occupation) which were built by the prosperous cloth and leather merchants of the time. The church of Saint-Nicolas-et-Saint-Hilaire is a fine example of 15th century Gothic and contains a remarkable organ-case.

10 Nave of the church of Saint-Nicolas-et-Saint-Hilaire, 15th c.
11 Windows in the house of the Chevalier Michel, 16th c.

LUNÉVILLE 2

LUNÉVILLE 3

LUXEUIL 4

LUXEUIL 6

MARVILLE 11

LUXEUIL 7

LUXEUIL 5

MARVILLE 10

METZ 5

METZ 6

MULHOUSE 9

METZ *Moselle.* K 5.

The city of Metz was one of the three famous Bishoprics (the others being Toul and Verdun) which Henry II besieged in 1552 during his war against the Emperor Charles V. The 13th-century cathedral is exceptionally large and shows a blend of traditional Lorraine styles and influences from the Champagne. The very high nave (130 feet) is lit by the famous 16th-century windows which have made the church famous. The cathedral opens onto the Place d'Armes which was designed by Blondel in the 18th century on the site of a former cloister. Although somewhat cold and severe in style, the square has a beautiful unity of style. Many other fine churches grace the city: the typically Champenois church of Saint-Vincent, built after the same design of the cathedrals of Toul and Verdun (1376), Saint-Martin with its curious narthex, etc. The Musée Central has very rich collections of Gallo-Roman sculpture for Metz played a very important role in the history of the late Empire, when it was on the frontiers of Romania. The museum is partly housed in the ruins of the Roman baths and contains a *Victory* which was found in the neighbourhood which seems to have been inspired by that set up by Augustus in the Curia Salia at Rome, besides a number of characteristic steles-shrines which were placed along roads like milestones and which used to contain the ashes of the dead. Other notable exhibits include the tomb of Louis the Pious, a 4th-century sarcophagus from the workshops at Arles, fragments from the chancel of Saint-Pierre-aux-Nonnains, and precious Merovingian sculptures.

1 The cathedral of Saint-Étienne, 13th c. 2 Crossing of the cathedral, 16th c. 3 Porte des Allemands, 12th-15th c. 4 Place d'Armes, by Blondel, 18th c.

MUSÉE CENTRAL

5 Gallo-Roman Victory. 6 Gallo-Roman stele with carving of an owl.

MOLSHEIM *Bas-Rhin.* L 6.

One of the most traditional Alsatian buildings may be seen at Molsheim: the *Metzig* which now contains both a museum and one of the most original shrines in Alsace: the Jesuit church which was built in a Gothic and Renaissance style in the early 17th century when most Jesuits were copying the Baroque of the Gesu in Rome. The Metzig used to house a slaughter-house under its arcades and guild-halls in the first storey. The Jesuit church is the work of Christopher Wamser (1619), the architect of Leopold of Austria, the prince-bishop of Strasbourg. The non-conformity of the building is increased by the curious stucco decorations in the transept.

7 The Metzig, the old slaughter-house, 1554. 8 Stucco decoration in the transept of the church of the Jesuits, by Jean Kuhn, 1632.

MULHOUSE *Haut-Rhin.* L 8.

Mulhouse has no pretensions to be an art centre. Its museums are devoted to craftsmanship and the decorative rather than the fine arts. Only the Town Hall has remained in its former state, with its façade decorated by the Swiss artist C. Bockstorffer.

9 The Town-hall, 1552.

MURBACH *Haut-Rhin.* L 8.

With its red sandstone apse, the ancient Benedictine abbey church nestling in the depths of a lonely valley has a strangely original and striking beauty. It was founded in the 8th century and the abbey was one of the richest and most powerful in the whole of Europe for a time. Now abandoned, all that remains of it are its apse with narrow pilaster, its choir with two towers and the transept. By the audacious verticality of its lines it is one of the most original examples of the Romanesque in the Rhine valley.

10 Apse of the abbey church, c. 1175. 11 South portal, lions, 12th c.

METZ 1

METZ 2

METZ 4

MOLSHEIM 8

METZ 3

MOLSHEIM 7

MURBACH 10

MURBACH 11

183

1

10

13

NANCY *Meurthe-et-Moselle.* K 6.

It was Stanislas Leczinsky, the dethroned king of Poland Louis XV's son-in-law and Duke of Lorraine who made Nancy into a masterpiece of 18th-century town-planning with its three famous squares: the Place Stanislas, the Place de la Carrière and the Place d'Alliance. An astonishing galaxy of artists, Emmanuel Héré the architect, Jean Lamour the metal-worker, and the sculptors Guibal and Adam all collaborated under Stanislas' direction, making Nancy into a unique example of the quintessence of the Louis XV style, without a single hint of affectation. Since the 11th century, Nancy had been the capital of the Dukes of Lorraine but the Porte de la Craffe is all that remains of the medieval city.

The ducal palace was destroyed and burnt on several different occasions and the surviving Porterie is built in a Flamboyant and Renaissance style. Emmanuel Héré, the architect of the three squares in the city, was a disciple of Boffrand, and transformed what had been a medieval city into a classical city while giving the Louis XV style a certain joyful, exuberant quality. Jean Lamour built the great railings for the squares, inlaying them with gilt, and the balconies which underline the windows in the squares are like metal embroidery over the stone façades. Guibal, a sculptor from Nîmes, completed the decoration with his great fountains of Neptune and Amphitrite. The two main squares are linked by a triumphal arch which was erected in honour of Louis XV and modelled on the arch of Septimius Severus at Rome. The Government Palace and the Town Hall (magnificent balustrade on the staircase by Jean Lamour) have superb façades opening onto the squares.

Two churches have served as the last resting places for the Dukes of Lorraine: first, the church of the Cordeliers, the official mausoleum, with the tombs of the dukes by Ligier Richier and Mansuy Gauvain (16th c.) as well as the ducal chapel modelled on the Medici chapel at Florence; secondly, the church of Notre-Dame du Bon Secours, which is the private resting place of the Duke Stanislas who modestly preferred to be buried apart from the Dukes of the French royal blood. The beautiful tomb of Catherine Opalinska was built by Nicolas-Sebastien Adam in a style reminiscent of Bernini. Lastly (without mentioning the 18th-century cathedral with its remarkable Treasury) the church of Saint-Epvre is a solemn and luxurious basilica in the neo-Gothic style by Morey (1871).

The town also gave rise to the school of Nancy which was founded by the glass-maker Gallé (1846-1904) and which played a vital part in the decorative arts of the late 19th century.

Two of the most eclectic and richest museums in France add to the renown of Nancy: that of the Beaux-Arts contains paintings, and the Musée Historique Lorrain in the Ducal palace covers the whole art of Lorraine, ranging from engraving (Jacques Callot, a native of Nancy) to painting (Georges de La Tour and Deruet), and includes ceramics (Lunéville, Niderviller), sculpture (statuettes by Cyfflé), tapestry (Galerie aux Cerfs) and popular art (costumed wax figures).

1 Porte de la Craffe, 14th-15th c. 2 Doorway (Porterie) of the Ducal Palace, 1512. 3 Place Stanislas, 18th c., facing the triumphal arch by Héré, 1757. 4 Railings by Jean Lamour. 5 Fountain of Neptune, by Guibal. 6 Town Hall, by Héré. 7 Place de la Carrière, by Héré, 18th c. 8 Ceiling of the ducal chapel of the church of the Cordeliers, 1632. 9 Tomb of Catherine Opalinska, by Nicolas-Sebastien Adam, 18th c. church of Notre-Dame du Bon Secours.

MUSÉE HISTORIQUE LORRAIN

10 Jacques Callot (1592-1635): Beggar, engraving. 11 Claude Deruet (c. 1588-1660): Diane chasseresse. 12 Georges de La Tour (1593-1652): Woman with the flea. 13 Evangeliary of Saint-Gauzelin, cathedral Treasury, 9th c.

2

9

3

4

6

5

7

8

12

11

185

NEUWILLER-LÈS-SAVERNE *Bas-Rhin.* L 6.

More interesting than the two main churches in the town is the little Romanesque sanctuary with its two superimposed chapels, one consecrated to Saint Sebastian (above) and the other to Saint Catherine, both dating from the early 11th century. The square capitals are bare in one chapel and decorated with animals and interlacing patterns in the other. A beautiful series of Basle tapestries (*Life of Saint Adelphe*, 15th c.) is exhibited in the upper chapel. Both chapels are rather curiously connected to the apse of the church of Saint-Pierre-Saint-Paul. A Benedictine basilica on the Cistercian pattern (12th-13th c). The old collegiate church of Saint-Adelphe which became a Protestant church in the 16th century, is in a very fine Rhenish Gothic style of the 12th century.

1 Upper chapel of Saint-Sebastien.

OBERNAI *Bas-Rhin.* L 7.

The prettiest villages in Alsace are Obernai, Hunspach, Eguisheim, Oberseebach, Riquewihr and Turckheim. They are often girdled with ancient ramparts, and surrounded with vineyards and have kept their charm and welcoming appearance throughout the centuries.

2 View of the old village of Obernai.

ORBAIS *Marne.* I 6.

The church was built in a pure Champagne Gothic style in the 12th century for a Benedictine abbey and was completed in 1200. The choir with its wide ambulatory served as a model for that of Notre-Dame de Reims and, like the latter, would appear to be the work of Jean d'Orbais.

3 Interior of the church, 12th c.

ORBAIS 3

OTTMARSHEIM *Haut-Rhin.* L 8.

Of purely archaeological interest, the 11th-century church of Ottmarsheim was built on a octagonal ground-plan in imitation of the octagon of Aix-la-Chapelle. The interior is domed, cradle-vaulted and rib-vaulted and is a unique example of its kind in France. It was saved from ruin by Prosper Mérimée.

4 Benedictine abbey church, 11th c. **5** Church interior.

LE PAILLY *Haute-Marne.* J 8.

Although the towers of an earlier château have survived, Le Pailly is a Renaissance style building which has been sadly neglected by the authorities. It is still rich in sculptures in the interior and contains fine chimneys and vaulting.

6 The château, by Nicolas Ribonnier, 1560.

PHALSBOURG 8

PHALSBOURG *Moselle.* L 6.

The name of the town means "Palatine fortress" for it was the gateway to Alsace and was surrounded with fortifications by Vauban. Two fine gateways with sculpted reliefs of trophies still remain.

7 Porte de France, 1680. **8** Porte d'Allemagne, 1680.

PHALSBOURG 7

POMPIERRE *Vosges.* K 7.

The portal and tympanum of the church are all that remain of the original Romanesque church and show great affinities with the Limousin style. The carving of the figures under the arches is rough but expressive, and the archivolts and colonnettes are very Burgundian in style.

9 Portal of the church, 12th c.

NEUWILLER-LES-SAVERNE 1

OBERNAI 2

LE PAILLY 6

OTTMARSHEIM 5

POMPIERRE 9

OTTMARSHEIM 4

1

8

REIMS *Marne*. I 5.

The city of Reims is fortunate in having not only one of the most famous of all French cathedrals, a masterpiece of High Gothic, but also a superb example of the Gothicised Romanesque style in the church of Saint-Rémi. The latter, former Benedictine abbey church, has a nave 375 feet long — like that of Notre-Dame in Paris. Severely Romanesque and austere in style, the nave is terminated by a finely carved choir with splendid windows which show the beginnings of the pointed Gothic style. The cathedral itself is the second largest in France (Amiens being the first in size) but it owes its beauty to its unity of style for it was begun in 1211 and completed by the end of the century. Its façade is particularly Champenois for it is ornamented with stained-glass windows in the tympana of the portals. The tapestry collection is only second in importance to that at Angers. The famous statuary has been praised and admired so much that it is worth the visitor's effort to try to look at it with fresh eyes and forget the over-reproduced Smiling Angel in order to appreciate the scene of the Annunciation as a whole, with its magnificent Gothic draperies, next to the classically-inspired scene of the Visitation. The diversity of style to be seen in the sculpture of the region was due to the presence of numerous workshops which were all active at the same time, but essentially it is not different from that of the sculpture at Chartres and Amiens, in the Ile-de-France and Picardy. Another important but earlier monument in the city is the splendid Gallo-Roman triumphal arch which is the finest in France after that at Orange. Despite the fact that the city has been largely rebuilt owing to extensive war damage, a number of old houses dating from the Middle Ages to the 18th century have miraculously survived. One, the hôtel Le Vergeur, a 15th-century dwelling, has now become the Musée du Vieux-Reims. Another was dismantled and removed to the sculpture museum: the remains of this fine old Gothic house, known as the Maison des Musiciens, may be seen side by side with such splendid sculptures as the well-known tomb of the Roman general Jovinus. The Musée des Beaux-Arts is one of the most comprehensive of all French provincial museums. It contains thirty paintings by Corot as well as examples of the work of many of the greatest French painters (Le Nain, Poussin, Philippe de Champaigne, David, Daumier, Pissarro, Renoir), a tapestry collection, drawings and famous portraits by Cranach.

5

10

I Porte Mars, Gallo-Roman triumphal arch, early 3rd c.

CHURCH OF SAINT-RÉMI

2 Façade, 12th c. 3 Nave, 11th c. 4 Cloister, detail, 12th c.

CATHEDRAL OF NOTRE-DAME

5 Capital with vine-patterns and vineyard scene (Chapiteau des Vendanges), 13th c. 6 Façade, 13th c. 7 The Annunciation and the Visitation. 8 Saint John the Baptist. 9 Nave.

MUSÉE DES BEAUX-ARTS

10 Maison des Musiciens, detail: musician, 13th c. 11 Mathieu Le Nain (1607-1677): Venus in Vulcan's forge. 12 David (1748-1825): Young girl in the nude. 13 J.-B.-C. Corot (1796-1875): Spring landscape. 14 Renoir (1841-1920): la Lecture du rôle.

2

4

3

6

7

9

12

I I

14

I 3

189

RIQUEWIHR *Haut-Rhin.* L 7.

Few other Alsatian towns are as charming and pretty as Riquewihr. The main streets are lined with lovingly tended old houses which once belonged to rich wine-growers in the late 16th and early 17th centuries. The town was surrounded by a double line of ramparts, the first was the Dolder, which may still be seen, and the second, the Obertor, has no longer survived.

1 View of the roofs of the town. 2 The "Sinnbrunnen" fountain, 1620.

RONCHAMP *Haute-Saône.* L 8.

The chapel was recently rebuilt by Le Corbusier and its curving lines are designed in harmony with the surrounding landscape. By contrast, the well-lit interior is austere in the straight severity of its lines, but the boldness of the architect has not diminished the spiritual significance of the building which is often visited by pilgrims, usually from Germany and Holland.

3 South façade of the chapel of Notre-Dame-du-Haut, by Le Corbusier, 1955. 4 Interior of the chapel.

ROSHEIM *Bas-Rhin.* L 6.

The church of Saint-Pierre-Saint-Paul was built in ten years, almost certainly under the auspices of Frederick Barbarossa, and is the most perfect and complete Romanesque church in Alsace. Traditional narrow pilasters run round the walls, also decorated with highly original and refined sculpture. According to M. Hans Haug, the high-relief sculpture is the earliest in Alsace. On the façade, the central pediment is flanked by acroteria (ornamental summits) representing men being devoured by lions, and the fronton itself carries the figure of a bird. The apse around the axial window is carved with low-relief symbols of the Evangelists in a style which has direct affinities with that of certain Poitevin churches. The small town also contains the only surviving Romanesque house in Alsace but its interest is historic rather than aesthetic.

5 View of the church of Saint-Pierre-Saint-Paul, 1160. 6 Fronton of the main façade, with acroteria. 7 Apse.

ROUFFACH 8

ROUFFACH *Haut-Rhin.* L 8.

Every French province can offer examples of bad restoration and the church of Notre-Dame (or Saint-Arbogast) at Rouffach in Alsace is no exception. It was built in 1320 and then over-restored in the 19th century, although it was a fine example of early Gothic decorated with stylish sculptures by the master-craftsman Woelfelin (some gargoyles are now in Colmar museum). A number of old houses may be seen in the town.

8 Tour des Sorcières (Witches' Tower), 13th-15th c., and façades of two houses, 1575 and 1715.

SAINT-DIÉ *Vosges.* L 7.

The two churches of this modern town are joined by a fine Renaissance cloister. The cathedral is partly Romanesque and has been rebuilt in red sand-stone, and the church of Notre-Dame which survived the war is built in the sober Rhenish Romanesque style.

9 Cloister of the cathedral, 15th-16th c.

RIQUEWIHR 2

RIQUEWIHR I

RONCHAMP 3

RONCHAMP 4

ROSHEIM 7

ROSHEIM 5

ROSHEIM 6

ST-DIÉ 9

191

SAINT-MIHIEL *Meuse.* J 6.

The town was the birth-place of two great families of artists, the Richiers who were sculptors and the Bérains who were decorators and ornament-painters. One of the town's two churches, Saint-Sépulcre, contains a masterpiece by Ligier Richier the Elder: the Entombment, and the other, Saint-Michel, part of a now lost group, the Passion of the Virgin, in once-polychromed walnut wood. These two masterpieces show Richier's great elegance of style, noble but slightly affected attitudes and a Germanic sense of pathos and sorrow which is almost exaggerated. But the stone and wood carving is among the very best of its time.

1 Ligier Richier (1506-1567): The Fainting Virgin, church of Saint-Michel. **2** Ligier Richier: detail of the Entombment, 1540, church of Saint-Sépulcre.

SAINT-NICOLAS-DE-PORT *Meurthe-et-Moselle.* K 6.

With its star-vaulting, its twin-bay transept, and choir without an ambulatory, the basilica of Saint-Nicolas is one of the most important Flamboyant churches in Lorraine and even the whole of France. The nave was completed in 1514.

3 Vaulting of the basilica of Saint-Nicolas, 16th c.

SAINT-THIERRY (near Reims) *Marne.* I 5.

Like many other churches in Champagne, that of Saint-Thierry is decorated with a purely ornamental projecting porch supported by slender colonnettes, like the gallery of a cloister. The church together with some arches of the Chapter Room was saved from the destructions wrought by a Reims architect in the 18th century. The château he built can hardly be said to compensate for his ravages.

4 Projecting front porch of the church, 12th c. **5** Chapter house, late 12th c.

SAVERNE *Bas-Rhin.* L 6.

The Cardinal Louis de Rohan, famous for his part in the scandal of Marie-Antoinette's diamond necklace, was as bold and ostentatious in his building projects as in his private life, and commissioned the architect Nicolas de Salins to build him the gigantic pink sandstone palace at Saverne. In the town, a very fine house dating from 1605 may be seen at 80, Grande-Rue.

6 North façade of the château, late 18th c. **7** Renaissance House, 1605.

SÉLESTAT 8

SÉLESTAT *Bas-Rhin.* L 7.

The originality of the church of Sainte-Foy is due to the fact that it was a subsidiary to Sainte-Foy-de-Conques, and that it brought the style of Rouergue to Alsace. Very fine tapering stone clock-tower with spire, restorations and additions. The red-sandstone and grey granite church of Saint-Georges was built between the 12th and 15th centuries. Two of the many ancient dwellings in the town deserve mention: the hôtel de l'abbaye d'Ebersmunster (1541) for its portal and courtyard, and the house of the architect Ziegler (1544).

8 Bell-tower of the church of Sainte-Foy, 12th c.

ST-MIHIEL 2

ST-MIHIEL 1

ST-NICOLAS-DE-PORT 3

ST-THIERRY 4

ST-THIERRY 5

SAVERNE 7

SAVERNE 6

11

12

13

14

STRASBOURG *Bas-Rhin.* L 6.

As its name indicates (Strasbourg: Strasse-Burg), Strasbourg was at the centre of so many warlike encounters that it is almost miraculous that its cathedral should have survived so nearly intact. Its 460 feet high spire, Jean Hultz's masterpiece, was built in 1439 and has successfully withstood all the bombardments suffered by the city and still soars over the old roofs of the many ancient timbered houses. Its pink sandstone façade was the work of Erwin de Steinbach who was unable to finish the church. Building continued from the 13th to the 15th century but the cathedral kept the purest and boldest Gothic style to be seen in the whole of France.

Many of the sculptures on the façade are in fact casts, for the originals are now exhibited in the Musée de l'Œuvre Notre-Dame. They include such famous pieces as *Le Séducteur et les Vierges folles* (The Seducer and the Foolish Virgins) — note the monsters, symbols of the Vices, behind the Seducer — the *Church* and the veiled *Synagogue*, the *Death of the Virgin*, etc. The nave is as richly decorated as the exterior and is lit by splendid 13th and 14th-century stained-glass windows; the Gothic pulpit is a masterpiece of its kind. During Holy Week twelve fine 18th-century tapestries depicting scenes in the *Life of the Virgin* are hung in the church. It was here that Louis XV married Maria Leczinska in 1726.

The Musée de l'Œuvre Notre-Dame has been installed in a group of several ancient houses and contains a series of historic documents relating to the building of the cathedral as well as some of its sculptures. Also exhibited are a number of works by Alsatian painters such as Witz, Schongauer, Grünewald, Hans Baldung-Grien and Stosskopff.

The Château des Rohan was built in 1742 by Massol on the plans of Blondel and now houses the Musée des Beaux-Arts in the apartments of the prince-bishops. All we can do to give an idea of its richness is to say that it contains every style of painting from Giotto to Braque. The neighbouring Musée des Arts Décoratifs contains a fine collection of porcelain as a reminder of the importance of the Hannong workshops in the 18th century. Because of the fame of the cathedral and the museums of Strasbourg the tourist is likely to forget that the city is one of the most beautiful in Alsace with its great bourgeois mansions and the picturesque old houses of the Petite-France quarter.

CATHEDRAL OF NOTRE-DAME

I Façade by Erwin de Steinbach, 13th c. 2 The Seducer and the Foolish Virgins, 13th c. 3 South arm of the transept, the pillar of the Angels, 13th c. 4 The Synagogue, statue in the left-hand portal, 13th c. 5 Astronomical clock, restored by Schwilgue in 1838.

MUSÉE DE L'ŒUVRE NOTRE-DAME

6 Head of the Wissembourg Christ, stained-glass window, c. 1070. 7 Conrad Witz (died 1447): Saints Catherine and Madeleine. 8 Stosskopff (1597-1657): Still-life, glasses and pastry.

MUSÉE DES BEAUX-ARTS

9 El Greco (c. 1541-1624): Mater Dolorosa. 10 Jean Tassel (1608-1667): the wood sawyers.

MUSÉE DES ARTS DÉCORATIFS

11 Paul Hannong, plate from the dinner service of the Cardinal de Rohan, 1760.

12 Courtyard of the hôtel du Corbeau, 14th c. 13 Maison Kammerzell, 1467, restored. 14 Palais Rohan, 1742.

1

2

3

4

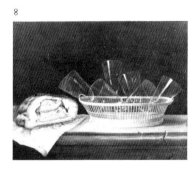

5

6

8

9

7

10

THANN 1

TROIS-FONTAINES 6

TROIS-FONTAINES 7

THANN *Haut-Rhin.* L 8.

Designed to charm and impress the pilgrim, the collegiate church of Saint-Thiébault is an elegant Gothic-Renaissance structure with a fine soaring choir, statues of apostles, apse and stained-glass windows (15th and 16th c.) and a tower with a perforated spire by the Basle architect Rémy Foesch (1516).

I Apse of the collegiate church of Saint-Thiébault. 2 Interior of the church.

TOUL *Meurthe-et-Moselle.* K 6.

The fact that Toul was one of the three historic bishoprics (with Metz and Verdun) explains the importance of the two churches (the cathedral and the collegiate) and their fine cloisters. The façade of the cathedral of Saint-Étienne was finished in 1496 and is late Flamboyant in style; the high windows are pointed with tapering gables. The severe cloister with its beautiful pointed bays is one of the largest in France. The second cloister belonging to the collegiate church of Saint-Gengoult was built in the 16th century in a late and exaggerated Flamboyant style. The Town Hall is a graceful 18th-century building.

3 Façade of the cathedral of Saint-Étienne, 1496. 4 Cloister of the cathedral, 13th-14th c. 5 Cloister of the collegiate church of Saint-Gengoult, 16th c.

TROIS-FONTAINES (Abbey of) *Marne.* J 6.

The Cistercian abbey was founded in 1116 and completed in the 18th century by very beautiful monastic buildings which are even more interesting than the remains of the Romanesque structure.

6 Abbey entrance, 18th c. 7 Portico facing the gardens.

TROYES *Aube.* I 7.

Now a museum-city, Troyes was an art centre as important as the Loire Valley or Fontainebleau during the Renaissance. Despite its modern buildings, it is still a town of churches, fine glass-factories, old wooden and *pisé* houses, and fine old mansions, all competing in interest and charm. It was the ancient capital of Champagne, and the birth-place of Pope Urban IV (1261) who was the son of a cobbler of Troyes, a centre of sculpture and stained-glass making during the Renaissance, and with its school of architecture could truly be considered as a city of the first rank.

The most beautiful and characteristic of its many churches are: the cathedral of Saint-Pierre-Saint-Paul which was begun in 1208, and added to at various times in the 15th, 17th and 19th centuries; three portals with sharp-pointed gables, a nave with twin aisles pierced with striking polychrome stained-glass windows which give the church the appearance of a glass cage; Saint-Urbain, the most beautiful church in Troyes (13th c.), a fine structure of delicately cut stone framing magnificent stained-glass windows, with tapering flying-buttresses of unparalleled lightness; the church of the Madeleine with its rood-screen, a masterpiece in the Flamboyant style by Jean Gailde in 1517.

8 North portal of the cathedral of Saint-Pierre-Saint-Paul, 13th c. 9 Nave of the cathedral, 13th c. 10 Rood-screen of the church of the Madeleine, 1517. 11 Church of Saint-Urbain: apse, 13th c.

THANN 2

TOUL 5

TOUL 3

TOUL 4

TROYES 9

TROYES 8

TROYES 11

TROYES 10

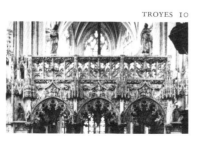

197

Saint-Jean-au-Marché has a fine Renaissance choir and stained-glass windows by Jean and Linard Gontier, both craftsmen from Troyes; Saint-Pantaleon with grisaille-stained-glass windows, like those of the church of Saint-Nicolas, by Jean Macadié, another artist of Troyes.

Some important sculpture: the *Christ de Pitié* (Christ of Pity) in the church of Saint-Nizier, the *Sainte Marthe* in the Madeleine, and some Virgins with typically sad expressions in the Musée Historique. The sculpture of Champagne always avoided theatrical grimace and attitudes and is characterised by a discreet pathos and profound sadness of expression.

One street in particular, the Rue des Chats, is lined with old timbered houses. The hôtels de Marisy, de Vauluisant and De Mauroy are among the finest examples of Renaissance civil architecture. The Hôtel-Dieu is famous for its monumental railing which was the work of a Parisian metal-worker, Pierre Delphin (1760). The museums contain a collection of classical French painting (Musée des Beaux-Arts), exhibits illustrating the history of Champagne (Musée Historique) and hosiery, which was the source of the city's prosperity.

1 Detail of a stained-glass window in the church of Saint-Nicolas. 2 Christ de Pitié, church of Saint-Nizier, 16th c. 3 Sainte-Marthe, church of La Madeleine, 15th c. 4 Hôtel de Marisy, 1530. 5 Hôtel de Mauroy, 1540. 6 Hôtel de Vauluisant, 1564. 7 Railings of the Hôtel-Dieu, by Pierre Delphin, 1760.

MUSÉE DES BEAUX-ARTS

8 Jean Malouel (c. 1370-1415): Descent from the Cross. 9 Watteau (1684-1721): The Charmer.

TROYES 9

TROYES 8

TURCKHEIM 10

TURCKHEIM *Haut-Rhin.* L 7.

Thanks to Turenne's victory at Turckheim, Alsace became part of France by the Treaty of Westphalia in 1648. The town has preserved its essentially Alsatian character and many well-kept 17th-century houses as well as three fortified gateways.

10 Main square and fountain.

TROYES 1

TROYES 3

TROYES 2

TROYES 5

TROYES 4

TROYES 6

TROYES 7

VIGNORY I

VIGNORY *Haute-Marne.* J 7.

The church at Vignory has hardly changed with the centuries and is a perfect example of the Romanesque style of Champagne. The three-storeyed nave is terminated by a great arch cutting it off from the choir with its radiating chapels and is vaulted in timber. The windows above the arch give the nave a stylistic resemblance to those of Cistercian churches and are devoid of all sculpture, achieving their effect by the pattern of openings alone.

1 Apse of the church, 11th c. 2 Nave, 11th c.

VILLEMAUR-SUR-VANNE *Aube.* I 7.

The wooden tower with three receding porch-roofs is one of the few to escape destruction in the 19th century and is an example of church towers that were frequently found in 19th century Champagne. A rood-screen, also in wood, cuts the church in half with its gallery supported by pilasters sculpted with scenes from the Passion and the life of the Virgin.

3 Wooden tower of the church, 16th c. 4 Wooden rood-screen in the church, 1521.

VILLEMAUR-SUR-VANNE 3

VIGNORY 2

VILLEMAUR-SUR-VANNE 4

VI

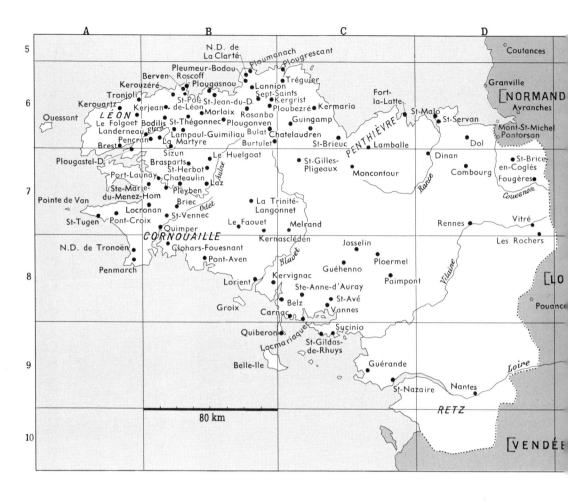

5

A   B   C   D

N.D. de
La Clarté
Pleumeur-Bodou

Ploumanach
Plougrescant
Coutances

Berven Roscoff
Kerouzéré
Plougasnou
Lannion
Tréguier

Granville
NORMAND

Tronjoli
Kerouartz
St-Pol St-Jean-du-D.
Sept-Saints
Kergrist

6

Kerjean
de-Léon
Ploubezré
Kermaria
Fort-
la-Latte

Avranches

Ouessant
LÉON
Morlaix
Rosanbo

St-Malo
St-Servan

Le Folgoet Bodilis St-Thégonnec
Plougonven
Guingamp

Mont-St-Michel
Pontorson

Landerneau
Lampaul-Guimiliau Bulat
Chatelaudren

Pencran La Martyre
Burtulet
St-Brieuc
Lamballe
Dol

Brest
Sizun
Le Huelgoat

PENTHIÈVRE
Dinan

St-Brice-
en-Coglès
Fougères

Plougastel-D.
Brasparts
St-Gilles-
Pligeaux

Combourg

7

Port-Launay
St-Herbot
Chateaulin

Moncontour
Rance

Couesnon

Ste-Marie-
du-Menez-Hom
Pleyben
Laz

Pointe de Van
Briec
Odet

La Trinité-
Langonnet

Rennes
Vitré

Locronan
St-Vennec

Les Rochers

St-Tugen
Pont-Croix
Quimper

Le Faouet
Melrand

Vilaine

N.D. de Tronoën
CORNOUAILLE
Clohars-Fouesnant

Kernascléden
Josselin

8

Pont-Aven
Blavet

Guéhenno
Ploermel
Paimpont

Penmarch
Lorient
Kervignac
Ste-Anne-d'Auray
St-Avé

LO

Groix
Belz
Vannes

Pouanc

Carnac
Quiberon

Sucinio

9

Locmariaquer
St-Gildas-
de-Rhuys

Guérande
Loire

Belle-Ile
St-Nazaire
Nantes

RETZ

80 km

10

VENDÉE

202

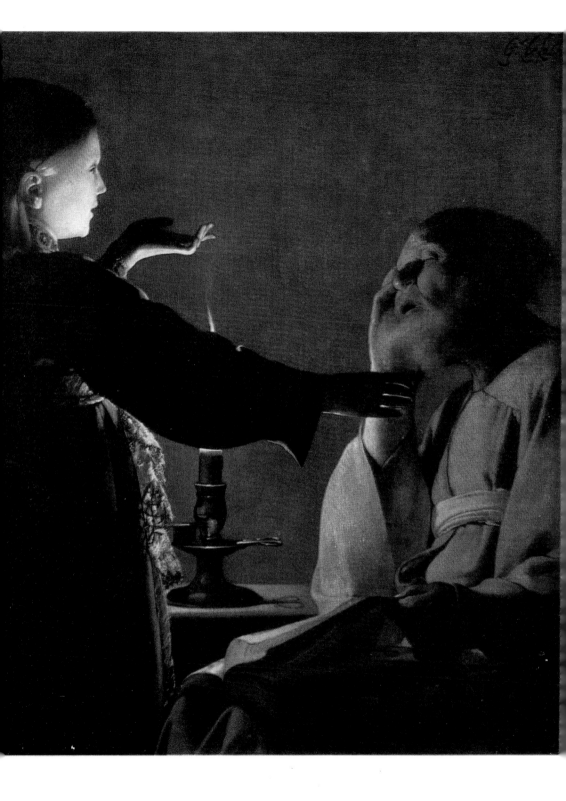

GEORGES DE LA TOUR (1593-1652), THE DREAM OF SAINT JOSEPH, MUSÉE DES BEAUX-ARTS, NANTES *(Giraudon)*

SAINT LIVERTIN, POLYCHROME WOOD STATUETTE, CHAPEL OF NOTRE-DAME-DU-HAUT, MONCONTOUR *(Hélène Jeanbrau)*

It is strange that in a region so ancient that it is famous above all for its druidic monuments and chamber tombs, the most important art and architecture is almost without exception of the Renaissance period. Romanesque art is rare and exceptional in Britanny. Some critics have spoken of naive art with regard to the granite calvaries and countless statues of Breton saints throughout the region, but this is oversimplifying matters since several different schools and workshops have been distinguished by experts. Other critics have spoken of an archetypal art, examples of something eternal in man, and of which, according to Plato, individual works are no more than reflections and copies.

BODILIS 6

BELZ *Morbihan*. C 8.

Only a few houses stand on the islet of Belz with its chapel dedicated to Saint Cado ("anglais de nation, prince de Glamorgan" as an old inscription states). The small jetty which links it to the mainland and which was said to have been built by the devil is protected by a calvary by the estuary. A few beautiful trees still survive in the centre of the island which is dominated by a simple monumental calvary. Beside the calvary, the chapel of the templars with Romanesque porch and arcades in the nave, and a small massive tower.

1 Monumental calvary, 1852. 2 Small calvary by the jetty.

BERVEN *Finistère*. B 6.

The church of Notre-Dame-de-Berven at Plouzévédé dates from the 15th and 16th centuries and is surrounded by an enclosure with a porch with three arcades. The tower with its superimposed balconies and lanterns (1576) is an ancient example of its kind. Very beautiful interior: stone choir screen surmounted by a rood-screen in carved wood, fine wall-plates and beams, choir-stalls and altarpiece. A statue of the Virgin should be noted in the centre of the Tree of Jesse.

3 Statue of Saint-Eloi, right aisle of the church. 4 Tower of the church of Notre-Dame-de-Berven, 16th c. 5 Sacred fountain.

BODILIS *Finistère*. B 6.

This humble little village has an interesting 16th-17th century church. Its most remarkable feature is the surprising group of caryatids under the porch, supporting the traditional series of figures of the apostles.

6 Caryatid in the porch of the church, 16th c.

BRASPARTS *Finistère*. B 7.

A fine group of parish buildings including a church (1551) with a spire and a turret and a fine Renaissance porch. In the interior, an ancient painted wooden Pietà. The cemetery is on a steep slope outside the original church precincts. The Pietà accompanied by the group of the Holy Women by the foot of the 16th-century calvary with its three crosses is highly unusual in its style and inspired a painting by Gauguin.

7 Paul Gauguin (1848-1903): Calvary, 1889, Brussels, Musée Royal des Beaux-Arts. 8 The Holy Women, calvary, 16th c.

BREST *Finistère*. A 6.

Apart from the old castle and the ramparts which still dominate the Penfeld, little remains of the old town of Brest. The great Breton port was severely damaged in the war and has become a "modern" city although its port is still as lively as ever. The Rue de Siam has been widened and is as animated as in the old days of its glory though its old character is gone.

9 Ramparts at Brest.

BRIEC *Finistère*. B 7.

The chapel of Saint-Corentin has a highly original vaulted beamed roof of perfect design and a very characteristic simplicity. Although not the richest, it deserves comparison with the finest of the kind.

10 Beamed roof of the chapel of Saint-Corentin, 17th c.

BELZ 1

BERVEN 3

BERVEN 4

BELZ 2

BERVEN 5

BREST 9

BRIEC 10

BRASPARTS 7

BRASPARTS 8

207

BULAT-PESTIVIEN *Côtes-du-Nord.* B 7.

The church of Notre-Dame de Bulat (15th-16th c.) has a porch sheltering the Twelve Apostles opening with a monumental arcade decorated in the Flamboyant style and divided by a slender column with entwined vine-motif decoration. Three pretty fountains. Although less important than the calvaries in Finistère, that at Pestivien (2/3 of a mile from Bulat) in one of the most attractive in the Côtes-du-Nord.

BURTULET *Côtes-du-Nord.* B 7.

The church of Saint-Servais is a massive and picturesquely melancholy structure on the summit of hill, among pine trees. Ancient statues including that of the founder in the interior.

3 Chapel of the church of Burtulet en Saint-Servais, 16th c.

CARNAC *Morbihan.* C 8.

Megalithic monuments, menhirs and dolmens abound throughout Britanny and are particularly numerous in the area around the gulf of Morbihan (more than 3,000 in the region of Carnac alone). The stone rows at Carnac are world-famous: rows at Menec, Kernario, Kerlescan etc. (q.v. Locmariaquer).
The church of Saint-Cornély at Carnac dates from the 17th century. On the left, a porch surmounted with a baldaquin (very rare). In the interior, painted wooden beams in the vaulting. On the façade, statue of the saint, patron of horned animals, between two oxen.

4 Row of menhirs, prehistoric period. **5** Church of Saint-Cornély, porch with baldaquin, 17th c.

CHATEAULIN *Finistère.* B 7.

Especially noted for the 15th-16th century chapel of Notre-Dame (restored). 16th-century calvary-ossuary (windows now blocked) and interesting Renaissance domed tower. Ancient statuary: Saint Catherine with her wheel, Saint Barbe, Saint Gregory holding a Greek cross and at the end of the church, a group sculpture of the Virgin and Child and Saint Anne. Note the knee of the Child which has been worn by the touch of generations of pious visitors.

6 Chapel of Notre-Dame, 16th c. **7** Virgin, Child and Saint Anne.

CHATELAUDREN *Côtes-du-Nord.* C 6.

Standing in its cemetery, the church of Notre-Dame-du-Tertre was founded in the 14th century and enlarged in the 15th and 16th centuries. Fine slated tower, and retable in gilt-wood. Remarkable 15th-century paintings on the wooden vaulting: only the upper part remains of the paintings in the nave and those in the chapel in the right transept have been saved by restoration. They are all the more interesting as painting is very rarely found in Breton churches. Scenes from the Old and New Testaments painted in a primitive style, one of the most famous being the remarkable frank scene depicting Noah succumbing to the effects of the juice of the grape.

8-9 Paintings in the church of Notre-Dame-du-Tertre, 15th c.

PESTIVIEN 1

BULAT 2

BURTULET 3

CARNAC 4

CHATEAULIN 7

CHATEAULIN 6

CARNAC 5

CHATELAUDREN 8

CHATELAUDREN 9

209

N.-D.-DE-LA-CLARTÉ I

NOTRE-DAME-DE-LA-CLARTÉ *Côtes-du-Nord*. B 6.

One of the prettiest of Renaissance chapels, and famous as much for its panoramic position by the sea as for the galaxy of artists it attracted. It was decorated with paintings of the Stations·of the Cross by Maurice Denis in 1931. Its porch is preceded by a calvary and has a single bay enclosed by a curious carved wooden screen.

I Porch of the chapel of Notre-Dame-de-la-Clarté, 1445.

CLOHARS-FOUESNANT *Finistère*. B 8.

The picturesque 15th-16th-century church in the village of Clohars-Fouesnant stands in its cemetery with an ancient calvary. A few hundred yards away may be seen one of the most beautiful sacred fountains in Britanny: the fountain of Drennec, ornamented with a Pietà.

2 Fountain of Drennec.

COMBOURG *Ille-et-Vilaine*. D 7.

The fortress at Combourg was first built in the 11th century and then enlarged and altered in the 14th and 15th centuries. It was here that the writer Chateaubriand (1768-1848) spent two years of his youth and nearly died of boredom despite the romantic nearby pond, as he himself related in his *Mémoires d'Outre-Tombe*.

3 Château of Combourg, 11th-15th c.

DINAN *Côtes-du-Nord*. D 7.

The "style" of the city is deservedly famous, for it is there that many ancient houses may still be seen in their original state and in a homogeneous quarter (Place de l'Apport, place des Cordeliers, Tour de l'Horloge) (It should be noted that it has not been thought necessary in this guide to illustrate the very numerous 15th-16th century houses which can be seen, all more or less isolated, in nearly every Breton town). Dinan's most famous and typical 15th-century street is the Rue de Jerzual which runs in a steep slope down to the river Rance.

The church of Saint-Sauveur has kept its Romanesque portal (12th c.) (the tympanum is modern) and was rebuilt in the Flamboyant style in the 15th and 16th centuries; the tower dates from 1605 and the fine beamed campanile from 1779.

The vast ramparts include the château of the Duchess Anne of Britanny with its 13th-century gateway and 105-foot high 14th-century keep. It has been transformed into an interesting museum, mostly devoted to folk-lore, and containing such rare exhibits as the heavy weights used for tithes in bronze and massive stone; charming collection of head-dresses; furniture, reconstructed interiors, etc. and some highly interesting and beautiful specimens of engraved wood-blocks used for printing popular images.

The centre of the town opens up into the Place du Champ-Clos, lined with many fine houses; the name of the square is in memory of the single combat fought by Du Guesclin against an English knight in 1364, as a result of which he not only saved his town but also won the heart of a fair lady. Du Guesclin is the almost legendary hero of Dinan and his heart is still kept in the church of Saint-Sauveur.

4 Old houses, Place des Cordeliers. 5 Rue and Tour de l'Horloge. 6 Church of Saint-Sauveur, 15th-16th c. 7 Château of Duchess Anne of Britanny, Porte du Guichet, 13th c. and keep, 14th c. 8 Engraved wood-block: mortuary image of Le Fas, 19th c.

DINAN 8

COMBOURG 3

CLOHARS 2

DINAN 4

DINAN 5

DINAN 7

DINAN 6

DOL I

DOL-DE-BRETAGNE *Ille-et-Vilaine.* D 6.

The greater part of the cathedral of Saint-Samson dates from the 13th century, but one of its three towers in unfinished. Magnificent nave, over 300 feet long and 65 feet high under the roof. The great rectangular 14th-century porch on the right flank of the church is perforated by wide arcades and crowned by a Flamboyant style balustrade. Some old houses with porches and columns; the Maison de la Guillotière (15th c.) has been transformed into a little regional museum.

I Porch of the cathedral of Saint-Samson, 14th c. 2 Nave of the cathedral, 13th c.

LE FAOUET 3

LE FAOUET *Morbihan.* B 7.

The town is built around a large square with a vast market-hall with a splendid beamed roof in the centre (late 16th c.). But the main interest of Le Faouet is its three great neighbouring chapels: Saint-Fiacre (2 miles to the south) which was built in about 1480 in the Flamboyant style, with a typical gabled tower; the rood-screen in the interior is decorated with outstandingly fine and varied stone-carving in which no motif is ever repeated twice; the church of Sainte-Barbe (1 ½ miles to the north-east) on a hill among chestnut-trees; built in 1498 in Flamboyant Gothic but transformed in character by the majestic granite staircase (1700) leading up to the oratory of Saint-Michel (loggia-sacristy by the landing); 4 miles to the north-east, in the village of Kervegan, the more modest 16th-century Flamboyant chapel of Saint-Nicolas, with a small stone tower with a gable flanked by a turret; the wooden rood-screen, painted in a naive Renaissance style should be compared with that in Saint-Fiacre (scenes from the legend of Saint-Nicolas; on the reverse, the Apostles).

3 Rood-screen of the chapel of Saint-Fiacre, carved wood, 15th c. 4 Fontaine Sainte-Barbe, 1708. 5 Chapel of Saint-Fiacre, 15th c. 6 Market-hall, 16th c. 7 Staircase of the chapel of Sainte-Barbe, 1700.

LE FOLGOET 13

LE FOLGOET *Finistère.* A 6.

The magnificent basilica of Notre-Dame was built due to the generosity of the Dukes of Britanny and the tower is one of the most beautiful in the Léon region. Very fine portals; in the south arm of the transept, a curious statue of Saint Christopher. The calvary dates from 1419. Statues of the Twelve Apostles in the porch. The venerated statue of Notre-Dame-du-Folgoët was crowned amid great ceremony on September 8, 1888 (annual forgiveness day). The interior contains a magnificent granite rood-screen.

8 The miraculous Virgin, stone, 15th c. 9 Basilica of Notre-Dame, early 15th c. 10 Front portal, 15th c. 11 Statues of the Apostles in the porch, 15th c. 12 Baptism of Christ, high relief in wood. 13 Granite rood-screen, 15th c.

DOL 2

LE FAOUET 4

LE FAOUET 5

LE FAOUET 6

LE FAOUET 7

LE FOLGOET 10

LE FOLGOET 8

LE FOLGOET 9

LE FOLGOET 11

LE FOLGOET 12

FOUGÈRES I

GUÉRANDE 5

GUIMILIAU IO

FOUGÈRES *Ille-et-Vilaine.* D 7.

Fougères is famous for its fortified walls (the town stood on the former frontier between Britanny and France), its castle, and its magnificent towers which have still survived (13th and 14th c.: Tour Melusine and Tour de Gobelin). Its other, equally interesting monuments include the churches of Saint-Sulpice and Saint-Léonard (15th and 16th c.), the 16th-century Town Hall with a remarkable doorway and the old houses of the Place du Marchaix (market).

1 The castle and the town of Fougères.

GUÉHENNO *Morbihan.* C 8.

The church has been rebuilt, but the calvary is one of the most important in the whole of Britanny. It has been dated at 1550 and is therefore older than that at Pleyben (1555) if not that of Troën which some authorities have dated from the early 15th century. (Guimiliau, 1581-88, Plougastel-Daoulas 1602-04, Saint-Thégonnec 1610). Both its composition and technique are unusual but criticism should be careful in view of numerous restorations. In front of the calvary an isolated column surmounted with Saint Peter's cockerel, and bearing the instruments of the Passion. The massive ossuary behind the calvary also appears as the tomb of the Resurrection. Unlike many others now covered with lawns and flowers, the cemetery has kept all its old tombs.

2 Calvary, 16th c. 3 Statues of the ossuary. 4 The ossuary, 16th c.

GUÉRANDE *Loire-Atlantique.* C 9.

The interesting but somewhat dead town of Guérande stands behind its walls with four doorways and six towers in a region of salt-marshes. Its streets are still lined with old houses splendidly built in stone and the town can have changed little from the time when Balzac described it as the setting for his novel *Beatrix*. The church of Saint-Aubin was founded in 852 but has been often altered. The capitals are Romanesque and quite remarkable for their style. The Moulin du Diable on the plateau of Guérande is one of the finest surviving windmills in France and a fine piece of architecture in its own right.

5 Moulin du Diable.

GUIMILIAU *Finistère.* B 6.

The parish church and its enclosure at Guimiliau is one of the richest in France. The main feature is its calvary (1581-1588) and its prodigiously life-like figures, the gestures of the personages and the treatment of the draperies being beautifully handled with great art. The cornice and the platform contain more than two hundred different personages and form 25 different scenes from the life of Christ. With the exception of the west tower, the church was rebuilt in the 18th century. The south porch is a fine example of Breton Renaissance architecture: note the two caryatids flanking the Christ at the back of the porch which bear a curious resemblance to figures of Adam and Eve.

6 Detail of the Calvary: Christ washing feet of his disciples. 7 Detail of the porch: the Birth of Eve. 8 Baptistery with baldaquin, carved wood, 17th c. 9 Calvary 1581-1588. 10 Saint-Yves, polychrome wood, 18th c.

GUÉHENNO 2

GUÉHENNO 3

GUIMILIAU 6

GUEHENNO 4

GUIMILIAU 7

GUIMILIAU 8

GUIMILIAU 9

215

GUINGAMP *Côtes-du-Nord.* C 6.

The beautiful part-Gothic, part-Renaissanceba silica of Guingamp was rebuilt at various dates. Old houses, Place du Centre, and the 16th-century fountain of "La Plomée".

I Portal of the basilica of Notre-Dame-de-Bon-Secours, 16th c.

HUELGOAT *Finistère.* B 7.

Huelgoat is mostly known for its rocks. In the village: a three gabled-church dating from 1591; in the interior a statue of Saint Yves standing between a rich man and a pauper (similar statues in a somewhat different style may also be seen at Saint-Herbot and Tréguier etc.). The Renaissance-style chapel of Notre-Dame-des-Cieux has a porch with twin doors, curious painted bas-reliefs around the choir (The work-shop at Nazareth, the Massacre of the Innocents) and under the side-altars.

2 Saint-Yves, church of Huelgoat. 3 Massacre of the Innocents, polychrome bas-relief in the chapel of Notre-Dame-des-Cieux.

JOSSELIN *Morbihan.* C 8.

The castle at Josselin belonged to the Rohan family from the 14th century onwards (their proud family motto is "Roi ne suis, prince ne daigne, Rohan suis"). The original fortress was built in the 11th century by Guethenoc, viscount of Porhoët, whose son was named Josselin. As the Rohan family had supported France in the war against Britanny the fortress was dismantled by Duke François II of Britanny but his daughter Anne made reparation to the family who were then able to build the present admirable *corps de logis*. The keep and five of the nine towers were then destroyed on Richelieu's orders but the castle has still kept its massive west ramparts and the beautiful decorations on the inner façade have been preserved.

4 Façade of the castle facing the canal, 14th c. 5 Façade on the courtyard, late 15th c.

9   10

KERGRIST *Côtes-du-Nord.* B 6.

A very elegant manor of the 15th century, flanked by 17th-century turrets overlooking the courtyard; facing the gardens, a magnificent terrace overlooking the valley of the Léguer.

6 Façade of the château facing the courtyard, 15th and 17th c.

KERJEAN *Finistère.* B 6.

The château of Kerjean is the most sumptuous residence in the Léon region and was begun in 1533 and completed by the end of the century. The main building is in the High Renaissance style and is surrounded by a fortified enceinte.

7 Cour d'honneur of the château, and well surmounted with dome and lantern, late 16th c. 8 Entrance portico, late 16th c.

II

KERMARIA *Côtes-du-Nord.* C 6.

The chapel at Kermaria is known as "Kermaria an Isquit" (House of the health-giving Virgin). This splendid building was first built in the 13th century and then enlarged in the 15th and 18th centuries. Slate tower. The inside of the porch is decorated on each side by the traditional statues of the Apostles in polychrome stone. The frescoes along the nave, with the scene of the Danse Macabre (in which the dead and the living take part in a Dance of Death) is unique in Britanny. A large wood carving of the Christ (14th c.) over the main altar, and many ancient statues.

9-10-11-12-13 Polychrome wood statues of saints. 14 Statues of the Apostles under the porch, 13th c. 15 Wooden Christ, 14th c., and wood-vaulting of the chapel. 16 Danse Macabre, detail, frescoes in the nave, 15th c.

12   13

HUELGOAT 2

HUELGOAT 3

JOSSELIN 4

JOSSELIN 5

KERGRIST 6

KERMARIA 15

KERJEAN 7

KERJEAN 8

KERMARIA 14

KERMARIA 16

KERNASCLEDEN *Morbihan.* B 7.

The church at Kernascleden which was consecrated in 1453 is rich in art: three porches, beautiful stained-glass windows, stone rib-vaulting, rare fresco-decorations in the vaults and walls of the choir (restored); in the right transept a large panel (the lower half in bad condition) of Hell, featuring the bodies of the Damned impaled on stakes (a theme frequently found in 15th-c. German wood-cuts and paintings by Hieronymus Bosch).

1 Fresco in the vault, 15th c. 2 Hell, fresco in the transept, 15th c. 3 Great porch of the chapel, 15th c. 4 Small porch, 15th c.

KEROUARTZ *Finistère.* A 6.

Standing on the left bank of the Aber Wrac'h river at the end of a magnificent drive (like most manors of its kind), the château of Kerouartz is a magnificent example of the Breton Renaissance style in architecture (17th c.): façade with crenellated doorway, turrets, towers and fine dormer-windows, and fine terraced gardens at the back.

5 Main façade of the château, 17th c.

KEROUZÉRÉ *Finistère.* B 6.

The château was built between 1425 and 1458 and is a splendid example of the old fortresses of Léon which became transformed into luxurious residences, surrounded by magnificent trees. Although massive in structure — the outer walls are nearly 10 feet thick — the style has great elegance.

6 The château, 15th c.

KERVIGNAC *Morbihan.* B 8.

The chapel of Notre-Dame-de-Pitié (1553) was entirely destroyed together with the village in 1945 and a new church was built. Very simple in style, it is built on the plan of a Greek cross: it would have rather a "barn-like" appearance because of its varnished wood walls were it not for the hundred-odd glass-tile windows decorated with themes of the Rosary running around the building half-way up the walls, giving the interior the necessary meditative atmosphere.

7 The Nativity and Adoration of the Shepherds and the Magi, stained-glass in the chapel by N. Loire, 1959.

LAMBALLE *Côtes-du-Nord.* C 6.

The descendants of the duke of Penthièvre also held the title of Prince de Lamballe (similarly, the descendants of the Rohans were also known as Princes of Josselin). The village has an important collegiate church, Notre-Dame, on the side of a hill (13th-c. nave, church completed in the 14th-15th c.), with an interesting little Flamboyant rood-screen in the right aisle. The church of Saint-Martin which was formerly a priory and which is now greatly restored has a timber-roofed spire and an unusually shaped small roof over the side porch.

8 Church of Notre-Dame, 13th-15th c. 9 Capital in the porch, 13th c.

KERVIGNAC 7

KERNASCLEDEN 1

KERNASCLEDEN 2

KERNASCLEDEN 3

KERNASCLEDEN 4

KEROUARTZ 5

KEROUZÉRÉ 6

LAMBALLE 8

LAMBALLE 9

219

FORT-LA-LATTE 5

LAZ 6

LOCRONAN 12

LAMPAUL-GUIMILIAU *Finistère*. B 6.

The doorway of the parish enclosure is dominated by a very simple calvary with three crosses (1669). The tower of the church was begun in 1573 and the south porch dates from 1533. Interesting interior decoration: first, the splendid triumphal beam crossing the nave, supporting the crucifix and entirely decorated with painted (and recently repainted) carvings, the side illustrated showing scenes of the Passion; on the left of the choir, retable sculpted in high-relief (18th c.) with scenes of the Birth of the Virgin and the Martyrdom of Saint-Miliau. At the end of the church an Entombment with large painted stone statues (1676). **1** Detail of polychrome wooden retable, 18th c. **2** Beam in the nave, 16th c.

LANDERNEAU *Finistère*. B 6.

The picturesque old bridge (Pont de Rohan) over the river Elorn is still covered with slate-roofed houses. The church of Saint-Houardon has a tower with a dome and a very fine Renaissance porch (1604). **3** Porch of the church of Saint-Houardon, 1604. **4** Pont de Rohan, 1510.

FORT-LA-LATTE *Côtes-du-Nord*. C 6.

The main attraction is the picturesque old fortress built on two islets and connected by drawbridges to the mainland. **5** View of Fort-La-Latte, 13th-14th c.

LAZ *Finistère*. B 7.

18th-century church with picturesque tower in the cemetery of the small village, with a calvary dating from 1527; the left altar is surmounted by a large sculpted wood altarpiece with a striking scene of the Last Judgment. **6** Altarpiece of the Last Judgment, 18th c.

LOCQMARIAQUER *Morbihan*. C 8.

The megalithic remains at Locmariaquer are of great archaeological importance. The great broken *menhir* is the largest known of its kind and the remaining four fragments (there are supposed to have been five originally) have an overall length of 65 feet, one stone measuring 40 feet. In the same field, a short distance away, the Table des Marchands (Merchants' Table), a magnificent dolmen standing on a tumulus, 115 feet in diameter. The subterranean chamber is supported by seventeen supporting stone props, one at the back bearing incised drawings (an ear of corn?). Other fine dolmens with supporting stones in the same area. **7** Dolmen, prehistoric period. **8** Stone prop, in the subterranean chamber.

LOCRONAN *Finistère*. B 7.

With its square, its old granite houses with dormer-windows (15th and 17th c.), its well, and its square-towered church (begun 1422 and completed some fifty years later) the town of Locronan has preserved its old character and uniformity of style. The church is flanked on the left by a picturesque porch with a beamed roof and on the right by the Du Pénity Chapel (1495-1515) where the tomb of Saint Ronan may be seen (early 15th c., made for Duke Jean of Britany): it is supported by six massive stone angels. **9** Entombment, Du Pénity chapel, stone, 16th c. **10** Place de Locronan, church and houses, 16th c. **11** Place de Locronan, well and houses, 16th c. **12** Granite figure of an angel, detail of the tomb of Saint Ronan, 15th c.

LAMPAUL 1

LAMPAUL 2

LANDERNEAU 4

LOCQMARIAQUER 7

LANDERNEAU 3

LOCRONAN 9

LOCRONAN 10

LOCRONAN 11

LOCQMARIAQUER 8

221

LA MARTYRE 3

LOGUIVY-LÈS-LANNION (near Lannion) *Côtes-du-Nord.* B 6.

Saint Ivy came to Brittany from Great Britain in 685 and the church at Loguivy (a mile and a half from Lannion) is dedicated to him. Built in the 16th century in the parish enclosure, it has an exterior staircase, and a retable of the Three Magi (17th c.) dressed as Breton bag-pipe players. In the enclosure, a Renaissance fountain and leaning against the wall, the Gothic fountain of Saint-Ivy.

1 Church and tower staircase, 16th c.

LA MARTYRE *Finistère.* B 6.

Very fine parish enclosure; triumphal porch surmounted with a calvary (15th c.), ossuary-chapel (1699) beside the porch, church of Saint-Salaün (Solomon) of the 15th century. The building is characterised by its elegant basket-handle vaulted arches.

2 'Basket-handle' porches, 15th c. 3 Martyrdom, caryatid on the ossuary-chapel, 15th c.

MELRAND *Morbihan.* C 7.

One of the many attractions of the small town of Melrand is its curious well with sculpted heads. Also to be seen are the 17th-century church, the calvary and several Renaissance-style houses.

4 The well.

MONCONTOUR *Côtes-du-Nord.* C 7.

Standing on a promontory, Moncontour was originally a fortified town but its walls were razed by order of Louis XIII. A mile and a half to the south-east of the town, the chapel of Notre-Dame-du-Haut. Its statues of the healing saints have great charm and make it quite clear for which illnesses they should be invoked: the edifyingly calm Saint Meen for madness, Saint Lubin, with a stick in his hand, for rheumatism, Saint Hubert as protection against rabies, the small Saint Houarniaule against fear (he is shown holding a staff), Saint Mamert for illnesses of the intestines (he is holding his own before him) and Saint Livertin for headaches. It should be added that not all of these Breton saints figure in the official Roman list of saints.

5 Polychrome wood statues of healing saints, chapel of Notre-Dame-du-Haut.

MORLAIX 8

MORLAIX *Finistère.* B 6.

The viaduct or "Pont de Morlaix" has made the town famous; even if not a work of art, it has been popularised in a sailor's song and was held to be one of the most remarkable sights in its time (1861). Morlaix is an old town which has kept many fine houses, notably that of the Duchess Anne of Brittany. The former church of the Jacobins, built in the 13th century and later altered, has been transformed into a highly interesting museum of folk-lore. The 11th-15th-century church of Sainte-Melaine, with its tower of 1574 surmounted by a modern spire, has greatly suffered from war-damage. The church of Notre-Dame-du-Mur collapsed in 1806 but a very rare statue of the Virgin was saved from it: it opens up to reveal the figures of the Trinity and its two flaps are painted with scenes from the Life of the Virgin. It is now in the church of Saint-Mathieu.

6 The viaduct of Morlaix, engraving, 19th c. 7 Old houses. 8 The opening statue of the Virgin, church of Saint-Mathieu.

LOGUIVY 1

LA MARTYRE 2

MELRAND 4

S⁺ LUBIN   S⁺ MAMERT   S⁺ NEER   S⁺ HUBERT   S⁺ YVERTIN   S⁺ HOUARNIAULE   MONCONTOUR 5

MORLAIX 6   MORLAIX 7

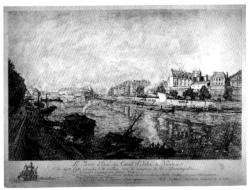

NANTES I

NANTES 2

NANTES *Loire-Atlantique.* D 9.

Nantes is the most important town in Brittany and has rivalled Rennes as the capital ever since the 10th century. After the ruinous wars of the 14th century, the house of Montfort vanquished that of Penthièvre and won *de facto* independence from France. But when Duke François II died (1480) he was succeeded by his daughter, the famous Duchess Anne, who married the King of France, Charles VIII, and then, after his death, Louis XII (1499). In 1500 one of her daughters Claude, married the Dauphin of France who became king François I in 1515 and the union of Brittany with France became confirmed in 1532.

The cathedral of Saint-Pierre-Saint-Paul was begun in 1434 (but only completed in 1893) and contains Michel Colombe's (1431-1512) masterpiece, the tomb of François II and his wife.

The ducal castle was begun by François II in 1466: with its enceinte it is a powerful stronghold and its towers once descended straight into the waters of a tributary of the Loire. In contrast to the exterior, the vast inner courtyard (once the setting for many festivals and tournaments) contains a Renaissance palace with a tower (known as the Couronne d'Or) ornamented with elegant Italianate loggias.

The city has greatly changed in appearance in the last twenty years (after suffering severe war damage) and the tributaries of the Loire and the Erdre were filled up to make spacious avenues. But the inhabitants still give the name of l'Ile Feydeau to a little cluster of aristocratic houses which were mainly built in the 17th century for rich ship-owners (rue Kervegan). Several 18th-century dwellings have still survived along the quaysides of the Loire and the theatre, with its lovely colonnade (1788) has remained intact.

I The old city of Nantes, 19th-c. engraving. The Ile Feydeau may be seen in the background. 2 Arms of Brittany, outer wall of the château. 3 Temperance, detail of the tomb of François II. 4 Tomb of François II and his wife Marguerite de Foix, by Michel Colombe (1431-1512). Commissioned by their daughter Anne and executed between 1502 and 1507. 5 Towers and enceinte of the ducal château, late 15th c. 6 Tower of La Couronne d'Or, at the angle of the Grand Logis. 7 Château courtyard: on the left the Grand Logis, and the Grand Gouvernement. 8 House on the Quai de la Fosse, 18th c. 9 La Psallette, music-school of the cathedral, 15th c.

NANTES 3

NANTES 4

NANTES 5

NANTES 7

NANTES 6

NANTES 8

NANTES 9

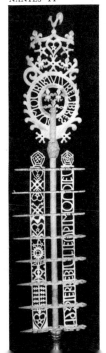

NANTES 10

NANTES 11

The château contains three museums: the Musée d'Art populaire régional (Popular regional art) in the Bâtiment du Grand Gouvernement with exhibits in iron, wood and ceramics; the Musée des Arts décoratifs (Decorative arts) in the Grand Logis (examples of all the various French and Breton styles of furniture, costumes and popular objects of the Napoleonic period); the Musée de la Marine (Naval Museum) or Musée Salorges in the Bâtiment du Harnachement: among its many fine exhibits are two figureheads, the *Chinois* and the *Négresse*, a model of the *Foudroyant*, a 66-gun vessel built in Nantes (18th c.) and various images and objects illustrating one of Nantes' main activities in the 16th and 17th centuries: the trading of slaves or "black ebony" as it was called.

The Musée municipal des Beaux-Arts is one of the great museums of painting in France. Its collection of over 2000 pictures includes a good selection of old foreign schools (the former Cacault Coll. was the basis for the collection), three important works by Georges de La Tour (17th c.), works by several Caravaggesque painters, paintings by Lancret, Nonnotte, Watteau, a surprising Greuze for the 18th century, examples of 19th-century French painting from Ingres to Delacroix and Courbet, works by Breton or Nantais painters such as Dezannay, Milcendeau and Maufra and a rich collection of moderns including works by Sérusier, Cottet and Maurice Denis and contemporary artists. The Breton sculptor Quillivic (born 1879) is represented by a very characteristic *Old Breton Woman at prayer.*

The Musée Dobrée (named after its founder) contains an eclectic collection covering the whole history of culture from prehistoric times to the 16th century: statues, ivory, paintings, drawings, manuscripts and especially fine relics of the old city of Nantes.

MUSÉE DES SALORGES

10 La Négresse, ship's figurehead (height about 10 feet). 11 Ensign of the sailors of the Loire, forged iron, 1790.

MUSÉE DOBRÉE

12 "Aristotle's fable", bronze aquamanile (vessel to contain water for guests to wash their hands at a meal), 15th c. 13 The Apothecary, corner post of a house, 15th c.

MUSÉE DES BEAUX-ARTS

14 Georges de La Tour (1593-1652), the Dream of Saint Joseph. 15 Georges de La Tour: The Hurdy-gurdy player. 16 Georges de La Tour: the Denial of Saint Peter. 17 Dirk van Baburen (c. 1570-1623): Singer. 18 Antoine Watteau (1684-1721): Recruits on their way to the regiment 18th c. copy. 19 Jean-Baptiste Greuze (1723-1805): Return from the Hunt: fowler tuning his guitar. 20 Dominique Ingres (1780-1867): Madame de Senones. 21 Gustave Courbet (1819-1877): the Corn sifters. 22 Alfred Manessier (born 1911): Salve Regina.

NANTES 13

NANTES 12

NANTES 14

NANTES 15

NANTES 16

NANTES 17

NANTES 18

NANTES 19

NANTES 20

NANTES 21

NANTES 22

227

OUESSSANT I

PLEUMEUR-BODOU 10

OUESSANT *Finistère*. A 6.

Despite the fierce winds sweeping over the island of Ouessant, the windmill has survived: it is built quite differently from the round windmills of northern Brittany with their rotating roofs for the entire structure turns on its axis with the wind.

1 Windmill of the island.

PAIMPONT *Ille-et-Vilaine*. C 8.

The great forest of Paimpont is more famous than the town of the same name: covering thousands of acres and full of hundreds of ponds it is known as the country of Brocéliande, immortalised in the old romances of chivalry. In the village: the ancient abbey chapel with an elegant silver reliquary containing relics of Saint Judicaël, a 7th century king of Britanny. To the south-west of the forest, at Campénéac, the romantic medieval château of Trecesson, rich in memories of King Arthur, Merlin the magician and Viviane.

2 Château of Trecesson, 15th c. **3** Silver hand-reliquary, church of Paimpont.

PENCRAN *Finistère*. B 6.

Interesting parish enclosure with triumphal porch and church of the 16th century; fine tower and old statues in the interior; calvary of 1521 and ossuary of the 17th century. The porch (1553) is in bad condition but the Nativity in the tympanum is very charming.

4 Porch of the church, Nativity, 1553. **5** Saint Madeleine, detail of the calvary, 16th c.

PENMARCH *Finistère*. A 8.

In Treoutré, church of Saint-Nonna (16th c.) in the Flamboyant style; large double-sloped roof with a little perforated tower. An enormous square tower was left unfinished; bas-reliefs of ships on the buttresses to remind the visitor as at Roscoff (q.v.) that the church was built by ship-owners; fish motifs on the arcades.
A few miles to the north, the Chapelle Notre-Dame-de-la-Joie in a desolate site protected from the sea by a sheltering wall. A little further north, in Plovan, ruins of the early 13th-c. chapel of Languidou with a rose-window in good condition.

6 Ship, bas-relief on the church of Saint-Nonna, 16th c. **7** Chapel of Notre-Dame-de-la-Joie, 16th c. **8** Church of Saint-Nonna, 16th c. **9** Ruins of the chapel of Languidou, 13th c.

PLEUMEUR-BODOU *Côtes-du-Nord*. B 6.

The ancient menhir near Pleumeur-Bodou was transformed into a Christian stele and was carved with a relief showing the instruments of Christ's Passion. Such Christianised menhirs are not uncommon in Brittany.

10 Sculpted menhir of Saint-Duzec, 1674.

PAIMPONT 2

PAIMPONT 3

PENCRAN 4

PENCRAN 5

PENMARCH 6

PENMARCH 7

PENMARCH 8

PENMARCH 9

PLEYBEN 1

PLEYBEN 2

PLEYBEN *Finistère*. B 7.

The religious architecture in the parish of Pleyben is among the most impressive in Brittany. Most recent in date is the monumental gateway (1725); the Flamboyant ossuary-chapel dates from about 1550; the exact date of the calvary is a matter of controversy but is now considered to be around 1555, the restoration work (signed by Yves Ozanne) being of the 17th century. The carving of the figures on the calvary is highly impressive and the scenes include the Visitation, the Flight into Egypt, the Agony in the Garden and the Descent into Limbo. The church itself is a remarkable 16th-century monument with its massive, square tower (Renaissance style, 1588-1591) and its contrasting Gothic tower with tapering spire, the prototype for a whole series of Breton church towers during the late 15th century. The carving along the wall-plate is particularly interesting: note the hunting scene, the corner figure of a bagpipe-player (on the right), and the dead man in his coffin, being fought over by an angel and a devil.

I Christ, detail of the calvary, 16th c. 2 Wall-plate in the church, detail. 3 The ossuary, 16th c. 4 The church of Saint-Catherine, 16th c. 5 The calvary, 16th c. 6-7 The Flight into Egypt, the Nativity, details of carvings on the calvary, 16th c.

PLOERMEL *Morbihan*.

The north porch of the church of Saint-Armel (16th c.) is covered with sculptures: apart from scenes from the life of Christ, they include many highly expressive realistic figures such as a cobbler and his wife and the musical sow (the same theme is found at Nantes and Chartres). The 16th-century sculptures on the beams in the Maison des Marmousets should also be seen.

8 Detail of the church porch, 16th c.

PLOUGASNOU 10

PLOUBEZRE *Côtes-du-Nord*. B 6.

More than a thousand old granite crosses still stand beside the waysides of Brittany. The five aligned crosses at Ploubezre at the beginning of the road to Tonquedec are unique.

9 Calvary at Ploubezre.

PLOUGASNOU *Finistère*. B 6.

Fine church tower with cantoned spire (16th c.). In the cemetery, a funerary chapel of 1580 built on a highly unusual triangular ground plan (it is now used as a tool store). A few hundred yards away, the small oratory of Pont-an-Gler, a resting place for pilgrims; stone roof supported by caryatids (the semi-naive style of caryatids in Breton ossuaries is a rich field for study).

10 Oratory of Pont-an-Gler, 1611.

PLEYBEN 3

PLEYBEN 4

PLEYBEN 5

PLEYBEN 6

PLEYBEN 7

PLOUBEZRE 9

PLOERMEL 8

231

PLOUGASTEL 1

PLOUGRESCRANT 7

PLOUMANACH 8

PLOUGASTEL-DAOULAS *Finistère*. A 7.

The church at Plougastel is of modern construction but the calvary (without an enclosure) has been restored after suffering war damage. It comprises some 150 carved figures and dates from 1602-1604. With the calvaries of Pleyben, Guehenno and Guimiliau (all of earlier date) it is the most important of its kind in Brittany. Like that of Pleyben, its style is more serene than that of Guimiliau as may be seen from the scenes of Christ washing the feet of His disciples or the Agony in the Garden.

1, 3, 4 Details from the calvary, 17th c.: Flight into Egypt, the Agony in the Garden, the Last Supper. **2** Summit of the calvary, 17th c.

PLOUGONVEN *Finistère*. B 6.

Interesting parish enclosure. The calvary, standing on an octagonal base, is one of the oldest (1554) if not the most important in Brittany. Note the double cross with the Holy Women above and the two sentinels below. A fine Renaissance fountain may be seen in the village.

5 Church and calvary, 1554. **6** Renaissance fountain.

PLOUGRESCANT *Côtes-du-Nord*. C 6.

The chapel of Saint-Gonéry and the three crosses standing by the entrance to the cemetery date from the 15th and 16th centuries. The church tower is crowned by a curious leaning spire (15th c.). Painted wooden vaulting in the interior.

7 The three crosses and the chapel of Saint-Gonéry.

PLOUMANACH *Côtes-du-Nord*. B 6.

The oratory of Saint-Guirec by the edge of the sea has kept its charm but, like so many others, it has lost its soul. A granite statue has replaced the earlier wooden figure of the saint, to which young girls came to worship before their marriage, and to stick pins in its nose to bring them good luck.

8 Oratory of Saint-Guirec.

PONT-AVEN *Finistère*. B 8.

It was at Pont-Aven, and then Le Pouldu, that Gauguin came to paint in 1886, and that a virtual colony of painters sprang up around him, including Émile Bernard (1868-1941), Paul Sérusier (1865-1891), Meyer de Haan (1852-1895), Maxime Maufra (1861-1918), Charles Laval (1862-1894). The Hôtel Le Gloarec where they first lived, and the *Bois d'Amour* that they painted (Sérusier painted the same landscape as Gauguin, on the latter's advice, in a "synthetic" style in 1888, calling his picture *The Talisman*) may still be seen but all traces of their stay have long since faded. Also in 1886, Émile Bernard painted his *Breton women in a field* a kind of "cloisonnisme" in painting. Above the Bois d'Amour, the Gothic chapel of Tremalo where Gauguin discovered the 15th-century wooden Christ which he used as a model for his *Yellow Christ*.

9 Chapel of Tremalo. **10** Paul Gauguin (1845-1903): Yellow Christ, 1889, private collection, Paris. **11** The Christ in the chapel of Tremalo.

PLOUGASTEL 2

PLOUGASTEL 3

PLOUGONVEN 5

PLOUGASTEL 4

PLOUGONVEN 6

PONT-AVEN 9

PONT-AVEN 10

PONT-AVEN 11

PONT-CROIX 2

QUIMPER 10

PONT-CROIX 1

PONT-CROIX *Finistère*. A 7.
The bell-tower with its spire (210 feet high) of Notre-Dame-de-Roscudon is one of the most beautiful 15th-century Breton church towers. It served as a model for that of Quimper cathedral (1854). The interior (partly 13th c.) is distinguished by the lightness of its construction; the richly decorated late 14th-century south portal is surmounted by a high pointed gable and is particularly elegant. A 17th-century Last Supper may be seen, curiously sited below the altar.

1 South portal of the church, 15th c. 2 Bell-tower of Notre-Dame-de-Roscudon, 15th c.

PORT-LAUNAY *Finistère*. B 7.
A remarkable parish enclosure and chapel (dedicated to Saint Sebastian) may be seen at Saint-Segal, two miles from Port-Launay, standing among the outbuildings of a farm. Above the porch, an interesting bas-relief depicting the saint's martyrdom; very curious masks carved in the granite base of the calvary. The interior of the chapel is profusely decorated; uninterrupted ornamentation (17th c.) of the main altar and the south transept, retable with large statues. In the left altar, twenty polychrome sculpted wood panels with scenes from the life of Christ (Flight into Egypt) and the history of the chapel of Notre-Dame-de-Lorette.

3 Interior decoration of the chapel of Saint-Sebastien, 17th c. 4 Parish enclosure of Saint-Segal, 17th c. 5 Base of the calvary, masks.

QUIMPER *Finistère*. B 7.
The ancient capital of the county of Cornouaille in Brittany is still known as Quimper-Corentin, and the cathedral is dedicated to Saint Corentin who is the city's patron saint. Fine Gothic structure with a 260-foot long nave. It was built in successive stages from 1240 to the 16th century, and the two high towers (260 feet) were only given their spires (designed after that at Pont-Croix) in 1854. The cathedral is at its most impressive when seen from the end of the street in front of it, lined with its old houses.

Quimper is also noted for its Musée Breton, devoted to the art and history of the county of Cornouaille, and the Musée des Beaux-Arts with an important collection of works by Breton artists and interesting examples of French and foreign painting from the 16th century to the school of Pont-Aven.

MUSÉE DES BEAUX-ARTS

6 Boudin (1824-1898): View of Quimper. 7 Cottet (1863-1925): Burned Breton church. 8 Chassériau (1819-1856): Mademoiselle de Cabarrus.

9 Rue Kéréon and cathedral towers. 10 Wall basin, Quimper faïence, Musée de Sèvres.

234

PORT-LAUNAY 3

PORT-LAUNAY 4

PORT-LAUNAY 5

QUIMPER 6

QUIMPER 9

QUIMPER 7

QUIMPER 8

RENNES *Ille-et-Vilaine.* D 7.

The "war of the Breton succession" in 1341 was fought between Rennes and Nantes, Penthièvre and Montfort; Nantes on the Loire was the least specifically Breton city. The Montfort family triumphed in 1364 at the battle of Auray but the famous Parliament of Brittany was definitively established at Rennes in 1561. The city was ravaged by the plague in 1632 and almost destroyed by a fire in 1720. There are now few remaining relics of the 15th- and 16th-century city and it is hard for the visitor to picture it as it must have been when the Dukes of Brittany came riding through the Porte Mordelaise on the day of their coronation.

After the great fire of 1720, a plan for the city was drawn up by the engineer Robelin, and the new city was designed and built in a somewhat severe style by the architect Gabriel (1667-1742) whose son, Jacques Gabriel (1710-1782) was to build the Place de la Concorde in Paris.

The Palais de Justice, the former Parliament House of Brittany, is the most majestic building in Rennes; it was built by Salomon de Brosse between 1618 and 1655 and fortunately survived the fire. The Grand' Chambre where the Parliament that so often defied the King of France used to meet is a nobly proportioned chamber with beautiful coffered ceiling, wall panelling and tapestries.

The Town Hall was built in a very pure Louis XV style (1732-1762) by Jacques Gabriel.

The church of Toussaints (1614-1651) was once a Jesuit chapel and is built in the style of the Counter-Reformation, its woodwork and retables being of the same style.

The cathedral with its classic façade (completed in 1844) replaced an earlier construction which collapsed in 1762, but the towers (begun in 1514 and completed in 1703) survived the disaster. The cathedral and the Toussaints chapel is still surrounded by a picturesque old quarter with fine 16th- and early 17th-century houses. The important hôtel de Blossac is famous for its staircase and dates from 1732.

The Musée de Bretagne, in the Palais des Musées, contains a very representative collection of Breton popular art of which only a few examples can be illustrated here; the Musée des Beaux-Arts is extremely rich in paintings ranging from the Florentine and Flemish schools and the 16th-century German school to Vuillard and Picasso.

1 Porte Mordelaise, 15th c. 2 Palais Saint-Georges. 3 Palais de Justice, by Salomon de Brosse, 1655. 4 Staircase of the hôtel de Blossac, 1742. 5 Cathedral, 19th c.

MUSÉE DES BEAUX-ARTS

6 Georges de La Tour (1593-1652): The New-born. 7 The Woman and the Two Ages, anonymous, 16th c. 8 P.-P. Rubens (1577-1640): Tiger and lion-hunt. 9 Veronese (1528-1588): Perseus delivering Andromeda. 10 J.-B. Chardin (1699-1779): Peaches and Grapes. 11 Paul Gauguin (1848-1903): Still-life with oranges.

1

2

3

4

5

6

7

8

9

10

11

12 Iron. 13 Butter markers. 14 Crucifix de Cancale, wrought iron. 15 The Wandering Jew, popular print, 19th c.

12

13

14

15

LES ROCHERS *Ille-et-Vilaine*. D 7.

The château of Rochers is some 4 miles from Vitré and is still haunted by the memories of Madame de Sevigné who spent many years on this family property. The Green Room (Cabinet Vert), Madame de Sevigné's room (preserved intact) and the gardens designed by Le Nôtre may be visited.

1 Château des Rochers, 14th and 17th c.

ROSAMBO *Côtes-du-Nord*. B 6.

The manor of Rosambo is situated in a valley some 4 miles from Plouaret, and is a finely designed series of 14th-, 17th- and 19th-century buildings surrounded by a spendid Le Nôtre garden.

2 Interior of the manor, 17th c. 3 Courtyard of the manor.

ROSCOFF *Finistère*. B 6.

The church of Notre-Dame-de-Croaz-Baz is crowned by a fine tower (1570) with a double row of bells, lanterns and a dome. The walls of the church are hung with pictures of ships as a reminder that Roscoff was once an important port and a "nest of corsairs" in the 16th century. Alabaster retable of English origin (late 15th c.). By the church, two ossuaries, one of the 17th century with 28 bays. The watch-tower looking over the port is called the "Tourelle de Marie Stuart" in memory of the Scots Queen who landed at Roscoff in 1548 at the age of five, as the fiancée of the French Dauphin, the future François II.

4 "Tourelle de Marie Stuart", 16th c. 5 Old house, dormer window with fronton, 16th c. 6 Bell-tower of Notre-Dame-de-Croaz-Baz, 16th c. 7 The Adoration, English alabaster retable, detail, 15th c. 8 Ossuary, 17th c.

ROSAMBO 2

LES ROCHERS 1

ROSAMBO 3

ROSCOFF 4

ROSCOFF 5

ROSCOFF 6

ROSCOFF 7

ROSCOFF 8

ST-AVÉ I

SAINT-AVÉ *Morbihan.* C 8.

The chapel of Notre-Dame-du-Loc (15th c., at Saint-Avé-d'en-Bas, 2 ½ miles from Vannes) lost its tower in a hurricane. In the interior, remarkable wall-plates, and a main beam with a calvary and figures surmounted by a wooden dais. Unusual calvary and fountain.

I Boundary cross. 2 Fountain. 3 Calvary.

SAINT-BRICE-EN-COGLÈS *Ille-et-Vilaine.* D 7.

The château of Rocher-Portail, a vast dwelling of a perfect balance and elegance of style, some distance from Saint-Brice-en-Coglès, dates from 1608. Built in a cheerful rose-coloured brick, standing amidst beautiful groves of trees, with a water-filled moat which is more picturesque than defensive, Rocher-Portail seems designed for gracious living rather than defence, like the châteaux of the Loire. In the left wing, the arcaded gallery on the ground floor is a perfect setting for a banquet or festival.

4 Château of Rocher-Portail, early 17th c.

SAINT-BRIEUC *Côtes-du-Nord.* C 6.

The cathedral of Saint-Étienne at Saint-Brieuc is one of the most important in Britanny. It was first built in the 12th century, then destroyed and rebuilt in the 14th and 15th centuries. It is a massive fortress-like construction, built on an irregular ground plan, and surmounted by a heavy crenellated tower; the generally severe aspect of the church is lightened by the splendid Flamboyant rose-window on the south front.

5 Cathedral of Saint-Étienne, 15th c. façade.

SAINT-GILDAS-DE-RHUYS *Morbihan.* C 9.

The exterior apse and the choir in the interior are the most perfect surviving parts of the 11th-century abbatial church of Saint-Gildas, the most important Romanesque monument in Britanny. The church was largely rebuilt in the 16th century. Abelard was the abbot of the monastery founded by Saint Gildas in the 6th century from 1125 to 1140. Interesting tombstone of Saint Goustan (6th c.)

6 Apse of the church, 11th c.

SAINT-GILLES-PLIGEAUX *Côtes-du-Nord.* C 7.

Interesting double fountain below the village.

7 The fountain.

ST-AVÉ 2

ST-AVÉ 3

ST-BRIEUC 5

ST-BRICE-EN-COGLÈS 4

ST-GILLES-PLIGEAUX 7

ST-GILDAS-DE-RHUYS 6

ST-HERBOT 1

SAINT-HERBOT *Finistère*. B 7.

The church of Saint-Herbot, on the outskirts of Huelgoat dates from the 15th and 16th centuries and its monumental square tower with high windows (1516) was often copied. Like Saint Cornély, Saint Herbot is the patron saint of horned animals and his tombstone may be seen in the choir which is enclosed by a richly decorated, finely carved wooden "chancel". Remarkable porches; fine circular perron at the north gable end. Fine double-fronted calvary of 1571 (with Saint Veronica on the reverse side) and a small ossuary (1558) attached to the south side. In the church, image of Saint Yves flanked by the rich and the poor man. The saint is set in a niche with shutters which is very unusual, and faces the image of Notre-Dame-de-Bonne-Nouvelle surrounded by cherubs.

1 Tombstone of Saint Herbot, detail, 16th c. 2 Saint Yves. 3 Choir screen, sculpted oak, 16th c. 4 The church, 16th c. 5 Monumental steps of the church. 6 Corsair, misericord.

SAINT-JEAN-DU-DOIGT *Finistère*. B 6.

The name of this pretty village with its parish enclosure is derived from a relic of the finger of Saint John which is kept in the church. Monumental doorway in a fine Gothic style.

7 Parish enclosure, 14th c., and Renaissance fountain.

12

13

14

SAINT-MALO *Ille-et-Vilaine*. D 6.

Saint-Malo, the "corsair's town" — and the birth-place of Jacques Cartier (1494-1556), the discoverer of Canada and the founder of Quebec, who was far from being a pirate — was more than half destroyed during the war. But the ramparts survived and thanks to an enlightened policy of collaboration between the city officials and the architect Arretche, the city has regained its former splendour. The famous old high-roofed houses of the city shipowners and corsairs have been rebuilt brick by brick and the old streets have been reconstructed in the "spirit" of the original town so that Saint-Malo is now one of the most interesting walled cities in France.

Besides Jacques Cartier, other famous natives of Saint-Malo were the two great corsairs Duguay-Trouin (1673-1736) and Surcouf (1773-1827) who were granted privateers' warrants by the King of France, and two famous Romantics - Chateaubriand (1768-1848) who is buried in a nameless grave on the Grand-Bé facing the sea, and the Abbé Lamennais (1794-1854), another tormented soul of the time.

8 The château and the Place Chateaubriand. 9 The Grand-Bé, tomb of Chateaubriand. 10 General view of the city. 11 The reconstructed city. 12 Jacques Cartier, bronze statue by Baveau, 1905. 13 The Abbé Lamennais, 19th-c. engraving. 14 Chateaubriand, 19th-c. engraving.

ST-HERBOT 2   ST-HERBOT 3   ST-HERBOT 4

ST-HERBOT 5   ST-HERBOT 6

ST-JEAN-DU-DOIGT 7

ST-MALO 8

ST-MALO 9

ST-MALO 10   ST-MALO 11

243

ST-POL I

SAINT-POL-DE-LÉON *Finistère*. B 6.

The tower of the Chapelle du Kreisker (240 feet high) is a marvel of architectural balance and daring (15th c.) and is modelled upon that of Saint-Pierre at Caen. The basilica with its 14th-century towers was inspired by the church at Coutances; fine rose-window, delicately carved baptismal font and choir stalls (1502), marble main altar in Louis XV style (1770) with two angels, and a particularly curious polychrome carved wood palm in the shape of a crozier (17th c.), ending, according to custom, in a pyxis in the form of a corolla (highly unusual) containing the Holy Sacrament.

1 Pyxis, polychrome carved wood, 17th c. **2** Detail of a choir-stall, 16th c. **3** Kreisker, bell-tower, height 240 feet., 15th c. **4** Rose-window in the façade, 14th c. **5** Porch, 16th c. **6** House in the Grande Rue, 15th c.

ST-POL **2**

ST-SERVAN 7

SAINT-SERVAN *Ille-et-Vilaine*. D 6.

Despite 17th-century alternations, the Tour Solidor, a continuation of the town of Saint-Malo, is an excellent example of 14th-century fortress architecture (it dates from 1382). The little city is rich in convents and charitable institutions and a street is named after Jeanne Jugan (1792-1879), the poor and humble cleaning woman who became the founder of the order of the Little Sisters of the Poor (Petites Sœurs des Pauvres).

7 Tour Solidor.

SAINT-THÉGONNEC *Finistère*. B 6.

ST-THÉGONNEC 13

The building and decoration of the important parish enclosure continued during two centuries. All that now remains of the former church is the tower (1563). The semi-circular triumphal doorway is crowned by lanterns and dates from 1587. The calvary with its three crosses dates from 1610 and is ornamented with scenes of the Passion treated in an exceptionally lively and realistic manner. The fine Renaissance style ossuary (1676) has been transformed into a chapel; in the crypt under the altar, polychrome wood sculptures of the Entombment, with life-size figures (1699-1707). In the church, a beautiful sculpted pulpit, the upper parts painted and gilded (1683). The interior decoration is almost excessively lavish, for beautifully worked wainscotting, retables and choir stalls were added in the 17th and 18th centuries. In a niche with shutters, statue of Notre-Dame-du-Bon-Secours with the Tree of Jesse, facing the statue of Saint Thegonnec.

8 Pulpit, 1683. **9** Calvary and ossuary, 17th c. **10** General view of the parish enclosure. **11-12** The mocking of Christ and Christ carrying the Cross, details of the calvary, 1610. **13** The Entombment, polychrome wood, by J. Lespaignol, 1699.

ST-POL 3

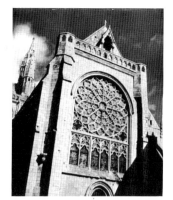

ST-POL 4

ST-POL 5

ST-POL 6

ST-THÉGONNEC 8

ST-THÉGONNEC 9

ST-THÉGONNEC 10

ST-THÉGONNEC 11

ST-THÉGONNEC 12

245

SAINT-TUGEN *Finistère*. A 7.

The Flamboyant Gothic chapel (1515-1530) of Saint-Tugen in the village of Primelin has a highly unusual feature: its square tower was left unfinished and complemented by a bell turret. Inside, superb carved wood vaulting. Ancient statues (Saint Sebastian, Saint Tugen and the mad dog), ex-votos of more recent date, richly decorated altar of Notre-Dame-de-Grâce in gilt wood (1694) bearing the medallions of Louis XIV and Marie-Thérèse. The baptismal chapel is decorated with paintings in a markedly naive style representing the Sacraments (dated 1699 and 1702). Sacred fountain. Saint Tugen had the power of curing rabies. A small cell may still be seen by the entrance to the chapel for "urgent cases" awaiting their cure. The calvary nearby dates from 1821.

1 Baptismal font, 1699-1702. 2 Altar of Notre-Dame-de-la-Grâce, 1694. 3 Church tower, 16th c.

ST-VENNEC 4

SAINT-VENNEC *Finistère*. B 7.

Two extremely interesting and stylistically unusual calvaries, that of Notre-Dame-de-Quillinen-en-Briec and that of Saint-Vennec-en-Quemeneur, may be seen on the road from Chateaulin to Quimper, half way and about 8-10 miles from both towns, standing amid trees near their chapels. Each calvary surmounted by three crosses standing on a triangular base. Somewhat mutilated state of the carving which includes the figure of the Virgin and Saint John standing above a curious group, rather like caryatids, who have been supposed to represent the Vices (?).

4 Church and calvary of Saint-Vennec.

SAINT-ANNE-D'AURAY *Morbihan*. C 8.

A little town of 1,600 inhabitants dominated by its modern basilica. One of the most important centres of pilgrimage in Britany ever since the mother of the Virgin appeared to the labourer Yves Nicolazic in 1623. The cloister (1640) is all that remains of the earlier buildings. Numerous votive images of great interest to connoisseurs of "naive" painting, dating from the 17th c. to the present day, hung on the walls of the chapel and in the treasury.

5-6-7-8-9 Details of ex-voto paintings in the basilica.

STE-MARIE-DU-MÉNEZ-HOM 11

SAINTE-MARIE-DU-MENEZ-HOM *Finistère*. B 7.

The beautifully simple chapel of Sainte-Marie stands on the slopes of Menez-Hom, the summit of the Montagne-Noire from where a magnificent view may be obtained. Rich 18th-century decorations in the interior; the calvary dates from 1544.

10-11 Details of the interior decoration of the chapel of Sainte-Marie, polychrome wood carvings, 18th c.

ST-TUGEN 1

ST-TUGEN 2

ST-TUGEN 3

STE-ANNE-D'AURAY 5

STE-ANNE-D'AURAY 6

STE-ANNE-D'AURAY 7

STE-ANNE-D'AURAY 8

STE-ANNE-D'AURAY 9

STE-MARIE-DU-MÉNEZ-HOM 10

SEPT-SAINTS I

TRÉGUIER II

TRÉGUIER 12

SEPT-SAINTS *Côtes-du-Nord.* B 6.

The chapel of Sept-Saints (in the village of Sept-Saints in the commune of Vieux-Marché) was rebuilt in 1708, partly over a dolmen which forms the crypt and a votive chapel (where the images of the "seven sleepers" of Ephesus are said to have been found; the seven small figurines are now on the modest low altar). Fine retable with large statues of the seven saints (Maximilian, Maloh, Martiny, Denis, John, Sérapion and Constantine). Even more surprising than the fact that part of the church (right transept) has been built on a dolmen which can still be clearly seen, is the fact that the chapel was once tied to the ancient and esoteric traditions of the church of Ephesus and has now become not only an international but also an interdenominational centre of pilgrimage — very unusual in traditionally minded Catholic Britanny.

I Altar of the Seven Saints (Sept-Saints).

SIZUN *Finistère.* B 6.

The architecture of Sizun is extremely interesting despite the fact that it is partly of recent date. Monumental gateway to the cemetery flanked by an ossuary chapel in the same style. Church with a 16th-century south porch, main structure rebuilt in the 17th century, the main porch and bell-tower and the spire are of 1723-1735. Impressive retable, secondary altars set at angles; luxurious decoration.

2 Ossuary and monumental gateway, late 16th c. 3 Windows with caryatids, detail of the ossuary.

SUCINIO *Morbihan.* C 9.

With its ramparts, six towers and monumental doorway, the château of Sucinio is a striking and romantic sight. It is situated at the far extremity of the gulf of Morbihan on a wind-swept promontory and its walls descended straight into the sea in the 13th century. Only the walls now remain but immense fire-places may still be seen in the inner buildings.

4 The château of Sucinio, 13th c.

TRÉGUIER *Côtes-du-Nord.* C 6.

Tréguier was the birth-place of Saint Yves (Yves Helori, 1253-1303) and Ernest Renan (1823-1892). The saint is buried in the cathedral where we may see: a moving figure of Christ on the Cross (14th-c. wood-carving) in the Chapelle du Duc, and the figures of Saint Yves standing between the rich and the poor man (a favourite Breton theme) in the south transept: the saint is shown listening to the poor man's suit and ignoring the rich man with his purse (Saint Yves was a lawyer). The house where Renan was born has been preserved in its original state and transformed into a museum. The basilica-cathedral, dedicated to Saint Tugdual, is designed after the earlier churches on the same site. The main structure was built in the 14th and 15th centuries in typical Flamboyant style; 13th-century west porch, those on the south side, of the 14th and 15th centuries. The massive, so-called "Hastings" tower, flanked by a round turret, is a relic of the Romanesque structure. Despite its late date (1450-1479) the cloister with its 46 arcades covered by a wooden vault is still in the radiant Gothic style. Interesting and elegant 1914-1918 war memorial facing the former bishop's palace, its simplicity in striking contrast to the usual banality of such monuments; the figure of the "Pleureuse" (mourner) by F. Renaud. 16th-century Gothic style rustic chapel of Notre-Dame at Port-Blanc, some 6 miles from Tréguier; built on the flank of a hill with a sloping roof almost touching the ground.

5 Cathedral of Saint-Tugdual, 14th-15th c. 6 Christ on the Cross, wood carving, 14th c. 7 Cloister, 1479. 8 Chapel of Notre-Dame-de-Port-Blanc, 16th c. 9 Saint Yves and the Rich and the Poor Man, 1765. 10 War memorial by F. Renaud. 11 Ernest Renan (1823-1892), Musée de Rennes. 12 Renan's house.

SIZUN 2

SIZUN 3

SUCINIO 4

TRÉGUIER 5

TRÉGUIER 7

TRÉGUIER 6

TRÉGUIER 8

TRÉGUIER 9

TRÉGUIER 10

249

LA TRINITÉ-LANGONNET *Morbihan.* B 7.

16th-century Flamboyant Gothic church. Elegant polygonal apse, rich interior decoration, fine vaulting. The nearby sacred fountain with balustrades is dedicated, like the church, to the Holy Trinity and is of the 17th century.

1 Fountain, 17th c.

TRONJOLI 2

TRONJOLI *Finistère.* A 6.

The château of Tronjoli near the village of Cléder (2 miles from Plouescat) is traditional in style but its balustrades and elegant Renaissance windows give it a graceful touch.

2 Château of Tronjoli, 16th c.

NOTRE-DAME-DE-TRONOEN *Finistère.* A 8.

Chapel of Notre-Dame-de-Tronoën, 6 miles to the west of Pont-l'Abbé. Fine porch and tower with two small spires. Most interesting of all is the early 15th-century calvary with its wide base and small figures. Perhaps the oldest of all the Breton calvaries, in which "craftsmanlike candour is combined with audacity in the most striking manner" (Henry Queffelec). This judgment is confirmed by the astonishing carving of the Virgin in her child-bed.

3 The Virgin in child-bed, detail of the calvary, 15th c. **4** Calvary of Notre-Dame-de-Tronoën, 15th c.

VAN (Pointe du) *Finistère.* A 7.

15th-century chapel of Saint-They with nearby fountain containing statue of the saint situated overlooking the sea by the Pointe du Van, near the famous promontory of the Pointe du Raz.

5 Fountain and headland of Van.

POINTE-DU-VAN 5

VANNES *Morbihan.* C 8.

Vannes is an ancient aristocratic city, dating from the time of Nominoé who was made a count by Charlemagne and who united Britanny in the 9th century (after 826). The city is linked with memories of the Revolution and the defeat of Quiberon Bay in 1795. The 13th-century ramparts with the old wash-houses at the foot of the walls, and the cathedral of Saint-Pierre (15th and 16th c.) in the background still give the town a medieval air.

6 Absidial chapel of the cathedral, 16th c. **7** The ramparts, 13th c.

VITRÉ *Ille-et-Vilaine.* D 7.

Vitré was for long a frontier town between Britanny and France which explains its extremely impressive remparts and fortress (château altered in the 14th-15th c.) The château is still surrounded by old houses which give the town its medieval aspect; particularly noteworthy is the Faubourg Rachapt whose name (Rachat; redemption) dates from the Hundred Years War.

8 Old houses at Vitré. **9** Château of Vitré, 19th-c. engraving, Musée de Rennes.

250

LA TRINITÉ-LANGONNET 1

N.-D.-DE-TRONOEN 3

N.-D.-DE-TRONOEN 4

VITRÉ 8

VANNES 6

VITRÉ 9

VANNES 7

251

VII

VAL DE LOIRE

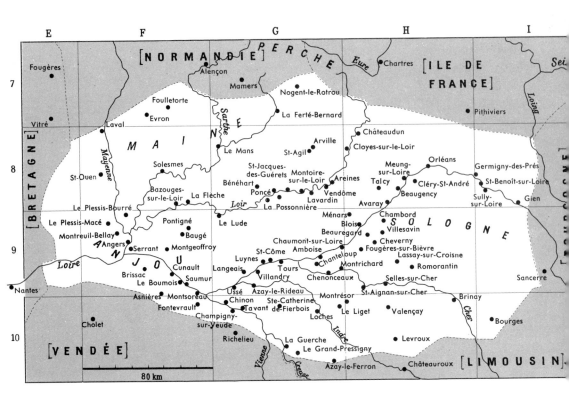

TAPESTRY OF THE APOCALYPSE BY NICOLAS BATAILLE, DETAIL, 14TH C., MUSÉE DES TAPISSERIES, ANGERS *(Connaissance des Arts-Bonnefoy)*

STAINED-GLASS WINDOW IN BOURGES CATHEDRAL, THE NEW COVENANT, LOWER HALF, C. 1215 *(Reproduced from « Le Vitrail français », Éditions des Deux-Mondes)*

The valley of the Loire was a pleasure garden for the French kings throughout the 16th century. Life could be nothing but sweet in such surroundings, among the gently swelling hills and along the peaceful, winding rivers of the valley. It is a country of fine stone and fine châteaux filled with memories of the kings of France and famous love stories immortalised by poets.

AMBOISE 1

AMBOISE 2

AMBOISE *Indre-et-Loire.* G 9.

The history of the château of Amboise begins in 1492 when Charles VIII ordered a fortress-palace to be built which explains the massive Tour des Minimes which may still be seen flanking the elegant royal *corps de logis*, both standing on a height above the river Loire. When the king returned from his Italian campaign in 1496 he decided to rebuild the palace in the Italian style and summoned Italian architects, sculptors and gardeners to carry out the work and filled the palace with Italian furniture and works of art but he died two years later without having completed what was to be the first great monument of the French Renaissance. The work was carried on by François I who continued the Italianising process by inviting Leonardo da Vinci to Amboise in 1516 and it was there that the great artist died in 1519 in his nearby residence of Clos-Lucé. The palace was the scene of the tragic events which followed La Renaudie's famous conspiracy in 1560 which was an attempt to kidnap François II in order to remove him from the influence of the Guise family. Some 1500 conspirators were beheaded, quartered or hanged as an example from the balconies overlooking the Loire, before the amused eyes of the king and his court. Louis XIII only came to Amboise to hunt, Louis XIV transformed the palace into a prison, part of the buildings were demolished during the First Empire and the remains now belong to the Count of Paris, the Pretender to the French throne. The chapel of Saint-Hubert has survived intact and is a fine example of the Flamboyant Gothic style with a famous portal with the figures of Saints Christopher and Hubert standing above the lintel.

1 Chapel of Saint-Hubert, lintel above the portal, 15th c. 2 Leonardo da Vinci (1452-1519) : Self-portrait, Biblioteca Reale, Turin. 3 The château: Tour des Minimes and Logis du Roi, 15th c. 4 Salle des États, 15th c. 5 Church of Saint-Denis, 12th c.

AMBOISE 4

AMBOISE 3

AMBOISE 5

I

9

ANGERS *Maine-et-Loire.* F 9.

The city of Angers contains a variety of rich treasures: the Cathedral of Saint-Maurice (12th-13th c.) its two spires flanking a tower that was added in the 16th century, remarkable capitals and beautiful stained-glass, old buildings such as the 15th-century Logis Barrault, now the Musée des Beaux-Arts with a fine collection of paintings and the complete *œuvre* of the sculptor and medallion-portraitist David d'Angers (1788-1856), the beautiful Renaissance-style hôtel Pincé, and the Maison d'Adam (16th c.) with its façade covered in small sculptures. Typical examples of "Angevin" or "Plantagenet" vaulting can be seen in the cathedral of Saint-Maurice and the church of Saint Serge, characterised by the high swelling of the groin-vaulting. But the city's main attraction is its château and the collection of tapestries. The old château of the Foulques family, the counts of Anjou (10th-12th c.) was destroyed and then rebuilt by Saint-Louis, and then lost some of its storeys during the reign of Henri III but it still remains an impressive structure over 125 feet high with twelve towers. A museum has recently been built on the upper storey next to a keep and a charming 15th-century chapel. In it, the famous series of the Tapestries of the Apocalypse are now on view to the public. They were made by Nicolas Bataille between 1375 and 1380 and were rescued from a rubbish dump in the 19th century by the bishop of Angers who bought them for 300 francs in 1843. The collection which was bequeathed to the museum comprises seventy pieces (there were originally 92) and their total length is 330 feet. Marvellous as they are, they seem to have lost some of their mysterious evocative quality since they left their original home in the cathedral for the museum.

1-2 Tapestries of the Apoclaypse, by Nicolas Bataille, 14th c., Musée des Tapisseries. 3 Towers of the Château du Roi René, 1238. 4 Chatelet and chapel, 15th c. 5 Maison d'Adam, 15th c. 6 Tour Saint-Aubin, 12th c. 7 Cathedral of Saint-Maurice, tympanum of the main portal, 13th c. 8 Church of Saint-Serge, Angevin vaulting, 13th c. 9 David d'Angers (1788-1856): Alfred de Musset, medallion portrait, Musée David d'Angers.

2

4

3

5

6

7

8

261

AREINES I

AREINES *Loir-et-Cher.* G 8

The little Romanesque country church of Areines is famous for the admirable series of frescoes that were discovered in it some twenty years ago. They date from the building of the church and their fine stylised drawing and delicate colouring have survived in an admirable state.

1 Fresco in the church: head of a woman, 12th c.

ARVILLE *Loir-et-Cher.* G 8.

The pilgrims' hostel and chapel at Arville is one of many that the Templars built along the main highways during the Middle Ages for they were the protectors and bankers of the pilgrims. The order was suppressed by King Philip the Handsome in 1307 when it had become too rich and powerful.

2 *Commanderie* of the Templars at Arville, 12th c.

ASNIÈRES (Abbaye de) *Maine-et-Loire.* F 9.

The gleaming white ruins at Asnières are those of a 12th-century abbey. The choir has still kept its Angevin vaulting which has the same purity of line as that in the church of Saint-Serge at Angers.

3 Ruins of the abbey Church, 13th c.

AVARAY *Loir-et-Cher.* H 8.

The château of Avaray is flanked by four 13th-century towers and overlooks an ornamental pond. After various vicissitudes in its history it was rebuilt in the 18th century in the Louis XIII style.

4 The château, 13th and 18th c.

AZAY-LE-FERRON *Indre.* G 10.

The château of Azay-le-Ferron is both a fine example of architecture and of interior decoration from the 15th to the 19th century. Each successive proprietor altered the decoration somewhat according to the taste of the day. Now both a residence and a museum, the château is especially visited for its park and its outstanding examples of Empire and Restoration furniture.

5 The château, 15th-18th c. 6 Salon in Restoration style, 19th c.

AZAY-LE-RIDEAU 8

AZAY-LE-RIDEAU *Indre-et-Loire.* G 9.

The architecture of the château of Azay-le-Rideau illustrates the transition from the Gothic to the Renaissance style for the fortifications have become mere ornamentation, the round towers have been transformed into elegant turrets, the rampart walk a graceful balcony, and the moats into an ornamental pond. It was built between 1518 and 1529 by the banker Gilles Berthelot in the river bed of the Indre. Like Catherine Briçonnet at Chenonceaux, it was his wife who supervised the building: this explains the extreme refinement of the interior with its straight staircase. The château is now a museum of the Renaissance.

7 The château, side view, 16th c. 8 Courtyard of the château, 16th c. 9 Great chamber, François I fireplace, 16th c.

262

ARVILLE 2

ASNIÈRES 3

AVARAY 4

AZAY-LE-FERRON 5

AZAY-LE-FERRON 6

AZAY-LE-RIDEAU 9

AZAY-LE-RIDEAU 7

BAUGÉ *Maine-et-Loire*. F 9.

The old houses and 15th-century castle of Baugé are a reminder of the times of good king René, the son of Yolande of Aragon, the Queen of Sicily and the arms of Anjou and Sicily may still be seen on the spiral staircase in the château. A fine collection of brass and brightly coloured porcelain pharmaceutical vases may be seen in the Hôpital Saint-Joseph which also has a fine painted ceiling. The chapel of the Incurables (17th c.) contains the Croix d'Anjou, a double armed cross known as the Croix de Lorraine ever since the 16th century.

1 The château, 16th c. 2 Pharmacy of the Hopital Saint-Joseph, 17th c.

BAZOUGES 3

BAZOUGES-SUR-LE-LOIR *Sarthe*. F 8.

On of the prettiest villages on the Loire with its castle with two crenellated towers, watermill, partly Romanesque church, and an old house known as the Maison du Pilon. The castle was built by a chamberlain of Louis XII and François I named Beaudouin de Champagne, and is surrounded by a fine French garden.

3 Castle and watermill, 16th c.

BEAUGENCY *Loiret*. H 8.

The bridge at Beaugency was the only one to cross the Loire between Blois and Orleans until the present century. The town was consequently an important strategic point and the scene of many battles in the past, being liberated from the English by Joan of Arc in 1429. The famous 450-yard-long bridge has still survived and many old buildings may still be seen in the town (Romanesque and Renaissance styles), especially in the Place du Martroi. The now restored Town Hall was built in 1526; the square keep known as the Tour de César is a good example of military architecture of the period.

4 Town Hall, 16th c. 5 Keep, 11th c.

BEAUREGARD (at Cellettes) *Loir-et-Cher*. H 9.

The main attraction of this little castle, well situated on a hill, is its gallery of 363 17th-century portraits. This unique picture gallery is paved with Delft tiles representing soldiers of the army of Louis XIII with a precision of detail that will enchant all students of military history.

6 The château, 16th-17th c. 7 Coffer in the ceiling of the "Cabinet des grelots", 17th c. 8 Delft tiling in the picture gallery, 17th c.

BÉNÉHART *Sarthe*. G 8.

The château façade is flanked by two turrets and pierced by a rhythmic succession of dormer-windows; in the centre of the façade, hexagonal staircase-tower.

9 The château, 16th c.

264

BAUGÉ 1

BAUGÉ 2

BEAUGENCY 4

BEAUGENCY 5

BEAUREGARD 6

BEAUREGARD 7

BÉNÉHART 9

BEAUREGARD 8

BLOIS I

BLOIS 2

BLOIS *Loir-et-Cher*. H 9.

Before Versailles was built, Blois was the royal palace *par excellence*. Charles d'Orléans, the poet-king, Louis XII, François I and Gaston d'Orléans all added a wing in the respective styles of their time. The first two wings are in the Gothic-Renaissance transitional style, the third is in the Renaissance style and the last, by Gaston d'Orléans who wished to destroy the rest of the château, is in the classical style. Blois was the setting for many historic events such as royal births and deaths, and the murder of the Duke of Guise by Henry III in 1588. Gaston d'Orléans' wing is remarkable particularly for being built in brick and stone — the first time the two were combined in French architecture. The octagonal staircase with its galleries is the most noteworthy feature of the François I wing, and the Loges recall an Italian Renaissance palace but the openings which depend upon the interior ground plan are ordered without any attempt at symmetry according to the French tradition of the time.

I The "Loges", façade of the wing of François I, 16th c. 2 Portal of the wing of Louis XII, late 15th c. 3 Wing of Louis XII. 4 Wing of François I. 5 Wing of Gaston d'Orléans, 17th c. 6 Hôtel d'Alluye, 16th c. 7 Antoine Caron (c. 1515-c. 1593): Arrest and execution of Thomas More, 16th c., Musée du château.

LE BOUMOIS (at Saint-Martin-de-la-Place) *Maine-et-Loire*. F 9.

With its towers, ochre-red brick and slate roofs the château of Le Boumois is medieval in appearance but it was built by the Lord René de Thory in 1515 and contains a pre-Renaissance style *logis* opening onto an inner courtyard. It was the birthplace of a hero of the naval battle of Aboukir in 1798, the knight Aristide du Petit-Thouars who died at the age of 28 on board his ship *Le Tonnant*. Sculpted door-way, pink brick pigeon-house, carved ceilings, early 16th-century tower.

8 The château, 1515. 9 Doorway with the arms of the Lords of Thory, 16th c. 10 Interior of the pigeon-house, 16th c.

266

BLOIS 3

BLOIS 4

BLOIS 5

BLOIS 6

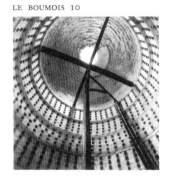

BLOIS 7

LE BOUMOIS 10

LE BOUMOIS 8

LE BOUMOIS 9

267

1

2

3

4

BOURGES *Cher.* I 10.

Although the cathedral of Bourges is one of the most beautiful in France, the main attraction of this city is its large number of old houses and in particular, that of the famous merchant Jacques Cœur. The Palais Jacques Cœur, as it is called, is far more sumptuous than any other bourgeois residence that was ever built at the time and is one of the very few perfect examples of Gothic secular architecture to have survived. It was built by Jacques Cœur, Charles VII's treasurer, in ten years, with every imaginable refinement of decoration and comfort. The façade is famous for its sculptures of servants waiting in the windows for the return of their master, on each side of the main doorway. The Palais was the private residence, offices and warehouse of the great merchant and the bas relief carvings of exotic trees and plants in the courtyard are a discreet reminder of his voyages to the Orient. The later Cujas and Lallemant *hôtels* were also built by rich merchants who had settled in Bourges; the first dates from 1515 and now contains the Musée du Berry, the second was altered and enlarged during the 15th, 16th and 17th centuries by successive owners. The hôtel des Échevins should be visited also for its fine Renaissance spiral staircase in an octagonal tower. The cathedral of Saint-Étienne is a splendid example of pure Gothic and has a number of original features such as its size (400 feet long, 120 feet high) its nave with double aisles and no transept, its five portals, each different in style to avoid any suggestion of monotony, its double-arched flying buttresses, its magnificent stained-glass windows (1215-1225) with their dominant blues and reds, and lastly its enormous late 12th-century crypt lit by twelve windows and supported by fine Gothic pillars.

1-2 Palais Jacques Cœur, details of the façade, servants awaiting their master, 15th c. 3 Inner courtyard of the Palais, 15th c. 4 Fire-place in the Palais, 15th c. 5 South front of the cathedral of Saint-Étienne. 6 Façade of the cathedral. 7 Detail of the south portal of the cathedral. 8 Cathedral crypt and tomb of the Duke of Berry. 9 Stained-glass window from the cathedral: detail: The Apocalypse: Vision of the Eternal god, Musée du Berry. 10 The museum, hôtel Cujas, 16th c. 11 Tournier (1604-1670): Reunion. 12 Nicolas Poussin (1594-1665): Virgin and Child. 13 School of Mignard, 18th c.: Pastoral.

5

6

7

8

10

9

11

12

13

269

BRINAY *Cher.* H 10.

The church of Saint-Aignan (11th c.) contains a marvellous series of frescoes running round the choir in two registers, depicting the childhood of Christ and his early life. They are painted on vermilion-yellow and blue-green grounds in a subdued and harmonious style, and both the attitudes of the figures and the colouring contribute to an overall impression of calm and serenity. They were discovered in 1913 under a thick coat of white-wash.

1 Church of Saint-Aignan, fresco-painting of the Flight into Egypt, 12th c. 2 Detail of the paintings: the Reaper.

BRISSAC *Maine-et-Loire.* F 9.

The château of Brissac was built early in the 17th century by Jacques d'Angluze, son of the architect of Fontainebleau; the main façade flanked by two feudal towers is Renaissance and the other is placed at right angles and is built in the Louis XII style. The château still belongs to the descendants of the Duke of Cossé-Brissac and is one of the most majestic in Anjou.

3 The château Renaissance style façade, 1621.

CHAMBORD *Loir-et-Cher.* H 9.

François I was the creator of this enormous château in the heart of the Sologne region, in an immense hunting domain surrounded by walls more than twenty miles long. The château has more than 400 rooms, 70 inner staircases, enormous terraces, and is particularly famous for the blinding white of its walls, its pseudo-medieval appearance and Renaissance decoration, its 365 chimneys, the 100 foot high lantern in the centre of the roof, and its double-spiral staircase. The whole castle provided a perfect setting for the sumptuous life of the megalomaniac and intriguing king and his court who were able to watch the progress of the royal hunt through the vast forest from the heights of the great terraces of the château. Henri II completed his father's work and added his initials to Diana's crescent in the royal coat of arms. It was at Chambord that Molière first staged his play the *Bourgeois Gentilhomme* for Louis XIV, and it was Louis XV who offered the château as a gift to that other great megalomaniac, the Maréchal de Saxe as a reward for his services to the crown when once again the building was the scene of lavish hunts, great balls and court intrigues. After the Maréchal's death, Chambord became the property of the Duke of Berry's posthumous son before finally becoming the vast, empty museum that it is now.

4 The château, aerial view, 1533. 5 Detail of the double-spiral staircase. 6 Terraces and chimneys of the château. 7 Lantern, height 100 feet.

CHAMPIGNY-SUR-VEUDE 8

CHAMPIGNY-SUR-VEUDE 9

CHAMPIGNY-SUR-VEUDE *Indre-et-Loire.* G 10.

The Bourbon-Montpensier chapel at Champigny illustrates the history of this great royal dynasty with its splendid sculptures and stained-glass. The château had been destroyed by Richelieu after he had acquired it for he feared that its splendour would eclipse that of his own residence. Only the chapel was saved, thanks to the Pope's intercession: with its peristyle, tombs, and magnificent stained-glass windows with their superbly beautiful violet-blue tints it is one of the finest surviving examples of Renaissance art at its climax.

8 Apse and stained-glass windows of the chapel, 16th c. 9 Doorway of the Sainte-Chapelle, 16th c.

BRINAY 1

BRINAY 2

BRISSAC 3

CHAMBORD 4

CHAMBORD 5

CHAMBORD 7

CHAMBORD 6

CHANTELOUP I

CHATEAUDUN 5

CHANTELOUP (at Saint-Denis-Hors) *Indre-et-Loire*. G 9.

The pagoda at Chanteloup, in the midst of woods a few miles from Amboise, is a reminder of the vogue for *chinoiserie* during the reign of Louis XV; it stood in the grounds of a vast château that had been built by Choiseul in his exile, in imitation of Versailles, and which was razed to the ground in 1823.

1 Pagoda of Chanteloup, by Le Camus, 1778.

CHATEAUDUN *Eure-et-Loir*. H 8.

The château of Châteaudun is the finest surviving example of 15th-century secular architecture in France. Its *corps de logis* of three storeys fortified by slim buttresses towers some 200 feet above the Loir and despite several fires it has still kept its original appearance thanks to skilful restorations. The keep is one of the earliest to be built on a circular plan and contains fine 15th-century wooden beams. The Sainte-Chapelle contains a number of statues by local sculptors of the late 15th century which had been collected by Dunois, the Bastard of Orléans and companion in arms of Joan of Arc, after he had been given the château by his brother Charles d'Orléans. The old town contains several old churches and old corbelled houses with sculpted pilasters.

2 The château, 15th c. 3 Wing of the château, 16th c. and loggias of the main staircase, Renaissance period. 4 Inner courtyard of the château: on the left: the keep, 12th c., flanked by the Sainte-Chapelle, 15th c.; on the right: part of the Longueville wing and staircase, 15th c. 5 Portal of the church of Notre-Dame-de-Champdé, 1519.

CHAUMONT-SUR-LOIRE *Loir-et-Cher*. G 9.

The north façade of the château of Chaumont towers over the Loire and the nearby village. It was built on the site of a former fortress between 1465 and 1510 but its towers and, in particular, its four-storeyed Tour d'Amboise still give it a medieval appearance. The courtyard is in a less severe, Renaissance style and offers a magnificent view over the Blésois. The ownership of the château was disputed by Catherine de Medicis and Diane de Poitiers after the death of Henri II and Madame de Staël lived in it during her exile from Paris on the orders of Napoleon, but she had few pleasant memories of her stay, perhaps because of the oppressive summer heat — whence the name Chaumont (literally: hot mount).

6 Aerial view of the château, 16th c. 7 Cour d'honneur, 1510.

CHENONCEAUX *Indre-et-Loire*. G 9.

Feminine in its history as well as in its jewel-like proportions and style, Chenonceaux was originally a square château built by Catherine Briçonnet on the foundations of a former mill that stood on the granite bed of the Cher. In 1547, Diane de Poitiers was given the château by Henri II and built a bridge linking it to the far side of the river. After the king's death Catherine de Medicis received Chenonceaux in exchange for Chaumont and added two storeys to the bridge giving the château its present enchanting aspect.

8 Aerial view of the château, 16th c. 9 Lodge of the château, 1521.

CHATEAUDUN 2

CHATEAUDUN 4

CHATEAUDUN 3

CHAUMONT 6

CHAUMONT 7

CHENONCEAUX 8

CHENONCEAUX 9

273

CHEVERNY 4

CHEVERNY *Loir-et-Cher*. H 9.

The early 17th-century château of Cheverny was built and decorated for the family whose descendants still live in it, and its Louis XIII style has survived without alterations to the present day. The walls, doors and ceilings are all covered with the original decorative paintings of the period. The master of the works was Jean Mosnier (1600-1656). The paintings of scenes from the life of Don Quixote on the ground floor are particularly lively and charming; the mythological scenes decorating the Chambre du Roi are more conventional in spirit.

1 The château, 1634. 2 Great staircase, 17th c. 3 The Abduction of Helena, Gobelins tapestry, 17th c., Salle des Gardes. 4 Jean Mosnier (1600-1656): detail from the Life of Don Quixote, painted panel in the dining room.

CHINON 5

CHINON *Indre-et-Loire*. G 10.

It was to Chinon that Joan of Arc went to plead with King Charles VII in 1429 and it was from the bridge on the Vienne that she must have caught her first sight of the lovely old town and its enormous castle. From the ramparts a magnificent view may be obtained of the old slate roofs of the town, huddling closely together, the city walls (now without their crest), and the Tour de l'Horloge (Clock Tower) of the 12th and 14th centuries. The town contains many old houses, especially in the Rue Voltaire and above all in the Place du Grand Carroi.

5 Town and castle of Chinon. 6 Tour de l'Horloge, 12th and 14th c. 7 Old house, Rue Voltaire, 15th c.

CLOYES 10

CLÉRY-SAINT-ANDRÉ *Loiret*. H 8.

The basilica of Cléry-Saint-André was erected by Louis XI following a vow he had made during the siege of Dieppe in 1443 and is dedicated to the cult of a statue of the Virgin found by labourers in 1280. As the king's vow was followed by a victory, he gave orders that he should be buried in the church, and he still lies with his wife in the tomb built by the Orleans sculptor Bourdin. The main structure is in the Flamboyant Gothic style except for a 14th-century square tower (a remnant of the earlier church destroyed by the English), and the Renaissance Chapelle Saint-Jacques.

8 Basilica of Notre-Dame-de-Cléry, 15th c. 9 Tomb of Louis XI, by Bourdin, 1622.

CLOYES-SUR-LE-LOIR *Eure-et-Loir*. H 8.

This little town inspired Zola for his novel "La Terre" and is dominated by the important 15th-century tower of the church of Saint-Georges.

10 Tower of the church of Saint-Georges, 15th c.

CHEVERNY 1

CHEVERNY 3

CHEVERNY 2

CHINON 6

CHINON 7

CLÉRY 8

CLÉRY 9

CUNAULT 2

CUNAULT 3

CUNAULT 4

CUNAULT *Maine-et-Loire*. F 9.

The Romanesque remains at Cunault are, with those of Saint-Benoît at the far end of the province, the finest and most unforgettable in the whole of the Val de Loire. Standing only a few yards from the Loire, the church of Notre-Dame is in a fine state of preservation, having been carefully and tastefully restored some 30 years ago. The remains of important fresco-paintings have been discovered on the walls, vaults and on some pillars and arches. That of Saint Christopher is the largest (about 10 feet high) and most expressive to have been preserved and its splendour makes it all the more regrettable that so much of the frescoes' former magnificence has been lost for ever. Very fine and varied capitals, many still showing their original painting. Exceptionnally beautiful apse and ambulatory. A 13th-century statue in the round of the Virgin in the tympanum of the main portal.

I Church of Notre-Dame, 12th c. 2-3 Capitals in the church, 12th c. 4 Saint Christopher, wall painting, 12th c. 5 Choir of the church, 12th c. 6 Virgin in Majesty, tympanum, 13th c.

ÉVRON *Mayenne*. F 7.

The church of the Benedictine abbey of Évron was built between the 12th and 14th centuries. Romanesque tower and main nave; the remainder of the structure is radiant Gothic. Old stained-glass windows, fine Aubusson tapestries, and a 12th-century fresco in the vault of the Chapelle Saint-Crépin.

7 Nave of the abbey church, 12th-14th c. 8 Virgin of Notre-Dame-de-l'Épine, life-size reliquary statue, wood and precious metal plate, polished stone and enamel, 13th c.

LA FLÈCHE *Sarthe*. F. 8.

Henri IV spent a part of his youth at La Flèche where he founded a Jesuit College in 1607; it later became a school and then a military school in 1808, being known as the *Prytanée*. The building dates from between 1620 and 1653 and is completed by a Louis XVI hôtel and contains a fine Baroque doorway and an interesting chapel. The Town Hall by the edge of the Loire makes a picturesque ensemble with the old bridge.

9 Portal of the Prytanée, 17th c. 10 Bridge and Château des Carmes (now Town Hall), 15th c., altered.

276

CUNAULT 6

CUNAULT I

CUNAULT 5

ÉVRON 8

ÉVRON 7

LA FLÈCHE 9

LA FLÈCHE IO

FONTEVRAULT-L'ABBAYE *Maine-et-Loire.* F 10.

The Romanesque kitchen of the abbey of Fontevrault is unique of its kind and famous as much for its practical design as for its architectural worth. The abbey was for both men and women and one of its most famous inmates was Gabrielle de Roche-chouart-Mortemart, the "queen of abbesses" and the sister of Madame de Montespan. Now a prison since the 19th century the abbey is worth visiting for its church, capitals, cupola-vaulting, chapter house, refectory, cloister (restored by the Monuments Historiques commission) and the tomb of the Plantagenets who were both counts of Anjou and kings of England.

1 Tour d'Évrault and exterior of the old kitchens, 13th c. 2 Cloister, 15th c. 3 Nave of the abbey church, 13th c.

FOUGÈRES 4

FOUGÈRES-SUR-BIÈVRE *Loir-et-Cher.* H 9.

The Gothic military fortress at Fougères is an anachronism since it was built in the mid- 15th century. The Renaissance style windows are of later date. Sober-styled gallery with flattened arches.

4 The château, 14th c.

FOULLETORTE (at Saint-Georges-sur-Erve) *Mayenne.* F 7.

The façade of the château of Foulletorte shows the stylistic transition from the Renaissance to Classicism: dormers with triangular central pediments, *avant-corps* with columns etc. Built in dark granite in the late 16th century, the château is surrounded by water.

5 Cour d'honneur of the château, 1590.

GERMIGNY-DES-PRÉS *Loiret.* I 8.

The church of Germigny-des-Prés is the only church of the time of Charlemagne to survive in France but it suffered from over-restoration in 1869. It served as an oratory for the bishop Théodulfe, the abbot of Saint-Benoît-sur-Loire. The visitor should now try to imagine the church as it must have been at the time of Theodulfe. It had the ground-plan of a Greek cross with four apses, was crowned by a curious lantern-tower and lit by windows filled with translucent alabaster like the mausoleum of Galla Placidia at Ravenna, and decorated with highly coloured glass mosaics, only those in the main apse still surviving.

6 Church of Germigny, c. 806. 7 Ark of the Covenant, mosaic in the main apse, 4th c.

GIEN *Loiret.* I 8.

The town of Gien was heavily bombed in 1940 and the reconstruction of the town and its monuments is a highly remarkable blend of modern and regional styles. The 15th-century (restored) château now contains the Musée de la Chasse à Tir (Museum of shot-gun hunting) which includes a fine series of paintings by François Desportes in a large hall with superb beams.

9 The town of Gien, bridge, 15th-c. château, modern church. 10 François Desportes (1661-1743): Still-life with game, Musée de la Chasse à Tir.

FONTEVRAULT 1

FONTEVRAULT 2

FONTEVRAULT 3

FOULLETORTE 5

GERMIGNY 7

GERMIGNY 6

GIEN 10

GIEN 9

LE GRAND-PRESSIGNY *Indre-et-Loire.* G 10.

Grand-Pressigny was an important centre for chipped-flint industries during the Neolithic period and the château, with its fine Renaissance façade, now contains a particularly well laid-out and instructive Museum of Prehistory. The square keep beside the château is a relic of an earlier 11th-century castle and is crowned by 15th-century machicolation.

1 The keep, 12th and 15th c.

LA GUERCHE-SUR-CREUSE *Indre-et-Loire.* G 10.

Charles VII built the château of La Guerche along the banks of the river Creuse for Antoinette de Maignelay, the cousin of Agnes Sorel and his first mistress. Enormous underground store-rooms with fine vaulting, under the château.

2 The château, 15th c.

LANGEAIS *Indre-et-Loire.* G 9.

The castle of Langeais was built in five years in the 15th century and has survived intact together with its original furnishings and interior decoration. It is a striking example of early Renaissance civil architecture of an almost military sobriety of style. Its chief interest lies in the medieval furnishings which are a perfect evocation of the times of the lord who built Langeais: Jean Bourré, Comptroller of Finances under Louis XI.

3 Lodge of the castle, 1465. 4 Bed room, 15th c.

LASSAY 6

LASSAY-SUR-CROISNE *Loir-et-Cher.* H 9.

The well preserved fresco in the little village church provided the model for the restoration of the castle of Moulin, prettily built with diamond-shaped red and black brick.

5 Fresco in the church, Saint Christopher and, in the background, the castle of Moulin, 15th c. 6 The castle of Moulin, 15th c., restored.

LAVAL 9

LAVAL *Mayenne.* F 8.

Numerous old houses have preserved the authentic ancient character of the town (Rue des Orfèvres, Grande-Rue and Rue du Pont-de-Mayenne). The château has a fortress-like exterior but contains a charming Renaissance courtyard and a very eclectic museum. Its most interesting features are the extraordinary beams in the keep and the main hall, 100 feet long and crowned by a wooden pointed barrel-vault. The church of Notre-Dame d'Avesnières on the outskirts of the town is partly Romanesque and partly Renaissance and has a remarkable 12th-century apse. Four highly original and imaginative historical personages were born at Laval: Ambroise Paré the surgeon, Alain Gerbault the sailor, Henri Rousseau, Douanier, the painter, and Alfred Jarry, the creator of Ubu.

7 The old castle and the bridge, 12th-16th c. 8 Apse of the church of Notre-Dame d'Avesnières, 12th c. 9 Alfred Jarry (1873-1907): Pa Ubu.

LA GUERCHE 2

LE GRAND-PRESSIGNY 1

LANGEAIS 3

LANGEAIS 4

LASSAY 5

LAVAL 7

LAVAL 8

281

LEVROUX 3

LAVARDIN *Loir-et-Cher*. G 8.

A great deal of imagination is required on the part of the visitor in order to imagine the ancient 11th-12th-century fortress and the church of Saint-Genest, with its badly damaged 12th- and 16th-century frescoes, in their former glory. But what little does remain of the two buildings is still highly impressive.

1 Column of the church, 12th c. **2** Fresco in the church of Saint-Genest, 16th c.

LEVROUX *Indre*. H 10.

The name of the town is due to a leper, a city father, who was cured by Saint Martin in the Middle Ages and a figure of a leper losing his skin may still be seen carved on the old wooden house near the church of Saint-Sylvain. The church is partly Romanesque and the severity of its façade, flanked by two towers, is only lightened by the sculptures of the tympanum.

3 Corner post of old wooden house, 15th c.

LE LIGET (Charterhouse) *Indre-et-Loire*. G 10.

All that now remains of the charterhouse of Liget, some 6 miles from Loches, are the foundations of the 12th-century monastery but the pleasant residential buildings and arcades of a great cloister still remain of the 18th-c. building together with its vast terrace and noble doorway. The most artistically noteworthy building is the Chapelle Saint-Jean standing in a nearby field in the midst of a wood. Its rotunda shape is extremely unusual for Romanesque architecture in the 12th century. Its walls are painted with six large frescoes of exquisite colouring, the best-preserved showing the Death of the Virgin, admirable in its balance, its majesty and serenity, and the Prophet Jesse holding the stem of the symbolic tree.

4-5 Frescoes of the Chapelle Saint-Jean, the Death of the Virgin, and the prophet Jesse, 12th c.

LOCHES *Indre-et-Loire*. G 10.

Were it not that Agnes Sorel, Charles VII's mistress, had stayed at Loches for a time the history of this rocky fortress would be one of unrelieved grimness for it was devoted to war and imprisonment in the course of its career. Its mile-and-a-half-long walls surround a superb 12th-century square keep and three so-called "beak" towers, named after their angular, spur-like shape. The buildings served as a state prison and contained the famous iron cages in which the prisoners were unable to stand upright. Cardinal La Balue who had been implicated in the Duke of Burgundy, Charles the Bold's treason against Louis XI was shut up in the dungeons for eleven years and Lodovico Il Moro spent eight years there before dying almost immediately after his release. The Royal Logis were built in a somewhat lighter style and date in part from the 14th, in part from the 15th century. The city has kept much of its medieval charm and contains a treasure of Romanesque architecture, the collegiate church of Saint-Ours, with unique pyramid vaulting dating from 1168. Interesting frescoes in the crypt. Other historic buildings include the Maison du Centaure, the Porte Picois, and the Town Hall; the Tour Saint-Antoine is a remarkable relic of a Renaissance church, with its double balustrade and perforated lantern.

6 Keep, 12th c., and pointed towers, 13th c. **7** Tour Saint-Antoine and loggia of Anne of Britanny, 16th c. **8** Logis Royaux, 15th c. **9** Church of Saint-Ours, inner portal, 12th c. **10** Towers of the church of Saint-Ours, 12th c.

LAVARDIN 1   LAVARDIN 2

LE LIGET 4   LE LIGET 5

LOCHES 6

LOCHES 7   LOCHES 8

LOCHES 10

LOCHES 9

LE LUDE *Sarthe.* G 9.

The château can be seen to have been built at three different successive periods for it is a mixture of Louis XII, François I and Louis XVI styles. Situated high over the Loire, it is worth visiting for its sumptuous rooms, which are still inhabited.

1 The château, wing of François I, by Jean Gendrot, 16th c.
2 Fresco in the Oratory, the Triumph of Chastity, Italian art, 16th c. restored.

LUYNES 3

LUYNES *Indre-et-Loire.* G 9.

Still inhabited by the family that built it the castle is a fortress almost entirely from the 13th century. In the neighbourhood, six arches of a Gallo-Roman aqueduct may be seen.

3 The castle, 13th and 15th c.

LE MANS 10

LE MANS *Sarthe.* G 8.

Le Mans is extremely rich in historic buildings and monuments. The cathedral of Saint-Julien is partly Romanesque but magnificently Gothic in its overall aspect and has a fine apse with double flying buttresses and a Gothic choir as high as that of Notre-Dame of Paris. The decoration of the tympanum and uprights of the 13th-century Romanesque south portal is stylistically related to that at Chartres. Two beautiful Renaissance tombs in one of the chapels; 13th-century stained-glass and 16th-century tapestries are among the treasures of the church. The 13th-century church of Notre-Dame-de-la-Couture is quite different in spirit and once was part of a Benedictine abbey. Angevin or Plantagenet vaulting (in the high barrel style), and a white marble Virgin attributed to Germain Pilon and dated 1571. Many old houses throughout the old town: the so-called house of Queen Bérengère contains a fine collection of ceramics and popular art. The Musée de Tessé in the old bishop's palace is rich in paintings and has very varied collections of gold- and silver-work, sculpture, tapestry and drawings among other works of art. Le Mans owed its past splendour to the Plantagenets, Counts of Anjou and kings of England, who spent many years in the city in the mid 12th century. Of the Gallo-Roman enceinte that then protected the city, some 400 yards of wall flanked by eight towers and sally-ports may still be seen.

4 Apse of the cathedral of Saint-Julien, 13th c. 5 Gothic choir of the cathedral, 13th c. 6 South portal, Romanesque, 12th c. 7 Maison de la Reine Bérengère, early 16th c. 8 Germain Pilon (1535-1590): Virgin, Notre-Dame-de-la-Couture, 1571.

MUSÉE DE TESSÉ

9 David (1748-1825): the Conventionnel Gérard and his family.
10 Enamel plaque of Geoffroy Plantagenet, 12th c.

LE LUDE I

LE LUDE 2

LE MANS 5

LE MANS 6

LE MANS 4

LE MANS 8

LE MANS 9

LE MANS 7

MÉNARS *Loir-et-Cher.* H 9.

Like so many earlier royal favourites, Madame de Pompadour wanted to possess a *pied-à-terre* in Anjou. She found it in a 17th-century building at Ménars and soon had it completed by Gabriel. At her death the property passed to her brother Marigny who commissioned Soufflot to complete the work. The lavish interior decorations of the time of the Marquise have unfortunately long since disappeared but the magnificent park has remained intact.

1 Façade of the château overlooking the gardens, 17th and 18th c.

MEUNG-SUR-LOIRE *Loiret.* H 8.

Two great medieval poets had a connection with the town of Meung for it was the birthplace of Jean de Meung who was co-author of the Roman de la Rose, and François Villon spent one of his frequent stays in prison in the keep of the city. The church has kept its fine 11th-century tower, built in the purest Romanesque style.

2 Church of Saint-Liphard, 11th-c. tower and 12th-c. keep.

MEUNG 2

MONTGEOFFROY (at Mazé) *Maine-et-Loire.* F 9.

The classical style château of Montgeoffroy was built in the space of only three years for the Maréchal de Contades by the architect Barré. Two great Parisian cabinet makers, Garnier and Blanchard were commissioned for the furnishings. The property has remained in the family ever since and has remained intact. With its fine paintings (Rigaud, Desportes, Drouais), its tapestries and works of art the château gives a perfect picture of the life of the time when it was the residence of Louis XVI's marshal.

3 The château, by Barré, 1775. 4 Salon, 18th-c. furniture.

MONTOIRE-SUR-LE-LOIR *Loir-et-Cher.* G 8.

A short and narrow road hemmed in by massive stone walls leads the visitor from the main road to the Priory of Saint-Gilles where Ronsard was once a lay abbot. All that remains of the original 11th-century structure are the apse and two minor apses of the transept and the beginning of the nave. Important fragments of painted decoration in the semi-dome of the apse and the arms of the transept have been preserved in good state. A curious feature of the decoration is that the same subject - Christ in majesty in a mandala has been repeated three times (fresco and distemper). The painting of the east apse is a masterpiece of Romanesque art and is dated late 11th century, the other two from the second half of the 12th century.

5 Apse of Saint-Gilles, 11th c. 6 Christ in Majesty, fresco in the apse, late 11th c. 7 Angel, fresco in the apse, 12th c. 8 Saint Gilles and the hind, polychrome wood statue, 12th c.

MONTRÉSOR 9

MONTRÉSOR *Indre-et-Loire.* H 10.

The site that Foulques Nerra chose for one of his residences dominates the pretty valley of the Indrois as might be expected. The present château contains several treasures: an *Adulterous Woman* attributed to Veronese, a massive mahogany staircase, etc. The village church has a fine Renaissance portal.

9 The château, south façade, 15th c.

MÉNARS I

MONTGEOFFROY 3

MONTGEOFFROY 4

MONTOIRE 5

MONTOIRE 7

MONTOIRE 8

MONTOIRE 6

MONTREUIL-BELLAY I

NOGENT-LE-ROTROU 4

NOGENT-LE-ROTROU 5

MONTREUIL-BELLAY *Maine-et-Loire*. F 9.

Montreuil was a fortress in the time of Foulques Nerra before becoming a residential château, and has still kept some of its 15th-century buildings. The Petit-Château has a kitchen with pyramid vaulting like that of Fontevrault. In the Château-Neuf: fine staircase overhung by palm-leaf vaulting.

I The château, 15th c.

MONTRICHARD *Loir-et-Cher*. G 9.

King Louis XII of France was married in the church of Sainte-Croix in the little town of Montrichard. The castle belonged to his father-in-law Louis XI. Fine 12th-century square keep, several Renaissance buildings, church of Nanteuil.

2 Bridge, church and keep.

MONTSOREAU *Maine-et-Loire*. F 9.

The Renaissance château of Montsoreau is beautifully situated on the Loire, almost by the confluence with the river Vienne, and was the setting for Alexandre Dumas' novel "La Dame de Montsoreau". The Lady of Montsoreau was involved with her husband Charles de Chambes in the assassination of Bussy d'Amboise, during the massacres of Saint-Bartholomew in 1579.

3 The château, 15th c.

NOGENT-LE-ROTROU *Eure-et-Loir*. G 7.

The town is rich in Renaissance houses, all of which were built after Nogent had been burned by Charles VII in 1449. But the attraction of the town also lies in its château of Saint-Jean which survived the destruction of the old town and became the property of Henry IV's minister Sully in 1624.

4 Entrance lodge to the château of Saint-Jean, 11th and 13th c.
5 Tomb of Sully, by Boudin, 1642.

ORLÉANS *Loiret*. H 8.

The cathedral of Sainte-Croix is a rare example of a successful pastiche of styles. It was rebuilt by Henry IV when all that remained of the earlier church were the apse and some 12th- and 13th-century ruins. Reconstruction continued during the 18th and 19th centuries and the final result is a beautiful church in an entirely Gothic style. Besides being destroyed during the siege by the English which began on October 12, 1428 and ended when the city was relieved by Joan of Arc on May 8, 1429, Orleans was also badly damaged during the last war, but it has been skilfully reconstructed. The Renaissance façade of the Town Hall has been partly restored, and its doorways with caryatids are of the highest interest. The fine Musée des Beaux-Arts owes its chief interest to its collection of French 17th- and 18th-century portraits, its drawings and prints, and a fine painting by La Tour: *Saint Sebastian with a lantern*.

6 Apse of the cathedral of Sainte-Croix, 13th c. 7 South transept of the cathedral.

MUSÉE DES BEAUX-ARTS

8 Deruet (1588-1660): the Four Elements: Water. 9 Velazquez (1599-1660): Saint Thomas. 10 Perronneau (1715-1783): Portrait of M. Chevotet, pastel. 11 Georges de La Tour (1593-1652): Saint Sebastian with a lantern.

MONTRICHARD 2

MONTSOREAU 3

ORLÉANS 6

ORLÉANS 7

ORLÉANS 9

ORLÉANS 10

ORLÉANS 11

ORLÉANS 8

289

LE PLESSIS-BOURRÉ 2   LE PLESSIS-BOURRÉ I

LE PLESSIS-BOURRÉ (at Écuillé) *Maine-et-Loire.* F 9.
The castle of Le Plessis-Bourré was one of three (the others being
at Jarzé and Vaux) built for his own use by Louis XI's treasurer
after he had supervised the building of Langeais for the king.
Le Plessis is the most interesting of the three and has survived
in its original state. It shows the fine taste of its creator and
has kept a remarkable unity of style and decoration.
I The castle, 1473. 2 Ceiling of the Salle des Gardes, detail, 15th c.

LE PLESSIS-MACÉ *Maine-et-Loire.* F 9.
The château has kept the grim aspect of a medieval fortress but
the courtyard is decorated in an elegant Renaissance style with
its sculpted balconies and Flamboyant chapel.
3. The château, 11th and 15th c.

PONCÉ-SUR-LE-LOIR *Sarthe.* G 8.
The Renaissance staircase is one of the wonders of this château
which was altered during the 18th century: its stone panels are
decorated with 130 different motifs, carved directly in the stone.
The church of Saint-Julien dates from the 12th century and the
interior was once completely painted but only a few fragments
of the original decoration have survived in a rather damaged
state (on one pillar, strikingly unusual painting of a violin player
and a female dancer symbolising the vice of Lust). The frescoes
in the choir have been repainted.
4 Coffered ceiling over the staircase of the château, 16th c. 5 Church
of Saint-Julien, 12th c.

PONTIGNÉ *Maine-et-Loire.* F 9.
Several churches in the neighbourhood of Baugé are distinguished
by their curious twisted steeples (Fontaine-Guerin, Le Vieil-
Bauge, Mouliherne) - a particularity of the Angevin-Plantagenet
style. Apart from its steeple, the church of Saint-Denis of Pontigné is worth visiting for its remains of Gothic paintings and its
fine barrel-vaulting.
6 Twisted steeple of the church of Saint-Denis, 12th c. 7 The
Resurrection of Lazarus, wall-painting, 13th c., restored.

LA POSSONNIÈRE (at Couture-sur-Loir) *Loir-et-Cher.* G 8.
The walls of the manor where Ronsard was born in 1524 are
decorated with religious and profane inscriptions; his arms of
three silver fishes on an azure ground are repeated several times
in the Italianate sculpted decoration of this house which Loys
Ronsard, the soldier-scholar, built on his return from the Italian
campaigns.
8 The manor house, view from the courtyard, 16th c. 9 Great
fireplace bearing the arms of Ronsard, 16th c.

LE PLESSIS-MACÉ 3

PONCÉ 4

PONCÉ 5

LA POSSONNIÈRE 8

PONTIGNÉ 6

PONTIGNÉ 7

LA POSSONNIÈRE 9

ROMORANTIN I

ROMORANTIN 2

ROMORANTIN *Loir-et-Cher.* H 9.

That many-sided genius, Leonardo da Vinci, had designed a prefa-
bricated palace to be built at Romorantin for Louise de Savoie,
the mother of François I, and it was here that the king spent
his youth. The angles of two streets in the town are graced by
two curious 16th-century houses. The Maison du Carroir Doré
is flanked by two corner posts bearing carvings of the Annunciation on one, and Saint Michael overcoming the dragon on
the other.

1 Maison de la Chancellerie, corner of Rue du Milieu, 16th c.
2 Corner post of the Maison du Carroir Doré, corner of Rue
Saint-Pierre, 16th c.

SAINT-AIGNAN-SUR-CHER *Loir-et-Cher.* H 9.

The modest collegiate church is famous for its Romanesque
capitals which show a great variety of very different subjects
and styles, ranging from the archaic to the most sophisticated.
In order to decorate the capitals the Romanesque sculptors had
recourse to an extensive decorative grammar in which the same
themes were often repeated but always renewed. The capitals
of Saint-Aignan comprise such motifs as serpent spirals, a deer
with very short legs followed by a hunter armed with a bow,
a kind of siren-bird with one bird's leg and the other leg ending
in a cloven hoof - typical of the strange monsters that the Romanesque artists created to astound the faithful. But the Romanesque
capitals are not the only attraction of the church: note the Romanesque and Gothic paintings of the crypt and the courtyard
of the Renaissance château.

3 The château, 16th c. 4 Porch and bell-tower of the church
late 12th c. 5 Capital in the choir of the church: hunting scene,
12th c. 6 Capital in the choir: Judgment of Solomon, 12th c.
7 The chapel of Noyers, 12th c.

ST-BENOIT-SUR-LOIRE 14

SAINT-BENOIT-SUR-LOIRE *Loiret.* I 8.

The monastery at Saint-Benoît is more than a mere historical
monument for the monastic life of the Benedictine order began
there again in 1944. From the 9th century onwards, Saint-Benoît
was known for its important monastic school whose writing
classes drew several illustrious pilgrims. The basilica was built
between 1067 and 1218 and is a fine example of Romanesque
art free from all regional influences. The horizontal stress of the
nave is offset by the strong horizontals of the choir in the purest
style. The famous capitals of the porch are as fine as those in
the nave. The church contains the relics of Saint Benedict whose
body was brought back from Monte Cassino in the 7th century,
and they have been ceaselessly venerated ever since in what
may be considered one of the spiritual centres of modern France.
The poet Max Jacob is now buried near the church, according
to his wish.

8 Porch and tower of the basilica, 10th c. 9 Corinthian columns
of the porch, 11th c. 10 Apse, 11th c. 11 Aisle and ambulatory,
12th c. 12-13-14 Capitals, 11th c.

ST-AIGNAN-SUR-CHER 5

ST-AIGNAN-SUR-CHER 6

ST-AIGNAN-SUR-CHER 3

ST-AIGNAN-SUR-CHER 4

ST-AIGNAN-SUR-CHER 7

ST-BENOIT-SUR-LOIRE 9

ST-BENOIT-SUR-LOIRE 8

ST-BENOIT-SUR-LOIRE 10

ST-BENOIT-SUR-LOIRE 12

ST-BENOIT-SUR-LOIRE 11

ST-BENOIT-SUR-LOIRE 13

ST-COME 1

ST-OUEN 4

STE-CATHERINE-DE-FIERBOIS 5

SAINT-COME *Indre-et-Loire.* G 9.

The priory of Saint-Côme is a centre for the study of Romanesque art and itself has fine remains of the architecture of the period. The poet Pierre de Ronsard was prior at Saint-Côme where he died in 1585; his tomb has been restored and may be visited.

1 Priory of Saint-Côme, semi-domed apse of the church, 12th c.

SAINT-JACQUES-DES-GUÉRETS *Loir-et-Cher.* G 8.

The church of Saint-Jacques, which belonged to an Augustine abbey, lies on the old pilgrim's route to Compostella and is decorated with a series of mural paintings. The paintings herald the beginning of the Gothic style in the almond-shaped eyes of the figures, in the languid grace of their gestures and the treatment of the draperies. The colours are original and delicate and include a fine blending of mauve, blue-green and copper tones.

2 Martyrdom of Saint James, fresco, 13th c. 3 Christ in majesty, fresco, 13th c.

SAINT-OUEN *Mayenne.* F 8.

The château was built by Anne of Britanny's confessor and includes fine examples of Louis-XIII style sculpture in the dormers of the *corps de logis*, the coping on the square tower, the inner staircase, and the fireplaces, all carefully preserved in their original state.

4 Staircase tower of the château, early 16th c.

SAINTE-CATHERINE-DE-FIERBOIS *Indre-et-Loire.* G 10.

The charming Flamboyant Gothic church of Fierbois contains memories of Joan of Arc, like so many other churches along the Loire, for it was there that the saint found Charles Martel's sword with the five crosses. The interior contains a highly realistic Entombment and a Flamboyant style carved wooden confessional.

5 Entombment, polychrome stone, 15th c.

SAUMUR *Maine-et-Loire.* F 9.

The château of Saumur illustrates the transition between medieval military architecture and the Renaissance style, and with its four great corner towers, dominates the whole of the town. It contains an equestrian museum and also an enchanting museum of decorative arts which has been arranged with the utmost taste. The exhibits come from the collection of the Count of Loir and include an important series of ceramics. The Town Hall has an unusually fortified aspect for it was once part of the enceinte of the town. The Maison de la Reine de Sicile owes its name to Yolande of Aragon, mother of King René and wife of Louis II of Anjou, King of the Two Sicilies. This fine manor has now been restored after being badly damaged in 1940. The town contains two Romanesque churches: Saint-Pierre with its Angevin nave (Saint-Florent tapestry) and Notre-Dame de Nantilly flanked by a Flamboyant chapel which was Louis XI's oratory and which contains twenty-seven tapestries which are displayed in rotation, the most famous being the *Bal des Sauvages* (16th c.), the *Tree of Jesse* (1529) and the *Siege of Jerusalem* (16th c.).

6 The château, 14th and 16th c. 7 Room of Rouen and Nevers faïences in the Musée des Arts Décoratifs, ceramic collection. 8 House of the Queen of Sicily (Maison de la Reine de Sicile, early 15th c. 9 Town Hall, early 16th c. 10 Tapestry in the church of Notre-Dame de Nantilly, *Bal des Sauvages,* c. 1500.

ST-JACQUES-DES-GUÉRETS 2

ST-JACQUES-DES-GUÉRETS 3

SAUMUR 6

SAUMUR 8

SAUMUR 9

SAUMUR 10

SAUMUR 7

295

SELLES-SUR-CHER *Loir-et-Cher.* H 9.

The originality of the church of Saint-Eusice lies in the sculpted frieze running round the apse. It would appear that this type of rather crude sculpture, dating from the 10th-12th centuries and also found at Andlau (Bas-Rhin) and Saint-Paul-les-Dax (Landes) was inspired by medieval ivory carvings. The church has been restored but the south wall and its fine Romanesque capitals have survived in their original state. The nave has a wooden ceiling.

1 Apse of the church of Saint-Eusice and upper frieze with scenes from the life of the hermit-saint, 12th c. 2 South aisle, 12th c. capitals.

SERRANT (at Saint-Georges-sur-Loire) *Maine-et-Loire.* F 9.

The château has a highly original ground plan, is flanked by large domed towers, and is built in brown schist and white stone. It has preserved a handsome unity of style although it was built over a period of more than two centuries. The furniture and interior decoration have been faithfully preserved; most noteworthy are the fine panelled staircase, the library with its 20 000 volumes, the Empire-style rooms and the chapel, built by J. Hardouin-Mansart, with the tomb of Maréchal de Vaubrun.

3 The château, 16th-18th c. 4 Panelled staircase, after a design by Philibert de l'Orme, 16th c. 5 Tomb of Maréchal de Vaubrun, by Coysevox, late 17th c.

SOLESMES *Sarthe.* F 8.

The Benedictine priory of Solesmes was founded in 1010 and had a chequered history, but it recovered its former splendour in the 19th century thanks to Dom Guéranger (1806-1875). The present grandiose and somewhat pompous buildings which tower above the Sarthe were built between 1896 and 1901 but the old priory, of which they are an extension, is a more graceful edifice of the 18th century. The abbey church still has its old choir and transept (11th and 15th c.). In the transept: the famous statues of the "Saints of Solesmes"; in the north arm the rather over-decorated Belle Chapelle; in the right arm: an Entombment (1496) with a fine Saint Magdalene attributed to Michel Colombe.

6 Old priory and abbey of Saint-Pierre, 18th c. 7 Saint Magdalene, attributed to Michel Colombe, 1496.

SULLY-SUR-LOIRE *Loiret.* I 8.

The extraordinary walnut beams of the keep have been preserved in a perfect state for six hundred years and are a witness to the skill of the carpenter Trévenin Foucher who carved them in 1363 in the shape of a reversed ship's hull. The fact that they survived for so long is due to the careful way in which the wood was treated before being used. The feudal castle contains a 17th century *corps de logis* where Henry IV's powerful minister Sully resided.

8 The castle, 14th c.

SULLY 8

SELLES-SUR-CHER 2

SELLES-SUR-CHER 1

SERRANT 3

SERRANT 5

SERRANT 4

SOLESMES 6

SOLESMES 7

TALCY *Loir-et-Cher.* H 8.

Two ladies from the small town of Talcy inspired two poets in the 16th century. The first was Cassandre, the daughter of Florentin Salviati, the cousin of Catherine de Medicis, and builder of the château in 1520. Ronsard had fallen in love with her after meeting her at a ball given by François I and immortalised her in his verse; the other was Cassandre's own daughter Diane who was loved by the poet Agrippa d'Aubigné. Although its style is Renaissance, the château has a somewhat rustic appearance; its fine architectural féatures include the main doorway, the courtyard, the pigeon-house with 1500 cells, and a winepress which is still in use. The interior is still decorated with simple but graceful furniture of the period and there is nothing to suggest the atmosphere of a museum.

I Courtyard, well and gallery, 16th c. **2** Pigeon-house, 16th c. **3** Room of Catherine de Medicis, 16th c.

TAVANT *Indre-et-Loire.* G 10.

The parish church of Saint-Nicolas contains some of the most important and oldest Romanesque frescoes in France (early 12th c. or even late 11th c.). The frescoes in the crypt are quite outstanding, not because of their size for they are less than a yard high (isolated subjects on each groined vault) but because of the liveliness of their style, their strong colouring and expressiveness. The crypt itself with its six low pillars is so small that one can touch the ceiling with one's hand. Note the three images of David in the paintings: playing the harp, fighting the lion, and dancing; also, the themes of Original Sin, Psychomachia, the Roman Pilgrim and the famous figure of Lust.

4 Lust piercing its flank with a spear, fresco, 12th c. **5** David playing the harp, fresco, 12th c. **6** Crypt of the church, 12th c.

TAVANT 6

TOURS *Indre-et-Loire.* G 9.

The city of Tours is the main centre for tourists in Touraine. The city was badly damaged during the last war but its fine cathedral, some old *hôtels*, and the excellent Musée des Beaux-Arts have survived intact except for some minor restorations. The cathedral contains examples of all the different phases of the Gothic style, from the 12th-century apse to the 16th-century façade. Its fine stained-glass windows escaped war damage. Old houses with wooden beams, some built of brick and wood, others in brick and stone, or carved stone like the hôtel Gouin, date from the 15th to the 18th centuries. The churches of Saint Gatien and Saint Martin, the latter the patron saint of the town, have fine cloisters. The Museum is in the former 18th-century archbishop's palace with its silk wall hangings and panelling, and contains a collection of paintings and furniture from the former château de Chanteloup, now destroyed.

7 Hôtel Gouin, 16th c. **8** Cloister of La Psalette, 16th c. **9** Fontaine de Beaune, 1511. **10** Apse of the cathedral of Saint-Gratien, 13th c. **II** Nave of the cathedral, 15th c.

TOURS 9

TALCY 2

TALCY 3

TAVANT 4   TAVANT 5

TALCY 1

TOURS 7   TOURS 8

TOURS 10   TOURS 11

299

TOURS 1

TOURS 2

TOURS (suite)

MUSÉE DES BEAUX-ARTS

1 Rembrandt (1606-1669): The Flight into Egypt, 1625. **2** Largillière (1656-1746): Self-portrait, 1690. **3** Mantegna (1431-1506): The Agony in the Garden, 1459.

TOURS 3

USSÉ *Indre-et-Loire*. G 9.

The fairy-tale castle of Ussé is built in gleaming white stone, and the severity of its outer towers is offset by the charm of its inner courtyard facing the river Indre. The small chapel in the park bears the initials C and L, the Christian names of the architect and his wife (Charles d'Espinay and Lucrèce de Pons) inserted in a pure Renaissance-style decoration.

4 View of the castle, 15th c., restored. **5** Courtyard of the castle, 15th c. **6** Doorway of the chapel, 16th c.

VALENÇAY *Indre*. H 10.

The main façade of the château is composed of a number of different elements set in juxtaposition: from right to left they are: the Old Tower, crowned with a dome, then a graceful *corps de logis* with pilaster decorations, the keep with four turrets and beautiful dormers, a smaller *corps de logis* and finally a low tower. The whole château was built in a century, between 1540 and 1650. The other wing of the château, set at right angles to the main building, dates from the 18th century. A museum in the grounds contains souvenirs of Talleyrand who was owner of the château for a time.

7 Château and main keep, 16th and 17th c.

VENDOME *Loir-et-Cher*. G 8.

The church of the Trinity is a dependance of an abbey founded in the 9th century by Georges Martel, son of Foulques Nerra. Its Flamboyant façade is almost an excessive example of the style, but the Trinité is the finest church to be seen in the region, with its remarkable stained-glass, its choir screen, capitals and several polychrome statues which all date from the Gothic period.

8 Façade of the church of the Trinity, by Jean de Beauce, 16th c. **9** Slaughtering of a sow, misericord in the choir stalls, 12th c. **10** Virgin and Child, stained-glass, 12th c., church of the Trinity.

USSÉ 5

USSÉ 6

USSÉ 4

VALENÇAY 7

VENDOME 10

VENDOME 8

VENDOME 9

VILLANDRY *Indre-et-Loire.* G 9.

The gardens of Villandry are the most beautiful in France and are a work of art in themselves, so perfectly have they been restored on the basis of the original designs left by the great garden designers of the 16th century such as Du Cerceau. The kitchen garden, ornamental garden by the foot of the château and pond are set on three successive terraces. The château itself consists of a 14th-century keep to which a Renaissance style corps de logis was added by François I's secretary Jean Le Breton, the creator of Villesavin (q.v.). With their clipped hedges and yew trees, ponds, waterfalls, and grottos full of statues, the gardens form a kind of brocaded carpet around the château, and are the work of Doctor Carvallo who transformed the former English garden into a French garden against the background of the village and its Romanesque church, during the period between the two wars. He also gathered a fine collection of Spanish paintings including works attributed to such great masters as Velazquez, El Greco and Zurbaran, in the interior of the château.

1 The château and gardens.

VILLESAVIN (near Bracieux) *Loir-et-Cher.* H 9.

While supervising work on the château of Chambord for his royal master, François I, Jean Le Breton built himself a graceful dwelling at Villesavin. The main lines of the building are classical although the decoration is entirely Renaissance in style. The building contains an old kitchen, a large 16th-century pigeon house, and a white marble, 17th-century Italian fountain.

2 White marble fountain, 17th c., and courtyard of the château, 1537.

VILLESAVIN 2

VILLANDRY 1

VIII

BOURGOGNE - FRANCHE-COMTÉ

I   J   K   L

[CHAMPAGNE]

[LORRAINE]

7   Montereau

Vallery

Fleurigny

Sens

Château-Landon

80 km

Plombières

Neuvy-Sautour

Montigny-sur-Aube

Pontigny

8   Appoigny

Tanlay

Tonnerre

Langres

Auxerre

Ancy-le-Franc

Chatillon-sur-Seine

Chauvirey-
le-Châtel

Fontenay

St-Fargeau

Montréal-en-Auxois

Bussy-Rabutin

Ratilly

Semur-en-
Auxois

Gray

9   Vézelay   Avallon

Flavigny-sur-Ozerain

Montcley

Clamecy

St-Père-sous-Vézelay

Donzy-le-Pré

Bazoches

Dijon

Besançon

Varzy

Saulieu

St-Réverien

Citeaux

Dôle

Ornans

La Charité-sur-Loire

Arc-et-Senans

Montbenoit

Nevers

Sully

Beaune

10   Autun

Arbois

La Rochepot

Pierre-en-Bresse

Chalon-sur-Saône

Lons-le-Saunier

Perrecy-les-Forges

FRANCHE-

Brancion

Moulins

Chapaize

Tournus

11   Paray-le-Monial

Farges

Montceaux-l'Etoile

Blanot

Fléchères

St-Claude

Cluny   Berzé-la-Ville

COMTÉ

Anzy-le-Duc

Neuilly-en-Donjon

La Clayette

Mâcon

Semur-en-Brionnais

Bourg

[AUVERGNE]

St-Julien-de-Jonzy

Brou

Genève

12   Vichy

[SAVOI

St-Paul-de-Varax

Annecy

Villefranche

13   [LYONNAIS]

[DAUPHINÉ]

Aix

BOURGOGNE

FRESCO PAINTING IN THE PRIORY CHAPEL, MARTYRDOM OF SAINT VIN-
CENT, DETAIL, 12TH C., BERZÉ-LA-VILLE

TAPESTRY OF THE ADORATION OF THE MAGI, DETAIL, FLANDERS,
15TH C., TREASURY OF THE CATHEDRAL OF SAINT-ÉTIENNE, SENS
(Giraudon)

*Burgundy was a kingdom in the time of the Merovingian kings
and never forgot its past splendour. Romanesque art flourished
in the province and Saint Philibert of Tournus is its most
glorious example. With Cluny and Citeaux, Burgundy became
the cradle of Cistercian art which soon created hundreds
of Houses like that of Sainte-Madeleine at Vézelay where
Saint Bernard preached the Second Crusade in 1146 —
the most perfect and most pure example of the style.
The golden age of Burgundy was from the 14th to the 15th century
but it was a brief splendour for the House of Burgundy died
with Charles the Bold in 1477. Claus Sluter sculpted statues
of angels and the Prophets of the Well of Moses during the
reign of Philip the Bold and when his duke died in 1404 was
still alive to carve his tomb — the glory of the museum at
Dijon. During the reign of the astonishing art patron Philip
the Good, the Burgundian court was an extraordinarily brilliant
centre of the arts. We should not forget that Burgundy, Flanders
and the Franche-Comté were then a single domain, whose
dukes styled themselves Grand Dukes of the West. Even
to-day, Dijon has kept its air of a proud capital city.*

307

ANCY-LE-FRANC *Yonne.* J 8.

The château was built by the Clermont family in 1546 and is the work of Italian artists and shows the beginnings of the Classic Renaissance style in French architecture. Serlio drew up the plans of the château and was responsible for the Italianising decoration with pilaster and scallop decorations. Niccolo dell'-Abbate, Primaticcio and Méguassier, a French painter of the School of Fontainebleau, decorated the rooms in the château with a refinement and lavishness which makes their work even more interesting than the architecture. The frescoes, medallions and pannelling have all been preserved in excellent condition.

1 Courtyard of the château, 16th c. 2 Chambre des Arts, medallions by Primaticcio, 16th c.

ANZY-LE-DUC *Saône-et-Loire.* J 11.

The Romanesque church of Anzy-le-Duc and its enchanting octagonal tower seem to have been taken as models by the abbot Renaud de Semur for the building of the Madeleine of Vézelay. But unlike Vézelay, the church of Saint-Martin has preserved all its architectural features of the time, including its fine capitals and Romanesque frescoes.

3 Tower of the church of Saint-Martin, 11th c. 4-5 Capitals, 12th c.

APPOIGNY *Yonne.* J 8.

Church built in 1220 by Guillaume de Seignelay, bishop of Auxerre; the fine rood-screen dates from 1606 and was built on the orders of another bishop, François de Donadieu.

6 Rood-screen of the collegiate church, 1606.

APPOIGNY 6

ARBOIS *Jura.* L 10.

Highly interesting church of Saint-Just in a very pure regional, romanesque style. The church was recently restored and is crowned by a fine square tower.

7 Church of Saint-Just, 12th c., tower of 1528.

ARC-ET-SENANS 10

ARC-ET-SENANS *Doubs.* L 10.

The architect Claude-Nicolas Ledoux was imprisoned between 1793 and 1795 because his projects risked bankrupting the Treasury. He was a man of genius and visionary imagination. After carrying out a mission of inspection in 1773, he had proposed the building of an ideal but practical city, dedicated to the manufacture of salt, to Louis XV. The buildings of the Royal Salt Factory are still to be seen at Arc-et-Senans, for the factory was put into operation, but only half of the city (circular in design with a diameter of about 400 yards) was built. The entrance gate, the director's lodge, and the ornaments are all worthy monuments of one of the greatest French architects.

8 Claude-Nicolas Ledoux (1736-1806): The Director's Lodge of the Salt Factory of Chaux, 1780. 9 Entrance porch. 10 Sculpted urn motif. 11 Overall plan of the salt factory.

ANCY-LE-FRANC 2

ANCY-LE-FRANC I

ANZY-LE-DUC 3

ANZY-LE-DUC 4

ANZY-LE-DUC 5

ARBOIS 7

ARC-ET-SENANS 8

ARC-ET-SENANS 11

ARC-ET-SENANS 9

I

AUTUN *Saône-et-Loire.* J 10.

The tympanum of the cathedral of Autun was signed by Gislebertus in 1135. For the theme of the Last Judgment, he had carved a group of scenes with extremely elongated human figures, often naked, of extraordinary tragic expression. The tympanum is the finest known of its kind for the Romanesque period for it has the triple merit of being signed by its artist, being in a perfect state of preservation, and being a thing of beauty in itself. The cathedral was built in the Cluniac style in 1121, over the remains of Saint Lazare, and was completed 25 years later. The tunnel-vaulting of the nave and the fluted pilasters are, like those at Paray-le-Monial, harbingers of the Gothic style although they still belong to Burgundian Romanesque. The capitals constitute a kind of Bible in stone and follow the same themes as those at Saulieu (q.v.). The decoration of the cathedral was completed in the 15th century by Cardinal Rolin who was responsible for the fine stained-glass window of the Tree of Jesse in a side-altar (1515). Much of the cathedral's precious sculpture is now in the Musée Rolin which was the house of the chancellor Rolin, the famous lawyer who made the prosperity of his native town. Among the exhibits are one of the finest French primitives, the painting of the *Nativity* by the Master of Moulins (Jean Prevost?), sculpted capitals, and a very beautiful 15th-century Virgin with richly carved draperies.

The town of Autun existed well before the time of Gislebertus and many Roman monuments still recall the splendour of the town during the reign of Augustus. The theatre could hold 30 000 spectators, and the two gateways (Saint-André and Porte d'Arroux) were part of the original Roman fortifications with sixty-two towers, all now destroyed. The richness of numerous Roman patrician dwellings is attested by a number of superb mosaics, now in the Musée Rolin.

1 Porte Saint-André, Roman period. 2 Tympanum of the main portal of the cathedral of Saint-Lazare, by Gislebertus, 1135. 3 Detail from the left side of the tympanum, the Resurrection of the Dead. 4 Nave of the cathedral. 5 Capital of the south aisle, detail, Saint Vincent protected by two eagles.

MUSÉE ROLIN

6 Fragment from the lintel of the north portal of the cathedral: Eve in hiding, 12th c. 7 Sculpted detail: the Three Magi, 12th c. 8 Capital: the Flight into Egypt, 12th c. 9 The Vierge Bulliot, known as the Virgin of Autun, 15th c. 10 The Master of Moulins (15th c.): The Nativity.

9

10

2

4

3 BESOGEIRO GERINERLIOR AVA

5

6

7

8

AUXERRE 4

AVALLON 6

BAZOCHES 7

AUXERRE *Yonne.* J 8.

From the edge of the river Yonne a superb view may be obtained of the apses of several churches of the city, the finest being those of the cathedral Saint-Etienne, and the abbey church of Saint-Germain. This last is partly Romanesque, partly Gothic in style and contains a Carolingian crypt where 9th-century frescoes were discovered in 1927. The cathedral is entirely Gothic and was begun in 1215 in the style of Champagne. The façade is Flamboyant, and the original nave was so light and high that the piers supporting it had to be doubled. Splendid stained-glass windows in the choir, with their medley of grisaille, reds and blues (13th c.). In the crypt: a fresco painting of the Christ of the Apocalypse mounted on a horse - the only known example of this theme in painting (11th c.). Not the least interest of the cathedral is its sculpture, often praised or criticised for the almost excessive skill it displays. Particularly interesting are the medallions on the base, in the north portal, which resemble those of the cathedral of Orvieto, and in which religious sentiment was subordinated to purely artistic considerations. The bishop's palace (now the Préfecture) contains a beautiful gallery of 18 Romanesque arcades supported by colonnettes with sculpted capitals.
1 Cathedral of Saint-Étienne, façade of the 13th c., 14th c. 2 Medallion on the base, north portal, Adam and Eve expelled from Paradise, 13th c. 3 Bracket: Lust, 13th c. 4 Fresco in the crypt: Christ of the Apocalypse, 11th c. 5 Gallery in the Préfecture, 12th c.

AVALLON *Yonne.* J 9.

The columnar statue in the portal of the church of Saint-Lazare, the only survivor of eight, resembles those of Saint-Loup de Naud (q.v.) and Chartres (q.v.) but as the 11th-century church is earlier in construction than the two churches of the Ile-de-France, its style is probably of Burgundian inspiration.
6 A prophet, columnar statue in the main portal of the church of Saint-Lazare, 11th c.

BAZOCHES *Nièvre.* J 9.

The château of Bazoches was rebuilt by Vauban on the foundations of the original 13th-century castle and its towers offer a view reaching as far as Vézelay. The church in the village contains the tomb of the famous marshal, whose heart is kept in the Invalides.
7 The château, 13th-17th c.

BEAUNE *Côte-d'Or.* K 10.

The medieval architecture of the town has been greatly restored but its famous Hospice has remained a masterpiece of hospital architecture, of outstanding refinement and grace, as it was in the time of its creation by Nicolas Rolin, the great patron of Autun. He had chosen the style of building, the colours of the decoration, the tapestries, and had commissioned Rogier van der Weyden for the famous *Polyptych of the Last Judgment*, and his wishes are still respected by the nuns who continue the charitable work for which the Hospice had been built. The collegiate church of Notre-Dame should also be visited: its style is Burgundian Romanesque but the porch with its three Gothic bays dates from the 14th century. The small cul-de-sac of the same name leads to an annex containing the beautiful tapestries of the *Life of the Virgin* (15th c.) which had been commissioned by Nicolas Rolin's son, the Cardinal. Among the marvels of the Hospice, particular mention must be made of the roofs with their varnished tile roofs overlooking the *cour d'honneur*, the tunnel-vaulted beams of the roof of the patients' ward, the tapestries and Nevers faïences in the pharmacy.
8 Cour d'honneur of the Hospice, 15th c. 9 Patients' Ward. 10 Rogier van der Weyden (1400-1464): Polyptych of the Last Judgment. 11 Porch of the church, 14th c. 12 Impasse Notre-Dame.

AUXERRE 5

AUXERRE 3

AUXERRE 1

AUXERRE 2

BEAUNE 8

BEAUNE 9

BEAUNE 10

BEAUNE 12

BEAUNE 11

313

6

3

1

13

8

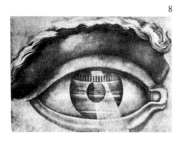

BESANÇON *Doubs.* L 9.

The "old Spanish town" of Besançon where Victor Hugo was born is an ancient Roman town with many striking monuments (Porte Noire, theatre and arena). The town owed its prosperity to Nicolas Perrenot de Granvelle, chancellor of the emperor Charles V, in the 16th century. From the same period dates the chancellor's palace with its Italianising courtyard that is one of the masterpieces of the town. The palace now contains the Musée Franc-Comtois and a famous series of tapestries of Charles V. The Palais de Justice dates from 1585 and was built by the architect Hugues Lamoin who was born at Gray and mostly worked at Dijon. The town still has kept many old bourgeois houses of the 16th century, including the Maison Mareschal (1516) which has a rather Gothic character. When the Franche-Comté was definitively given back to France by the treaty of Nymwegen in 1678, its finest fortifications were built on designs by Vauban; a well restored part of this citadel overlooks the river Doubs from a height of more than 300 yards. The city was enriched by many fine buildings in the 18th century: the Hopital Saint-Jacques, the church of the Madeleine, numerous *hôtels*, Claude-Nicolas Ledoux's theatre (hideously "embellished" in the 19th c.) and Nicole's Préfecture built after the designs of the architect Victor Louis. The watch-making industry at Besançon dates from 1713 when some 80 Swiss watchmakers all took refuge in the city after having been exiled for their rather too audacious political opinions. The two main attractions of the Musée des Beaux-Arts are the collection of French 18th-century drawings and the paintings of the most famous artist to be born in the region - Gustave Courbet.

1 Porte Noire or Triumphal Arch of Marcus Aurelius, Roman period, in the background, tower of the cathedral of Saint-Jean, 18th c. 2 Spanish house, rue de la Monnaie, 16th c. 3 Porte Rivotte, 1546, forepart of the 17th c. 4 Pharmacy of the Hopital Saint-Jacques, 1702. 5 Courtyard of the Palace of Nicolas Perrenot de Granvelle, 1547. 6 Watch tower of the citadel, 17th c. 7 The Préfecture, by Louis, 1778. 8 Cl.-N. Ledoux (1736-1806): Symbolic representation of the auditorium of the theatre of Besançon, engraving.

MUSÉE DES BEAUX-ARTS

9 F.-A. Vincent (1746-1816): Portrait of Bergeret de Grancourt. 10 François Boucher (1703-1770): Chinese fishing scene. 11 Fragonard (1732-1806): Garden with pine trees in Rome, drawing. 12 Courbet (1819-1877): The sleep-walker. 13 Clock with mannekin-strikers, German, late 16th c., incised and gilded copper.

2

4

7

5

9

11

10

12

315

BERZÉ-LA-VILLE *Saône-et-Loire.* K 11.

Of all French Romanesque frescoes, those in the Cluniac priory of Berzé like those at Auxerre are the only paintings to have really been executed "al fresco" according to the Italian technique, i.e. with water colours on a layer of wet plaster. They were discovered in 1877 and have preserved all the freshness of their dark colours on a blue back-ground. The themes are treated in an Oriental style and both the drawing and the stiffness of the figures' attitudes are reminiscent of the art of Byzantium and Ravenna.

1 Fresco in the apse of the upper chapel, Martyrdom of Saint Vincent, early 12th c. 2 Christ in Majesty.

BLANOT *Saône-et-Loire.* K 11.

The high tower surmounting the crossing of the transept of the modest little Romanesque church of Blanot is of architectural interest because of its Lombard arcading.

3 The church, early 11th c.

BRANCION *Saône-et-Loire.* K 11.

This feudal village is now almost deserted and has been preserved by the efforts of a few local historians. It contains the remains of a fine 10th-century castle, partly rebuilt in the 14th century, a sober Romanesque church in yellowstone, with a solid square tower covered with "lauzes" (12th c.), and in the church, 14th century frescoes in a good state of preservation.

4 Church of Saint-Pierre, 12th c. 5 Fresco in the church, Pilgrims arriving in Jerusalem, 14th c.

BROU 11

BROU 12

BROU *Ain.* K 12.

The monastery of Brou, near the gates of the town of Bourg, is a magnificent example of the transition from the Flamboyant to the Renaissance style. Those who prefer the sobriety of Romanesque architecture may be indifferent to its splendour, but the richness, dynamism and exuberance of its design and its sculpture cannot fail to excite the enthusiasm of connoisseurs of the style. Its sculptors seem to have defied the laws of matter and gravity by blending sculptures in the round, high- and low relief with unequalled audacity. The church and its treasures are the result of a vow made by Marguerite de Bourbon and accomplished by her daughter-in-law, Margaret of Austria. Magnificent white limestone façade, a luminous nave, stone rood-screen, seventy-four oak choir-stalls (1532) and three tombs of which the most beautiful, in our opinion, is that of Margaret of Austria, white marble retable of the Annunciation in the chapel of Sainte-Marguerite, and stained-glass windows in the chapel, are among the treasures of the church. The regional museum of the Ain department has been installed nearby in the monastery buildings, which have a fine cloister dating from 1506. The whole of the architecture here is of the 16th century, without a single exception.

6 Church of Brou, 16th c. Façade. 7 Rood-screen. 8 Choir-stalls, 1532. 9 Tomb of Margaret of Austria. 10 Sybils, detail of the tomb of Philibert le Beau. 11 Detail from the altar of the Annunciation, in the chapel of Sainte-Marguerite. 12 Margaret and her patron saint, stained-glass window in the chapel.

BERZÉ-LA-VILLE 1

BERZÉ-LA-VILLE 2

BLANOT 3

BRANCION 5

BRANCION 4

BROU 6

BROU 8

BROU 10

BROU 9

BROU 7

317

BUSSY-RABUTIN I

CHAPAIZE 2

CHAUVIREY-LE-CHATEL II

BUSSY-RABUTIN (near Laumes) *Côte-d'Or.* K 9.

The spirit of the Grand Siècle (17th century) survives in the bitter-sweet captions underlining the portraits of the mistresses and enemies of Roger de Bussy-Rabutin which may be seen in the gallery of the château. This famous cousin of Madame de Sevigné was a noted rake and a notorious pamphleteer and it was here that he finished his adventurous and amorous career. The façade of the château, which was built on his orders, is of a very beautiful classic simplicity.

I Façade of the château, 1649, wings of the reign of Henri II.

CHAPAIZE (at Saint-Gengoux-le-National) *Saône-et-Loire.* K 11.

The countryside around Cluny is filled with tall and massive, but elegant, church towers decorated with narrow pilasters, and often supported by cupolas on squinches. The 115 foot-high tower of the church of Chapaize is a masterly prototype of the style.

2 Tower of the church of Saint-Martin, late 11th c.

LA CHARITÉ-SUR-LOIRE *Nièvre.* I 10.

The two beautiful towers of the Romanesque church at La Charité can be seen long before reaching the town. One, the Tour Sainte-Croix, is high and pointed while the other is more squat but they are both equally elegant with their arcading and narrow pilasters. The immense church was once part of a Benedictine priory that was famous in the whole of Christendom and was a dependency of its neighbour at Cluny. The sculpted decoration of the portals and nave shows Burgundian Romanesque art at its most perfect.

3 Tour Sainte-Croix and river Loire, 11th c. 4 Detail of the lintel of a portal: Adoration of the Magi, 11th c. (now removed to the south crossing of the transept).

CHATILLON-SUR-SEINE *Côte-d'Or.* K 8.

It was here that the wonderful discovery was made in 1947 of the great "Vix treasure" which is now the pride of French museums. When a nearby tumulus was excavated, the discovery was made of a chariot bearing the remains of a young woman wearing all her jewels. At her sides were several pieces of funerary furnishings and the great bronze crater, the largest ever to be found. We now know that this crater dates from the second half of the 6th century B.C. and that it was probably made by Greek bronze workers in the south of Italy and had been imported into Burgundy for sale in an important local market. It was cast in one piece and its relief decoration was probably made from a wax-cast. This treasure is not the only attraction of the Musée de Châtillon (formerly Hôtel Philandrier, built in a pure Burgundian Renaissance style) for it also contains a fine Entombment which was given to the church of the Cordeliers by the Lord of Romprey in 1527. The church of Saint-Vorlès at Châtillon dates for the most part from the 10th century.

5 Church of Saint-Vorlès, 10th c.

MUSEUM

6 Vix crater, height 64 1/2 inches, 6 th c. B.C. 7 Detail of the lid. 8 Detail of frieze on the neck of the crater. 9 Detail of the handle of the crater, Gorgon's head flanked by volutes. 10 Entombment, c. 1527.

CHAUVIREY-LE-CHATEL *Haute-Saône.* L 8.

The chapel of Saint-Hubert is part of a now ruined castle, and was built in a traditional Gothic style in 1484. The main altar has a fine stone retable of the same period.

II Retable of the chapel of Saint-Hubert, 15th c.

LA CHARITÉ-SUR-LOIRE 3

LA CHARITÉ-SUR-LOIRE 4

CHATILLON-SUR-SEINE 7

CHATILLON-SUR-SEINE 9

CHATILLON-SUR-SEINE 6

CHATILLON-SUR-SEINE 8

CHATILLON-SUR-SEINE 5

CHATILLON-SUR-SEINE 10

319

CITEAUX (at Saint-Nicolas-les-Citeaux) *Côte-d'or.* K 10.
Without having to see the few wretched remains of the buildings, the name of Citeaux alone is enough to remind one of the importance of the great abbey that Saint Bernard, founder of the Cistercian order, founded in 1098 and inhabited in 1114.
1 Façade of the former abbey library, 15th c.

CLAMECY *Nièvre.* J 9.
The church of Clamecy is a vast Gothic structure with a Flamboyant façade and a three-tiered nave. Similar in type to those at Auxerre (q.v.), and Nevers (q.v.), it was begun in the early 13th century and finished in the 14th and 15th centuries. Numerous old houses still line the winding streets of the old town.
2 Façade of the collegiate church of Saint-Martin, 14th-15th c.

LA CLAYETTE *Saône-et-Loire.* K 12.
The pretty château of La Clayette is surrounded by a lake formed with the waters of the Genète and has been partly modernised. The graceful turrets heighten its fairy-tale quality.
3 The château, 14th c.

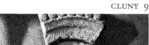
LA CLAYETTE 3

CLUNY 9

CLUNY *Saône-et-Loire.* K 11.
Cluny is one of the most famous names in Romanesque art and the church of Cluny was once the vastest in Christendom (nave 175 yards long, 5 steeples, 2 towers) and the most powerful and influential of its type. All that now remains of the great structure are a tower and a museum but they attest to the former importance of Cluny just as much as the numerous famous Cluniac churches of the region. Cluny was first and foremost a school of Romanesque architecture in which every tendency came together, and which was little marked by local Burgundian influences. The third of the abbey churches, Saint-Pierre-Saint-Paul de Cluny, was founded in the 9th century but building continued until the end of the 12th century. All we can now see is the tower of the Holy Water, part of the nave, and, in the Musée du Farinier, the finest of the capitals from the choir, decorated with the Seasons, the tones of plain chant, the Rivers of Paradise, the Virtues, etc. Already close to the Gothic in style, they are characterised by their elegance, refinement, intense expression and admirable perfection of technique. Many of the houses that are the glory of the town are of the same period: the church of Saint-Marcel has a fine octagonal Romanesque tower, while the façade of the palace of Pope Gelasius is Gothic (13th c.) Cluny is likely to disappoint the visitor however, unless he visits the stone remains displayed in the Musée du Farinier, for the abbey became too rich and fell into decadence after the 14th century. It was damaged during the Revolution, largely destroyed when its stones were sold with the blessing of the authorities. Thus not even Viollet-le-Duc himself would have been able to restore it to its former glory.
4 Tower of the Holy Water (Clocher de l'Eau-bénite) of the abbey church of Saint-Pierre-Saint-Paul, 12th c. 5 Interior of the Musée du Farinier, museum of sculpture, 13th c. 6-7-8 Capitals of the abbey church, 12th c. 9 Agnus Dei, keystone of the vault of the abbey church, 12th c. 10 Tower of the church of Saint-Marcel, 12th c. 11 Romanesque house, 12th c.

CITEAUX 1

CLUNY 4

CLAMECY 2

CLUNY 11

CLUNY 10

CLUNY 5

CLUNY 6

CLUNY 7

CLUNY 8

321

1

DIJON *Côte-d'Or.* K 9.

In 14th-century France three capital cities fought one another for primacy: Paris, Avignon, and Dijon in Burgundy. The states of the Duke of Burgundy comprised Burgundy itself, the Franche-Comté and a large part of the Netherlands and constituted a powerful threat to the French king. The wealth of the Dukes seemed unlimited and was constantly increased by a series of brilliant marriages. The four most famous Dukes who succeeded one another, Philip the Bold, John the Fearless, Philip the Good, and Charles the Bold, all left traces of their rule in the buildings which make Dijon one of the main artistic centres of modern France.

The palace of the Dukes of Burgundy contains an astonishing kitchen dating from 1433 which is as famous as that at Fontevrault, and various rooms in which Burgundian art treasures are exhibited; the palace itself was begun in the 14th century and was decorated by the greatest artists from Versailles in the 17th and 18th centuries, when it was the meeting place of the "states of Burgundy" from 1674 onwards. Mansart, Gabriel and Verberckt were among the artists who took part in the work. But it was above all in their tombs that the dukes of Burgundy wished to perpetuate their memories, like the Egyptian pharaohs of old. In 1383 Philip the Bold built the Charterhouse of Champmol to contain the tombs of his family and invited the sculptor Claus Sluter from Holland to undertake the work. Although the Charterhouse was destroyed in 1793, his portal flanked with the kneeling figures of Philip the Bold and his wife Margaret of Flanders (1394) has still survived, as has also the Well of Moses (Puits de Moïse) which was the base for a calvary originally painted and gilded by Jean Malouel. Sluter's genius influenced the whole of medieval art: brilliant as it is, the Well of Moses is eclipsed by the statue of the prophet Jeremiah whose intensity of expression has never been equalled. The other tombs of the dukes are now in the Musée des Beaux-Arts. The most interesting churches in Dijon include Saint-Bénigne. Now all that remains of the original 11th-century abbey is a crypt with a groined vault and barrel-vaulting and a chapter house, for it was rebuilt in the Burgundian Gothic style in the 14th century. The church of Saint-Michel was built in Flamboyant Gothic in the early 16th century and was completed by the addition of two towers in the 17th century. Notre-Dame is a Gothic masterpiece, built between 1230 and 1251 after the examples of the cathedrals of Soissons and Laon. Its flat, rectangular façade, which was once ornamented with gilded statues, opens into a deep porch which is unique of its kind. The nave is surrounded by a gallery above the high windows, of an elegance which in no way diminishes its solidity, and ends in a pointed apse.

1 Ducal palace, Tour de Bar, 14th c., and Bellegarde staircase, 1614. 2 Abbey of Saint-Bénigne, monks' dormitory, 13th c. (now an archaeological museum). 3 Façade of the church of Notre-Dame, 13th c. 4 Façade of the church of Saint-Michel, 16th-17th c. 5 Le Présidial, 14th c. 6 Hôtel Chambellan, keystone of the vault of the spiral staircase, 1490. 7 Staircase of the hôtel Magnin, 17th c. 8 François Rude (1784-1855): Fountain (Fontaine du Barenzai). 9 Hôtel de Berbis, and entrance of the Rue Vénerie.

8

2

3

4

9

5

6

7

The Musée des Beaux-Arts, contains many of the works which were the pride of Burgundy: the Salle des Gardes (period of Philip the Good) contains the finest works from the Charterhouse of Champmol, including Melchior de Broederlam's retable (1399), which shows traces of Sienese influence. The museum also contains examples of Burgundian sculpture and gold-and silver-work of the 15th and 16th centuries. Important modern works including Manet's *Fille du Bar*, and a collection of sculptures by Pompon (1855-1933).

Claus Sluter's work may also be seen in the archaeological museum; the Musée Magnin is devoted to French painting, and Rude's works are displayed in the church of Saint-Étienne, now a museum. As was to be expected, the town was enriched by a number of fine courtiers' mansions in the period of its greatest splendour, under its dukes. Among the finest, mention should be made of the hôtel Chambellan, the Présidial, the hôtels Milsand and De Vogüe, etc., for their portals, their staircases, their rooms, and their great architectural and sculptural interest. The whole city is a witness to the high degree of civilisation and art attained in the 15th century, in which Flemish, Italian and French influences all combined.

CHARTERHOUSE OF CHAMPMOL

1 Claus Sluter (died 1406): Philip the Bold, statue from the portal of the Charterhouse, 15th c. 2 Sluter: Well of Moses, 15th c. 3 Sluter: the prophet Jeremiah.

MUSÉE DES BEAUX-ARTS

4 Sluter: Tomb of John the Fearless, 15th c. 5 Mourner, from the tomb of John the Fearless. 6 Melchior de Broederlam (born c. 1388): Retable of the Charterhouse of Champmol. 7 The Master of Flémalle (Robert Campin c. 1380-1444): Nativity. 8 Richard Tassel (c. 1580-1660): Portrait of Catherine de Montholon.

5

8

DOLE 10

DOLE 9

DOLE *Jura.* L 10

The town of Dôle contains many fine works by artists of the Franche-Comté: first, the church of Notre-Dame in a fine Flamboyant style, although built in the 16th century, the Sainte-Chapelle with its façade by Hugues Le Rupt and doorway with its fine chiselled railing decorated by the goldsmith Anatole Chastel (1611), and the Hôtel-Dieu with its Italianate outer balcony (1683) and two-storied cloister by the architect Boyvin.

9 Doorway of the Collège de l'Arc, 16th c. 10 Hôtel-Dieu, by Boyvin, 1683.

3

2

1

4

7

6

DONZY-LE-PRÉ (at Saint-Martin-du-Pré) *Nièvre.* I 9.

The tympanum of the church of Saint-Martin deserves to be more widely known for it contains a curious representation of the Virgin in Majesty under an arcade, flanked by an Angel and Saint-John the Baptist. This highly original work is of capital importance for the history of Burgundian art, and was restored in 1939.

1 Tympanum and south portal of the church of Saint-Martin-du-Pré, 12th c., restored.

FARGES *Saône-et-Loire.* K 11.

The church dates from the first third of the 11th century and is supported by thick round pillars without capitals like those in the church of Saint-Philibert at Tournus (q.v.). In the nave, the slightly pointed vault is further proof that the pointed arch appeared in Burgundian Romanesque art before the Gothic period.

2 Nave of the church, 11th c.

FLAVIGNY-SUR-OZERAIN *Côte-d'Or.* K 9.

Apart from being a centre of manufacture for anisette-flavoured sweets, the little town of Flavigny is of great historic interest and its ramparts (Porte du Val and Porte du Bourg) surround many old Gothic houses. Of the ruins of an old abbey only the Carolingian crypt is of any interest. The church of Saint-Genest contains a fine Renaissance rood-screen, and a famous Burgundian statue of an angel.

3 Carolingian crypt of Sainte-Reine, 9th c. 4 Angel of the Annunciation, 15th c., church of Saint-Genest. 5 Nave and rood-screen of the church of Saint-Genest, 13th-14th c.

FLÉCHÈRES 6

FLÉCHÈRES (at Fareins) *Ain.* K 11.

The design of the château dates from the early 17th century and has been attributed to Du Cerceau. The high slate roof, in the Henri IV style, is in contrast to the medieval moat below. The decoration of the fireplaces and the arabesque ornamentation of the ceilings justifies a visit of the apartments.

6 The château, by J. Sève after design by Du Cerceau, 1610.

FLEURIGNY *Yonne.* J 7.

The château of Fleurigny is a beautiful dwelling of the Renaissance period, with towers of an earlier château (14th c.). Its noble architecture is enriched by painted panelling, a superb fireplace, a chapel with sculpted panel vaulting, and a stained-glass window by Jean Cousin.

FLEURIGNY 7

7 Lintel of the chimney in the Salle des Gardes, 16th c. 8 The Seminary, 17th c.

FLEURIGNY 8

FONTENAY *Côte-d'Or.* K 8.

The role of window lights in Cistercian religious architecture was always symbolic and constituted the sole decoration. Those at Fontenay are particularly striking by their aesthetic perfection and are as intellectually satisfying as a Bach fugue. The seven windows above the doorway symbolise the Seven Sacraments, and there are five openings in the triumphal arch preceding the choir. Above the altar, two rows of five windows symbolise the Holy Trinity, and there are another three openings in the north crossing of the transept. The play of light and shade is sufficient decoration in itself. Apart from this vast church, so severely Cistercian in its style, the cloister of the abbey has been restored, with its Romanesque arches supported on short coupled pillars with capitals. The abbey of Fontenay was formerly used as a paper factory but has been beautifully restored by its present owners.

Abbey church, 12th c. 9 The nave looking towards the front. 10 The nave looking towards the choir. 11 Transept and statue of Notre-Dame de Fontenay, 13th c. 12 The cloister.

DONZY-LE-PRÉ 1

FARGES 2

FLAVIGNY 4

FLAVIGNY 3

FLAVIGNY 5

FONTENAY 12

FONTENAY 9

FONTENAY 10

FONTENAY 11

327

GRAY 2

GRAY I

GRAY *Haute-Saône*. L 9.

With its many-coloured tiled roof and its white façade with pink marble columns in the arcade, the Town Hall of Gray is in perfect keeping with the style of this pretty little town. The museum is devoted to Prud'hon who fled to Gray at the end of the Revolution and contains some 18th-century French and Flemish works.

1 Town Hall, by Pierre Arnoux, 1568. 2 P.-P. Prud'hon (1758-1823): Queen Hortense, black and white chalk drawing, museum.

MONTBENOIT *Doubs*. L 10.

The ancient abbey of the Augustine monks was founded in the 12th century but only completed in the 16th. The cloister dates from 1445 and is in an early Gothic style. The 16th-century choir of the church contains stalls which are famous for their satirical decorations which were intended to be a daily reminder for the monks of the dangers of earthly passions. Without quite reaching the level of great art, the carvings are remarkable for the liveliness, verve and realism of the scenes depicted.

3 Choir-stalls of the abbey church, the Humiliation of Aristotle, 1527. 4 Choir-stall: Women fighting.

MONTCEAUX-L'ÉTOILE *Saône-et-Loire*. J 11.

The tympanum of the church is so finely sculpted that the artist is supposed to have worked afterwards at Vézelay, a full master of his art. The angels with their symmetrically deployed wings display a rare mastery.

5 Tympanum of the church portal, the Ascension, c. 1120.

MONTCLEY *Doubs*. L 9.

The extraordinary château of Montcley immediately recalls the style of Cl.-N. Ledoux by its semi-circular façade and portico with Ionic columns. It was, in fact, built by Bertrand in 1778 under the influence of Ledoux who was working nearby at Besançon and Arc-et-Senans (q. v.). The château is in a perfect state of preservation and has kept its original furnishings and decoration.

6 Façade of the château, by Bertrand, 1778. 7 Rear façade seen from the gardens.

MONTIGNY-SUR-AUBE *Côte-d'Or*. K 8.

Although only one of its three wings has survived, the north façade and the seignorial chapel of the château of Montigny show it to have been one of the great achievements of Renaissance civil architecture in France. The style is markedly Italianate for only Serlio could have inspired the motifs in the coffered ceiling of the chapel and the beautiful rhythm of the forty-four columns on the ground floor of the façade. The chapel is lit by three rose-windows and contains the tomb of the Amoncourt family, the founders of the château.

8 North façade of the château, 16th c. 9 Interior of the chapel, 16th c.

MONTRÉAL-EN-AUXOIS *Yonne*. J 9.

The fine qualities of the 12th-century church in this pretty feudal village — one of the favourite residences of the Dukes of Burgundy — were acknowledged by Viollet-le-Duc. The church contains very beautiful choir-stalls, carved with an elegant simplicity by the brothers Rigoley in the 16th century. They may be compared to those in the church of Montbenoît, but the satire in the reliefs is harsher and less naive in tone.

10 The Baptism of Christ, choir-stall in the church, by the brothers Rigoley, 1522. 11 Original Sin, choir-stall.

MONTBENOIT 4

MONTBENOIT 3

MONTCEAUX-L'ÉTOILE 5

MONTCLEY 7

MONTCLEY 6

MONTIGNY-SUR-AUBE 8

MONTIGNY-SUR-AUBE 9

MONTRÉAL-EN-AUXOIS 11

MONTREAL-EN-AUXOIS 10

NEUILLY-EN-DONJON *Allier.* J 11.

The sculptures of the portal of the little Romanesque church at Neuilly represent the Adoration of the Magi in the tympanum, and the Feast at the House of Simon to the right of the Original Sin on the lintel. The elongation of the figures recalls the style of the carvings at Autun and Anzy-le-Duc (q.v.).

1 Tympanum of the church portal, 12th c.

NEUVY-SAUTOUR *Yonne.* J 8.

The church is entirely Renaissance in style and has two fine pilastered portals which are a compromise between the styles of Champagne and Burgundy. In the church, a high cross decorated with 16th-century statues.

2 Portal of the church, 16th c.

NEVERS *Nièvre.* I 10.

The two main churches in Nevers illustrate every aspect of medieval church architecture: Saint-Étienne is Romanesque and has a remarkable apse and nave; the cathedral of Saint-Cyr with its double apse is partly Romanesque and partly Gothic. Both churches are of the highest interest and are in perfect harmony with the beautiful old town and narrow quiet streets leading to the beautiful square of the Ducal Palace, lined with uniform-style houses overlooking the Loire. The Renaissance Palace has been restored to its former splendour and stands next to the elegant 18th-century archbishop's palace.

Nevers was a ducal city and owes its celebrity to its faïence manufacture which was established by the Duke Louis de Gonzague in 1575 after his return from Italy. The factory was at first strongly influenced by the faïences of Urbino but then developed a style of its own and flourished until the Revolution. Spun-glass and enamel-work were also specialities in the town. Examples of these local products may be seen in the Musée Frédéric-Blandin. The Porte de Croux is a remnant of the original 14th-century fortifications of the town and has been transformed into an archaeological museum.

3 Apse of the church of Saint-Etienne, 12th c. **4** Nave of the church, 12th c. **5** Apse of the cathedral of Saint-Cyr, 13th c. **6** Porte de Croux, 14th c. **7** Ducal Palace, 16th c. **8** Archbishop's palace, 18th c. **9** Nevers faïence plate, 17th c., Musée Frédéric-Blandin. **10** Large vase in Nevers faïence, height 34 inches., 17th c., Musée Frédéric-Blandin.

ORNANS 12

ORNANS 11

ORNANS *Doubs.* L 10.

Most of Courbet's paintings, which his critics thought so irreverent in style, were inspired by the countryside and the peasants of Ornans. A small museum has been devoted to his memory by his native town but many of his favourite subjects are rather to be seen in the surrounding landscape.

MUSÉE COURBET, in the Town Hall.

11 Courbet (1819-1877): Self-portrait at Sainte-Pélagie. **12** Courbet: Landscape near Ornans.

NEUILLY-EN-DONJON 1

NEVERS 4

NEUVY-SAUTOUR 2

NEVERS 3

NEVERS 5

NEVERS 6

NEVERS 7

NEVERS 8

NEVERS 9

NEVERS 10

PARAY-LE-MONIAL *Saône-et-Loire.* J 11.

Only the basilica of the Sacré-Cœur at Paray-le-Monial can give us an idea of how the mother abbey-church of Cluny must have looked before it was destroyed, when it was the largest church in all of Christendom (before Saint-Peter's had been built in Rome). Paray-le-Monial was built on the same plan as Cluny under the direction of Saint Hugues and was begun in 1109. It is a model of Cluniac architecture and distinguished by its severe simplicity. Although its storeyed apse may recall the Romanesque style of the Auvergne, its façade and nave are purest Burgundian. The two towers over the façade date respectively from the 11th century (south tower), and the 12th but the north tower is the most decorated of the two. The nave is so close in spirit to the Gothic style that it is almost surprising to see its Romanesque elements. The vaulting is carried by pilasters and columns which soar up to a height of 80 feet, and the ambulatory and three chapels are supported by pilasters as in the classical orders of architecture. The aisles have pointed barrelvaults according to the technique used in Burgundian Romanesque from the 11th century onwards. Although the church was consecrated to the cult of Sainte-Marguerite-Marie Alacoque in 1875, when it became a basilica, it managed to preserve its original identity and escape the banal decoration that has disfigured many other places of pilgrimage.
The Town Hall contains a museum of local antiquities and was the house of a rich Renaissance draper.
Basilica of the Sacré-Cœur, 12th c. **1** The apse and tower. **2** Capitals. **3** Ambulatory. **4** Town Hall, 1525.

PERRECY-LES-FORGES *Saône-et-Loire.* J 11.

The cherubims surrounding God in his mandala in the tympanum of the church of Perrecy have six wings each and are a peculiarity of Burgundian art. They have a strangely beautiful dragon-fly appearance and are of the same date as the portal of Montceaux-l'Etoile.
5 Tympanum of the church portal, God in Majesty; on the lintel: the Passion, c. 1120.

PIERRE (at Pierre-de-Bresse) *Saône-et-Loire.* K 10.

The Dijon artist Jean Dubois took part in the decoration of the château at Pierre which is characterised by its four towers crowned by slate domes with high campaniles. Beautiful railings and a finely proportioned pink marble staircase.
6 The château of Pierre, 17th c.

PIERRE 6

RATILLY 9

PONTIGNY *Yonne.* J 8.

The enormous abbey church of Pontigny has survived intact and still seems to huddle close to the ground in the bare landscape. In length (over 300 feet) it is nearly the equal of Notre-Dame in Paris, and its Romanesque style, its Cistercian simplicity and wide ambulatory supported by cross-ribbed vaulting (13th c.) make it one of the most beautiful churches in the region. It was a meeting place for intellectuals early in the present century thanks to the Decades organised by the philosopher Desjardins. The entrance porch preceding the church is a frequent feature in the great Burgundian abbey churches, but few have survived in as good a state.
7 The abbey church, 12th-13th c. **8** The porch. 12th c.

RATILLY (near Treigny) *Yonne.* I 9.

The château is built in curious yellow sandstone and has kept all the medieval characteristics of a fortified dwelling and now stands surrounded by tall trees.
9 The château, 13th c., restored.

PARAY-LE-MONIAL 4

PARAY-LE-MONIAL 1

PARAY-LE-MONIAL 3

PARAY-LE-MONIAL 2

PERRECY-LES-FORGES 5

PONTIGNY 8

PONTIGNY 7

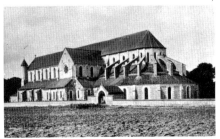

LA ROCHEPOT (or La Roche-Pot, at Nolay) *Côte-d'Or*. K 10.

The recently diverted road no longer runs past the château of Rochepot with its many-coloured, tiled roof, perched up on its rock overlooking the village. It was the birth-place of Philippe Pot whose tomb is a masterpiece of Renaissance sculpture and has now been removed to the Louvre (see page 140). The château was damaged but rebuilt and restored by M. Sadi-Carnot and has kept its medieval character.

I The château, 15th c., restored.

SAINT-CLAUDE *Jura*. L 11.

The church was begun in 1380 and completed in the 15th century without being touched by the then prevailing taste for the Flamboyant style. It has survived in its originally massive simplicity and is an example of the true style of the Franche-Comté. A sculptor from Geneva, Jean de Vitry, carved the admirable choir-stalls which are of a mastery and variety unequalled in 15th-century French art.

2 Back of the choir-stalls, by Jean de Vitry, 15th c.

SAINT-FARGEAU *Yonne*. I 9.

When the Grande Demoiselle (Mademoiselle de Montpensier) was exiled to the château of Saint-Fargeau by Louis XIV she brought all the arts of the capital with her when she asked Le Vau to rebuild the courtyard. The château is built in rose-coloured brick and is partly medieval, but it was rebuilt in the Renaissance and the 17th century. The pretty little village it overlooks has a 15th-century belfry, a Gothic church and, in the interior, a 15th-century polychrome stone Pietà.

3 Angle of the *cour d'honneur*, by Le Vau, 1652.

SAINT-JULIEN-DE-JONZY *Saône-et-Loire*. J 12.

The Romanesque tympanum of the portal of the otherwise modern church of Saint-Julien bears a striking resemblance to that at Charlieu (q.v.) and was probably by the same hand for the movement of the angels and the rich carving of the stone show an equal mastery.

4 Tympanum of the church portal, 12th c.

SAINT-PAUL-DE-VARAX *Ain*. K 12.

Like those of Charlieu, Montceaux-l'Étoile or Perrecy-les-Forges (q.v.), the Romanesque church of Saint-Paul has a tympanum with a Christ in Majesty flanked by two angels above a remarkable carved lintel. It is to be hoped that this masterpiece will soon be restored.

5 Tympanum of the centre portal of the church, 11th c.

SAINT-PÈRE-SOUS-VÉZELAY *Yonne*. J 9.

The various parts of the church illustrating the three phases of the Gothic style are no longer intact but the essential elements have been preserved such as the gable on the façade with its vertical figures of Christ, the Virgin and several saints, including a very beautiful Saint-Étienne (underneath the Christ). The draperies and faces are sculpted with great distinction and their air of benevolent dignity is particularly striking. The archaeological museum contains various prehistoric, Gallo-Roman and Merovingian antiquities found in the neighbourhood.

6 Gable of the church of Notre-Dame, 13th c. 7 Narthex, 14th c.

LA ROCHEPOT I

SAINT-CLAUDE 2

ST-FARGEAU 3

ST-PAUL-DE-VARAX 5

ST-JULIEN-DE-JONZY 4

ST-PÈRE-SOUS-VÉZELAY 7

ST-PÈRE-SOUS-VÉZELAY 6

335

ST-RÉVERIEN I

SAINT-REVERIEN *Nièvre.* J 9.

So many country churches in France are rich in treasures that it is difficult to choose between them. The church at Saint-Réverien has a fine Romanesque nave which escaped successive restorations, and a doorway flanked by winged cherubims of Byzantine inspiration.

I Cherubim of the portal, 12th c.

SAULIEU *Côte-d'Or.* J 9.

The capitals of the basilica of Saulieu take pride of place over the gastronomic fame of the town, the museum with its collection of animal sculptures by Pompon, a native of the town, and even the basilica of Saint-Andoche itself, which has been so damaged and so restored that it has lost the original aspect of the Romanesque church that was consecrated in 1119. All that needs to be mentioned here are the choir and the aisles, famous for their capitals. The three types of decoration are biblical scenes, animal and floral motifs. They are all distinguished by a highly personal style, their slightly mocking tone, vigorous design, and a handiwork which seems to have been deliberately rough despite the astonishing skill they display. Most astonishing are the compositions which run right round the corbels of certain capitals. Each one seems to be a living illustration of the Medieval Bible.

2 Detail of the porch, 12th c. 3 North aisle of the basilica of Saint-Andoche, Balaam on his she-ass stopped by the angel of Jehovah, 12th c. 4 South aisle, the Hanging of Judas. 5 The owl of Minerva-Athena. 6 View of the basilica from the square.

SEMUR-EN-AUXOIS 10   SEMUR-EN-AUXOIS 8

SEMUR-EN-AUXOIS *Côte-d'Or.* J 9.

The various elements such as sculpture and stained-glass of the beautiful Gothic church of Semur-en-Auxois rival the façade for elegance. The façade dates from the 14th century and a graceful porch was added in the 15th, but it lost its statues during the Revolution. The choir is decorated with foliated capitals of a great elegance and the triforium above is punctuated with equally interesting masks. Going back even further in date is the notorious Bleds portal (13th c.) with its confused and agitated sculpture which depicts the life of Saint Thomas without ever reaching the level of real art; more interesting are the arch mouldings. In the Lady Chapel, the fine stained-glass windows, somewhat archaic considering their date (1250), were lucky enough to please Viollet-le-Duc when he restored the church.

7 Façade of the church of Notre-Dame, 14th-15th c. 8 Detail of the Bleds portal, late 13th c. 9 Choir of the church, 13th c. 10 Stained-glass window of the Butchers' Guild, 15th c.

SAULIEU 2

SAULIEU 6

SAULIEU 5

SAULIEU 3

SAULIEU 4

SEMUR-EN-AUXOIS 9

SEMUR-EN-AUXOIS 7

337

SEMUR-EN-BRIONNAIS *Saône-et-Loire.* J 12.

Semur is the capital of the Brionnais, a region filled with the Romanesque churches built at the instigation of Saint Hugues who was the abbot of Cluny and a member of the noble Semur family. All these churches are built in a yellow limestone which is very easily carved, thus explaining the similarity of styles and technique that have been found. In the church of Semur the Small Portal has similar arch-mouldings to those of Charlieu. The tympanum of the main doorway is as nearly always, decorated with the themes of Christ in Majesty and the Evangelists, and the lintel of Semur is as crowded with carving as in other churches of the Brionnais, and depicts the story of Saint Hilary.

1 Apse of the church, 12th c., and tower, 13th c. **2** Saint-Hilaire condemned at the Council of Selencié in 539, lintel over the main portal, 12th c. **3** Petit Portail (Small Portal), 12th c.

SENS *Yonne.* I 7.

The town of Sens stands on the frontiers of Burgundy and is of considerable importance in the history of Gothic art. Saint-Louis was married and Thomas Becket preached in its vast cathedral, which lost a tower in the 19th century, and Abélard was condemned in the nearby 13th-century Synodal Palace. The sculpture decorating the façade as high as the top of the tower (19th-century additions) is somewhat mutilated but the portal consecrated to Saint-Étienne is an important link between the art of the Ile-de-France and that of Burgundy at the beginning of the Gothic period. The vast luminous nave was so admired by Corot that he devoted his last painting to it — a magnificent gold-yellow composition with a single patch of red in the center.

SENS 6

The superb stained-glass windows which decorate the nave date from the 12th to the 17th centuries. The main themes are *Life of Saint Eustache, Life of Saint Thomas of Canterbury* and the *Tree of Jesse* (1500), and it is known that the famous stained-glass artists of Troyes came to work in Sens in 1500. Equally famous are the Flemish tapestries of the Treasury. A few remains of the Roman ramparts and several wood-beamed Renaissance houses recall the remote past of the town.

4 Façade of the cathedral Saint-Etienne, 13th c., and Palais Synodal. **5** Main portal, late 12th c. **6** J.-B.-C. Corot (1787-1822): Interior of the cathedral of Sens, Louvre Museum. **7** The Adoration of the Magi, Brussels tapestry, 15th c. Cathedral Treasury.

SULLY-LE-CHATEAU *Saône-et-Loire.* K 10.

Sully is more of a palace than a castle but despite its date (16th-17th c.) and its Louis XIV style façade it is still surrounded by anachronistic moats. Its beautifully designed classic courtyard is ornamented with arched windows and the building is generally attributed to Nicolas Ribonnier, the architect of the château of Pailly.

8 North façade of the château, 18th c.

TANLAY *Yonne.* J 8.

In comparison to Ancy-le-Franc, the château of Tanlay shows the liberation of the French classic Renaissance style from Italian influence. The domes crowning the corner towers are in the tradition of the Burgundian châteaux. The château was completed in 1643 by Le Muet, an architect from Dijon, and with its outbuildings is typically French in style. The 17th-century furnishings, wall hangings, woodwork and works of art in the apartments are of an exceptional unity of style and consistent high quality and were originally due to Patricelli d'Hemery, Mazarin's Superintendant of Finances. Frescoes in the château symbolise the religious troubles which were to end in the Massacre of Saint-Bartholomew.

9 Portail-Neuf of the château and bridge with obelisks, 17th c. **10** Facade facing the park, 17th c.

SEMUR-EN-BRIONNAIS 1

SEMUR-EN-BRIONNAIS 2

SENS 4

SENS 5

SENS 7

TANLAY 9

SULLY-LE-CHATEAU 8

TANLAY 10

TONNERRE *Yonne.* J 8.

The Hospital of Tonnerre was founded by Margaret of Burgundy more than a century before the creation of the Hospice at Beaune. The hospital contained a great hall more than 300 feet long with oaken barrel vaulting which may still be admired, seven centuries later. At the end of the hall, to the right, is the chapel which contains another masterpiece, an Entombment, by two little known sculptors, Jean Michel and Georges de la Sonnette. The work was offered as a gift in 1454 by a rich citizen of Tonnerre, Lancelot de Buronfosse. The treatment of the old man on the left of the group - Saint Nicodemus - shows an obvious stylistic affinity with Sluter's *Well of Moses* in its similar richness of draperies, gravity, severity of expression, and uncompromising beauty.

1 Beams of the great hall of the Hospital, length 250 feet, 1293.
2 Entombment, detail, 15th c., in the Chapelle du Revestière.

TOURNUS *Saône-et-Loire.* K 11.

The main road leads to the sober and majestic Romanesque church of Saint-Philibert. The façade by its simplicity might almost be a defensive wall for its only decoration is its narrow pilasters. The squat and massive two-storied narthex is supported by columns without capitals and leads into a nave which seems reduced to its essentials for it is devoid of all decoration although the small rose-coloured brick shows traces of paintings. The very simplicity of the church as it is now is satisfying in itself. The vaulting of the nave is characterised by its tunnel-vaults supported by transverse ribbing — a system not found elsewhere. Certain of the abbey buildings are now in course of restoration and are worth visiting. In the Hôtel-Dieu, the 17th-century pharmacy contains fine wood-work and a collection of faïence jugs.

3 Tower of the church of Saint-Philibert, 11th c. 4 North aisle of the church, 11th c. 5 The low-church of the narthex, 11th c. 6 Stone sculpture inset in a pier of the upper chapel of the narthex, 11th c.

VALLERY 7

VALLERY *Yonne.* I 7.

The famous sculptors Jean Sarrazin and Philibert de l'Orme came to work at the humble village of Vallery in the château of the Princes of Condé. The château has since been destroyed and all that remains of its past splendour is the tomb in the church.

7 Jean Sarrazin: Caryatids of the tomb of Henri II of Condé, 17th c.

VARZY *Nièvre.* J 9.

The 14th-century church of Saint-Pierre stands next to a surprising little museum: the first contains a very beautiful Renaissance tryptych while in the second, some fine pieces of medieval sculpture, faïence, glass- and enamel-ware may be seen.

8 Tryptych of Sainte-Eugénie, detail, 1537, north crossing of the church of Saint-Pierre. 9 Head of Christ, wood carving, 14th c., Musée Municipal.

TONNERRE 1

TONNERRE 2

TOURNUS 5

TOURNUS 3

TOURNUS 6

VARZY 8

VARZY 9

TOURNUS 4

341

VÉZELAY *Yonne.* J 9.

Like Notre-Dame in Paris, the château of Pierrefonds and the city of Carcassonne, Vézelay may have suffered from Viollet-le-Duc's restoring zeal but there is no denying his careful spirit of research and the result is that the great basilica, dedicated to Saint Madeleine and founded in 864, must be considered as an outstanding example of the architecture of its time. The outer narthex had most suffered the ravages of time and was restored in the 19th century but the inner narthex, dating from 1152, survived intact and is famous for its sculptures of the Pentecost and the Mission of the Apostles in the centre portal, with the figure of Christ who seems to be borne on the wind, lifting the folds of his vermiculated robe. The small flanking portals are equally fine and offer an admirable view of the aisles of the basilica. On each side of the central pier the bi-coloured keystones of the vault inspired by those of Saint-Philibert of Tournus and Cordoba should be noted. The luminous choir is in a Romanesque-Gothic style dating from 1215 and contrasts with the earlier parts of the basilica. The capitals and the recess of the tympanum are decorated with an impressive variety of sculptures. The Madeleine of Vézelay was consecrated in 1102 and building continued for more than a century, mostly under the direction of the abbot Renaud de Semur who was born at Semur-en-Brionnais, which would explain the Brionnais style of Vézelay for it was directly inspired by the church at Anzy-le-Duc. The sculpture is entirely Cluniac in style. All in all, we can only be grateful to Viollet-le-Duc for having preserved one of the finest churches in Burgundy, once the point of departure for pilgrimages to Saint-James of Compostella.

1 Vézelay, view of the town. 2 Water-colour by Viollet-le-Duc, 19th c. 3 The narthex, 12th c. 4 Centre portal of the narthex. 5 Christ of the Pentecost, centre portal. 6 Nave and vaulting, 12th c. 7-8 Capitals in the nave, 11th c. 9 Detail of the tympanum.

4

5

7

6

8

IX

POITOU - SAINTONGE - ANGOUMOIS

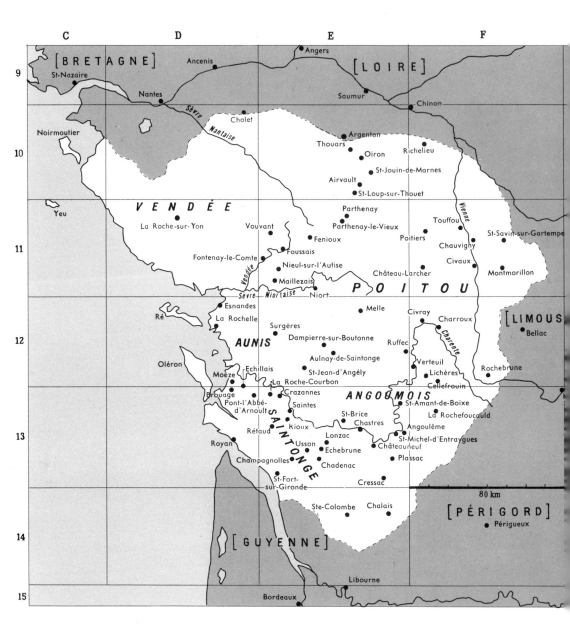

CAPITAL IN THE CHOIR OF THE CHURCH OF SAINT-PIERRE, 12TH C.,
CHAUVIGNY *(Fronval)*

FRESCO IN THE CHURCH OF SAINT-SAVIN, ENOCH'S PRAYER, 11TH-
12TH C., SAINT-SAVIN-SUR-GARTEMPE

*Although the countryside between Poitiers and the Atlantic
is considered to be comparatively poor in "tourist attractions",
it has some of the finest masterpieces of Romanesque art in
the whole of Europe: including such grandiose monuments as
the churches and cathedrals of Angoulême, Aulnay, Poitiers
and Saint-Savin and more than a hundred more modest churches
to excite the passion of the art-historian and lover of beauty.*

349

AIRVAULT 1

AIRVAULT *Deux-Sèvres*. E 10.

The church of Airvault was built in 1100 by the abbot Pierre de Sainte-Fontaine and is one of the most characteristic examples of the Poitevin Romanesque style. It was completed in the 13th century by vaulting in the Angevin Gothic style. The tomb of the abbot-architect is a good example of Poitevin sculpture in the 12th century. The figured capitals are highly original, being almost in the style of the region of Berri. The Gendarmerie is an ancient abbey of the 12th and 17th centuries. The town also contains old houses with wooden beams and a Gothic bridge over the river Thouet.

1 Lower storey of the narthex in the church of Saint-Pierre, 12th c.

ANGOULÊME *Charente*. E 13.

The cathedral is practically the only sight of interest in the town; in any case it is the most famous (if only because of its notorious restorer, Abadie). The Town Hall with its arcaded courtyard is a plagiaristic work of the 19th century and only the two towers belong to the original château. There is a modest museum in the town, but the walk along the ramparts is superb. The cathedral of Saint-Pierre has a flat façade in a purely Angevin style (gables and towers are a 19th-c. addition) with 75 statues, including figures of dancing angels under the centre bay, and a Christ in Majesty in a mandala. The five-tiered bell-tower is of great beauty. The single nave, without aisles is covered by cupolas resting on pendentives: this was one of the bishop Girard's, the architect's, most important creations for the nave was too wide for barrel-vaulting but we do not know if this was an original solution or the result of the influence of Oriental architecture.

2 Façade of the cathedral of Saint-Pierre, 12th c., restored in the 19th c. 3 Apse and square tower (180 feet high), 12th c. 4 Central bay of the façade: Christ in Majesty, 12th c. 5 Interior of the cathedral, 12th c. 6 Detail of the façade: Saint George, 12th c.

ANGOULÊME 6

AULNAY-DE-SAINTONGE *Charente-Maritime*. E 12.

The region of Saintonge is rich in Romanesque churches but that at Aulnay is the finest of them all. It owes its fine state of preservation to the quality of its grey-blue stone and hard gold-yellow limestone. The church is set among cypresses and at first sight, the harmony of its elements reveals the Romanesque style at its finest for the purity and simplicity of the lines, the grace and richness of the decoration, the overall impression and every detail make the building an undoubted masterpiece. The upper intrados of the south portal contains a curious motif of kneeling Atlantes with one hand raised, wide staring eyes, in a style reminiscent of the Orient and Egypt. In the archivolts, a sculpted bestiary including the figure of an ass playing the hurdy-gurdy. In the interior, the famous "elephants capital" was considered to be so strange by the sculptor himself that he thought it necessary to write underneath it "Hi sunt elephantes". This variety of inspiration is not the only merit of Aulnay for the air of monastic simplicity is even more striking than the plastic detail which is only surpassed by the church of Saint-Jouin-de-Marnes.

7 Façade of the church of Saint-Pierre, early 12th c. 8 Portal of the south transept, moulding: Bestiary. 9 Bay and tympanum, on the façade: Crucifixion of Saint Peter. 10 South aisle, capital of the Elephants. 11 Portal of the south transept, intrados, Atlantes.

AULNAY 7

ANGOULÊME 4

ANGOULÊME 2

ANGOULÊME 5

ANGOULÊME 3

AULNAY 10

AULNAY 8

AULNAY 11

AULNAY 9

351

CELLEFROUIN 4

CELLEFROUIN 3

BROUAGE *Charente-Maritime.* D 13.

The little fortified town of Brouage rises out of the surrounding marshes like a mirage. The history of the town is the following: in the Middle Ages it was the most important salt-market in Europe and one of the finest ports of France; in 1640, at Richelieu's instigation, it became a fortress with a garrison of six thousand soldiers but the marshes became filled with sand, the climate degenerated and the town was abandoned. The city is now a kind of museum-piece, unique of its kind. A 17th-century enceinte still surrounds the fortified town which contains a warehouse, an arsenal, a cannon-ball foundry, a church, of course, and some houses. The site is so little known that the tourist may still "discover" it.

1 Enceinte of the town, each side, 1900 yards in length, 1640.
2 The warehouse, galleries in brick and stone, 17th c.

CELLEFROUIN 5

CELLEFROUIN *Charente.* F 12.

All that remains of the abbey that once rose in the Middle Ages above the surrounding marshes is the church of Saint-Pierre with the oldest façade in the whole region of Angoulême. It is absolutely bare, without sculpture, and depends for its effect on the rhythm of its vertical buttresses and its pointed pediment. The church has lost its former height because it has sunk in the ground. The pillars should be admired although they have been eroded by humidity, and some fine capitals have also survived. In the cemetery overlooking the village a fine graveyard turret on a stepped base, crowned by a cone with projecting scales. Such turrets, known as "dead men's lanterns", served as beacons to pilgrims and indicated the presence of a cemetery and are a frequent feature of the region (q.v. Château-Larcher, Fenioux, etc).

3 Dead men's lantern, 12th c. 4 Façade of the church of Saint-Pierre, 12th c. 5 Hand of consecration, base of the wall in the south transept.

CHADENAC *Charente-Maritime.* E 13.

The almost Oriental subtlety of the lines of the Romanesque façade of the church contrasts with the rigour of the construction: three tiers of arcades, richly decorated recesses. The beauty and strangeness of the wild beasts shown devouring a lamb in the side arcades are in the same spirit as that of the reptilian monsters devouring the foolish Virgins.

6 Façade of the church, 12th c. 7 Recess of the portal, 12th c.
8 Recess of the portal, a reptile attacking a Foolish Virgin, 12th c.
9 Capital of the nave, 12th c.

CHALAIS *Charente.* E 14.

The beautiful polyfoil portal of the church of Saint-Martial faces a 14th-century château which was altered in the 18th century. The decoration of the recesses is completely geometric and the portal may be compared to that of Aubeterre, now in ruins.

10 Portal of the church of Saint-Martial, late 12th c.

BROUAGE I

BROUAGE 2

CHADENAC 6

CHADENAC 8

CHADENAC 9

CHADENAC 7

CHALAIS 10

CHAMPAGNOLLES 1

CHAMPAGNOLLES *Charente-Maritime.* E 13.
Apart from its fine and rather squat apse, the church at Champagnolles is worth visiting for the somewhat daring subjects of the corbels supporting the cornice (similar to those at Givrezac).
1 Apse of the church, 12th c.

CHARROUX *Vienne.* F 12.
All that remains of the greatest Poitevin abbey of the 11th century is the admirable octagonal lantern-tower which crowned the choir of the church and which escaped destruction in the 19th century. The chapter house has been transformed into a museum and contains sculptures from the portal and some beautiful reliquaries. All the visitor can now do is to try to imagine the ancient church as it must once have stood, with its round porch-tower similar to that of Saint-Bénigne in Dijon.
2 Lantern-tower, so-called "tower of Charlemagne", early 11th c.
3 Chapter house of the former abbey of Saint-Sauveur: Wise Virgin, 13th c. 4 Prophet, 13th c.

CHASTRES (at Saint-Brice) *Charente.* E 13.
The abbey church of the Augustines has been ruined both by the Protestants and by time. It was founded in the 11th century and has still kept its polyfoil portal, its high façade and its nave covered by three domes, but it is now used as a barn.
5 Portal of the church of Saint-Martial, late 12th c.

CHATEAU-LARCHER *Vienne.* F 11.
"Dead men's lanterns" are fairly rare in France and they used to signal the presence of a cemetery. That at Château-Larcher has kept its altar-table destined for open-air services. The village church is built in rose-coloured brick which glows as the sun sets, and is flanked by a fortified tower. The portal is slightly pointed which is highly unusual for Poitevin architecture which remained faithful to semi-circular arches during the whole of the 12th century.
6 Dead men's lantern, 13th c. 7 West façade of the church of Notre-Dame, and fortified tower, 12th and 14th c.

CHATEAU-LARCHER 6

CHATEAUNEUF *Charente.* E 13.
We should forget the recoating of the façade of the church of Saint-Pierre in order to admire its harmonious proportions which are reminiscent of those of Abbaye-aux-Dames at Saintes, and especially the statue of the mounted Constantine, the finest in the region, shown trampling the female figure of Heresy (now destroyed) under his horse's hooves. Prosper Mérimée was responsible for the preservation of the church.
8 Façade of the church of Saint-Pierre: the horseman Constantine, 12th c.

CHARROUX 3   CHARROUX 4

CHARROUX 2

CHASTRES 5

CHATEAU-LARCHER 7

CHATEAUNEUF 8

CHAUVIGNY *Vienne*. F 11.

Amid the ruins of several keeps and a château overlooking the Vienne from a limestone spur, stands the most astonishing of the three churches of Chauvigny. The church of Saint-Pierre is a kind of sculpted picture-book of hell, in a style that is as naive as it is barbaric and the artist has left his name under a capital which bears the inscription "Gofridus me fecit". Gofridus, who was obviously obsessed by demons and monsters, must certainly have been a local artist and his work is a treasure of popular art of the 12th century and stands poles apart from the refined sculptures of the church at Aulnay which had been executed by learned monks. In his figures, Gofridus has represented Man being ruled by the devil, the spirit of evil, until his salvation by the Incarnation, when the Virgin's face is shown lighting up with a crudely drawn smile. We cannot call the work beautiful, and the red outlines added in the 19th century certainly have not helped matters, but we must admit that it is astonishing. The apse has a peculiarity which has puzzled many antiquarians for the roof is lined with parapets decorated with several bas-reliefs of an earlier date than the church.

Also to be seen at Chauvigny are the 11th-century church of Saint-Martial, now a barn, and the church of Notre-Dame, a Romanesque structure partly rebuilt in 1860.

1 Apse of the collegiate church of Saint-Pierre, mid-12th c.
2 Nave. **3** Columns in the choir. **4** Capital in the choir, four-legged man. **5** Capital, the Annunciation. **6** Capital, winged lion.

CIVAUX 7

CIVAUX 8

CIVAUX *Vienne*. F 11.

We no longer know the reason for Civaux's importance in the Merovingian period but the presence of thousands of tombs ranged in seven successive layers proves the existence of a Christian community. Certain authorities maintain that it was the site of a Merovingian coffin industry. The polygonal apse of the church is also Merovingian. The cemetery with its ancient still erect tomb-stones should be worth excavating. The worn and archaic capitals are similar to those at Chauvigny.

7-8 Capitals of the church of Saint-Gervais-Saint-Protais, 12th c.

356

CHAUVIGNY 4

CHAUVIGNY 5

CHAUVIGNY 6

CHAUVIGNY 1

CHAUVIGNY 2

CHAUVIGNY 3

357

CIVRAY *Vienne*. F 12.

If we take the façade of the church of Notre-Dame-la-Grande at Poitiers (q.v.) as being the most typical representative of the Poitevin style, that of Saint-Nicolas at Civray must be considered as the second most characteristic, with its "screen" filled with sculptures in a relatively harmonious composition dominated by heavy horizontals between two clusters of angular columns. The bell-turret, the decoration of the tympanum and the paintings in the inner walls and vault are modern and regrettable, but the various themes of the sculpted ornament are worth noticing. They include: the Virtues, the Virgins, Samson and Delilah, Samson and the lion, the Heavenly Musicians, a horseman, etc. They had all been detached in the 19th century for the façade was falling into ruins. The nine statues in the south archivolt do not seem to have found their original home.

1 Façade of the church of Saint-Nicolas, late 12th c. 2 Detail of the recess of the portal.

CRAZANNES *Charente-Maritime*. E 13.

Besides its magnificent Flamboyant Gothic doorway — alone, enough to justify a visit — the Renaissance manor house at Crazannes has also kept its beautiful corner-turret, its transomed windows, oak ceilings, etc. The pinnacle above the doorway is richly sculpted with highly original comic figurines.

3 Doorway of the manor, 15th c.

CRESSAC *Charente*. E 13.

Although much restored, the paintings in the chapel of the Templars at Cressac are still worth seeing for they depict the departure of knights for the Holy Land and various events of their everyday and legendary life: knight defending a lady from a griffon, etc.

4 Romanesque painting in the chapel of the Templars: Knight, late 12th c.

DAMPIERRE-SUR-BOUTONNE *Charente-Maritime*. E 12.

The château was built by the Clermont family in the early 16th century and has now lost its wings, but its finest part — the gallery of the façade with two flanking towers — has survived. Its two storeys with flattened arches are separated by a finely sculpted frieze. The ceiling of the upper storey is renowned for its pendant knob-bosses, all different in style, and for its coffers with various pessimistic mottoes (the baron of Dampierre had been disgraced for having written criticisms of Diane de Poitiers, mistress of Henri II).

5 Façade of the château, 16th c. 6 Gallery and coffered ceiling, 16th c.

ÉCHEBRUNE *Charente-Maritime*. E 13.

The centre polyfoil arch above the main portal of the church might appear to be an Arab motif or a variation on the scallop theme, but like the signboard of an inn, it indicated a stage on the pilgrims' way to Compostella. Beautiful corbels under the cornice.

7 Façade of the church, 12th c.

ÉCHILLAIS *Charente-Maritime*. D 12.

At Échillais, as at Échebrune (q.v.) and elsewhere in the Saintonge region, a strange capital figure seems to stand guard to the left of the centre portal as if to forbid the unworthy to enter the church: the glutton, a narrow eyed monster who seems to be devouring the column (similar figures may be seen as holding beam-ends in their mouths in Breton churches). Carved façade: fine corbels, geometric motifs in the blind arcading, etc.

8 Façade of the church, 12th c. 9 The glutton, figure capital, left of the centre portal.

CRESSAC 4

CRAZANNES 3

CIVRAY 2

CIVRAY 1

DAMPIERRE 6

DAMPIERRE 5

ÉCHEBRUNE 7

ÉCHILLAIS 9

ÉCHILLAIS 8

359

ESNANDES *Charente-Maritime.* D 12.

An entire system of fortifications was added to the Romanesque church in the 15th century for its situation by the sea made it too easily exposed to attack. A rampart-walk surrounds the church and the small recessed portal seems crushed beneath the weight of the warlike superstructure.

1 Church, 12th-13th c., fortified in the 15th c.

FENIOUX *Charente-Maritime.* E 11.

The "dead men's lantern" at Fenioux is a curious vestige of Romanesque art and served as a model for the monuments that his admirers raised to Maurice Barrès on the Colline Inspirée at Sion-Vaudémont. Other such lanterns are found in the region at Saint-Pierre-d'Oléron, Cellefrouin, Pranzac, Brigueil, Pamplie, Journet, Aubigny, and Château-Larcher (q.v.). In each case, the charnel house is overlooked by a lantern whose light used to keep watch over the dead and guide pilgrims.
Equally striking is the church at Fenioux: with its tower, its two stacked lanterns and the sculptures of the façade it is the prettiest church of the Saintonge region after those of Saintes and Aulnay.

2 Dead men's lantern, 12th c.

FONTENAY-LE-COMTE *Vendée.* E 11.

Fontenay-le-Comte was the artistic capital of the Poitou during the Renaissance and has kept many old houses of this period as well as a motto attributed to François I; "Fontaine et source d'esprits heureusement doués" (Fountain and spring of fortunately endowed spirits), which has been inscribed on the beautiful fountain of Quatre-Tias (or "tuyaux": pipes) with its fronton finely carved in the Renaissance style. The church of Notre-Dame was rebuilt after the Revocation of the Edict of Nantes on Romanesque foundations, and has a fine Gothic-style tower dating from 1700. In the portal, a fine and little-known Virgin surrounded by arch-moulding in the Flamboyant style with figures of the Wise and the Foolish Virgins.

3 The church of Notre-Dame, steeple by François Leduc de Toscane, 1700. 4 Portal, and Virgin with Child, 15th c.

FOUSSAIS *Vendée.* E 11.

According to an inscription in Latin, the sculptor Giroud Audebert from Saint-Jean-d'Angély is the artist of the large bas-reliefs of the church at Foussais. The themes of the reliefs are "Descent from the Cross" and "Feast at the House of Simon". The portal contains carving of traditional themes such as sirens, acrobats, apostles, abbots, etc.

5 Moulding of the main portal, 12th c. 6 Detail of the portal, siren.

LICHÈRES *Charente.* F 12.

The little church of Saint-Denis stands surrounded by centenarian linden trees in the midst of a field by the little village of Lichères. Its south transept collapsed in the 18th century and was unfortunately over-restored. The exterior of the church resembles other churches of the Charente region by its design and decoration but the interior is Poitevin. The calvary is carved in a very fine grained stone and has survived in a perfect state. The tympanum of the portal is set over a curiously flattened arch or arched lintel like that of Campagne-Mouton, and contains carvings of a lamb surrounded by lions, birds and monsters. The ground by the church has risen by a yard since the building of the church yard and excavations have shown the first pillar on the left to have a finely moulded base.

7 View of the church of Saint-Denis, 12th c. 8 Tympanum of the portal, Agnus Dei.

FENIOUX 2

ESNANDES 1

FONTENAY-LE-COMTE 4

FONTENAY-LE-COMTE 3

FOUSSAIS 6

FOUSSAIS 5

LICHÈRES 7

LICHÈRES 8

361

LONZAC *Charente-Maritime.* E 13.
Galiot de Genouillac, Grand-Master of Artillery in the reign of
François I, owned a château at Assier in the Lot and a chapel
with his tomb which bore the motto "J'aime fortune". In the
sepulchral chapel of his wife at Lonzac he changed the motto
to "J'aime fort une". The chapel of Catherine d'Archiac is more
than an example of her husband's taste for puns for it is a very
beautiful example of Renaissance architecture.
I Doorway of the chapel, 1530.

MAILLEZAIS *Vendée.* E 11.
The great church of Maillezais was an abbey church founded
in the 10th century, then being a cathedral, and then a fortress of the
Protestants. All that remains of it after its chequered history
are a few ruins in which the finest Romanesque mingles with
admirable groin-vaulting. Rabelais took refuge in the church,
Agrippa d'Aubigné the Protestant commanded it when it was
a stronghold. In the neighbouring village, the church of Saint-
Nicolas has curious capitals on the façade and figures of birds
perched on Atlantes in the small portal.
2 Ruins of the abbey church of Saint-Pierre, 13th c. **3** Portal of
the church of Saint-Nicolas, 12th c., restored.

MELLE *Deux-Sèvres.* E 12.
Of the three churches of the town that of Saint-Hilaire is the most
esteemed for a variety of reasons, the first being the figure of a
horseman above the south portal. This theme is frequently found
in the region and represents the emperor Constantine, the bene-
factor of the Church, and it might be that the famous equestrian
statue of Marcus Aurelius originally served as a model. But
only the long-necked horse is authentic here. The apse is covered
with round tiles; fine square tower and interesting rustic-style
capitals signed "Aimerious". The arcade above the south side
portal of the church of Saint-Pierre has a beautiful Christ seated
between the mutilated figures of two saints. The third church,
Saint-Savinien, has become a prison.
4 Church of Saint-Hilaire, apse, 12th c. **5** Church of Saint-Hilaire,
horseman above the north portal. **6** Church of Saint-Pierre,
south side portal, 12th c.

MOEZE *Charente-Maritime.* D 12.
A verse from the Gospels ending with the line "Hosanna in
excelsis" is engraved in the entablature of a little temple with
Corinthian columns in the village cemetery. This Renaissance
structure is unique of its kind (other Hosanna-crosses are far less
important); the parish church has a pretty notched spire (16th c.).
7 Hosanna Cross, known as Temple of Moeze, 1563.

MONTMORILLON *Vienne.* F 11.
The *Octogone* is the main monument of this interesting but little-
known town. This octagonal-shaped dome contains the two
storeys of a Romanesque funerary monument and the pediment
of the facade is decorated with square columns flanked on three
sides by very curious statues representing the Annunciation,
the Visitation, Lust, the Apostles, etc.
As at Saint-Savin, the church of Notre-Dame towers over the
Gartempe river. It has kept some of its Romanesque elements,
including the apse, despite 18th-century restorations. The frescoes
in the crypt dedicated to Saint Catherine show the Virgin surrounded by saints and scenes from the life of Saint Catherine. The
style of the frescoes is Romanesque, with certain Gothic elements.
Ochre, green and violet are used for the subjects, and the background is painted in bands of white and blue-grey.
8 Fresco of the crypt of Sainte-Catherine, 1200. **9** The *Octogone*,
sepulchral chapel c. 1180. **10** Porch of the *Octogone*, detail: figure
of Lust.

MONTMORILLON 8

LONZAC 1

MAILLEZAIS 2

MAILLEZAIS 3

MELLE 4

MELLE 5

MELLE 6

MOEZE 7

MONTMORILLON 9

MONTMORILLON 10

NIORT 3

OIRON 6

PLASSAC 11

NIEUL-SUR-L'AUTISE *Vendée.* E 11.

The visitor to the church at Nieul must make allowances for the parts restored by Viollet-le-Duc in 1870. The tower and all the upper part of the façade and the apse are modern but nonetheless the church is still one of the finest examples of the Poitevin Romanesque. The two registers of the three blind arcades offer one of the most splendid and probably the most ancient illustrations of this style. The cloister (11th c.) has survived intact and is curious for its low elevation, stressed by its thick pillars. In the square facing the church, the fine former hostelry of the church, now the presbytery.

1 Façade of the church, 11th c. 2 Cloister, 11th c.

NIORT *Deux-Sèvres.* E 11.

The English "Plantagenet" style of architecture is well illustrated at Niort by the keep of the castle that was built by Henry II of England, the husband of Eleanor of Aquitaine. It has now been transformed into a museum of Poitevin costume. The old Town Hall has a very beautiful Renaissance dormer window, and is built on a triangular ground plan. It now contains a display of regional antiquities.

3 Keep, 12th-14th c.

OIRON *Deux-Sèvres.* E 10.

One of Perrault's fairy-tale characters, the Marquis of Carabas, really existed and lived in the château of Oiron. This admirable building is partly Renaissance, partly 17th-century and has a courtyard with flattened arches and twisted columns which give it a charming touch of fantasy. In the church, splendid tombs of the Gouffier family. The interior of the château is worth visiting for its ceilings, fireplaces, and 16th- and 17th-century frescoes. In 1525 the chatelaine established a manufacture of faïence, known as Saint-Porchaire or "Henri II", of which a few beautiful pieces may be seen in the Louvre.

4 Left wing of the château, 16th c. 5 Fireplace of the Galerie des Fêtes, 16th c. 6 Faïence of Oiron or Saint-Porchaire, 16th c.

PARTHENAY *Deux-Sèvres.* E 11.

The four churches of Parthenay are evidence of the former importance of this picturesque town by the river Thouet. The fine machicolated gateway of Saint-Jacques leads into the city at the end of the old bridge. The old quarter contains many 14th and 15th-century wooden houses. The church of Notre-Dame-de-la-Couldre, like that of Aulnay, has a fine portal with elongated figures. In the church of Saint-Laurent, two curious capitals carved with scenes of the Weighing of Souls and the Resurrection.

7 Porte Saint-Jacques, 13th c. 8 Notre-Dame-de-la-Couldre, portal, 12th c.

PARTHENAY-LE-VIEUX *Deux-Sèvres.* E 11.

The finest carved horseman in the whole region of Poitou may be seen on the pearl-grey façade of the church of Saint-Pierre, facing the figure of Samson slaying the lion. The figure of the lordly horseman with a falcon on his wrist, his cape billowing in the wind, and the figure of Heresy lying trampled beneath his horse's hooves, would appear to be the portrait of Guillaume Larchevêque, the lord of Parthenay.

9 Church of Saint-Pierre, façade, 12th c. 10 Left arch of the façade, the horseman Constantine, 12th c.

PLASSAC *Charente.* E 13.

The church of Plassac overlooks superb vineyards and is crowned by a very fine conical steeple covered with brick scales. Façade with three storeys of arcades.

11 Apse of the church and tower, 12th c.

NIEUL I

NIEUL 2

OIRON 5

OIRON 4

PARTHENAY 7

PARTHENAY 8

PARTHENAY-LE-VIEUX 9

PARTHENAY-LE-VIEUX 10

365

3

2

I

POITIERS *Vienne.* F 11.

The city of Poitiers has been rebuilt no less than seven times on its hill, and it is one of the richest towns in France for historical buildings. The long list begins with the Hypogeum of the Martyrs, a subterranean chapel built by the abbot Mellebaude in the 4th century in the early Christian cemetery. The Baptistère Saint-Jean also dates from the 4th century: it is the oldest surviving Christian edifice in France and contains Merovingian tombs and important Romanesque frescoes. Saint-Hilaire-le-Grand and Notre-Dame-la-Grande are the two outstanding Romanesque churches of the city. The first is highly unusual of its kind because of its side tower, triple aisles and raised choir, its domes like those of Puy-en-Velay, its narrow aisles, and its altar-tomb. The second, on the contrary, is a model of the Poitevin style with its squat and heavy façade, similar to that of Saint-Jouin-de-Marnes (q.v.), covered with sculptures like an Indian temple, and with its scaly bell-turrets. The interior of Saint-Hilaire like that of Notre-Dame has kept its marbled agate pillars. The visitor should try to imagine the façade of Notre-Dame as it was when it was painted in the 12th century, when it was a kind of picture-book in stone for the passer-by or pilgrim.

Saint-Porchaire still has a fine Romanesque porch and bell-tower; the rest of the church is pointed Gothic. Sainte-Radegonde has kept its Romanesque apse, crypt and ambulatory but even finer is the late 15th-century porch at the foot of the bell-tower, with its statues of the patrons of the town under a dais. The cathedral Saint-Pierre is often overlooked to the profit of the other churches of Poitiers but it has magnificent soaring naves and aisles covered with fine Angevin-style vaulting. The stained-glass windows and the choir are famous.

The secular monuments are no less fine than the churches: most interesting is the Palais de Justice, followed by the hôtel Fumée with Renaissance windows surmounted by Gothic arches on its façade.

The Palais de Justice was partly reconstructed by the Duke Jean de Berry and is flanked by the Tour Maubergeon, a square *corps de logis* which was never completed, flanked by four round towers surmounted by secular statues. The Salle des Pas-Perdus (Waiting room) in the Palais is 50 yards long and covered by a wooden vault which was restored in the 19th century. At the end of the hall, a triple fireplace surmounted by Gothic windows with fine tracery.

1 Hypogeum of Mellebaude or the Martyrs, detail of sculpture, 4th c. 2 Baptistère Saint-Jean, apse, 4th c. 3 Interior of the Baptistery, 4th c. 4 Fresco in the Baptistère Saint-Jean, an emperor, c. 1120. 5 Church of Saint-Hilaire-le-Grand, apse, 11th c. 6 North aisle of Saint-Hilaire. 7 Notre-Dame-la-Grande, façade, 12th c. 8 Cathedral of Saint-Pierre, nave, 13th c. 9 Salle des Pas-Perdus, Palais de Justice, 13th-15th c. 10 Tour Maubergeon, exterior, 14th c. 11 Tour Maubergeon, interior, 14th c. 12 Church of Sainte-Radegonde, portal, late 15th c. 13 Hôtel Fumée, 15th c. 14 Musée des Beaux-Arts: Minerva of Poitiers, 1st c.

14

4

5

7

6

8

9

11   10

12

13

PONT-L'ABBÉ-D'ARNOULT *Charente-Maritime.* D 13.

Apart from the 15th-century bell-tower and the upper part of the façade (13th c.) the church is decorated in a splendid Romanesque style full of geometric motifs. It was once part of an important Benedictine abbey. The tympana of the portals are unusual for the region: that on the right represents Saint Peter crucified head downwards, like a common thief. The corbels under the cornice are carved with masks similar to those at Rétaud (q.v.).

1 Façade of the church, detail, 12th c. 2 Corbelling of the cornice.

RÉ *Charente-Maritime.* D 12.

Although the isle of Ré is known more to holiday makers than to antiquarians its two churches are far from being devoid of interest. Saint-Martin was given ramparts designed by Vauban and the ruined Gothic church witnesses a former splendour. The more modest church at Ars is famous for its black steeple with a white base which dominates the whole island. A few wooden sculptures in the nave under the Gothic vaulting; Romanesque portal. The church of Saint-Étienne has a Romanesque portal now half below ground.

3 Church of Ars-en-Ré, 12th-13th c. 4 Ruins of the church of Saint-Martin-en-Ré, 13th c.

RÉTAUD *Charente-Maritime.* E 13.

The church at Rétaud is sister to that at Rioux and has an apse with seven sides decorated with pointed blind arches and surmounted with blind arcading and a cornice with very varied corbels of grimacing masks like those at Pont-l'Abbé-d'Arnoult. The resemblance to Moslem art seems very close, in particular that of Cordoba, since geometric motifs preponderate over to human figuration.

5 Apse of the church, 12th c. 6 Corbels under the cornice.

RÉTAUD 5

RICHELIEU *Indre-et-Loire.* F 10.

All that remains of a château that Cardinal Richelieu intended to be larger than that of Louis XIII at Versailles is a modest lodge. From this château came Michelangelo's sculptures of slaves, now in the Louvre. The Revolution and the sale of the stones to local builders destroyed the château in less than a century. But the model village designed on a regular plan, 750 by 500 yards long by Jacques le Mercier has still survived. The hôtel du Sénéchal (17 Grande-Rue) is typical of the houses of local dignitaries of the time. The Porte de Chinon is one of the three former gateways that have survived.

7 Aerial view of the town, 17th c. 8 Dome, former outbuildings of the château, 17th c. 9 Porte de Chinon, 17th c.

RIOUX 10

RIOUX *Charente-Maritime.* E 13.

The seven sides of the admirable apse with its Oriental-style decoration are separated by elegant colonnettes that taper upwards towards the roof. The brickwork is different for each side. Varied corbels. The whole church seems to have been inspired by Saint-Eutrope at Saintes.

10 Apse of the church, 12th c.

PONT-L'ABBÉ-D'ARNOULT 2

PONT-L'ABBÉ-D'ARNOULT I

RÉ 4

RÉTAUD 6

RÉ 3

RICHELIEU 8

RICHELIEU 7

RICHELIEU 9

ROCHEBRUNE I

LA ROCHE-COURBON 2

LA ROCHEFOUCAULD 3

ROCHEBRUNE (at Étagnac) *Charente.* F 12.

The château flanked by its four large towers has been well restored and is a fine Renaissance seignorial residence. A fine Renaissance fireplace may still be seen in the interior.

I The château, 16th c.

LA ROCHE-COURBON *Charente-Maritime.* E 13.

The château of "the Sleeping Beauty" at La Roche-Courbon has been saved from destruction by the writer Pierre Loti and has been perfectly maintained and restored by its present proprietor who has kept its style of the 17th and 18th centuries. Noble staircases and covered gallery overlooking the splendid gardens.

2 The château, 17th c.

LA ROCHEFOUCAULD *Charente.* F 13.

If it were not situated in a little-known region the château would be as famous as any of the Loire Valley for it is one of the purest examples of the Renaissance style. Two corner turrets flanking a fine façade with mullioned windows, a keep of earlier date (11th c.), a very beautiful Renaissance courtyard, galleries, staircase with palm-leaf vaulting. It was the home of the celebrated author of the *Maximes.*

3 Façade of the château, 16th c.

LA ROCHELLE *Charente-Maritime.* D 12.

The beauty and picturesqueness of the town of La Rochelle has appealed to countless artists including Corot. For eight hundred years the town never ceased to assert its personality and independence. It owes the quality of its architecture, its numerous wood-beamed houses, its vaulted porticoes, arcaded streets, richly sculpted Renaissance façades, classical *hôtels* to its rich ship-owners, and the varied treasures of its three museums to the generosity of local collectors. The port is dominated by three towers: the Tour Saint-Nicolas (1384) and the Tour de la Chaine (1375) by the harbour entrance, and the Tour de la Lanterne (1468), an enormous keep which once served as a lighthouse. The town's defences include the gateway of the Grosse Horloge with a 13th-century tower completed in the 18th century. The machicolated battlements of the ramparts are remains of the original 15th-century fortifications and are flanked by two elegant turrets. The town contains a superb 16th-century Town Hall with a courtyard which is a masterpiece of the Renaissance in the region: open gallery supported by thick Tuscan pillars, statues of the cardinal Virtues in niches, loggia, coffered ceilings make it the most beautiful Town Hall in the whole of France. Another fine Renaissance building is the house of Diane de Poitiers. The city is poor in 17th-century architecture (houses of the Mayor Guiton and the doctor Venette) but the cathedral of Saint-Louis was built by Gabriel and completed in 1784.

The town's history is illustrated in the three museums: the Musée des Beaux-Arts gives pride of place to two painters born in La Rochelle, Eugène Fromentin (1820-1876) and Bouguereau (1825-1905), the Musée d'Orbigny is rich in regional art, and the Musée Lafaille contains the natural history collection gathered by an amateur in its original 18th-century panelled rooms.

4 Town Hall, main façade and battlements, 15th c. 5 Courtyard of the Town Hall, 16th c. 6 Pavillon Henri IV, 16th c. 7 Porte de la Grosse Horloge, 13th and 18th c. 8 House of Diane de Poitiers, 16th c. 9 Musée Lafaille, natural history collection, 18th c. 10 J.B.C. Corot (1796-1875): The Port of La Rochelle.

LA ROCHELLE 6

LA ROCHELLE 4

LA ROCHELLE 8

LA ROCHELLE 7

LA ROCHELLE 5

LA ROCHELLE 10

LA ROCHELLE 9

ROYAN I

ROYAN *Charente-Maritime.* D 13.

The town was reduced to ashes by the bombardments in 1945 and has been entirely rebuilt. The interesting concrete church resembles the cathedral of Albi by its strong vertical linear rhythm.

1 Church of Notre-Dame, by Guillaume Gillet, 1958.

RUFFEC *Charente.* E 12.

The decoration of the Romanesque façade of the church of Saint-André is interesting: under the gable, a fine Christ in Majesty in a mandala, flanked by two dancing angels. The statues of saints along the string course have been badly damaged but the left portal has kept its curious tympanum with what has been taken to be a representation of Judith standing by the bed of Holofernes.

2 Church of Saint-André, façade, 12th c.

SAINT-AMANT-DE-BOIXE *Charente.* E 13.

Second to the cathedral of Angoulême by its great size, the abbey church of Saint-Amant is a monumental structure 250 feet long. Beautiful cupola over the crossing of the transept (14th c.). Very sober façade without figure sculpture but abounding with geometric motifs. The interior view into the magnificent cupola is highly impressive. The frescoes of the crypt date from 1320 and have been well restored and are now in the chapel of the south transept: Annunciation, Visitation, Nativity, Presentation in the Temple and Last Supper. In the immediate surroundings, numerous remains of abbey buildings still stand (remains of a cloister, etc.) amid farm buildings.

3 Façade of the church, 1170. **4** Scenes from the Childhood of Christ, fresco from the crypt, late 13th c.

SAINT-BRICE *Charente.* E 13.

Catherine de Médicis and Henri of Navarre, the future Henri IV, both met in the château in 1586 to discuss the future of the kingdom. The apartment has been preserved. Romanesque church.

5 The château, 14th c., altered.

SAINT-FORT-SUR-GIRONDE *Charente-Maritime.* E 13.

According to one writer, the centre moulding of the portal, representing horses' heads biting a bar symbolises "the image of fiery passions that religion alone can contain" but as the imagination of Romanesque sculptors knew no restraint, such interpretations of their themes must be treated with reserve.

6 Church of Saint-Fortunat, portal with horses' heads, 12th c.

SAINT-JEAN-D'ANGÉLY *Charente-Maritime.* E 12.

The "Jesuit" church at Saint-Jean d'Angély is a rarity for the region and has made the fame of the town which was once so important that its Cluniac abbey was surrounded by nine churches. The Jesuit-style church was never completed, and only the towers which were erected between 1741 and the Revolution have remained. All that the Huguenots left of the abbey church in 1568 were a few ruins of little interest. The interior contains a painting of "Christ on the Mount of Olives" by Chassériau. But the little town is still graced by its 16th-century belfry and the fountain of Pilori (1546) which came from a nearby château.

7 The towers, unfinished church, 18th c. **8** Fontaine du Pilori, 1546.

ST-AMANT-DE-BOIXE 4

RUFFEC 2

ST-AMANT DE BOIXE 3

ST-BRICE 5

ST-FORT-SUR-GIRONDE 6

ST-JEAN-D'ANGÉLY 7

ST-JEAN-D'ANGÉLY 8

ST-JOUIN-DE-MARNES 4

SAINT-JOUIN-DE-MARNES *Deux-Sèvres*. E 10.

The vast size of the church of Saint-Jouin (275 feet long), out of all proportion to the surrounding village, is due to the fact that it belonged to a former pilgrims' abbey. The original portal is similar to that of Notre-Dame-la-Grande at Poitiers (q.v.), but the spacious composition of the façade with its triangles breaking the monotony of the horizontal lines is lighter and more forceful. The sculptures are treated in a skilful, refined and personal style and include such themes as running horses, pilgrims on the march (string-course above the arcades), the supple figures of the Annunciation, the women with serpents symbolising Lust, etc. A few steps lead up to the immense and spacious three-storeyed nave, partly covered by Angevin vaulting. On the exterior, the supporting buttresses, which were added during the Renaissance, contrast with the Romanesque style of the structure and separate the church from an overhanging kitchen garden. Some large and now unused buildings of the classical style have survived beside the church as a reminder of the importance of this halting place for pilgrims in the Middle Ages. The church is a masterpiece of Poitevin architecture and is even more impressive than that of Aulnay (q.v.).

1 View of the church of Saint-Jouin, 12th c. 2 Church of Saint-Jouin, façade, early 12th c. 3 Detail of the façade: Pilgrims. 4 Sculpture on the façade: the Annunciation, 12th c. 5 Capital in the nave. 6 Capital in the transept.

ST-LOUP-SUR-THOUET 7

SAINT-LOUP-SUR-THOUET *Deux-Sèvres*. E 10.

This very fine château illustrates the transition from the Renaissance to the classical style under Henri IV. It was built by the grandson of the architect of Oiron, Artus Gouffier. A 15th-century keep, the relic of an earlier château, stands at the entrance to the drive.

7 The château, 1610.

ST-MICHEL-D'ENTRAYGUES 8

SAINT-MICHEL-D'ENTRAYGUES *Charente*. E 13.

Like Montmorillon, the kitchen of Fontevrault and the Saint-Sauveur chapel in the church of Saint-Honorat, the church of Entraygues is octagonal in plan but eight minor apses are here connected to the main structure in what must be an imitation of ancient baptisteries. Pilgrims on the way to Compostella used to rest here and fulfil their religious duties. Admirable tympanum showing a mastery of line and movement in the design of the figures. It would appear to have been the work of a passing artist which would explain its originality for it is unlike those usually found in the region. The interior is well lit by stained-glass windows of recent date, with red and yellow the predominating colours.

8 View of the church, 12th c. 9 Tympanum on the façade: Saint Michael and the Dragon, 12th c.

ST-JOUIN-DE-MARNES 3

ST-JOUIN-DE-MARNES 5

ST-JOUIN-DE-MARNES 6

ST-JOUIN-DE-MARNES 2

ST-JOUIN-DE-MARNES 1

ST-MICHEL-D'ENTRAYGUES 9

375

ST-SAVIN 3

ST-SAVIN 4

ST-SAVIN I

SAINT-SAVIN-SUR-GARTEMPE *Vienne.* F 11.

The church of Saint-Savin is the best preserved Romanesque church in France, and has the most intact Romanesque paintings in the world. Architecture, sculpture and painting are all of the same high quality. The church was officially classed as a national monument in 1836 by Prosper Merimée on the recommendation of an anonymous colleague and with its sober, massive radiating chapels is in perfect harmony with the surrounding landscape. The first thing to strike the visitor will be the paintings of the Apocalypse in the porch-tower; he will then ascend a few steps into the vast nave, as pure in style as that of a Roman basilica, with its vaults decorated with scenes from Genesis and Exodus. The paintings on the walls of the tribunes illustrate the Passion, those in the crypt, the martyrdom of Saints Savin and Cyprian. Admirable marbled columns in imitation of agate support the vaulting and lead to the chancel with its rounded end. The capitals are also fine and would suffice in themselves to ensure the fame of another church (capital with lion-figures). The painting of the frescoes with their golden tones is quite as fine as the drawing: note the undulating, restless lines of the draperies of the prophets. The six Romanesque altars of the chapels should also be mentioned.

I Apse of the church of Saint-Savin, late 11th c. 2 Nave. 3 Fresco in the nave: Building of the Tower of Babel. 4 The Creation of the Stars. 5 The Crossing of the Red Sea. 6 Eve being presented to Adam. 7 Fresco on the north wall of the narthex: The Woman and the Dragon of the Apocalypse. 8 Fresco in the crypt: Martyrdom of Saints Savin and Cyprian.

SAINTE-COLOMBE *Charente.* E 14.

Colomba was a young Spanish virgin who was fleeing from persecution and was decapitated when she reached Sens. The sober-styled church of Sainte-Colombe was built in memory of her journey through the region. The statue of the saint, facing that of Saint Peter on the other side of a window may be considered as a precursor of the columnar statues of the portal of Saint-Loup de Naud and Chartres cathedral (q.v.).

9 Sainte-Colombe, façade of the church, 12th c. 10 Saint Peter detail of façade of the church.

376

ST-SAVIN 5

ST-SAVIN 6

ST-SAVIN 7

ST-SAVIN 8

ST-SAVIN 2

STE-COLOMBE 9

STE-COLOMBE 10

377

SAINTES 1

SAINTES *Charente-Maritime*. E 13.

Saintes-la-Romaine was situated at the cross-roads of several great highways and has kept several important relics of her former grandeur. First, the triumphal arch, known as the arch of Germanicus, which stood in the centre of a bridge until 1845, and secondly the arena which could hold 20 000 spectators. Traces of Roman baths and aqueducts have also been found and an interesting archaeological museum now displays various treasures of the old Gallo-Roman city. New life was given to the city in the Middle Ages as proved by the three magnificent church towers which still rise above the surrounding buildings. The first, shaped like a fir-cone, dates from 1170 and belongs to l'Abbaye-aux-Dames which also has a very beautiful west portal with four sculpted mouldings, the richest in the region for its profusion of motifs. The Cluniac church of Saint-Eutrope has two superimposed naves and the crypt is the largest in France after that of Chartres and contains a choir with curious radial vaulting and fine capitals. The Flamboyant bell-tower (180 feet high) was erected by Louis XI.

The church of Saint-Pierre was sacked by the Protestants and all that now remains is the bell-tower with its superimposed flying-buttresses ending in a forest of pinnacles (270 feet high). Fine pointed doorway of the 15th century. The Musée Mestreau contains an interesting collection of local art and folk-lore. The Musée de Peinture has a *Portrait of Vauban* by Rigaud and an *Autumn* by Brueghel among other fine quality paintings by old masters.
1 Roman arena, late 1st c., and tower of the church of Saint-Eutrope, 15th c. 2 Triumphal Arch of Germanicus, 21 A.D. 3 Abbaye-aux-Dames, façade, 12th c. 4 Church of Saint-Pierre, late 15th c. 5 Crypt of Saint-Eutrope, 12th c.

SURGÈRES *Charente-Maritime*. E 12.

A beautiful Renaissance gateway decorated with the arms of the La Rochefoucauld family, the ancient lords of the château, opens into the park leading to the château of Surgères. All that now remains are the enceinte and a 16th-century building which is now the Town Hall. Facing the gateway, the Romanesque church with thirteen blind semicircular arcades set in two registers against the façade with geometrical decoration, under a bare fronton. The registers are divided by string-courses with curious corbels and the geometric severity of the structure is highly impressive. The overall impression produced by the château, the gateway, the doorway, and the walls is very striking.
6 Façade of the church, 12th c. 7 Renaissance gateway, altered in the 19th c.

THOUARS *Deux-Sèvres*. E 10.

The château is of a fine classical style but unfortunately cannot be visited. It was built in about 1635 by the La Trémoille family. Beside it, the pretty Sainte-Chapelle with a high portal surmounted by an elegant gallery. The church was completed in 1514. The church of Saint-Médard has a fine Romanesque main portal and was built between the 12th and 15th centuries. Nearby, the *hôtel* of the Président Tyndo, ornamented with a polygonal staircase-tower ringed with ornamental machicolation.
8 Church of Saint-Médard, main portal, 12th c. 9 Sainte-Chapelle, by André Amy, 1514. 10 Hôtel Tyndo, stair-turret, 15th c.

TOUFFOU (at Bonnes) *Vienne*. F 11.

The main part of the château is formed by an ancient 10th and 12th-century keep, which was flanked by four corner towers in the 14th century. A pretty Renaissance wing was later added, with five windows surmounted by interesting coats-of-arms on the pediments. In the so-called Tour Saint-Jean, Renaissance frescoes representing various agricultural activities.
11 The château, 10th, 12th, 15th-16th c.

TOUFFOU 11

SAINTES 2

SAINTES 3

SAINTES 4

SAINTES 5

SURGÈRES 6

SURGÈRES 7

THOUARS 9

THOUARS 10

THOUARS 8

379

USSON 1

VERTEUIL 2

USSON (at Égreteaux) *Charente-Maritime*. E 13.

The château of Usson was formerly situated at Échebrune but when it began to decay it was brought stone by stone to Égreteaux and faithfully rebuilt in the late 19th century. It is a fine example of Renaissance civil architecture.

1 Courtyard of the château, Renaissance period.

VERTEUIL *Charente*. F 12.

Apart from the very fine polychrome terracotta Entombment in the church, dating from the mid-16th century, and attributed to Germain Pilon, the triangular ground-plan of the château is interesting. It was restored but has preserved its machicolated corner towers.

2 The château, 16th c.

VOUVANT *Vendée*, E 11.

The north portal with its double porch under a single arch is one of the most original features of the church of Notre-Dame, but even its ruins have a certain charm. The sculpture is as interesting as in other churches of the region, the main themes treated being sirens, tritons, masks, the story of Samson and Delilah, Atlantes and fantastic beasts which were meant to instruct the faithful as much as to frighten them. The façade has highly original ornamentation on two registers: on the upper, apostles lifting their arms towards the Lord, on the lower, a representation of the Last Supper.

In the little town, remains of a tower thought to have been built by the fairy Mélusine in the 13th century, and part of a fortress.

3 Church of Notre-Dame, façade of the north transept, 12th c.
4 Archivolt of the great arch, Atlantes.

VOUVANT 3

VOUVANT 4

X

LIMOUSIN - AUVERGNE - PÉRIGORD

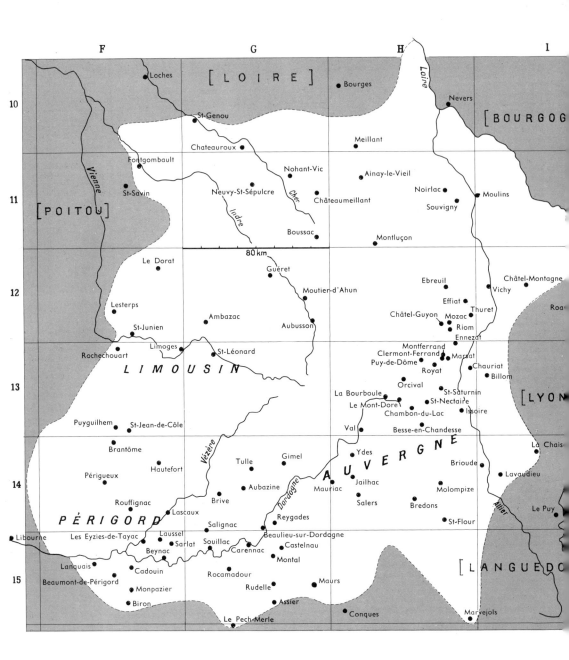

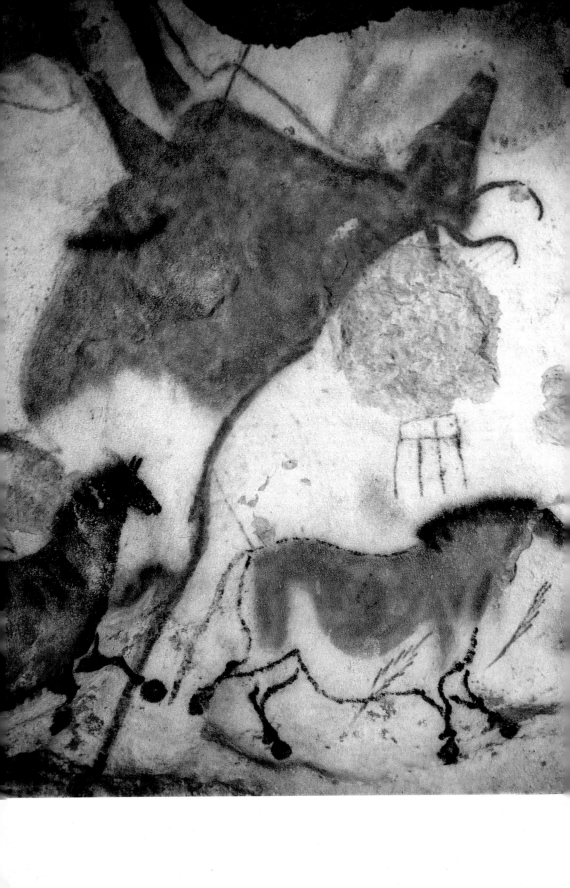

RELIQUARY OF SAINT-ÉTIENNE, LIMOUSIN ENAMEL, DETAIL, C. 1170,
GIMEL *(Belzeaux-Zodiaque)*

FRESCO IN THE CAVE AT LASCAUX, PREHISTORIC PERIOD, DETAIL
(Realités-Millet)

Geology has proved that the lovely mountains of the Auvergne are the oldest in France. The Périgord is a region of prehistoric caves and the home of Lascaux in the valley of Vézère where the world famous paintings, some 10,000 or 20,000 years old, are perhaps the finest, the most comprehensive and the most ancient witness to man's creative genius. Every succeeding period of civilisation — Romanesque, Gothic, and Renaissance — brought new riches to the region: Romanesque Virgins in the Cantal, exquisite reliquaries in enamel of Limoges, severe churches built with the stone lava of the Auvergne, and fairy-tale châteaux in the Périgord.

AINAY-LE-VIEIL I

AUBUSSON 6

AUBUSSON 5

AINAY-LE-VIEIL *Cher.* H 11.

The château has a polygonal fortified enceinte of the 14th century and a Renaissance courtyard of brick and stone of great charm. It has been partly restored, but with discretion.

1 Renaissance corps de logis of the château, 1500.

AMBAZAC *Haute-Vienne.* G 12.

The richness of the treasure of the abbey of Grandmont may be imagined by the fact that it possessed seven reliquaries of which one, that of Saint Étienne, may still be seen in the church of Ambazac. It is in the form of a church and symbolises the heavenly City. The enamelled base is divided into panels and is encrusted with various stones.

2 Reliquary of Saint Étienne de Muret, Limousin champlevé enamel, length 29 ½ inches, early 13th c.

ASSIER *Lot.* G 15.

The château and church of Assier were raised to the glory of Galiot de Genouillac, François I's Grand-Master of Artillery, and their decoration represents his exploits without any hint of modesty. All that remains of the château is the *corps de logis*, but the church is intact. The frieze that runs round it is a kind of comic-strip form of illustration of Genouillac's warlike feats. His statue, showing him leaning on his cannon with one foot resting on three cannon-balls, may be seen inside.

3 The château, 16th c.

AUBAZINE (or Obasine) *Corrèze.* G 14.

Fine Romanesque Cistercian abbey church, built between 1156 and 1176, with grisaille windows with interlacing patterns. The windows have been restored but they date from the late 12th century and are the most ancient in France. The church contains a Romanesque cupboard, a very rare surviving piece of Romanesque furniture, and the tomb of Saint-Étienne, 13th c.

4 Windows of the church, grisaille decoration, 12th c., restored.

AUBUSSON *Creuse.* G 12.

The little town of Aubusson has been renowned for its tapestry manufacture ever since the 8th century in the time of the Saracens. It was famous for the craft in the 15th century and during the Second Empire and was given a new lease of life during the last war by the artists who took refuge in it, among them Jean Lurçat, the master of modern tapestry design.

5 "Solaires", Aubusson tapestry by Jean Lurçat, length 13 feet, 6 inches, 1963. 6 "Coiffes de Vigne", Aubusson tapestry by Tourlière, length 11 feet 3 inches, 1963.

BEAULIEU-SUR-DORDOGNE *Corrèze.* G 14.

Large Romanesque church in the Auvergnat style with a fine south portal similar in composition and sculpture to that of Moissac (q.v.). The decentred cross behind the central Christ, shown seated with legs apart according to the archaic custom, is supported by two angels. The centre post of the portal is highly original, being formed of three combined Caryatids standing like Atlases with elongated arms.

7 South porch of the church of Saint-Pierre, 12th c. 8 Centre post of the south portal, 12th c. 9 Silver reliquary-Virgin, 12th c., Treasury of the church.

BEAULIEU 9

AMBAZAC 2

ASSIER 3

BEAULIEU 7

BEAULIEU 8

AUBAZINE 4

BEAUMONT-DU-PÉRIGORD 2

BEAUMONT-DU-PÉRIGORD 1

BEYNAC 5

BEAUMONT-DU-PÉRIGORD *Dordogne.* F 15.

The village has kept its character of a medieval stronghold with its groin-vaulted arcades and fortified church of Saint-Front. A few miles away, the beautiful Renaissance château of Barmes may be seen.

I Church and square, 13th-14th c. 2 Château of Barmes, 16th c.

BESSE-EN-CHANDESSE *Puy-de-Dôme.* H 13.

The village is built in dark basalt stone and contains Renaissance houses bearing coats-of-arms. The fine collegiate church has deteriorated so much that only the Romanesque nave and capitals are now worth attention. Among the capitals which are carved with ferocious figures, the most interesting are those illustrating the Minotaur, the Passion of Saint-André, in a more rustic style, and the curious capital of the three devils bearing away the soul of a dead man which might be a representation of the parable of Lazarus and the rich man; on the reverse of the last mentioned capital, the return of Tobias.

3 Capital of the nave of the collegiate church of Saint-André, 12th c. 4 15th c. houses.

BEYNAC *Dordogne.* F 15.

Charming château beautifully situated on a height overlooking the Dordogne. Delightful corbelled turrets, naive paintings of the 15th century and one of the 16th. A former fortress built in the 13th century and then transformed into an elegant residence, the pretty bays being added in the 16th century.

5 The Last Supper, fresco painting in the oratory of the château, 15th c.

BILLOM *Puy-de-Dôme.* I 13.

The ancient collegiate church of Saint-Cerneuf contains a Romanesque choir in the finest Auvergnat style. Later additions of various dates in the church. The choir is enclosed by very fine Romanesque railings with simple volutes. In the town, fountain and 16th-century belfry with wooden bell-turret.

6 Railings of the choir of the church of Saint-Cerneuf, 12th c.

BIRON (at Monpazier) *Dordogne.* F 15.

The château of Biron is one of the most complex and surprising in the region. It was first built in the 10th century, altered in the 12th-13th centuries, decorated in the Italianate style in the 15th (by Pons de Gontaut, brother of the bishop Armand, builder of the cathedral of Sarlat), completed with the addition of a *corps de logis* in the 17th. The fine Renaissance chapel was restored in 1954, and consists of two storeys. Inside, the very beautiful tomb of Pons de Gontaut (1524).

7 Courtyard of the château, *corps de logis* and Renaissance chapel. 8 Tomb of Pons de Gontaut-Biron, the Resurrection of Lazarus, 1524,

BOUSSAC *Creuse.* G 11.

Three famous names are linked with the history of the château of Boussac (an ancient fortified manor): those of George Sand, Merimée and the *Lady with the Unicorn*. It was here that the famous tapestry was discovered by George Sand, who had it classified by Merimée, the inspector of the Historical Monuments commission at the time. It may now be seen in the Musée de Cluny, Paris (q.v.). Less than a mile away from the château, a modest church containing remains of Romanesque frescoes, including one masterpiece: the Nativity (note the attempt at perspective and the harmony of the ochre tones).

9 The château, 15th-16th c. 10 The Nativity, fresco in the church of Boussac-Bourg, to the right of the axial window, late 12th c.

BESSE-EN-CHANDESSE 4

BESSE-EN-CHANDESSE 3

BIRON 8

BILLOM 6

BIRON 7

BOUSSAC-BOURG 10

BOUSSAC 9

389

BREDONS 3

BRANTOME *Dordogne*. F 14.

The 16th-century abbey is flanked by the two arms of the river and was the 16th-century retreat of Pierre de Bourdeiller, better known as Brantôme, the author of the famous *Chronicles*. The superb Limousin Romanesque bell tower with its gable dates from the original 11th-century abbey building (see Saint-Leonard). Behind the abbey, natural grottos with strange bas-reliefs (15th c.).

1 Bell-tower of the abbey-church, 11th c. **2** Rock bas-relief, the Crucifixion, in the grotto of the abbey, 15th c.

BREDONS *Cantal*. H 14.

Almost every church in the Cantal contains one or several precious wood-sculptures of the Romanesque period. The most usual themes are the Virgin in Majesty, with a rigorous frontal aspect, or saints like the Saint Peter of the Romanesque church of Saint-Timothée de Bredons.

3 Saint Peter, wood sculpture, 12th c.

BRIOUDE *Haute-Loire*. I 14.

The largest Romanesque church in the Auvergne with its 280-foot-long nave. The basilica was recently restored and important frescoes were found in the chapel of Saint-Michel and the gallery of the narthex. They are painted in sombre tones and the most important represents a frightening scene of Hell ruled over by an enormous green demon. Byzantine and even Asiatic influences have been detected in the painting.
Several figured capitals, and remarkable 14th-c. statues of the Virgin in childbirth, the Leprous Christ and Virgin with a bird.

4 Apse of the basilica of Saint-Julien, 12th c. **5** Columns and capitals, 12th c. **6** Hell, fresco in the chapel of Saint-Michel.

CADOUIN *Dordogne*. F 15.

The episodic richness of the Cistercian abbey of Cadouin was derived from its (false) Holy Shroud which it lost and regained on several successive occasions. During one of its lean periods, the abbey built the church with its agreeably simple façade. A second period of prosperity saw the addition of the highly exuberant Gothic cloisters with their profane, satirical, and even scabrous sculptures.

7 Façade of the church, 12th c. **8** The cloister, 15th c.

CARENNAC *Lot*. G 15.

Before he became the archbishop of Cambrai, Fénelon was the prior of the abbey of Carennac from 1681 to 1696. The abbey buildings date from the Romanesque period. The tympanum of the main portal represents Christ surrounded by the Apostles and the symbols of the four Evangelists; note the two angels prostrating themselves in the angles (cf. Cahors and Collonges). The cloister has kept a Romanesque gallery, but the others are in Flamboyant Gothic. A 16th-century Flemish Entombment of rare refinement and feeling may be seen in the church.

9 Tympanum of the portal of the church of Saint-Pierre, 12th c. **10** Gallery of the cloister, 12th c. **11** Detail of the Entombment, Flemish art, 16th c.

CASTELNAU 12

CASTELNAU (at Bretenoux) *Lot*. G 15.

The enormous red fortress of Castelnau dominates the Dordogne river where it meets with the Cère. This massive piece of medieval military architecture once held 1,500 men-at-arms and 100 horses.

12 The fortress, 12th-15th c.

BRANTOME 2

BRANTOME 1

BRIOUDE 6

BRIOUDE 4

BRIOUDE 5

CARENNAC 11

CARENNAC 9

CADOUIN 8

CADOUIN 7

CARENNAC 10

391

LA CHAISE-DIEU *Haute-Loire.* I 14.

The church is the last resting place of its creator, Pope Clement VI and has kept its sepulchral atmosphere to this day. Compared to the austere, anguishing atmosphere of the church, the famous painting of the *Danse Macabre* is almost serene. Every class of 15th-century society is represented in it, following in the wake of Adam: pope, emperor, cardinal, king, patriarch, knight, archbishop, a doctor of the Sorbonne, troubadour, peasant, friar and lastly a child and its mother. The frescoes are on the exterior of the choir screen and extend over a length of twenty yards. The church is built of granite in a very sober southern Gothic style and its only ornament is the great rood-screen bridging the nave. 14th-century choir-stalls and gaily coloured tapestries of the late 15th century.

1 The rood-screen, late 15th c. **2** Choir-stalls and tapestries. **3** Danse Macabre, detail, 15th c.

CHAMBON-DU-LAC *Puy-de-Dôme.* H 13.

Apart from its Auvergnat Romanesque church, somewhat sunk in the ground, with an interesting representation of the martyrdom of Saint Étienne on its tympanum, Chambon is worth visiting for its funerary rotunda, the mausoleum of the Lords of the Murols family. The Holy Sepulchre in Jerusalem would seem to have inspired its shape (cf. Montmorillon) which dates from the Merovingian period.

4 Funerary rotunda, 12th c. **5** Tympanum of the church, 12th c.

CHATEAUMEILLANT *Cher.* G 11.

The church of Saint-Genès has a portal in the Berrichon style and several unusual features: unusually high nave, six radiating chapels around the choir linked by twin arches of great elegance. **6** Choir of the church of Saint-Genès, 12th c.

CHATEL-MONTAGNE *Allier.* I 12.

The church of Notre-Dame was the former abbey church of a Benedictine priory and illustrates the encounter of two styles: the elegant Burgundian style as seen in the beautiful narthex-porch, and the Auvergnat style in the rough treatment of the granite and in the lines of the nave. The capitals are also in granite and their sculptures are correspondingly rough. In their stylisation and the humour of the acrobatic Atlantes they are similar to those of Mozac (q.v.).

7 Capital, Atlante, 12th c.

CHATEL MONTAGNE 7

CHAURIAT *Puy-de-Dôme.* H 13.

The great pilgrims' church of Chauriat has the most original south façade in the region: the stone marquetry decoration is in the best Mozarabic tradition and consists of gilded arkose, ochre-coloured or reddish-brown volcanic tufa, and black lava. The size of its octagonal bell-tower is only equalled by that of Saint-Saturnin (q.v.) and the apse is modern. As at Issoire (q.v.) the most interesting capital in the church is carved with a Last Supper, with the tablecloth coming down like a skirt over the legs of the Apostles.

8 Gable of the transept, south façade, 12th c. **9** Capital, the Last Supper, 12th c.

LA CHAISE-DIEU 1

LA CHAISE-DIEU 2

LA CHAISE-DIEU 3

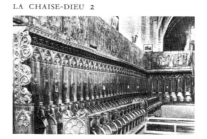

CHAMBON-DU-LAC 4

CHAMBON-DU-LAC 5

CHATEAUMEILLANT 6

CHAURIAT 9

CHAURIAT 8

393

CLERMONT-FERRAND *Puy-de-Dôme*. H 13.

Although it was built between the 6th and the 12th centuries, the church of Notre-Dame du Port (not to be confused with the Gothic cathedral of Notre-Dame) has a striking unity of style. It was admirably restored in 1843 by the architect Mallay. It is a typical church for its region (the Limagne) with its storeyed apse, the exterior decoration of pebbles encrusted in mortar, its harmonious design, majestic choir and beautiful but extremely complicated ambulatory. The sombre nave leads to the famous capitals of the choir which were mostly the work of Robert de Clermont (*see* the tympanum of Conques, and the apse of Saint-Nectaire). The capitals inspired by the Psychomachia (the work of the Spanish poet Prudentius, 6th c.) are by an unknown hand but the static force of their composition is astonishing. In the town, fine Renaissance fountain (Fontaine d'Amboise) and numerous old houses.

I Notre-Dame du Port, nave, 11th-12th c. **2** Side portal with saddle-backed lintel, 12th c. **3** Capital of the Psychomachia, 12th c. **4** Nave of the cathedral of Notre-Dame, 13th c. **5** Courtyard and doorway of the hôtel Savaron, 16th c.

LE DORAT 6

LE DORAT *Haute-Vienne*. F 12.

The portal of the church adorned by numerous festooned mouldings is similar to those of the church of La Souterraine in the same region, showing the same influence of Moslem styles on the Limousin Romanesque school. Fine cupola on pendentives over the crossing of the transept.

6 Polyfoil portal of the church, 12th c.

ÉBREUIL *Allier*. H 12

The large Benedictine abbey church at Ébreuil was built between the 10th and 12th centuries over the remains of Saint Léger. Its impressive porch-tower is as striking as its early Gothic apse and its timber-vaulted nave, but its most interesting features are the Romanesque frescoes on the gallery with scenes of the martyrdom of Saints Valerian and Pancratius.

7 Fresco of the gallery of the church of Saint-Léger, 12th c.

ÉBREUIL 7

EFFIAT *Puy-de-Dôme*. H 12.

The château was begun in 1627 for the Marquis d'Effiat but it was never completed. Among the historic documents kept in the château, a letter signed by the Marquise d'Effiat, beseeching Louis XIII to pardon his son, the "young and misled" Cinq-Mars for having conspired against the life of Richelieu. The gateway to the château is a fine example of Louis XIII style architecture. Superb furnishings; painted ceilings and park with ornamental ponds of the 17th century.

8 Gateway to the château, 1627. **9** Fireplace in the great salon: Vulcan's smithy, attributed to Le Nain, 17th c.

ENNEZAT *Puy-de-Dôme*. H 13.

The Romanesque-Auvergnat style is perfectly illustrated here by the narrow nave of the church of Saint-Victor with its massive pillars flanked by columns with figured capitals.

10 Nave of the church of Saint-Victor, 11th c. **II** Capital in the nave: the punishment of the usurer, 11th c.

CLERMONT-FERRAND 1

CLERMONT-FERRAND 2

CLERMONT-FERRAND 4

CLERMONT-FERRAND 5

CLERMONT-FERRAND 3

EFFIAT 8

EFFIAT 9

ENNEZAT 10

ENNEZAT 11

395

LES EYZIES-DE-TAYAC 1

LES EYZIES-DE-TAYAC *Dordogne*. F 15.

Situated in the heart of a rocky region renowned for its caves with stone-age rock drawings, Les Eyzies is now a centre for excursions. A museum has been installed in the village.

1 Deer and fish, engraved bone, Musée National de la Préhistoire.

FONTGOMBAULT *Indre*. F 11.

The perfect design of the apse of the Romanesque Benedictine abbey church is echoed by the choir which is one of the most beautiful in central France, and now restored by the monks who inhabit it.

2 Apse of the abbey church, late 11th c.

GIMEL *Corrèze*. G 14.

The reliquary protecting the remains of Saint Étienne is a late 12th-century work in which the Limousin enamel-worker daringly combined several different colours of enamel in each compartment. The figures have inlaid copper heads with enamel eyes. The dominant colours are green, blue, turquoise.

3 Reverse of the reliquary of Saint-Etienne, three angels and four Apostles, Limousin champlevé enamel, length 22 ½ inches, c. 1170.

GUÉRET *Creuse*. G 12.

The small provincial town of Guéret has a charming early Renaissance *hôtel* built by Antoine de Monneyroux, treasurer of the Comte de la Marche, and contains a museum which includes, among other attractions, a series of Limousin reliquaries of which the finest is the *châsse de Malval*. It is decorated with scenes depicting the life and martyrdom of Saint Étienne like the Gimel reliquary, but is certainly at least twenty years later in date. The figures and the mosaic decoration in blue and green on the reverse are enamelled on a golden vermiculated background.

4 Front view of the reliquary of Saint Étienne, known as the *châsse de Malval*, Limousin enamel, length 6 inches, late 12th c., Musée de Guéret. 5 Hôtel des Monneyroux, late 15th-early 16th c.

HAUTEFORT *Dordogne*. F 14.

Hautefort is undoubtedly the most beautiful château in the Périgord and one of the most impressive in the whole of France. Its setting is equally grandiose. It was built over medieval foundations in the 17th century by an architect from Perigord, Nicolas Rambourg.

6 The château, by Nicolas Rambourg, 17th c.

HAUTEFORT 6

ISSOIRE *Puy-de-Dôme*. H 13.

The church of Saint-Austremoine is as striking by the beauty of its proportions and the majesty of its great nave (240 feet long), and the design of its apse as it is repulsive for the orange and green badigeon that was applied in the 19th century. The visitor must try to forget its colouring in order to admire the figured capitals. The crypt has escaped being painted over and gives an idea of what the nave must have looked like before it was "restored".

7 Apse of Saint-Austremoine, 12th c. 8 The Last Supper, capital of the nave, 12th c. 9 Crypt of the church, 12th c.

FONTGOMBAULT 2

GIMEL 3

GUÉRET 5

GUÉRET 4

ISSOIRE 8

ISSOIRE 7

ISSOIRE 9

JAILHAC (near Moussages) *Cantal.* H 14.

The chapel of Notre-Dame-de-Claviers contains one of the most beautiful statues of the Virgin in Majesty: unequalled expressiveness, nobility of attitude, treatment of draperies make this hieratic figure one of the earliest masterpieces of Romanesque figurative sculpture.

1 Virgin in Majesty, known as Notre-Dame de Claviers, chapel of Notre-Dame de Claviers, 11th c.

LANQUAIS *Dordogne.* F 15.

King Henri II's favour did not last long enough for his mistress Isabeau de Rimeuil to be able to complete the château she was building for herself at Lanquais. The château has consequently been achieved in two quite different styles: the machicolated part is 15th-century and dates from Henri II's reign, and the other is so purely Renaissance that it is thought that the architects of the Louvre must have had a hand in its building.

2 The château, façade of the 15th c. 3 Fireplace and sculpted doorways, 16th c.

LAVAUDIEU 10

LESTERPS 11

LASCAUX (at Montignac) *Dordogne.* F 14.

The discovery of Lascaux in 1940 is an important date in the history of prehistoric archaeology. Although far from being one of the largest caves in France its walls are covered with paintings at least ten or twelve thousand years old or which have become famous the world over for their fine colouring and accomplished style. Scholars have stressed the way the various subjects have been arranged in compositions which include the figures of bulls (some 30 feet long), a herd of swimming deer, and in the "well" (closed to visitors), the scene of the "dead hunter" — exceptional as pictures of human figures from that epoch are practically unknown.

4-5-6-7-8 Frescoes in the caves of Lascaux.

LAUSSEL (near Marquay) *Dordogne.* F 15.

The region is full of prehistoric caves in one of which, the Abri de Laussel, the famous bas-relief figure of the "Venus of Laussel" was recently found among other humanoid figures. Nearby, a pretty Renaissance château.

9 Venus of Laussel, Aurignacian period.

LAVAUDIEU (4 1/2 miles from Brioude) *Haute-Loire.* I 14.

The cloister of the Benedictine abbey of Lavaudieu was saved from imminent collapse, although it was still intact, in 1948, and has been perfectly restored. It is unusual in having kept its beams and upper storey entirely built in wood. Semi-circular arches supported by alternate single and twin-colonnettes, some of which are spiral. In the chapter house a 13th-century fresco of the Virgin in Majesty has been uncovered.

10 Cloister of the Benedictine abbey, 12th c.

LESTERPS *Charente.* F 12.

Although the base of the porch-tower of the church is the earliest part of the structure (11th c.), the whole enormous tower is similar to that of the church at Ebreuil (q.v.).

11 Porch-tower of the church, 150 feet high, 11th c.

LANQUAIS 3

LANQUAIS 2

LASCAUX 4

LASCAUX 5

LASCAUX 6

LASCAUX 7

LASCAUX 8

LAUSSEL 9

LIMOGES *Haute-Vienne.* F 13.

The town of Limoges is famous the world over for its enamels and its porcelain. The cloisonné, champlevé (from the 12th c. onwards) or painted (from the 15th c.) enamels may be seen in an excellent museum. The manufacture of Limoges porcelain in France dates from 1768 and more than ten thousand ceramics of all ages and countries may be seen in the Musée Adrien Dubouché. The town has a Gothic cathedral built by Jean Deschamps, completed in the 19th century. Its main features are the bell-tower and the rather restrained Flamboyant Saint-Jean portal. The little Gothic church of Saint-Michel-des-Lions has its steeple crowned by a ball of incised copper.

1 Tower of the cathedral Saint-Étienne, 13th c. 2 Tower of Saint-Michel-des-Lions, 15th c. 3 Eucharistic coffer, champlevé enamel, 13th c., Musée Municipal. 4 Tureen and plate in Limoges porcelain, 19th c., Musée Adrien Dubouché.

MARSAT *Puy-de-Dôme.* H 13.

The heavy railings of the north side chapel of the church of Notre-Dame conceal a little Virgin in blackened walnut wood, with rather over-gilded draperies. It is a very beautiful example of Auvergnat Romanesque Virgins, with its rigid frontal aspect and long, stiff hands.

5 "Vierge noire", 12th. c.

MARSAT 5

MARVEJOLS *Lozère.* H 15.

The town of Marvejols was rebuilt by Henri IV in the early 17th century and the three fortified gateways date from the time. Two statues by the contemporary sculptor Auricoste in the town: one of Henri IV, and the other of the Beast of Gévaudan which terrorised the region in the 18th century.

6 Porte Soubeyran, 1610, and statue of Henri IV by Auriscote.

MAURIAC *Cantal.* H 14.

The tympanum of the Auvergnat church of Notre-Dame-des-Miracles is in a purely Languedoc style. Above the decapitated figures of the apostles, the Ascension of Christ, and signs of the Zodiac on the outer moulding, as at Ydes (q.v.). College founded in 1560, with portal with elegant Corinthian columns.

MAURS 9

7 Tympanum of the portal of the church of Notre-Dame-des-Miracles, 12th c. 8 Portal of the college, 1623.

MAURS *Cantal.* G 15.

The reliquary bust of Saint Césaire at Maurs has the same characteristic large flat hands with fingers of almost equal length as the Auvergnat Romanesque Virgins. The figure is covered with copper sheet and encrusted with stones and may be seen in the mediocre Gothic church of the village.

9 Reliquary-bust of Saint Césaire, wood and copper plating, 13th c.

MEILLANT *Cher.* H 10.

The 13th-century fortress of Meillant was decorated in an early Renaissance Italianate style by Charles I of Amboise, the favourite of Louis XI. This duality of styles has made it the most beautiful château in the region. The Tour du Lion bears emblems of the Chaumont (chaud mont) and the Amboise families and illustrates the transition from Flamboyant Gothic to the Renaissance style.

10 Tour du Lion, 16th c.

LIMOGES 1

LIMOGES 2

LIMOGES 4

MARVEJOLS 6

LIMOGES 3

MAURIAC 7

MEILLANT 10

MAURIAC 8

401

MOLOMPIZE I

MOLOMPIZE *Cantal*. H 14.

The wooden reliquary-statues of the Virgin in Majesty in the Cantal region are often covered with gold sheet and the Child is always shown from the front with large staring eyes, a half-smiling mouth and enormous hands. Only the draperies and the seat of the Virgin differ from statue to statue.

I Notre-Dame de Vauclair, Virgin and Child, painted wood, 29 inches high, in the chapel of the ancient château of Vauclair.

MONPAZIER *Dordogne*. F 15.

The town is built on a chess-board pattern and is a model of Medieval town-planning. Main square with Gothic arcades, known as "grandes cornières", and well preserved 13th-century houses.

2 Old market hall, 13th c.

MONTAL (at Saint-Jean-Lespinasse) *Lot*. G 15.

The lonely widow Jeanne de Balsac decided to decorate the fortress-château of Montal in the style of her time for her son Robert who was fighting in Italy with François I but the motto "Plus d'espoir" which was engraved under a window tells us that Robert never returned alive from the wars. During the Revolution, the fine Renaissance decoration added by Jeanne de Balsac was sold at auction, stone by stone, by a certain enterprising but unscrupulous Macaire. In 1908 a rich and devoted art-patron, M. Fenaille, bought back the stones which were dispersed all over the world, restored the château and presented it to the State. The courtyard is a masterpiece of the Italianate style with its busts of the Balsac family, frieze and dormer-windows.
Inside, an exceptionally fine staircase with a perforated centre wall and sculpted ceiling. The Salle des Gardes and bed-room have hangings and furniture of the period.

3 Inner courtyard of the Renaissance château.

MONTFERRAND *Puy-de-Dôme*. H 13.

The dead city of Montferrand is worth discovering for it contains a countless number of Gothic and Renaissance houses. Although its buildings are blackened with grime and in a state of abandon, every façade in the main streets conceals courtyards, staircases and bas-reliefs of great interest. Montferrand was annexed by Clermont in 1731, losing half its name (Clermont-Ferrand) and all its former activity.

4 Doorway of the Maison du Centaure, 11, rue du Languedoc, 15th-16th c. 5 Maison de Lucrèce, 28, rue Jules-Guesde, 15th c. 6 Staircase of the house of the Sire de Beaujeu (Hôtel d'Albiat), 13, rue du Languedoc, 15th c.

MOULINS *Allier*. I 11.

In the heart of the noble and calm old town, the visitor may see one of the glories of the French primitive school, the great painted tryptych of the *Virgin in Glory* by the Master of Moulins. The painting is exhibited in the sacristy of the cathedral and stands next to an interesting *Bethlehem Tryptych* attributed to Joss Van Cleeve (early 16th c.). The cathedral is built in the Flamboyant Gothic style and has beautiful stained-glass windows. The tomb of Henri of Montmorency may be seen in the Lycée Banville. In the municipal library, a manuscript Bible of the 12th century from the Benedictine monastery of Souvigny, with fine miniatures.

7 Centre panel of the tryptych of the *Virgin in Glory:* Virgin venerated by the Duke and Duchess of Bourbon, c. 1498, cathedral sacristy. 8 Jonas, page of the Souvigny Bible, 12th c. manuscript, municipal library. 9 Tomb of Henri II of Montmorency, chapel of the Lycée Banville, by François Anguier, 1652.

402

MONPAZIER 2

MONTAL 3

MONTFERRAND 4

MONTFERRAND 6

MONTFERRAND 5

MOULINS 7

MOULINS 9

MOULINS 8

403

MOZAC 4

MOZAC 3

MOUTIER-D'AHUN *Creuse.* G 12.

The extraordinary oak wood-work decorating the interior of the church is the work of Simon Baüer, an Auvergnat artist who worked there between 1673 and 1681. It has recently been cleaned and reveals a talent and a richness of imagination of the highest order. Fine Romanesque bell-tower of the church, and pretty pointed bridge over the Creuse (14th c.).

I Bridge over the Creuse, 14th c. 2 Wood-work in the choir by Simon Baüer, 1681.

MOZAC (or MOZAT) *Puy-de-Dôme.* H 12.

The Benedictine abbey church of Mozac was founded by Calmin and Namadie (later canonised) and is a virtual museum of Auvergnat sculpture. The different capitals are all in a perfect state and are all works of art, together with the Treasury, and are attributed to the sculptors who were working at Saint-Julien de Brioude between 1160 and 1165. In the Treasury, 16th-century painted wooden reliquary, the *châsse de Saint Austremoine*, and reliquary of Saint Calmin, a masterpiece of Limoges enamel and gold-work dating from about 1168.

3 The Holy Women in the tomb, capital taken down and placed in the apse, so-called Capital of the Resurrection, 12th c. 4 Reliquary of Saint Calmin, champlevé enamel, 34 inches long, 12th c.

NEUVY-SAINT-SÉPULCRE *Indre.* G 11.

When the lord of Déols came back in 1042 from a pilgrimage to the Holy Land he built the round church at Neuvy in imitation of the Holy Sepulchre in Jerusalem. Choir encircled by eleven columns with remarkable capitals carved by sculptors from a local Berrichon school.

5 Exterior of the church, 82 feet in diameter, 11th-12th c. 6 The columns in the choir, 12th c.

NOHANT-VIC *Indre.* G 11.

Village where Georges Sand retired to spend her peaceful old age. Beautiful 12th-century frescoes in the church of Saint-Martin de Vic, discovered in the 19th century and preserved through the efforts of Prosper Mérimée, then Inspector of the Historical Monuments Commission. Extremely expressive attitudes, dominant pale ochre and reddish-brown tones.

7 The Magi. 8 The Visitation, fresco in the church of Saint-Martin de Vic, 12th c.

NOIRLAC (near Saint-Amand-Montrond) *Cher.* H 11.

The buildings of an ancient Cistercian abbey may still be seen along the banks of the river Cher somewhat below the main road. The cloister is certainly the most beautiful of the order and illustrates the evolution of the Gothic style with its pointed arches in the earliest bays of the late 13th century and the 14th-century foliated cusps in the groin vaulting.

9 West wing of the conventual buildings and façade of the abbey church, 12th c. 10 Nave of the church, 12th c. 11 View of the gallery of the cloister, 13th c. 12 Chapter house and gallery of the cloister, 13th-14th c.

MOUTIER-D'AHUN 1

MOUTIER-D'AHUN 2

NOHANT-VIC 8

NEUVY-ST-SÉPULCRE 5

NEUVY-ST-SÉPULCRE 5   NEUVY-ST-SÉPULCRE 6

NOHANT-VIC 7

NOIRLAC 9

NOIRLAC 11   NOIRLAC 12

NOIRLAC 10

ORCIVAL *Puy-de-Dôme.* H 13.

The basilica of Notre-Dame is characterised by a refinement of the Auvergnat Romanesque style that could be seen in its early stages in the churches of Saint-Nectaire, Issoire and Clermont-Ferrand (q.v.). High apse, two-tiered octagonal belltower; the high elevation of the luminous nave and, especially, the aisles with their fine capitals — a precursor of the Gothic style. The apse has four radiating chapels, the even number being compulsory in churches dedicated to the Virgin.

I Apse and bell-tower of the church of Notre-Dame, late 12th c.
2 Aisle, 12th c.

LE PECH-MERLE 3

LE PECH-MERLE *Lot.* G 15.

The hill of Pech-Merle overlooking the little village of Cabrerets is famous for its prehistoric cave with enormous chambers with highly important Stone Age paintings on the walls. The high machicolated tower of the château of Gontaut-Biron dominates the river valley; it is now a little museum of prehistoric archaeology.

3 Château of Gontaut-Biron and mill, 15th c. 4 Rock painting in the cave of Pech-Merle.

PÉRIGUEUX *Dordogne.* F 14.

The enormous white, multi-domed basilica of Saint-Front owes more to the reconstruction work of M. Abadie, completed in 1901, than to the original design of its 12th-century architect. It has nevertheless a medieval appearance and the ground-plan of a Byzantine basilica with five cupolas supported by pendentives would appear to have been inspired by Saint Mark's in Venice. The church of Saint-Étienne de la Cité is a more authentic example of the Romanesque style of the Périgord. Altar decorated with a fine gilt-wood retable of the 17th century. In the pretty old quarter by the river Isle, the surprising Maison des Consuls with its machicolated gallery surmounted by high Renaissance dormers.

5 Church of Saint-Front, 12th-19th c. 6 Church of Saint-Étienne de la Cité, 12th c., restored. 7 Maison des Consuls, 15th and 16th c.

PUY DE DOME 8

PUY DE DOME *Puy-de-Dôme.* H 13.

The remains of an important Gallo-Roman sanctuary dedicated to Mercurius Dumias have been found at a height of more than 4,800 feet on the summit of the Puy de Dôme.

8 Ruins of the temple of Mercury, Gallo-Roman period.

PUYGUILHEM (at Villars) *Dordogne.* F 13.

The château of Puyguilhem is as finely sculpted as any along the Loire Valley and illustrates the early, heavily Italianate Renaissance style in France. The massive towers and façade are richly decorated with dormers with high pediments and a sculpted balustrade.

9 The château, 16th c.

ORCIVAL 1

ORCIVAL 2

LE PECH-MERLE 4

PÉRIGUEUX 6

PÉRIGUEUX 5

PÉRIGUEUX 7

PUYGUILHEM 9

407

REYGADES I

ST-GENOU II

ST-GENOU 12

REYGADES *Corrèze*. G 14.

The Entombment is not particularly original but its setting in the bare little railed chapel of the cemetery gives it a simplicity and expressiveness all of its own. Remains of gilt and polychromy on the figures; naive and touching expressions.

1 The Entombment, 15th c.

RIOM *Puy-de-Dôme*. H 12.

Riom would be a pretty town if it were not built in the sad grey Volvic stone used throughout the Auvergne, for it is rich in ancient *hôtels* (rue de l'Hôtel-de-Ville and rue de l'Horloge, for example) and well laid-out. Religious architecture is well represented by the Sainte-Chapelle of the Palais de Justice, built for Jean de Berry in 1390, with admirable 15th-century stained-glass. The façade of the church of Notre-Dame du Marthuret bears a replica of the statue of the Virgin with a bird (the original is inside).

2 Staircase of the hôtel Guimoneau. **3** Medallion on the staircase of the hôtel Guimoneau, 16th c. **4** Fountain of Adam and Eve, by Longueville, 16th c. **5** Virgin with a bird, church of Notre-Dame du Marthuret, 16th c. **6** Maison des Consuls.

ROCHECHOUART *Haute-Vienne*. F 13.

The château of Rochechouart is perched on a rocky peak and was reconstructed in the 15th century. Pretty inner courtyard. Gallery with flattened arches in the arcading and curious twisted columns. Fine 16th-century frescoes in the Salle des Chasses.

7 Gallery of the *cour d'honneur* of the château, 15th c.

RUDELLE *Lot*. G 15.

With its rampart walk and battlements the keep at Rudelle is a fine example of medieval military architecture but surprisingly, it contains a 14th-century fortified church - witness to the insecurity of the times.

8 Fortified church, 14th c.

SAINT-FLOUR *Cantal*. H 14.

An admirable view may be had from the town which is perched up on a rock. The cathedral is in a severe Gothic style and was built by Jean de Berry's architect, Hugues Joly, who preserved the military character of the city in his structure.

9 Façade of the cathedral Saint-Flour, completed in 1466. **10** Detail of the Beau Dieu Noir, Christ on the Cross, 12th c., cathedral.

SAINT-GENOU *Indre*. G 10.

A "dead men's lantern" like those found in many places in southwest France has been preserved in the old cemetery of a now no longer existing monastery. The abbey church has kept its Romanesque choir in the finest Berrichon style. Wonderful carved capitals.

11 Dead men's lantern, 12th c. **12** Choir of the abbey church, late 12th c.

RIOM 5

RIOM 3

RIOM 2

RIOM 4

RIOM 6

ROCHECHOUART 7

ST-FLOUR 10

ST-FLOUR 9

RUDELLE 8

409

ST-JEAN-DE-COLE I

ST-LÉONARD-DE-NOBLAT 4

ST-NECTAIRE 7

SAINT-JEAN-DE-COLE *Dordogne.* F 13.

One of the many villages whose charm is derived from the golden-coloured stone of which they are built. The church, château, houses and Gothic bridge are all in perfect harmony. The Périgord region is particularly rich in such beautiful villages.

I Château de la Marthonie, 15th c. 2 The church, 11th c.

SAINT-JUNIEN *Haute-Vienne.* F 12.

The late 12th-century limestone tomb of the young hermit Junien is the main interest of the church which was built between the 11th and 15th centuries. The figures in high-relief are almost carved in the round and the lines of the composition seem almost certainly to have been inspired by a reliquary casket.

3 Detail of the façade of the tomb of Saint Junien: the Elders of the Apocalypse, 12th c.

SAINT-LÉONARD-DE-NOBLAT *Haute-Vienne.* G 13.

The church of Saint-Léonard has the finest polyhedric faceted bell-tower of the Romanesque period in the whole of the Limousin. By using gables the architect made the transition from its square base to an octagonal tier. It was skilfully restored in the 19th century. The church is somewhat incongruous and was built between the 11th and 13th centuries.

4 Bell-tower of the church of Saint-Léonard, 12th c.

SAINT-NECTAIRE *Puy-de-Dôme.* H 13.

The proportions of the purely Auvergnat-style basilica are calculated with perfect precision and the structure was completed in thirty years, being finished in 1178. It is set on Mont-Cornadore and is adapted to the varying levels of its granite base. Tufa, trachyte and lava give it its autumnal colouring, animated by stone marquetry patterns. The interior is rich in treasures: a hundred and three finely carved capitals in the aisles and choir are of unequalled richness and are famous for their naivety of design and vigour of expression. The Treasury contains a traditional Romanesque Auvergnat Virgin in polychrome wood — the Notre-Dame du Mont Cornadore — 12th century Limousin champlevé enamel binding boards and most famous, the moving bust of Saint Baudime, plated with gold.

5 Basilica of Saint-Nectaire, 12th c. 6 The nave, 12th c. 7 Reliquary-bust of Saint Baudime, Limousin enamel, 12th c.

SAINT-SATURNIN *Puy-de-Dôme.* H 13.

Saint-Saturnin is the only church in the Auvergne which has kept its original belltower: an admirable stone pyramid crowning two tiers of twin-arcades. The church is situated on the edge of a precipice and its golden arkose and black lava give it an austere purity of appearance. No narthex or radiating chapels: its only ornaments are a few capitals.

8 Apse and tower of the church, 12th c. 9 Fountain built of lava, in front of the château, late 16th c.

SALERS *Cantal.* H 14.

A very pretty and typical Auvergnat town with numerous 15th-century turreted houses. In the Gothic-style church, a stone Entombment with life-size figures and remnants of its original colouring.

10 15th-century houses. 11 Entombment, polychrome stone, 1495.

410

ST-JEAN-DE-COLE 2

ST-JUNIEN 3

ST-NECTAIRE 5

ST-NECTAIRE 6

ST-SATURNIN 8

SALERS 11

SALERS 10

ST-SATURNIN 9

411

SALIGNAC I

SALIGNAC *Dordogne.* G 14.

Several houses with fine dormer windows of the Renaissance, often highly original in design. The nearby château of Salignac is a fine specimen of a medieval fortress.

1 Dormer window and tiled roof, 16th c.

SARLAT *Dordogne.* F 15.

The winding streets of the old town are rich in houses dating from the 14th to 17th century. Pointed windows of the hôtel Plamon, splendid Renaissance dormer of the hôtel La Boëtie, severe stone casements of the hôtel Malleville, curious Louis XII-style slate roof of the hôtel du Présidial.

2 Tour des Morts, 12th c. **3** Hôtel de Selves de Plamon, 14th c. **4** Hôtel La Boëtie, 16th c. **5** Hôtel du Présidial, 17th c.

SARLAT 4   SARLAT 3

SARLAT 5

SARLAT 2

SOUILLAC *Lot.* G 15.

The school of Romanesque sculpture of the Languedoc is characterised by an elaborate composition, lively elegance of attitudes and richness of detail inspired not so much from nature as from such highly elaborate decorative works as Byzantine ivories and Irish miniatures with their complicated interlacing patterns. This style of sculpture is most notably represented at Souillac, Cahors, Carennac, Moissac and Beaulieu. The ancient abbey church of Souillac has cupolas resting on pendentives in the Romanesque style of the Perigord and is free from all later additions.

6 Apse of the church of Sainte-Marie, late 12th c. **7** The prophet Isaiah, reverse of church portal. **8** Pillar decoration: monsters (Pilier des monstres). **9** The legend of the monk Theophilus.

SOUVIGNY *Allier.* H 11.

The church of the ancient priory at Souvigny is a particularly happy combination of the Romanesque and Gothic styles. From the first date the 11th-century capitals in the nave, from the second, the beautiful vaulting of the nave, the two tombs of the Bourbons (15th c.) and the curious cloister with alternating vaulting with off-centre key-stones in its sole surviving gallery. Very elegant 18th-century façade of the priory buildings facing the main square.

10 Façade of the church of Saint-Pierre, 15th c., and façade of the priory, 18th c. **11** South wall of the nave of the church of Saint-Pierre, and Romanesque capitals, 11th c. **12** Vaulting of the nave, 15th c. **13** Gallery of the cloister, 16th c.

SOUILLAC 6

SOUILLAC 8

SOUILLAC 9

SOUILLAC 7

SOUVIGNY 12

SOUVIGNY 10

SOUVIGNY 11

SOUVIGNY 13

413

THURET 1

TULLE 2

THURET *Puy-de-Dôme*. H 12.

The decorated tympanum of the church of Thuret is rare for the Dordogne where sculpture is generally confined to the capitals. The nave is covered by a surprising 15th-century Gothic vault. The capitals have been unfortunately painted over and it is to be hoped that they will soon be restored to their former state.

1 Saddle-back lintel of the south portal of the church, 11th c.

TULLE *Corrèze*. G 14.

The bell-tower of the church of Saint-Martin is composed of three different parts dating from the 12th, 13th and 14th centuries, and is crowned by a tall stone spire. The 12th-century cloister is well lit by trefoil windows but only two of its galleries have survived intact. The abbey buildings are completed by the house of the Abbot, a Renaissance building with four storeys of richly sculpted windows.

2 Gallery of the cloister, 12th c.

VAL (at Bort-les-Orgues) *Corrèze*. H 13.

The feudal château of Val stands on a site which seems to have remained unchanged since the Creation. The château was built on its rocky island in 1450 but the beautiful lake is artificial, having been made as a reservoir for the power station of the Électricité de France, in 1954.

3 The château, 1450.

YDES *Cantal*. H 14.

Small Romanesque bas-relief of the Annunciation on the portal of the church of Saint-Georges, and apse with curious corbels and capitals.

4 The Annunciation, bas-relief to the left of the portal of the church of Saint-Georges, 12th c. 5 Apse of the church, 12th c.

VAL 3

YDES 4

YDES 5

XI

LYONNAIS - SAVOIE - DAUPHINÉ

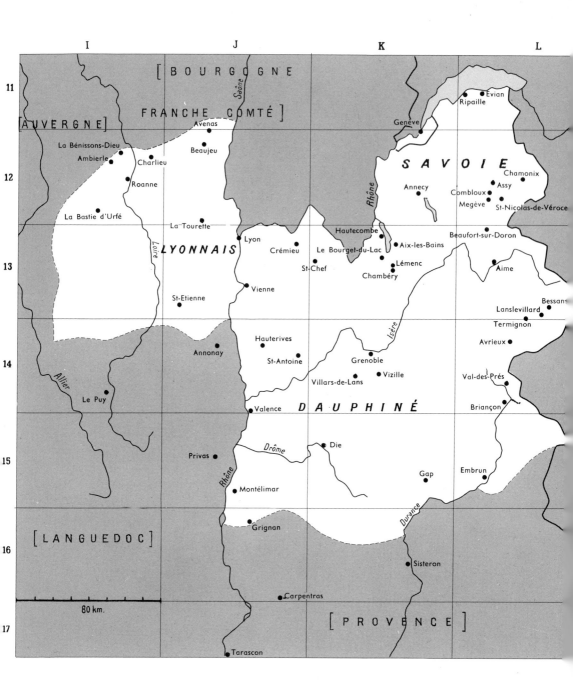

I   J   K   L

[B O U R G O G N E

FRANCHE COMTÉ]

[AUVERGNE]

Saône

Avenas

11

La Bénissons-Dieu

Beaujeu

Geneve

Evian

Ripaille

S A V O I E

Ambierle

Charlieu

Rhône

Chamonix

12

Roanne

Annecy

Assy

Combloux

Megève

St-Nicolas-de-Véroce

La Bastie d'Urfé

La Tourette

Loire

L Y O N N A I S

Lyon

Hautecombe

Beaufort-sur-Doron

13

Crémieu

Le Bourget-du-Lac

Aix-les-Bains

St-Chef

Lémenc

Chambéry

Aime

Vienne

Isère

St-Etienne

Lanslevillard

Bessans

Termignon

Hauterives

14

Annonay

St-Antoine

Avrieux

Grenoble

Vizille

Val-des-Prés

Allier

Villars-de-Lans

D A U P H I N É

Le Puy

Valence

Briançon

Drôme

Die

15

Privas

Rhône

Gap

Embrun

Montélimar

Durance

Grignan

[L A N G U E D O C]

16

Sisteron

80 km.

Carpentras

[P R O V E N C E]

17

Tarascon

SILK, EMPIRE STYLE, LYON, TASSINARI COLLECTION *(Connaissance des Arts - J. Guillot)*

GEORGES BRAQUE (1892-1963), THE VIOLIN, MUSÉE DES BEAUX-ARTS, LYON *(Camponogara)*

Lyon is as old as Paris and was chosen as the capital of Roman Gaul for its situation on the Rhone. Emperors were born and died there, such as Claudius and Caracalla, and two thousand years of intense living have made the famous city one of the richest and most interesting in France.

Grenoble is the city of Stendhal, and lies in a bend of the river Isère. It is famous as a cultural centre and for its fine museum of modern art.

At Chambéry, the Palace of the Dukes is a reminder of the long-lived splendour of the House of Savoy in the days of its independence, and the bulbous, greenish copper domes of the churches give the little villages a unity and an almost Byzantine quality which makes a curious contrast with the ultra-modern church recently built on the plateau of Assy.

419

ANNECY 6

ANNECY 5

AVENAS 11

AIME *Savoie.* L 13.

The church of Saint-Martin is a reminder that Savoy was once a Roman province for it is built in several successive styles including that of an ancient Roman temple, Merovingian crypt and Romanesque nave, the last being massive and very unusual. The frescoes are Romanesque.

1 Church of Saint-Martin, 11th-12th c. 2 Massacre of the Innocents, fresco in the church of Saint-Martin, 12th c.

AMBIERLE *Loire.* I 12.

When Michel de Changy died in 1479 he left a retable to the church of Ambierle. It had been painted and sculpted at Beaune by an anonymous artist in about 1466 and represented the members of Changy's family. All we now know of the painter was that he was a skilful pupil of Rogier van der Weyden, and greatly influenced by him. The polyptych is one of the finest examples of the Burgundian primitive school.

3 Nave of the abbey church. 4 The Master of Ambierle (15th c.): wing of the polyptych: Laurette de Jaucourt and her patron Saint Laurent, c. 1466.

ANNECY *Haute-Savoie.* K 12.

The picturesque town of Annecy owes its charm to its arcaded streets, its château and its beautiful lake with two other nearby châteaux: Duingt, built in the 11th century and altered in the 18th, and Menthon, of the Renaissance period. The churches of Annecy contain two fine paintings: a *Descent from the Cross* by Pourbus the Elder in the church of Saint-Maurice (1558), and the same theme treated by Caravaggio in 1609 in the cathedral.

5 Palais de l'Isle on the river Thion. 6 Château de Menthon, 16th c.

ASSY *Haute-Savoie.* L 12.

Formerly only a mountain resort, Assy is now a symbol of the renewal of religious architecture. Its church was built in 1950 by the architect Novarina in a style inspired by the chalets of Savoy and has been remarkably decorated by many of the greatest contemporary artists: Chagall, Lurçat, Léger, Matisse, Rouault, etc.

7 The church of Notre-Dame-de-Toute-Grâce, 1950. 8 View of the choir of the church: Jean Lurçat (1892-1966): tapestry: The Woman of the Apocalypse vanquishing the Dragon. 9 Germaine Richier (1904-1959): Christ on the Cross. 10 Georges Rouault (1871-1958): The mocking of Christ, stained-glass window.

AVENAS *Rhône.* J 12.

Fine altar in the form of a sarcophagus in the Romanesque church. The skilful composition of its façade represents Christ in a mandala surrounded by the twelve Apostles (only Judas is without the Gospel in his hands). A side of the altar shows Louis VII (1119-1180) dedicating the church to Saint Vincent.

11 Altar of the church of Saint-Vincent, sculpted stone, 12th c.

AIME 2

AIME 1

AMBIERLE 3

AMBIERLE 4

ASSY 8

ASSY 7

ASSY 9

ASSY 10

421

AVRIEUX *Savoie.* L 14.

The frescoes on the façade of the church at Avrieux are especially remarkable for their realistic design and colour and the treatment of the subject matter: the seven deadly sins are shown triumphing on Earth before being sent to Hell.

1 Greed and Lust, 15th c.

LA BASTIE-D'URFÉ *Loire.* I 12.

We owe the world's longest love story (*L'Astrée*, 1610-1627, 5,000 pages long) to the frustrated and platonic love of Honoré d'Urfé for the wife of his eldest brother, Diane de Chateaumorand, whom he finally married. The setting of the novel is the mysterious and little known region of Forez surrounding the château of La Bastie, a kind of large Italian country villa built in the Renaissance period by the Urfé family. As at Wideville (q.v.) a grotto with highly profane fountains serves as an antechamber to the chapel.

2 Staircase to the gallery, right wing of the château, 16th c.
3 Interior of the "Salle de fraîcheur" or grotto, 16th c.

BEAUFORT-SUR-DORON 4

BEAUFORT-SUR-DORON *Savoie.* L 13.

A pulpit and two fine retables in the church reveal the talent of Savoyard wood-sculptors in the 17th-18th centuries.

4 Church pulpit, 1722.

LA BÉNISSONS-DIEU *Loire.* I 12.

Modest remains of a Cistercian abbey founded in 1138. The roof has kept its patterns of varnished brick. Tower of the 15th century.

5 Abbey church, 12th c.

BESSANS *Savoie.* L 13.

As at Lanslevillard (q.v.), the frescoes in naive style depicting scenes from the life of Christ show the influence of Giotto.

6 Fresco in the chapel of Saint-Antoine, 16th c.

LA BÉNISSONS-DIEU 5

LE BOURGET-DU-LAC *Savoie.* K 13.

Among the buildings of an ancient Cluniac priory built in the 12th c. and altered in the 16th and 19th c. we may see a two-storeyed cloister with ribbed-vaults separated by beams, and the frieze of the old rood-screen, the finest piece of medieval sculpture in the whole of Savoy, executed in a very Burgundian style.

7 Cloister of the priory, 15th c. 8 Frieze from the former rood-screen, 13th c.

CHAMBÉRY *Savoie.* K 13.

Chambéry's greatest period was in the 15th c. when the duchy of Savoy extended from Nice to Lyons and Berne.
The Tour des Archives, the Portail Saint-Dominique, and especially the Sainte-Chapelle, are the surviving reminders of the city's former splendour. The Gothic apse of the chapel projects from behind its surrounding ramparts, and all its stained-glass windows have survived (the façade was added in 1650). The rest of the château is a 19th-c. reconstruction which followed a fire, and is designed after the château built by Victor-Amédée in 1786.

9 View of the château of the Dukes of Savoy; in the background, façade of the Sainte-Chapelle, 1641. 10 Détrier Venus, Gallo-Roman bronze, Musée Savoisien. 11 School of Savoy, c. 1488: Descent of Christ into Hell, Musée des Beaux-Arts.

CHAMBÉRY 10

422

AVRIEUX I

LA BASTIE-D'URFÉ 3

LA BASTIE-D'URFÉ 2

BESSANS 6

LE BOURGET-DU-LAC 8

LE BOURGET-DU-LAC 7

CHAMBÉRY 9

CHAMBÉRY II

CHARLIEU *Loire.* I 12.

The beauty of the ruins of the former Benedictine abbey of Charlieu and of its Burgundian sculpture, richly carved like some Byzantine ivory, is due even more to the quality of the stone (a crystalline limestone) than to the talent of the sculptor. The tympanum of the north side of the narthex shows a Christ in Majesty surrounded by the symbols of the Evangelists; on the lintel, the Virgin and the twelve apostles; in the left intrados, a curious figure representing Lust. On the tympanum of the window on the right, the Last Supper, carved without any attempt at perspective. Also of interest are the Romanesque and Gothic galleries of the cloister, the religious works of art in the church of Saint-Philibert, and the numerous old houses of the town whose name is derived, fittingly enough, from Cher Lieu (Beloved spot).
I Tympanum of the portal of the church of Saint-Fortunat, north side of the narthex, 12th c. **2** Tympanum above a window of the narthex, to the right of the former, 12th c. **3** Romanesque gallery of the cloister, chapter house, 12th c. **4** Gothic cloister, 15th c.

COMBLOUX 5

COMBLOUX *Haute-Savoie.* L 12.

Many little Savoyard towns are characterised by their pretty iron or copper bulbous spires like that of Combloux which was restored in the 19th century and belongs to a church built in 1704.
5 Bulbous spire of the church, 1829.

CRÉMIEU *Isère.* J 13.

The pretty little town of Crémieu has kept its fortifications which are a reminder that in olden times it was always likely to be attacked by the Dukes of Savoy. Apart from the ramparts and the old houses, the market hall with its vast beams spreading over three aisles and its great stone façade is of great interest. The Town Hall is installed in a former Augustinian priory and is flanked by a very pure style classical cloister enclosing a pretty garden.
6 The market hall, 15th c. **7** Cloister of the Augustine priory, 17th c.

EMBRUN 10

DIE *Drôme.* K 15.

The Gallo-Roman origins of the town may be detected in the Roman arch of the Porte Saint-Marcel, flanked by two medieval towers. The cathedral was largely rebuilt in the 17th c. but has kept its Romanesque porch decorated with ancient Roman columns.
8 Porte Saint-Marcel, 14th c. **9** The Sacrifice of Abraham, capital from the porch of the cathedral, 12th c.

EMBRUN *Hautes-Alpes.* L 15.

The town is magnificently situated on the flanks of the Mont Saint-Guillaume overhanging the river Durance. The ancient cathedral with its black-and-white stones is Lombard in style.
10 Porch of the former cathedral, known as "Le Réal", 12th c.

GAP *Hautes-Alpes.* K 15.

The museum which is particularly rich in local art and history contains the tomb of the Duc de Lesdiguières, a friend of the future Henri IV and a brilliant Protestant soldier who only became converted to Catholicism at the age of 81 when he was named Constable of France.
II Jean Richier (16th-17th c.): Tomb of François de Bonne, Duc de Lesdiguières (1541-1626), marble, Musée des Hautes-Alpes.

CHARLIEU I

CHARLIEU 2

CHARLIEU 4

CHARLIEU 3

CRÉMIEU 6

CRÉMIEU 7

DIE 8

GAP II

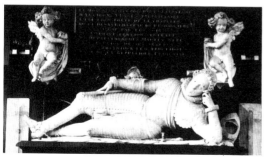

DIE 9

425

1

2

12

GRENOBLE *Isère.* K 14.

The lively town of Grenoble owes its character to its situation in a bend of the river Isère, and the nearby mountains with their ski-slopes. Its university and international colony of students add to the general gaiety of the town. The museum is rich in ancient works (Zurbaran, the French school of the 18th c.) and has also gathered one of the most representative collections of modern art since it acquired the Agutte-Sembat collection, famous for its paintings by the Fauves. Other artists represented include Matisse, Gauguin, Van Gogh, Dufy, Léger, Soutine, Marcoussis, Braque and Picasso. There are two private museums in the town, one devoted to Fantin-Latour (born in Grenoble in 1836), and another to Henri Beyle or Stendhal, also a native of the town (born in 1783). The Musée Stendhal has two original portraits of the writer and a number of his manuscripts are in the municipal library. The churches have suffered from much alteration and are of little interest except for Saint-André with its fine 13th-century tympanum, and the Merovingian crypt of Saint-Laurent which may be dated from the 7th century according to the style of some of its carved capitals. The Palais de Justice is built in the fine Renaissance style of the Dauphiné.

1 Carving on a capital of the crypt of Saint-Laurent, 7th c. 2 Façade of the Palais de Justice, 16th c.

MUSÉE

3 Claude Gellée *known as* Le Lorrain (1600-1682): Landscape.
4 Zurbaran (1598-1662): The Annunciation. 5 Bonnard (1867-1947): White interior. 6 Matisse (1869-1954): Interior with aubergines. 7 Soutine (1894-1943): Flayed ox. 8 Delaunay (1855-1941): Homage to Blériot. 9 Fernand Léger (1881-1955): The Tug. 10 Picasso (born 1881): Woman reading. 11 Vieira da Silva (born 1908): Landscape with towers.
12 De Dreux (1810-1860): Portrait of Stendhal, Musée Stendhal.

3

4

10

5

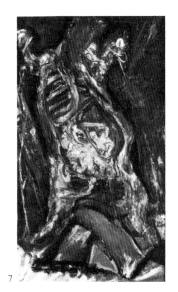

7

6

9

8

11

427

GRIGNAN *Drôme.* J 16.

It was to the château of Grignan that Madame de Sevigné wrote her famous letters to her beloved daughter. The château is as interesting as any of the Loire region and is built on the foundations of an earlier feudal structure. Gothic *cour d'honneur*, sumptuous Renaissance façade and terraces, and a fine Louis XVI wing. Madame de Sevigné died there in 1696.

1 The château, Renaissance façade. **2** Madame de Sevigné's bedroom, 17th c.

HAUTECOMBE 3

HAUTECOMBE *Savoie.* K 13.

The Benedictine abbey of Hautecombe was almost entirely rebuilt in the 19th c. It is known for its situation by the edge of the lake and its intellectual and monastic activity. It contains the tombs of the Dukes of Savoy. In the church, a fine *Annunciation* by the Piemontese painter Difendente Ferrari.

3 View of the abbey by the edge of the lake.

HAUTERIVES *Drôme.* J 14.

Famous for the fantastic "Palace" built by the Facteur (Postman) Cheval. One of the greatest and most poetic creations of "naive" art. Its fantastic and extravagant architecture and sculpture will fascinate some visitors and repel others. It was built over a period of thirty years by the postman Cheval who carefully collected stones during his rounds which he brought to the site in a wheel-barrow, or even in his pockets if they were small enough, and assembled into a vast structure some 100 feet long by 50 wide and as high as 40 feet, painstakingly transforming his dreams into solid reality.

4-5-6 Le Facteur Cheval (1836-1922): Le Palais Idéal (1878-1922).

LANSLEVILLARD *Savoie.* L 13.

In gratitude for a cure a native of the village commissioned a neighbouring artist to paint a series of pictures relating the life of his patron Saint Sebastian. They were painted on the walls of the chapel of Saint Sebastian in a spontaneous and charming naive style. Note the old-fashioned costumes of the figures, due to the isolation of the village.

7 Scenes from the life of Saint Sebastian, 15th c.

LÉMENC (neighbourhood of Chambéry) *Savoie.* K 13.

The church of Saint-Pierre has a Carolingian crypt with six columns around a baptistery (martyrium or ciborium) in the centre, and is an outstanding relic of early Christianity in the region. Nearby, the country-house, "Les Charmettes" is a reminder of Jean-Jacques Rousseau's liaison with Madame de Warens.

8 Baptistery in the crypt of the church of Saint-Pierre, early 9th c.

GRIGNAN 1

GRIGNAN 2

HAUTERIVES 6

HAUTERIVES 5

HAUTERIVES 4

LEMENC 8

LANSLEVILLARD 7

429

5

3

2

4

1

16

LYON *Rhône.* J 13.

Lyon, a city of mysticism and of commerce is also the capital of the silk industry and the birthplace of Guignol. Its two rivers are lined by fine houses in a uniform style which belonged to its powerful and rich bourgeoisie. The great church of Saint-Jean, the steps of the "canuts" (silk-weavers) of Croix-Rousse, the narrow streets of Ainay and the high walls of the convents of Fourvière give the old quarters an air of mystery and drama.

Of the many churches in the city, mention should be made of Saint-Martin d'Ainay, consecrated in 1107, for its very pure Romanesque style; the Flamboyant Gothic of the cathedral of Saint-Nizier; the primatial of Saint-Jean at the foot of Fourvière (12th-13th c.), for its historical importance, as it was the setting for many important events, including church councils and the deposition of the emperor Frederick II, etc. Its nave is 122 feet high, and the funerary sculptures in the Bourbon chapel rival those of Brou (q.v.) for quality. Lastly, the church of Notre-Dame de Fourvière which dominates the city, but its 1880-style is not to everyone's taste.

Many old houses of the 15th and early 17th century including the hôtel de Gadagne (late 15th c.), the Town Hall (1655), and the whole of the Louis XVI-style Place Bellecour with its pretty Corinthian columns.

The Palais des Arts in a former Benedictine abbey is one of the richest museums in France. Among the treasures of its varied collections: The *Drunken Bacchus*, a Roman mosaic, the Spanish *Reclining figure* (polychrome wood), and paintings of the 15th-century Flemish school, German, Italian and French works of the 16th century, and French paintings of the 19th century. The museum of textiles is unique of its kind and contains more than 300,000 specimens from Egypt and ancient Peru to the most recent masterpieces from all over the world.

1 The great Roman theatre. **2** Façade of the cathedral Saint-Nizier, 16th c. **3** Façade of the primatial church of Saint-Jean. **4** View of the quays along the Saône, apse of Saint-Jean and basilica of Notre-Dame de Fourvière. **5** Town Hall, 17th c.

MUSÉE DES BEAUX-ARTS

6 Greek art (6th c. B.C.): Kore. **7** Nino Pisano (13th c.): the Annunciation, polychrome sculpture. **8** Lucas Cranach (1472-1553): Portrait of a woman. **9** Géricault (1791-1824): The Madwoman. **10** Attributed to J.L. David: the Market-woman. **11** Delacroix (1798-1863): Woman with a parrot. **12** Puvis de Chavannes (1824-1898): The Sacred grove, mural painting, 1886. **13** Rodin (1840-1917): The Walking man. **14** Gauguin (1848-1903): Nave, nave, Mahana. **15** Van Gogh (1853-1890): Peasant-woman.

MUSÉE HISTORIQUE DES TISSUS

16 Philippe de la Salle (18th c.): Silk.

6

7

12

8

10

9

15

13

11

14

RIPAILLE (near Thonon-les-Bains) *Haute-Savoie.* L 11.

The château of Ripaille was the residence of the princes of Savoy since the beginning of the Middle Ages. In the 15th c. it was transformed into a priory by Amedée VII who retired there before becoming the anti-Pope Felix V. After ten years of bitter struggle, he came back there to die.

1 The château, 15th-18th c., restored in the 19th c.

SAINT-ANTOINE (at Saint-Marcellin) *Isère.* J 14.

The great church is built in a fine Gothic Flamboyant style. It contains the remains of Saint Antoine, and formerly drew many pilgrims to his shrine.

2 South entrance to the abbey, Henri IV period. 3 Façade of the abbey church, by Antoine Le Moiturier, 15th c.

SAINT-CHEF (near Flosaille) *Isère.* K 13.

The Romanesque church with its 15th-century façade in a bad state of preservation is without interest. But the spiral staircase at the end of the north transept leads to a high chapel containing an admirable Romanesque fresco of the *Celestial Jerusalem.* The angels with their soaring wings are famous and the influence of Byzantium modified by the Carolingian style may be seen in the expressions of the figures with their joined eyebrows.

4 The Celestial Jerusalem, fresco in the tribune of the church, late 11th c.

TERMIGNON *Savoie.* L 13.

The sculpted, painted, and gilded retables of the churches of the region are masterpieces of the Savoyard Baroque. The most visited are that in Notre-Dame de la Gorge (1707), three of the 17th century in Termignon, one very fine example dating from 1777 in Saint-Nicolas-de-Véroce.

5 Retable of the church at Termignon, 17th c.

LA TOURETTE 6

LA TOURETTE (at Éveux, near l'Arbresle) *Rhône.* J 12.

Dominican monastery of La Tourette by le Corbusier in concrete. Designed to produce effects of violent light and shade contrasts according to the architect's principle of the "music of light".

6 Façade of the monastery of La Tourette, by Le Corbusier, 1960.

VAL-DES-PRÉS *Hautes-Alpes.* L 14.

The church with its shingle roof is preceded by a pillared porch in the style of the massive arcades of the houses of the region of Briançon. The bell-tower with its two tiers of semi-circular arcades is Romanesque.

7 Church, bell-tower of the 12th c.

VAL-DES-PRÉS 7

VALENCE *Drôme.* J 14.

The Romanesque cathedral is a rare example of careful and respectful 17th-century restoration work. The Pendentif dates from the Renaissance: small funerary monument which once indicated the centre of the cloister. A few imaginatively decorated Renaissance houses still remain in the town. An attractive museum has been installed in the former bishop's palace (fine painted ceilings of the 16th c.). Apart from a collection of paintings of the Italian, Flemish and French schools, a hundred red-chalk drawings by Hubert Robert, made during his stay in Italy between 1755 and 1775.

8 The "Pendentif", 1548, and the tower of the cathedral, restored in the 19th c. 9 La Maison des Têtes, 16th c. 10 Hubert Robert (1733-1808): The painter drawing an antique vase, red-chalk drawing, museum.

RIPAILLE 1

ST-ANTOINE 3

ST-ANTOINE 2

TERMIGNON 5

ST-CHEF 4

VALENCE 10

VALENCE 8

VALENCE 9

433

VIENNE 2

VIENNE 1

VIENNE 4

VIENNE *Isère.* J. 13.

Vienne was one of the great cities of Roman Gaul and almost the equal of Lyon. It has kept several important remains of this period: the temple of Augustus and Livia, almost as well preserved as the "Maison Carrée" at Nimes (q.v.), the theatre, and the "spina" (obelisk or "Aiguille" as it is now known) of the Roman circus. The Roman museum of sculpture in the church of Saint-Pierre contains very fine sculptures (sarcophagi, busts) and Gallo-Roman mosaics.

Romanesque art is well represented by the church of Saint-Pierre, partly dating from the 16th century, and the church of Saint-André-le-Bas, with a museum of Christian art in its cloister. The cathedral of Saint-Maurice has masterly Gothic sculptures in the recesses of the portals.

1 Temple of Augustus and Livia, 25 B.C. 2 Fragment of Roman mosaic, Musée Lapidaire Romain, church of Saint-Pierre. 3 Apse of the church of Saint-Pierre, 10th c. 4 Cloister of Saint-André-le-Bas, 12th c. 5 Fragment of Romanesque sculpture, Musée Lapidaire Chrétien. 6 Mouldings in the portal of the church of Saint-Maurice, 14th-15th c.

VIZILLE *Isère.* K 14.

The French Revolution originated at Vizille when the States of the Dauphiné met there in 1788. The château was built by the rich and famous Duc de Lesdiguières and is now one of the residences of the President of the Republic. The main gateway is decorated by a fine bronze bas-relief (by Jacob Richier) representing the Constable on horseback (1622) (q.v. Gap).

7 The château, 1619, staircase of 1627.

VIZILLE 7

VIENNE 5

VIENNE 3

VIENNE 6

XII

GUYENNE - GASCOGNE

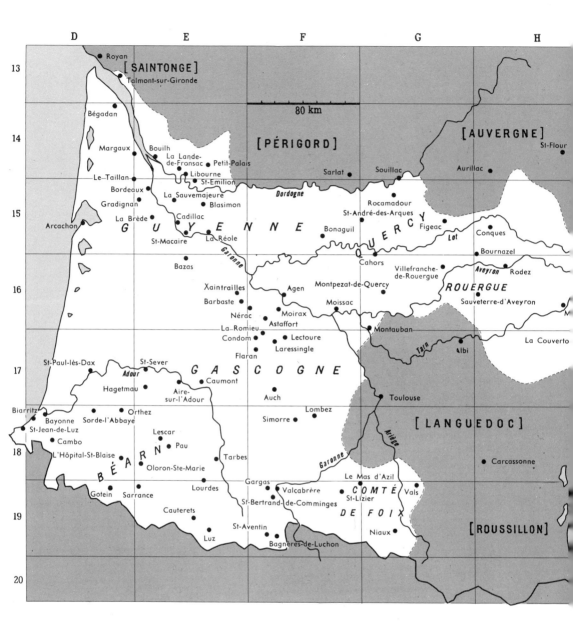

PISANELLO (C. 1395-C.1455), WOMEN DRAPED IN MANTLES, WATER-
COLOUR DRAWING, MUSÉE BONNAT, BAYONNE.

RELIQUARY-STATUE OF SAINTE-FOY, 12TH C., PRESBYTERY OF THE
ABBEY OF CONQUES (Georges de Miré)

*From the proud port of Bordeaux, with its surrounding vineyards,
its magnificent 18th-century architecture and the memory that
it once had Montaigne for its mayor, the road leads through
the lonely plains of the Landes, studded with strange fortress-
like churches, to the Béarn, where Henri IV was born in the
14th-century château of Pau, and from there to the mountains
of the Pyrénées. Saint-Bertrand de Comminges is one of the
most famous sites in these mountains where Roland met his
death. But even older are the neighbouring caves of the Gargas
where men made imprints of their hands on the walls, tens of
thousands of years ago, for reasons which have remained mysterious to us. In the county of Foix the palaeolithic caves of
Niaux are famous for their surprisingly realistic portraits
of "Bisons".*

*Gascony is a fascinating, rich province with a magnificent
variety of châteaux, old manor houses, fortress-strongholds
and arcaded town squares which all await the visitor.*

439

AGEN I

ASTAFFORT 7

BARBASTE 12

AGEN *Lot-et-Garonne*. F 16.

Between the 12th and 15th centuries, the town of Agen belonged more to the English crown than to France. After the old Gothic cathedral of Saint-Étienne had been destroyed its place was taken in the 19th century by the church of Saint-Caprais, built between the 11th and 16th c. The beautiful Romanesque capitals in the crossing of the transept are carved with scenes of the life of Saint-Caprais. Other capitals in the old chapter house; some carved with scenes from the childhood of Christ. But the main attraction of the town is the magnificent and moving *Self-portrait of Goya* which is as fine as any of Rembrandt's self-portraits. This simple but powerful picture was painted before Goya's deafness, and the bitter, visionary period of the "black paintings" and is simply a penetrating study of the young genius as seen by himself without illusions, and without artifice. The other painting by Goya in the town's municipal museum, the *Messe* is as daring in its composition as the *Junta of the Philippines* in the museum of Castres, with its central figures surrounded by a vast emptiness. Also in the museum, a fine collection of Gallo-Roman antiquities and the statue of *Venus* found in the Mas d'Agenais in 1876.

I Cathedral of Saint-Caprais, 11th-16th c. **2** Capital in the chapter house, 12th c.

MUSÉE MUNICIPAL

3 Vénus du Mas, Greek hellenistic art. **4** Francisco Goya (1746-1828): Self-portrait **5** Francisco Goya: La Messe des Relevailles.

AIRE-SUR-L'ADOUR *Landes*. E 17.

The main church in the town is largely Romanesque. Even more interesting, the church of the Mas d'Aire with its several very beautiful Gallo-Roman sarcophagi in the Romanesque crypt.

6 Sarcophagus of Sainte-Quitterie, white marble, 5th c.

ASTAFFORT *Lot-et-Garonne*. F 16.

Near Astaffort in the open countryside, a curious kind of pigeon-house standing on columns with mushroom-shaped capitals.

7 Pigeon-house near Astaffort.

AUCH *Gers*. F 17.

Two hundred steps lead up from the lower town of Auch to the old town overlooking the river Gers where the main monuments are to be found. Flamboyant Gothic cathedral with a majestic Renaissance façade with two towers. In the interior, a hundred and thirteen 16th-century choir-stalls sculpted in a fine Flamboyant style with religious and mythological themes. Stained-glass windows in the choir and the transept are among the finest of the Renaissance period. The whole of the cathedral has great unity of style and the interior is of a consistently high standard.

8 Cathedral of Sainte-Marie, façade 16th c. **9** Choir and stalls, 1550. **10** Entombment, 1500. **11** Arnaud de Moles: Adam and Eve, stained-glass window, 16th c.

BARBASTE *Lot-et-Garonne*. E 16.

The fortified mill at the end of a pretty Gothic bridge served as a manor house for Henri IV. Its four crenellated towers and its outer walls are the only authentic remains of the period.

12 Henri IV's mill, 14th-15th c.

AGEN 3

AGEN 5

AGEN 2

AGEN 4

AIRE-SUR-L'ADOUR 6

AUCH 9

AUCH 8

AUCH 11

AUCH 10

441

BAYONNE I

BAYONNE *Basses-Pyrénées.* D 18.

Although the museum with its collection of paintings gathered by the painter Léon Bonnat is the pride of the town, it is also famous for its fancy chocolates, its hams and the invention of the bayonet (called after the town). The Musée Basque is one of the richest ethnographic museums in France and has a section devoted to the Basque game of *pelota*. Cathedral with high windows with elegant tracery on the sides, and flanked by a beautiful unfinished Gothic cloister with remarkably vast twin bays. The Musée Bonnat is famous for its paintings by El Greco, Rembrandt, Rubens, Goya, Ingres and Degas among many others, and also for its collection of world-famous drawings. Italian, Flemish and French works of the 15th to 18th centuries are displayed in rotation.

I Cathedral of Sainte-Marie and cloister (1240), 13th-14th c.

MUSÉE BONNAT

2 Pisanello (c. 1395-1455): Ladies wearing mantles, water-colour. 3 El Greco (c. 1541-1624): Portrait of Cardinal Quiroga. 4 Watteau (1684-1727): Young girl seen in profile, drawing. 5 Ingres (1780-1867): Francesca de Rimini and Paolo Malatesta. 6 Degas (1834-1917): Portrait of Léon Bonnat.

BAZAS 7

BAZAS *Gironde.* E 16.

The most interesting part of the cathedral is the façade: it has three portals with deep recesses and the finest Gothic sculpture in the whole of the Gironde. The pediment with its scrolls above the façade is an unfortunate 18th-century addition, for the cathedral was built and rebuilt on many occasions from the Romanesque period onwards.

7 Façade of the cathedral, porch of late 13th c.

BÉGADAN *Gironde.* D 14.

The capitals in the apse and the corbels on the exterior are finely sculpted in the great tradition of the small Romanesque churches of the Saintonge region.

8 Apse of the church, 12th c.

BLASIMON *Gironde.* E 15.

BONAGUIL II

The Romanesque portal at Blasimon is the finest in the Gironde and the equal in beauty to that of Chadenac in the Charente-Maritime (q.v.). Elongated figures of Virtues trampling Vices underfoot with highly elegant draperies clinging to the lines of their bodies. Both the Virtues and the angels in the first bend of the arch lost their heads during the Revolution. Remains of the conventual buildings of the abbey.

9 Façade of the church of Saint-Maurice, 12th c. 10 Detail of the moulding of the portal, 12th c.

BONAGUIL *Lot-et-Garonne.*

The château was built by Béranger de Roquefeuil between 1485 and 1525 and has remained as an outstanding example of medieval military architecture. Its pointed keep resembles the prow of a ship and its russet coloured walls overlook a valley known as the "Val des légendes".

II The château, 1525.

442

BAYONNE 6

BAYONNE 2

BAYONNE 5

BAYONNE 3

BAYONNE 4

BÉGADAN 8

BLASIMON 10

BLASIMON 9

7

12

13

BORDEAUX *Gironde*. E 15.

Bordeaux is certainly the most beautiful city in France after Paris thanks to the abundance of its monuments which date from the 3rd to the 19th centuries. It was conquered by Caesar's legions in 56 B.C. and became an important Roman city but the only remains of this period are the ruins of the Palais Gallien, a vast amphitheatre. From the Merovingian period has survived the church of Sainte-Croix with a purely Romanesque façade and a north tower that was added by Abadie in the 19th century. Unfortunately its original façade, in the Girondin style, was "completed" by the addition of bell-turrets and gables, but nonetheless the primitive style of the original sculpture is interesting (figure of Lust). Apart from the Porte Cailhau and the Porte de la Grosse Horloge, the Middle Ages left Bordeaux with many churches: Saint-Seurin is a famous pilgrims' basilica with an off-set porch, fine south portal, and famous 11th-century crypt with Gallo-Roman capitals and the tomb of Saint-Fort. Saint-André is certainly the finest Aquitaine Gothic church in the city and the statues in the jambs of the Royal Portal are among the greatest masterpieces of the 13th century. In 1440 the archbishop Pey-Berland built the powerful isolated tower which was named after him. Another isolated tower, 427 feet high, flanks the church of Saint-Michel which has a choir similar to that at Poitiers. The church of Saint-Bruno has statues by Bernini and the 18th-century Saint-Paul seems a smaller version of the Gesù at Rome. The great architect of the 18th c. was Victor Louis. He first built a new theatre as the old one had been destroyed by fire some thirty-eight years previously. Thanks to this project, Victor Louis became the creator of the new city of Bordeaux, and his style was so carefully imitated and repeated by his pupils that the 18th-century civil buildings of the city all have an unusual unity of style. The neo-classic style Grand Théatre was completed in 1780. Its staircase inspired that by Garnier for the Paris Opéra. The fine Town Hall built in 1781 for the prince-archbishop of Rohan and the hôtel Boyer-Fonfrède and its staircase in the Place Jean-Jaurès are also by Victor Louis. He was not the only great architect of Bordeaux for other buildings were also designed by Jacques Gabriel and his son, Portier, Laclotte and others. The Gabriels built the fine quays which are almost as beautiful in their uniformity as those of Lyons, and the masterly Place de la Bourse, begun in 1731, with its Louis XV pilasters, pediments and scrolls. We should also mention the hôtel Saint-Marc and its round entrance lodge with Ionic columns (now the Hospices), the hôtel Saint-François (22, rue de Mirail) with its staircase with its scroll-pattern decorations on the rise, the hôtel Labottière (Laclotte, 1773) and its garden with trimmed hedges in the Rue David Johnston. The visitor should also walk around the Cours Xavier Arnodan and see the fine façades of the 18th-century *hôtels*. Bordeaux also has several fine museums: the Musée des Beaux-Arts with a good collection of French 18th and 19th-century painting, the Musée des Arts Decoratifs known for its ceramics collection, and the Musée de la Marine with exhibits illustrating local history.

1 Palais Gallien, 3 rd. c. 2 Portal of the church of Sainte-Croix, 11th c. 3 Detail of the arch-moulding: the Seven Deadly Sins, church of Sainte-Croix: Lust, 11th c. 4 Crypt of Saint-Seurin and tomb of Saint-Fort, 11th c. 5 Porte de la Grosse Cloche, 13th c. 6 Nave and choir of the cathedral Saint-André, 13th c. 7 Tour Pey-Berland, 15th c. 8 Aerial view of 18th-c. Bordeaux. 9 The Bourse (Exchange), 1749, altered in the 19th and 20th c. 10 Grand Théâtre, by Victor Louis, 1780. 11 Staircase of the Grand Théâtre.

MUSÉE DES BEAUX-ARTS

12 J.F. de Troy (1679-1752): An Abbot of the order of Saint Bernard. 13 Delacroix (1798-1863): Greece at Missolonghi.

1

4

3

5

2

10

6

11

9

BOURNAZEL 2

CAHORS 10

CAMBO 11

BOUILH *Gironde.* E 14.

The château of Bouilh was never completed but the beauty of its west wing, the semi-circle of out-buildings and the unfinished open colonnade on the façade make it all the more regrettable that its creator, the Marquis de la Tour du Pin, saw fit to economise by ordering his architect, Victor Louis, to stop work on it.

I The château, by Victor Louis (1737-1807), 18th c.

BOURNAZEL *Aveyron.* H 15.

Superb Renaissance château built for Jean de Buisson, lord of Mirabel. The triumph of the classical style can be seen in the colonnading and the sculptures of the metopes and the capitals of the pilasters.

2 The château, 16th c.

CADILLAC *Gironde.* E 15.

The château of the Dukes of Épernon has been saved from the grip of the Administration Pénitentiaire (French Prison service), has now taken on a new lease of life and is being restored. It is famous for its eight monumental fireplaces by Jean Langlois and was described as being one of the most beautiful and sumptuously furnished châteaux of the reign of Louis XIII. It is situated behind the fortified walls of the town and is flanked by two beautiful medieval gateways.

3 Château of the Dukes of Épernon, by Pierre Souffron, 1615. **4** Jean Langlois, fireplace, early 16th c.

CAHORS *Lot.* G 16.

Although the Pont Valentré, with its six great Gothic arches and its three beautiful square towers has been reproduced countless times on post-cards as the symbol of the town of Cahors, the most beautiful building is certainly the cathedral Saint-Étienne. Majestic cupolas on pendentives, single nave, apse without ambulatory, remains of frescoes in the vault, north portal in Romanesque style (removed from west front), as fine as those of Moissac and Beaulieu-sur-Dordogne (q.v.). The whole structure is a perfect example of the domed churches of the Aquitaine. The Christ on the tympanum of the centre portal is one of the finest and most mystical known.

Fine 16th-century cloister by the south side of the cathedral. The Archidiaconé (Archdeacon's house) Saint-Jean and hôtel de Roaldès are in the Renaissance style as well as several other houses in the Badernes quarter of the town.

5 Pont Valentré, 14th c. **6** North portal of the cathedral of Saint-Étienne, early 12th c. **7** Detail of the tympanum: Christ in majesty and dancing Angel, c. 1135. **8** Cathedral cloister, 16th c. **9** La Barbacane (Barbican). **10** Fresco in the vault of the cathedral, 14th c.

CAMBO *Basses-Pyrénées.* D 18.

Agreeable little town with a bracing climate; classical-style church with wooden gallery (reserved for men only) and several tombstones along its side, in typical Basque style.

11 Interior of the church, wooden galleries, 17th c.

BOUILH 1

CADILLAC 4

CAHORS 5

CAHORS 7

CAHORS 6

CAHORS 9

CAHORS 8

447

CAUMONT I

CAUMONT *Gers.* E 17.

Fine brick-and-stone Renaissance château. Birth-place of the Duc d'Épernon, favourite of Henri III. Pretty *cour d'honneur* with basket-handle arches.

I The château, c. 1530.

CONDOM *Gers.* F 17.

Small but ancient town with 18th-century houses lining its streets. Late Gothic cathedral with cloister with fine moulded vaulting (now a public passage). The Town Hall is in the former bishop's palace. Before it stands the former Bishop's chapel in Renaissance style.

2 Cloister of the cathedral of Saint-Pierre, 16th c. 3 Gallery of the Town Hall, 16th c.

CONQUES-EN-ROUERGUE *Aveyron.* H 15.

The town of Conques has survived almost intact since the Middle Ages. It became an important centre for pilgrims as the result of a theft committed in the name of piety when the remains of Sainte Foy (martyred at the age of twelve at Agen, 303) were brought to the town on January 14, 866 by a monk of the Benedictine abbey of Conques. The cult of the saint that followed brought prosperity to the city and produced a famous gold statue which is certainly the most precious ever to have been made by a medieval goldsmith and the pride of the Treasury of the church of Sainte-Foy. The saint is shown seated in majesty on a throne with forearms extended in a rigid hieratic posture, and its robe has been decorated by pilgrims with cameos, enamel, precious stones and other personal offerings of jewels. The statue is now exhibited in a modern chapel of the church where the Treasure is kept, but it has lost nothing of its mystery and magic quality. Although it is the "star" of the Treasure, the other objects are of great interest. The church itself is Romanesque and a simplified version of Saint-Sernin at Toulouse (q.v.). The tympanum with its scene of the Last Judgment is a masterpiece of early Romanesque sculpture. It is particularly worth-while to climb the ancient streets for a dramatic view of the dark red, still medieval church against the background of the arid landscape.

4 View of the church, 11th c. 5 Tympanum of the main portal, 11th c. 6 Nave of the church. 7 Capital in the triforium, 12th c. 8 Reliquary-statue of Sainte Foy, 12th c.

LA COUVERTOIRADE *Aveyron.* H 17.

Ancient Templars' hospice set in the bare landscape of the Aveyron. Its polygonal walls of the 14th century enclose a Renaissance village. Like Laressingle, a striking survival from the past.

9 View of the village, 14th and 16th c.

CONQUES 8

CONDOM 2

CONDOM 3

CONQUES 5

CONQUES 4

CONQUES 6

CONQUES 7

LA COUVERTOIRADE 9

449

FIGEAC *Lot.* G 15.

The town of Figeac has the distinction of being one of the richest in France for medieval houses. The Monnaie (mint), also used as a market hall, is the finest example to have survived. Church of Saint-Sauveur similar in style to that at Conques. Champollion, the archeologist, was born in the town.

1 Hôtel de la Monnaie, late 13th c.

FLARAN (at Valence-sur-Baïse) *Gers.* F 17.

The tiny Cistercian church of Flaran was founded in 1151 and has survived in good state. Graceful design, glowing gold-coloured stone, only three bays and a semi-circular apse — unusual for a Cistercian building. A single gallery of the cloister still remains as well as a very beautiful chapter house.

2 Apse of the abbey church, 12th c. 3 Chapter house, 12th c.

GARGAS *Hautes-Pyrénées.* F 19.

The rock paintings in the caves at Gargas are more moving and more human than elsewhere, and consist of the imprints of more than a hundred human hands surrounded by red or black pigment as though the artists had projected the colour over his hand as it was pressed against the rock, in what might have been an Aurignacian religious rite, many tens of thousands of years ago.

4 Hand impressions, Aurignacian period.

GOTEIN *Basses-Pyrénées.* D 19.

Typical Basque church with a tower with three gables of equal size symbolising the Holy Trinity.

5 Church tower with triple gable.

GRADIGNAN *Gironde.* E 15.

Majestic château of the period of Louis XVI attributed to the architect Victor Louis in the immediate neighbourhood of Bordeaux, near the beautiful remains of the 14th-century priory of Gayac.

6 Château de Tauzia, attributed to Victor Louis, 1780.

HAGETMAU *Landes.* E 17.

Modern church with crypt of the greatest interest: 12th-century columns with Romanesque capitals somewhat crudely carved but with lively figure subjects.

7 Crypt of the church of Saint-Girons, 12th c.

L'HOPITAL-SAINT-BLAISE *Basses-Pyrénées.* D 18.

Small church with geometrical stone tracery in the windows showing clear Arab influence. The cupola, painted with stars, is similar to that of Oloron (q.v.)

8 Tracery in window of the church, 12th c.

L'HOPITAL-ST-BLAISE 8

FIGEAC 1

FLARAN 3

FLARAN 2

GARGAS 4

GOTEIN 5

HAGETMAU 7

GRADIGNAN 6

451

LABRÈDE *Gironde*. E 15.

The main building of the château of Montesquieu was built in various styles, from the Gothic to the classical. It was here that Montesquieu, author of the "Esprit des Lois" spent his childhood and his most creative years. His library of seven thousand volumes, furniture and personal objects may still be seen. The château is built on a defensive polygonal plan surrounded by a moat and has kept its charm as an aristocratic country residence.

1 The château, 13th-17th c. 2 Montesquieu's bed-room.

LA LANDE-DE-FRONSAC *Gironde*. E 14.

The Romanesque church of La Lande-de-Fronsac (also known as La Lande-de-Cubzac) has a portal decorated with Byzantine-style interlacing motifs and a highly unusual tympanum, distinguished for its uncommon theme and technique: on the left, Saint John of Patmos leaning on the seven churches of Asia, in the centre, the Christ of Saint John's vision with a seven-starred circle in one hand and a sword in the other, and a pattern of interlacing tracery on the right. The wide-sleeved robe of the Christ, the representation of the stars as flowers, and the delicate tracery are the work of a highly original anonymous artist.

3 Portal of the church of La Lande-de-Cubzac: Saint John of Patmos, 12th c.

LARESSINGLE *Gers*. F 17.

The ghost-like Gascon village of Laressingle, huddled behind its Romanesque fortifications has been deserted by its inhabitants but has kept the ruins of its château, once the residence of the bishops of Condom, its keep and its church. Seen from a distance, its stone silhouette is one of the most striking sights in the region.

4 Walls of the village, 13th c.

LECTOURE *Gers*. F 17.

Interesting cathedral, attacked on several occasions during the wars of the 15th and 16th centuries. It was originally covered by two cupolas, now replaced by square rib-vaults. Another pointed arch separates the nave from the choir which once stood on a lower level. In 1540, some twenty Roman altars used for taurobolic sacrifices (sacrifices to the goddess Cybele which required the offering of bull's blood) were discovered on the site of the former altar. The altar steles and several fine examples of antique sculpture are now in the interesting lapidary museum. The Gothic fountain (known as Fontaine de Diane) in the Rue Fontélie is over seven hundred years old and is protected by 15th-century railings.

MUSÉE LAPIDAIRE

5 Taurobolic altar, 3rd. c. 6 Head of a Gaulish divinity.

LESCAR *Basses-Pyrénées*. E 18.

Lescar was the original capital of the Béarn (to which it gave its Latin name Beneharnum) and was a bishopric where the local sovereigns were buried. Beautiful cathedral with exterior altered in the 17th century; figure capitals in the nave, 17th-century choir-stalls with large figures of the apostles, evangelists and saints, and important 12th-century mosaic hunting scene (note the hunter with a wooden leg) similar to that at Sorde-l'Abbaye in the Landes (q.v.).

7 Nave of the former cathedral of Notre-Dame, and bishop's throne, 12th c. 8 Capital in the nave, 12th c. 9 Mosaic in the choir: hunting scene, c. 1125.

LESCAR 7

LABREDE 1   LABREDE 2

LARESSINGLE 4

LA LANDE-DE-FRONSAC 3

LECTOURE 5   LECTOURE 6

LESCAR 9

LESCAR 8

LOMBEZ *Gers.* F 18.

Like the cathedral of Albi the splendid church of Sainte-Marie is built in brick and is fortified with buttresses linked by powerful pointed arches. Very beautiful octagonal five-storeyed tower in the Toulousain style.

1 Tower and buttresses of the cathedral of Sainte-Marie, 14th c.

LOURDES *Hautes-Pyrénées.* E 19.

Famous for over a hundred years as the main pilgrimage centre in France. The new basilica was built recently to hold some of the three million worshippers who visit the shrine every year and is more a masterpiece of engineering than of architecture. The underground nave has undeniable abstract beauty. Picturesque medieval castle in the town.

2 Nave of the basilica of Pius X, by Vago, Le Donne and Pinsard, 1958.

LUZ *Hautes-Pyrénées.* E 19.

Romanesque church surrounded by a fortified wall to shelter the population of the village in times of war; beautiful Christ in Majesty above the main portal. The church was also visited by pilgrims on the way to Compostella.

3 Church of the Hospitallers of Saint John, 12th c.

MARGAUX *Gironde.* D 14.

Apart from being the name of the excellent claret, Château-Margaux is also a majestic Louis XVI-period château. On the façade, staircase leading to portico with Doric columns; on the rear side, horse-shoe staircase leading down to the gardens.

4 Château-Margaux, 18th c.

LE MAS-D'AZIL *Ariège.* F 19.

Famous large natural caves where rock-engravings and carved objects of such importance were found that the name "azilian" has been given to a period of Palaeolithic art.

5 Fawn with birds, carved bone, Azilian period.

MILLAU *Aveyron.* H 16.

The small industrial town of Millau is well situated in the centre of the touristic region of the Tarn gorges and is dominated by the pretty eight-sided Toulousain-style tower of its church. In the town, a highly elegant 18th-century wash-house surrounded by a surprising portico. Nearby, the well-preserved Louis XIV-style château of Sambucy, built for the royal favourite Mlle de Fontanges.

6 Tower of the church of Notre-Dame, 16th c. 7 Wash-house, 1759.

MOIRAX *Lot-et-Garonne.* F 16.

Well-restored church which originally belonged to a Cluniac abbey. Interesting architectural peculiarity: a cupola resting on squinches over the square choir, crowned by a lantern and decorated inside by carved 17th-century wood-work. The old walls of the village and the keep have not been restored.

8 Apse of the church, late 11th c.

LOMBEZ 1

LOURDES 2

LUZ 3

MARGAUX 4

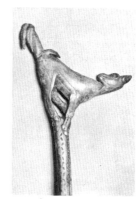

MAS D'AZIL 5

MILLAU 6

MILLAU 7

MOIRAX 8

2

4

MOISSAC *Tarn-et-Garonne*. F 16.

The town of Moissac is situated at the cross-roads of the regions of Languedoc, Guyenne and Quercy and was always an important centre of communications and trade. But far more interesting than the town itself and even its church of Saint-Martin are the remains of the abbey which was founded in the 6th century, and destroyed in the Revolution with the exception of the portal and the cloisters which are among the most outstanding masterpieces of Romanesque art ever to have been preserved.

Three different styles are evident: first, a classical style inspired by Antiquity, which gave rise to the palm-, rose- and scroll-patterns, then an Oriental style in the highly refined carving, almost as delicate as Byzantine ivory carving, with its imaginative and fantastic animal themes, and thirdly, the narrative style of Languedoc sculpture with its profusion of Biblical themes. According to the art-historian Émile Mâle, the sculpture of Moissac was inspired by the famous manuscript of the Apocalypse from the abbey of Saint-Sever (Bibliothèque Nationale, Paris). The theme for the sculpture of the south portal of the abbey church of Saint-Pierre is the Vision of the Apocalypse. In the top centre of the tympanum: fine, serene, hieratic figure of Christ surrounded by evangelical symbols, with figures of Elders in varied attitudes at his feet, and surrounded by interlacing, ornamental motifs, in a style reminiscent of that of Beaulieu-sur-Dordogne (q.v.). Figures of a suave Saint Peter and the prophet Isaiah in the jambs of the portal; intersecting figures of lions on the centre post; in the splay of the portal, scenes from the life of Christ including an Annunciation with an almost excessively human angel.

In the church, interesting Entombment of 1485, Romanesque Christ and a Pietà of 1476. The cloister is a marvel of harmony of white marble, red brick and greenness, and the pillars have seventy-six capitals all carved in a different style, some with geometric motifs, others with fantastic animal figures, but the majority have figure subjects and are carved in a technique ranging from the archaic to one of uttermost refinement.

1 Church of Saint-Pierre, façade, 12th c. 2 Tympanum of the south portal of the church of Saint-Pierre: Vision of the Apocalypse, 12th c. 3 Two Elders, detail of the lower register of the tympanum. 4 Jamb: Saint Peter. 5 Centre post: monsters. 6 Jamb of the portal. 7 Cloister, 12th c. 8 Capital with scroll decoration. 9 Figure capital: Announcement to the shepherds. 10 Virgin of Pity (Vierge de Pitié), polychrome stone, 1476.

3

6

1

5

10

9

8

7

MONTAUBAN 5

MONTAUBAN *Tarn-et-Garonne.* G 16.

Montauban offers the rare opportunity of being able to study the essential of an important artist's work in a single place for its famous Musée Ingres contains an outstandingly important collection of the painter's works, including some four thousand drawings and his personal effects, including his famous violin. Another native artist of the town, the sculptor Bourdelle, is also well represented in the same museum by forty sculptures and fifty drawings. Other works by contemporaries and pupils if Ingres include *The Negro Joseph* by Delacroix and Chassériau's *Alice Ozy.* Early 18th-century cathedral with one of Ingres' most interesting paintings, the *Vow of Louis XIII.* Apart from the museum which is set in the former 17th-century bishop's palace, most of Montauban's buildings are built in brick. Highly picturesque Place Nationale with arcades and elegant pilasters where a market is held daily.

1 Place Nationale, 17th c.

MUSÉE INGRES

2 Ingres (1780-1867): Portrait of Madame Gonse. 3 Ingres: The Dream of Ossian, detail, 1812. 4 Ingres: Reclining odalisque, drawing. 5 Bourdelle (1861-1929): Dying Centaur, bronze, 1914.

MONTPEZAT-DE-QUERCY *Tarn-et-Garonne.* G 16.

The treasury of the former collegiate church of Saint-Martin contains such incomparable pieces as the series of fifteen Flanders tapestries (16th c.) with scenes from the life of Saint Martin, reliquaries, religious objects and embroidery from the 14th to the 16th centuries. The church was founded in 1334 by the Cardinal des Prés whose tomb with his reclining white marble effigy may be seen in the choir.

6 Flanders tapestry: Saint Martin cutting his mantle (detail), 16th c. 7 Tomb effigy of Cardinal des Prés, white marble, 1366.

NÉRAC *Lot-et-Garonne.* F 16.

Old bridge spanning the river Baïse. Delightful château in the pure Renaissance style of the period of Henri IV: gallery with flattened arches supported by twisted columns and figure capitals. Four fountains in the town: Fontaine du Chevalier de Saint-Jean, that of Fleurette where the lady in love with the future Henri IV is supposed to have drowned herself, the Fontaine des Marguerites and that of the Dauphin.

8 View of the town and bridge. 9 Wing of the château facing the inner courtyard, 16th c.

NIAUX *Ariège.* G 19.

The famous palaeolithic paintings of bisons and horses in the caves of Niaux are more than ten thousand years old and have so much expression that the local inhabitants have given them such nick-names as "Henri IV" and the "cheval triste" (sad horse). The enormous caves are of the Madgalenian period and are almost as important as those of Altamira in Spain but the paintings are in black without any colour. The arrows traced on the bodies of the bisons are thought to have had a magical significance.

10 Bison, drawing in manganese oxide and bison fat, 13 000 B.C.

MONTAUBAN 4

MONTAUBAN 2

MONTAUBAN 3

MONTPEZAT 6

MONTAUBAN 1

MONTPEZAT 7

NIAUX 10

NÉRAC 9

NÉRAC 8

459

OLORON-SAINTE-MARIE *Basses-Pyrénées*. E 18.

The church of Sainte-Marie was built in three successive stages: it was begun in the Romanesque style then continued in High Gothic and the richly gilt wood-work, pulpit, crèche and organ were added in the 17th century. Most important of all is the portal. The originality of its composition and variety of its motifs defy strict classification, although it may be said to belong to the general tradition of Poitevin architecture. Two arch mouldings above the tympanum, the first symbolising the heavens with figures of the Elders of the Apocalypse, the second the earth, with rustic scenes from the daily life of the peasants of the region. The tympanum is divided into three parts, with the Descent from the Cross in the centre; in the left of the two semi-circular arcs below: two lions seated by the side of God to symbolise the Church persecuted but triumphant, in the right: two winged lions attacking a man. Gaston IV, the viscount of Béarn and creator of the church on his return from the Crusades had himself represented on horseback (like the Constantine-figures in the Poitou) to the right of the tympanum. The centre post rests on a plinth carved with figures of barbarian slaves in chains. The church of Sainte-Croix stands in the heart of the old quarter of the town but has been much restored although its Hispano-Mauresque cupola covered by flat stones has remained intact.

1 Tympanum of the portal of the church of Sainte-Marie, 13th c.
2 Plinth of the centre post, 12th c. 3 Crèche, gilt wood, 17th c.

ORTHEZ *Basses-Pyrénées*. D 18.

The river Gave de Pau runs through a steep ravine at Orthez and is spanned there by a 14th-century fortified bridge, rather like that at Cahors, with a pointed tower. The other tower which rises over the town is the keep or Tour Moncade, the sole remaining vestige of Gaston Phoebus's (Count of Foix) fortress. The charming house (so-called of Jeanne d'Albret) at 39, rue Bourg-Vieux, is in the Renaissance style.

4 Pont-Vieux, 14th c.

ORTHEZ 4

PAU *Basses-Pyrénées*. E 18.

Two kings were born in Pau: Henri IV of France and Bernadotte, king of Sweden. Pau was the capital of the Béarn since 1476 but it remained a very small town until the 19th century when it became a popular health resort for English tourists, because of its bracing mountain air. The château was built by Gaston Phoebus in the 14th century, altered by Catherine de Bourbon, Henri IV's sister in the 16th, and ruined by Louis-Philippe in the 19th. Fine south front, and graceful, trapezoidal *cour d'honneur*. The pride of the château is its exceptional tapestry collection, including fine pieces from Brussels and the Gobelins: *The Hunts of Maximilian*, the *Lucas Months*, *Story of Saint John the Baptist*, *Arabesque Months*, *Fables*, etc. Part of the château is now the Musée des Beaux-Arts and contains several important paintings including a *Saint Francis* by El Greco and the well-known *Cotton exchange* by Degas.

5 South front of the château, 16th c. 6 Great reception room and tapestries.

MUSÉE DES BEAUX-ARTS

7 El Greco (1541-1614): Saint Francis. 8 Edgar Degas (1834-1917): Cotton exchange at New Orleans. 9 Berthe Morisot (1840-1895): Young woman sewing.

OLORON-STE-MARIE 3

OLORON-STE-MARIE 1

OLORON-STE-MARIE 2

PAU 5

PAU 7

PAU 6

PAU 8

PAU 9

461

PETIT-PALAIS I

PETIT-PALAIS *Gironde.* E 14.

The charming church of Saint-Pierre has a façade and ground-plan surprisingly similar to those of the churches of the Saintonge. Richly carved façade with three tiers of arcades, some polyfoil, and original sculpted motifs including figures of a woman, a man, a goat and a leopard.

I Façade of the church of Saint-Pierre, 12th c.

LA RÉOLE *Gironde.* E 15.

The Town Hall at La Réole is one of the few remaining secular Romanesque buildings in France. The ground floor was originally used as a market hall. First storey with six twin-windows, second storey and gables of the 14th century. The 18th-century Benedictine abbey nearby is of less interest although it has an elegant double flight staircase.

2 Town Hall, 12th c. 3 Staircase of the Benedictine abbey, 18th c. 4 Railings of the abbey, by Blaise Charlut (died 1792), wrought iron.

ROCAMADOUR *Lot.* G 15.

Although it has been exposed to the open for seven centuries the admirable fresco on the outer wall of the chapel of Saint-Michel has kept its bright colours and its clear-cut lines. Two themes are represented: an Annunciation in a Hellenistic style, and a Visitation in a Syrian style.

5 The Annunciation, fresco of the chapel of Saint-Michel, late 12th c.

RODEZ *Aveyron.* H 16.

The severe, cold and grey city of Rodez, huddled around its red sandstone cathedral, is built on the site of a highly important former Gallo-Romain city. Many important archaeological remains have been found on the site and are now in the Musée Fenaille. Among the most interesting are a group of anthropomorphic sculpted menhirs which are probably the oldest of their kind to have been found in France. Every phase of the Gothic style may be seen in the architecture and decoration of the magnificent cathedral Notre-Dame which was begun in 1277 and finished in about 1577. From the last period date the exuberant Flamboyant crowning of the tower and the majority of the interior ornamentation: organ case, stone rood-screen, retables and tombs.

Like Toulouse, although to a lesser degree, the old quarter is rich in old *hôtels:* canonical house in the Place Adrien-Rozier, Maison de l'Annonciation in the Place du Bourg and, especially, the Maison d'Armagnac, built between 1525 and 1530 in the style of François I.

6 Tower of the cathedral of Notre-Dame, 280 feet high, 14th and 16th c. 7 Nave and choir-stalls of the cathedral, 16th c. 8 Choir screen, stone, chapel of Saint-Sepulcre, 16th c. 9 Entombment, polychrome stone, 16th c. 10 Musée Fenaille: Menhir statue of Saint-Sernin, Gallo-Roman period.

LA ROMIEU II

LA ROMIEU *Gers.* F 17.

Interesting little medieval city with walls and fortified gateways, fortified church with rampart-walk, cloister at the foot of the collegiate church, arcaded square. The fine Gothic arches with tracery in the cloister are now being skilfully restored.

II Gallery of the cloister and apse tower of the church, 14th c.

LA RÉOLE 3

ROCAMADOUR 5

LA RÉOLE 4   LA RÉOLE 2

RODEZ 6

RODEZ 7

RODEZ 8

RODEZ 9

RODEZ 10

SAINT-ANDRÉ-DES-ARQUES *Lot.* G 15.

In 1954 the sculptor Zadkine discovered a considerable number of frescoes in the small church which seem to date from the late Gothic period, according to the costumes of the figures.

1 Frescoes in the choir of the church, late 15th c.

SAINT-AVENTIN *Haute-Garonne.* F 19.

Late 11th-century church in pure Romanesque style with tympanum carved with figures of apostles brandishing their emblems, as at Valcabrère (q.v.). The Virgin and Child is of great beauty.

2 Virgin and Child, 12th c.

ST-BERTRAND-DE-COMMINGES 4

SAINT-BERTRAND-DE-COMMINGES *Haute-Garonne.* F 19.

The city had two great periods in its history: first, in the Gallo-Roman period, secondly in the Romanesque period when it was the rendezvous for pilgrims from all over Europe, on the last stage of their journey to Saint James of Compostella. The city became the residence of the bishop Bertrand who built it much as we see it to-day. After the great pilgrimages had waned away, the city lost its importance and relapsed into the slumber of the centuries, dreaming of its past glories. Among its finest monuments are the cloister, mostly Romanesque in style and built in rose-coloured stone, the enormous church with its rood-screen and seventy sculpted choir-stalls dating from 1535, and its medieval and Renaissance houses.

3 Carved choir-stalls, 1535. 4 Romanesque galleries of the cloister and pillar of the Evangelists (second from left). 5 Renaissance house, 16th c.

ST-ÉMILION 7

SAINT-ÉMILION *Gironde.* E 15.

The whole region is now covered by vineyards, including the remains of a convent founded by the Dominicans in the late 13th century of which one wall survives with Gothic arcades. The town is built on two hills and is surrounded by massive walls. Narrow winding streets and old houses. On one hill a monolithic church built in the 12th century. The height of its nave makes it the vastest in France. Overlooking it is the beautiful collegiate church. The fine church of the Cordeliers (Franciscan Friars) with its Gothic-style choir is now carefully maintained by the neighbouring wine firm.

6 Town and collegiate church, 14th c. 7 Cloister of the church of the Cordeliers, 13th c. 8 Wall of the Dominican convent, 13th c. 9 Monolithic church, 12th c.

ST-LIZIER 10

SAINT-LIZIER *Ariège.* F 19.

The town is fortunate enough to possess two cathedrals: one by the walls of the city, the other in the town itself, which was an important Romanesque foundation. The Romanesque cathedral of Saint-Lizier is of great interest, especially for its cloister with alternating single and paired columns in marble and very fine capitals carved with interlacing motifs and figure subjects.

10 Cloister of Saint-Lizier, 12th c.

ST-ANDRÉ-DES-ARQUES 1

ST-AVENTIN 2

ST-BERTRAND-DE-COMMINGES 3

ST-BERTRAND-DE-COMMINGES 5

ST-ÉMILION 8

ST-ÉMILION 6

ST-ÉMILION 9

465

SAINT-MACAIRE *Gironde.* E 15.

The ancient town of Saint-Macaire should be visited soon before its 15th-century arcades, its 14th-century houses and its ramparts with their three well-preserved gateways fall into ruin and oblivion. Kept in a good state of preservation is the 12th, 13th-and 14th-century church which is built on a highly original trefoil ground-plan.

1 Church of Saint-Sauveur. 2 Place du Mercadieu, 15th c.

SAINT-PAUL-LES-DAX *Landes.* D 17.

The frieze running round the Romanesque apse of the otherwise modern church is one of the curiosities of the Landes region. Dating from the 11th century it illustrates scenes from the life of Christ in a simple Romanesque style with all the figures depicted in a rigid frontal aspect. In the Last Supper the twelve apostles have almost identical faces, only their hair-styles being varied. The way in which the dishes are shown on the table without any attempt at perspective is an indication of the early Romanesque style.

3 Apse of the church, 11th c. 4 Last Supper, detail from the sculpted frieze, 11th c.

SAINT-SEVER *Landes.* E 17.

Although the old abbey church has been rebuilt on several occasions as the result of various disasters it has kept its Benedictine plan and its magnificent choir (six radiating chapels of decreasing size, tribunes in the transepts, columns in antique marble, highly unusual and very fine capitals in the style of Cordoba). In the town, 17th-century abbey buildings and grain market in the former church of the Jacobin friars. The importance of the town was due to the fact that it lay on the pilgrims' route to Compostella. It was here that the famous manuscript of the Apocalypse (now in the Bibliothèque Nationale, Paris) was found.

5 Capital in the church of Saint-Sever, 12th c.

SARRANCE *Basses-Pyrénées.* E 19.

The former Premonstratensian abbey of Sarrance has a church and cloister in the Henri IV style - a rarity which should gladden the heart of anyone who may be sated by a surfeit of Romanesque buildings! The polygonal bell tower and the pointed slate roofs over each arcade of the cloister are of great elegance.

6 Bell tower and cloister of the Premonstratensian abbey, early 17th c.

SARRANCE 6

LA SAUVEMAJEURE *Gironde.* E 15.

Exceedingly interesting ruins of the former abbey that lay on the pilgrims' route to Compostella. Although built in the 12th century the abbey church is already in the Gothic style. The carving of the capitals in the apse is of the highest interest. Some of the shafts of the columns bear curious carved medallions representing the apostles with the instruments of their martyrdom. Fine church of Saint-Pierre on a neighbouring hill: 12th-century statues and frescoes in the apse, restored in the 19th century.

7 Capital in the abbey church: Daniel in the lion's den, 12th c.
8 Sirens. 9 Medallion on the shaft of a column, 12th c.

SAUVETERRE-D'AVEYRON 10

SAUVETERRE-D'AVEYRON *Aveyron.* H 16.

Arcaded or "covered" squares are frequently found in towns in the Rouergue region but that of the small medieval stronghold of Sauveterre is in a more complete state and more regular in pattern than the others.

10 Arcaded square of Sauveterre.

ST-MACAIRE I

ST-MACAIRE 2

ST-PAUL-LES-DAX 4

ST-PAUL-LES-DAX 3

ST-SEVER 5

LA SAUVEMAJEURE 7

LA SAUVEMAJEURE 8

LA SAUVEMAJEURE 9

467

VALCABRÈRE 8

VALCABRÈRE 9

SIMORRE *Gers.* F 18.

The striking red-brick fortified Gothic church of Simorre is the most beautiful of its kind in Gascony even though it was restored by Viollet-le-Duc somewhat audaciously. In the interior, beautiful stained-glass windows dating from the 14th to 16th century and early 16th-century choir-stalls carved in a somewhat rustic style, almost certainly by local artists.

I Apse of the fortified church, early 14th c. **2** Detail of the choir-stalls, early 16th c.

SORDE-L'ABBAYE *Landes.* D 18.

The abbey was destined to be destroyed on several occasions but it has kept some of its 16th-century buildings which now have a romantic charm under their covering of ivy, and its Romanesque church with their capitals carved in a somewhat rustic but very lively style. The choir is paved with a beautiful Gallo-Roman mosaic — a reminder that the abbey was founded on the site of a Roman villa — with themes similar to those of Piazza-Armerina in Sicily.

3 Mosaic in the choir of the church, hunting the hare, Gallo-Roman period. **4** Capital in the choir, the Passion, 12th c.

LE TAILLAN *Gironde.* D 14.

In a wine-growing country, the cellars and wine-stores are often works of art in themselves like the superbly proportioned wine cellar in the Château de la Dame Blanche on the road to Médoc.

5 Wine cellar in the château de la Dame Blanche, 17th c.

TALMONT-SUR-GIRONDE *Charente-Maritime.* D 13.

The beautifully situated church at Talmont overlooks the estuary and has suffered from the sea wind. Its design is interesting: as at Rioux (q.v.) and Rétaud (q.v.) the polygonal apse is decorated with pilastered blind arcades. In the Middle Ages the church lay on the route to Compostella and pilgrims would continue their journey from there by boat.

6 The church of Sainte-Radegonde, apse, 12th c.

VALCABRÈRE *Haute-Garonne.* F 19.

The main apse with its conch and the minor apses clustering round it give an air of elegance to the former cathedral Saint-Just which was built with the materials of an ancient Gallo-Roman town. The use of marble for the statues in the portal is another reminder of the ancient past of the site (note the nobility of the attitudes and expressions of the statues). Columnar statues of Saints Étienne, Just and Helena, with scenes of their martyrdom illustrated on the capitals.

7 Apse of the church of Saint-Just, 12th c. **8-9** Columnar statues of the side portal, 12th c.

VALS *Ariège.* G 19.

The site of the church is stranger than may be supposed from the photograph here for entrance to the church is by a steep staircase cut in the rock. In the choir, Romanesque frescoes discovered in 1956.

10 Romanesque church, 12th c. **II** Frescoes in the choir, possibly 12th c.

SIMORRE 2

SIMORRE 1

SORDE-L'ABBAYE 3

SORDE-L'ABBAYE 4

TALMONT-SUR-GIRONDE 6

LE TAILLAN 5

VALS 11

VALCABRÈRE 7

VALS 10

VILLEFRANCHE-DE-ROUERGUE *Aveyron.* G 16.

The small town of Villefranche seems to have remained unchanged with time. The market is still filled with peasants from the surrounding region, the streets are as chaotically paved as ever and still lined with old houses with Gothic arcades or Renaissance façades and the Place Notre-Dame has kept all its medieval atmosphere. In the collegiate church, fine choir-stalls carved by André Sulpice and completed in 1487; in the chapel of the Black Penitents (Penitents Noirs) a curious wooden campanile and an exuberantly carved gilt wood 17th-century retable. But the main interest of Villefranche is its Charterhouse which escaped destruction in the Revolution by becoming a hospital. Large and small cloister, chapter house, refectory and chapels have all survived. It was begun in 1451 and completed in eight years, whence its unity of style — pure Gothic. All the openings in the small cloister are different from one another. The "maisons" of the inmates of the charterhouse have also survived intact. In the refectory, a preacher's pulpit carved in the Flamboyant style.

1 Place Notre-Dame. **2** Window of a Renaissance house. **3** Courtyard of the great cloister of the Charterhouse, 15th c. **4** Small cloister. **5** Preacher's pulpit, refectory, 15th c.

XAINTRAILLES *Lot-et-Garonne.* E 16.

Birth-place of Joan of Arc's faithful companion of the same name who rebuilt the old 12th-century château around its square keep on the hill.

6 The château, 12th-15th c.

VILLEFRANCHE-DE-ROUERGUE 2

VILLEFRANCHE-DE-ROUERGUE 3

VILLEFRANCHE-DE-ROUERGUE 1

XAINTRAILLES 6

VILLEFRANCHE-DE-ROUERGUE 5

VILLEFRANCHE-DE-ROUERGUE 4

XIII

LANGUEDOC - ROUSSILLON

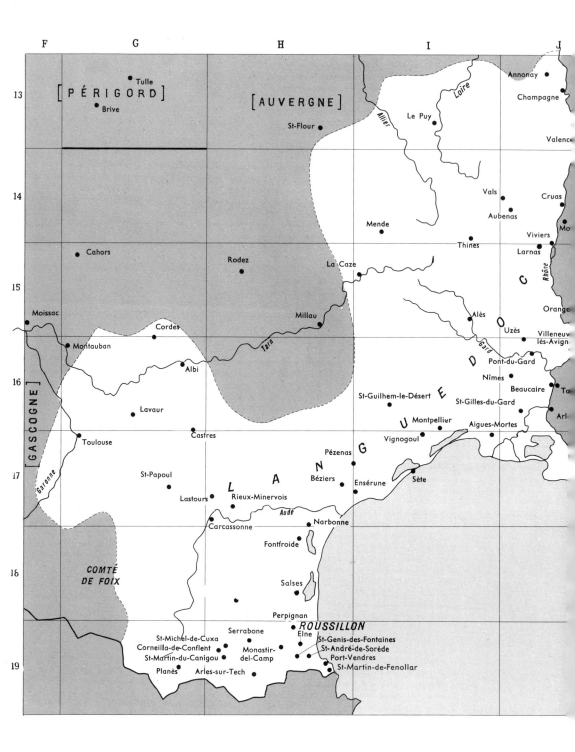

F   G   H   I   J

13

[P É R I G O R D]   [A U V E R G N E]

Tulle
Brive
St-Flour

Annonay
Champagne
Le Puy
Valence

14

Vals
Cruas
Aubenas
Mende
Viviers
Mo
Thines
Larnas

Cahors
Rodez
La Caze

15

Moissac
Millau
Alès
Orange
Uzès
Villeneuv
lès-Avign
Cordes
Montauban
Pont-du-Gard

16

Albi
Nîmes
Beaucaire
St-Guilhem-le-Désert
St-Gilles-du-Gard
Ta
Lavaur
Montpellier
Arl
Toulouse
Castres
Vignogoul
Aigues-Mortes

17

St-Papoul
Pézenas
Béziers
Ensérune
Sète
Lastours
Rieux-Minervois
Aude
Carcassonne
Narbonne

18

COMTÉ
DE FOIX
Fontfroide
Salses

Perpignan

ROUSSILLON
St-Michel-de-Cuxa
Serrabone
Elne
St-Genis-des-Fontaines
Corneilla-de-Conflent
Monastir-
del-Camp
St-André-de-Sorède
St-Martin-du-Canigou
Port-Vendres

19

Planès
Arles-sur-Tech
St-Martin-de-Fenollar

[GASCOGNE]

Garonne

Tarn

L A N G U E D O C

Rhône

Gard

Loire

Allier

472

MADAME VIGÉE-LEBRUN (1755-1842), THE EMPRESS ELISABETH-ALEXIEVNA, MUSÉE FABRE, MONTPELLIER *(Giraudon)*

FRANCISCO GOYA (1746-1828), THE JUNTA OF THE PHILIPPINES, DETAIL, MUSÉE GOYA, CASTRES *(Giraudon)*

It was administrative history rather than geography that created the enormous province of Languedoc and yet there is a common bond which links its furthest parts together — its Romanesque sanctuaries at Notre-Dame du Puy, in Velay where pilgrims from the east would meet on the way to Compostella, later to meet again at Saint-Sernin in Toulouse, the capital of the region.

Nîmes and the Pont-du-Gard survive as reminders of the Roman presence in the Rhone valley, and the walls of Carcassonne and Aigues-Mortes speak of the feudal ages and the Crusades.

Montauban and Albi are the birth-places of two of France's greatest artists, Ingres and Toulouse-Lautrec, and jealously preserve their memory in magnificent museums. The spirit of Catalonia still survives in the region of Perpignan, whether in the frescoes of Saint-Martin-de-Fenollar or in the ancient "sardane" dances.

AIGUES-MORTES I

AIGUES-MORTES *Gard.* I 17.

The 13th-century walls which have survived intact belong to an abandoned port which was once by the sea (like Brouage in the Charente-Maritime, q.v.). The moat that surrounded the rectangular enceinte has been filled in but the Tour de Constance, a keep built by Saint-Louis, towers over the battlements. Aigues-Mortes is one of the most curious towns in France and is particularly impressive seen from a distance.

I View of the walls, 13th c.

ALBI *Tarn.* G 16.

There is nothing rose-coloured or charming about Albi for it is a grim fortress with walls the colour of the dried blood of Albigensian heretics who were so ruthlessly slaughtered in the Middle Ages. The cathedral has nothing of the traditional Gothic in its style for it is closer in aspect to the modern church of Royan (q.v.) yet it is a masterpiece of the Aquitanian Gothic with its single brick-built nave and smooth sides, round buttresses and high lanceolated windows. With its narrow slit windows and 290-foot-high fortified tower the cathedral might be a fortress rather than a church and indeed it was built as such by the archbishop of Albi, Bernard de Castanet, who was resolved to defend it against the heretics. Although his project for the cathedral dates from 1276 it took more than a century for it to be completed, but the finished structure still kept a remarkable unity of style, only broken by the Gothic crowning of the tower and the famous white stone "Baldaquin" in the Flamboyant style. The exuberant porch was once described by Jean Jaurès as being "like a knot of lace around the pommel of a sword" and no better words can be found to describe it. The tower and the porch were added in the late 15th-century by Louis d'Amboise who wanted to make the building look like a church again. The low windows and the crowning intersecting arches were added by César Daly in the 19th-century. The contrast between styles is even more marked inside: the severe and undecorated old nave has been doubled by a second church separated by a rood-screen and a stone screen sculpted like a fossilised shell. According to Marcel Aubert the Burgundian-Flemish style of this sculpture would have come to Albi via Spain. Frescoes were then added to the walls and the vaulting giving the interior a sumptuous and somewhat stifling atmosphere.

ALBI 5

The Palais de la Berbie is inseparable from the cathedral and equally intact, having been begun in the 12th-century and completed five centuries later, during which time terraces, watch-towers, galleries and rich interior decoration were added to it. It is now a beautiful and famous museum of modern painting dominated by the work of Toulouse-Lautrec who was born in the region. The collection of his works on view is outstanding.

2 View of the cathedral of Sainte-Cécile, 14th c. 3 View of the choir, 15th c. 4 Saint Judith, detail of the choir-screen, 15th c. 5 Fresco of the Last Judgment, detail, 16th c. 6 Palais de la Berbie, 12th c.

MUSÉE D'ART MODERNE, PALAIS DE LA BERBIE

7 Henri de Toulouse-Lautrec (1864-1901): Self-portrait. 8 Toulouse-Lautrec: Page with drawings from a school exercise book, 1875. 9 Toulouse-Lautrec: Doctor Tapié de Celeyran. 10 Toulouse-Lautrec: the Salon in the Rue des Moulins.

ALBI 2

ALBI 3

ALBI 4

ALBI 6

ALBI 8

ALBI 7

ALBI 9

ALBI 10

477

ARLES-SUR-TECH I

ARLES-SUR-TECH *Pyrénées-Orientales.* H 19.

Although the Gothic cloister in white marble is the most immediately charming feature of the Cluniac abbey church of Sainte-
Marie, the interior contains several treasures: some pieces of
11th-century sculpture, 15th-century silver reliquary-busts, etc.
The church is unusual in being orientated towards the west
rather than the east.

I Abbey cloister, late 13th c.

AUBENAS 2

AUBENAS *Ardèche* J 14.

The old town of Aubenas with its steep and winding stone streets
overlooks a bend in the river Ardèche and is dominated in its
turn by a fortress-château that was elegantly altered in the 17th c.
The forms and colours of the glazed tiles of its roof add a touch
of fantasy to its sober aspect.

2 Doorway of the château, 14th-17th c.

BEAUCAIRE *Gard.* J 16.

Like Tarascon on the other side of the Rhône, the town of
Beaucaire was a citadel of Catholicism in an area that had been
greatly influenced by the Reformation. Château built by the
Counts of Toulouse with a curious triangular keep which has
survived intact. Town Hall by Mansart (1683) and the church
of Notre-Dame-des-Pommiers, a highly successful work of the
18th century by an architect from Avignon.

3 The keep of the château, 13th c. 4 View of Notre-Dame-des-
Pommiers, 18th c.

CARCASSONNE 7

BÉZIERS *Hérault.* H 17.

Béziers is a rich wine-growing city and is built on a hill dominated
by a fortified Gothic cathedral. Interesting Musée Fabregat:
paintings and a collection of Greek vases.

MUSÉE FABREGAT

5 Greek art: interior of a cup. 6 Bernard Van Orley (1493?-1542):
Virgin and Child.

CARCASSONNE 8

CARCASSONNE *Aude.* H 17.

Thanks to Viollet-le-Duc the walled citadel of Carcassonne has
regained its medieval aspect. The view from a distance is
highly picturesque and seen from nearby it might almost be a
careful reconstruction made for a film: not a single battlement is
missing. The church of Saint-Nazaire has kept most of its original
stones and has a Gothic choir with magnificent stained-glass
windows of later date that give it the appearance of a glass casket.
Pillars flanked with fine statues. The "stone of the siege" is carved
with a relief of the 13th c. which is a precious "document" on
medieval military art. The tomb of the bishop Radulphe has
been recently uncovered and shows the figure of the bishop
with an almost Buddha-like smile, standing on a very fine sculpted
plinth. The museum contains a fine Chardin.

7 The château and ramparts, seen from the Porte d'Aude. 8 The
City of Carcassonne, water-colour, 19th c. 9 Choir of the church
of Saint-Nazaire, 14th c. 10 Bas-relief on the siege, 13th c.
11 Tomb of Bishop Radulphe, 1266. 12 J.-B. Chardin (1699-1779):
Still-life, Musée des Beaux-Arts.

BEAUCAIRE 4

BEAUCAIRE 3

BÉZIERS 5

BÉZIERS 6

CARCASSONNE 9

CARCASSONNE 11

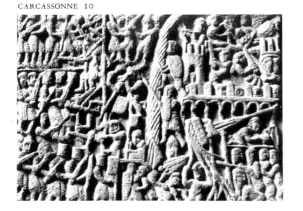

CARCASSONNE 10

CARCASSONNE 12

LA CAZE 6

LA CAZE 7

CASTRES *Tarn.* G 16.

The Musée Goya (in Mansart's Town Hall, with gardens by Le Nôtre which should be seen from the first floor) is one of the most important museums of Spanish painting and contains Goya's great *Junta of the Philippines,* an amazing, spacious composition in which the shadowy figures seem to have emerged out of the surrounding emptiness. The immense painting is now exhibited in a furnished room which might almost be an antechamber for the hall in the painting. Beside it, a self-portrait by Goya, seen wearing spectacles. The collection also includes Goya's *Caprichos,* a few primitives and several 17th-century Spanish paintings.

MUSÉE GOYA

1 Garcia de Benabarre (late 15th c.): Adoration of the Magi. 2 Velazquez (1599-1660) and Mazo: Portrait of Philip IV. 3 Francisco Goya (1746-1828): Self-portrait with spectacles, c. 1788. 4 Goya: Don Francisco del Mazo, c. 1815. 5 Goya: Ferdinand VII presiding over the Junta of the Philippines, 1815.

LA CAZE *Lozère.* I 15.

The château of La Caze stands in the wildest part of the Tarn gorges and according to legend was built by Soubeyrane Alamand for her eight daughters the "nymphs of the Tarn" whose portraits may be seen on the ceiling of a room. The corridors of the château are paved with pebbles from the river and although the building has been restored it has kept its disturbing and somewhat oppressive charm.

6 The château, 15th c. 7 Painted ceiling: the eight nymphs of the Tarn, 15th c., restored.

CHAMPAGNE *Ardèche.* J 13.

Hispano-Arabic influences are frequently found in the Languedoc region and may be seen in the church of Champagne, in the cupolas on squinches over the nave and in the triforium with its trefoil arches in the style of Cordoba.

8 Cupolas on squinches over the nave, 12th c. 9 Triforium with trefoil arches, 12th c.

CORDES *Tarn.* G 16.

Although somewhat exploited by tourism, the perfectly preserved old town of Cordes is still worth "discovering". It is a perfect example of military and civil architecture, built in two years by the Count of Toulouse, between 1222 and 1224. The perfect survival of the houses is due to the fine quality of the stone used. Gothic houses may be seen in every street. The Maison du Grand-Fauconnier on one side of the pretty Place de la Halle, the Maison du Grand Écuyer and the Maison du Grand Veneur are in a perfect Tuscan style and were built by the architects of Cosimo de Medicis. The gateways of the double enceinte, the church of Saint-Michel and the staircase of the Pater Noster seem to have remained unchanged for the seven centuries of their existence.

10 Staircase of the Pater Noster. 11 Façade of the Maison du Grand-Fauconnier, 14th c.

CORNEILLA-DE-CONFLENT *Pyrénées-Orientales.* H 19.

Remarkable Romanesque church with Virgin in majesty in a mandala in the marble portal. Several Romanesque wood-carvings of the Virgin in the interior. Tower with narrow-pilasters (q.v. Cruas). Floor of pink marble.

12 Portal of the church, 12th c.

CASTRES 1

CASTRES 5

CASTRES 2

CASTRES 4

CASTRES 3

CHAMPAGNE 9

CHAMPAGNE 8

CORDES 11

CORDES 10

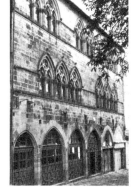

481

ENSÉRUNE 7

LARNAS 12

LASTOURS 13

CRUAS *Ardèche.* J 14.

Small town with church in an archaic Romanesque style inspired by Byzantine art. The apse and the bell-tower are decorated with high arcades (as at Saint-Guilhem-le-Désert and Uzès, q.v.). **1** Apse of the church, 11th c. **2** The crypt, 11th c. **3-4** Capitals, 11th c.

ELNE *Pyrénées-Orientales.* H 19.

The cloister of Elne is a perfect specimen of Romanesque art at its apogee but is perhaps less directly moving than others. It was built between the 12th and 14th centuries. Capitals of the paired columns decorated with fantastic animals or narrative scenes, showing great richness of inspiration. They seem to have been painted originally. Only the south tower of the cathedral by the cloister is Romanesque.

5 Gallery of the cloister, late 12th-14th c. **6** Tombstone, 13th c.

ENSÉRUNE *Hérault.* I 17.

The site of the acropolis of Ensérune has been inhabited since 600 B.C. Vestiges of a pre-Roman oppidum have been found and are now on view in the local museum.

7 Marble torso, Greek art, Musée National d'Ensérune.

FONTFROIDE *Aude.* H 18.

Fontfroide, the great Cistercian abbey of the Languedoc (q.v. Sénanque, Silvacane and Le Thoronet) is set in the midst of a wild and steep-sided valley, and consists of various buildings dating from the 11th to 17th centuries, restored in the early 20th century. The vast buildings are given unity by the grey, pink and yellow sandstone in which they were built, in a transitional Romanesque-Gothic style. The cloister is famous for its pointed bays surmounted by either one vast *oculus* or three small *oculi* (round windows, sometimes called "bull's eyes").

8 Cloister and bell-tower of the church, 13th c. **9** Vaulted hall, 13th c. **10** Nave of the abbey church, 13th c. **11** Entrance porch, 17th c.

LARNAS (near Saint-Montand) *Ardèche.* J 15.

The small 12th-century church shows several pre-Romanesque elements in its structure, forming a link between the style of the Massif Central and that of the Rhône valley.

12 Church, 12th c., apse restored.

LASTOURS *Aude.* H 17.

Four inaccessible, towering castles were built on the rocky peaks at Lastours by the lords of Cabaret during the 12th and 13th c. Their names are: Quertinheux, Fleur Espine, Tour Régine and Cabaret.

13 Ruins of the four castles, 12th-13th c.

LAVAUR *Tarn.* G 16.

Old Cathar town which suffered greatly during the Crusades of Simon de Montfort. Massive blood-coloured cathedral with a pretty Flamboyant style portal.

14 Portal of the cathedral Saint-Alain, Adoration of the Magi, 15th c.

CRUAS 2

CRUAS 3

CRUAS 4

CRUAS I

ELNE 5

FONTFROIDE II

ELNE 6

FONTFROIDE 9

FONTFROIDE 8

FONTFROIDE IO

LAVAUR I4

MENDE 1

MENDE *Lozère*. I 14.

Old medieval town with houses classified as national monuments. 14th-century bridge with a centre arch that has resisted the floods of the river Lot throughout the centuries. The Gothic cathedral is built in yellow stone. Its 13th-century crypt of Saint-Privat is one of the oldest in France.

1 Façade of the cathedral Saint-Pierre, 14th-16th c. **2** Pont Notre-Dame, 14th c.

MONASTIR-DEL-CAMP (near Thuir) *Pyrénées-Orientales*. H 19.

The Priory is as completely Catalan in style as it is in name and was founded by Charlemagne. 11th-12th-century church with a beautiful cloister.

3 Cloister of the priory, 1307.

MENDE 2

MONASTIR·DEL·CAMP 3

MONTPELLIER 4

MONTPELLIER 5

MONTPELLIER *Hérault*. I 16.

With its fine promenade, one of the best museums in France, old *hôtels* in every street of the old quarter, Montpellier is the most famous town in southern France after Aix-en-Provence and Avignon. It also has a 14th-century cathedral of Saint-Pierre, the 18th-century buildings of its Faculty of Medecine, founded in 1221, and a Jardin des Plantes created by Henri IV.

The striking Jardin du Peyrou with its aqueduct and water tower was built during the 18th century and is worthy of any great capital city. The Musée Fabre was founded by a pupil of David and is famous for its collection of drawings (including three by Raphaël), its fine works by European masters and its French paintings of the 18th and 19th centuries, with works by Greuze, Delacroix, Courbet and Bazille — the last a native of Montpellier. The unity of style of the *hôtels* in the old city is due to the fact that it was almost entirely rebuilt by Louis XIII after the siege of 1622. Many of the small winding streets are lined by the façades of the classical-style *hôtels* with their spacious courtyards and fine staircases discreetly hidden behind walls. Among the finest are the *hôtels* Bonnier de la Mosson, Saint-Côme, and the hôtel des Trésoriers de France, all of the 17th and 18th centuries.

4 Water tower of the Jardin du Peyrou, 18th c. **5** Courtyard of the hôtel Bonnier de la Mosson, 18th c.

MUSÉE FABRE

6 Raphaël (1483-1520): drawing. **7** Sebastien Bourdon (1616-1671): The Man with black ribbons. **8** Aved (1702-1766): Madame Crozat. **9** J.-B. Monnoyer (1664-1699): Still life. **10** Mme Vigée-Lebrun (1755-1842): the Empress Elisabeth-Alexievna. **11** Delacroix (1798-1863): The Women of Algiers. **12** Courbet (1819-1877): Bonjour, M. Courbet. **13** J.-F. Bazille (1841-1870): View of the village of Castelnau.

MONTPELLIER 7

MONTPELLIER 6

MONTPELLIER 8

MONTPELLIER 10

MONTPELLIER 11

MONTPELLIER 9

MONTPELLIER 13

MONTPELLIER 12

485

NARBONNE *Aude*. H 17.

The cathedral of Saint-Just was never completed but what there is of it is a masterpiece. Only the choir and the apse were built and their undecorated piers rise to a height of 150 feet — only surpassed by that of the naves of Amiens and Beauvais. A purely Nordic, skilful and elegant type of construction, dating from the late 13th-early 14th century like that of the cathedrals of Clermont-Ferrand, Limoges, and Toulouse. The interior is decorated with fine tapestries and paintings.

The Palais des Archevêques is a curious blend of civil and military architecture of the Romanesque, Gothic and "Viollet-le-Duc" periods (the pseudo-Renaissance façade dates from the 19th c.). It is now the Town Hall and the old, sumptuous apartments of the archbishop-dukes of Narbonne now contain the beautiful collections of the Musée d'Art et de Céramique. It was also in this building that Cinq-Mars made his tragic appearance before his judges who accused him of conspiring against Richelieu in 1642. The most important lapidary museum in France is in the Église Lamourguié, an archaic Gothic church which provides a perfect setting for the exhibits. Gaulish, Roman, Visigothic and Saracen exhibits. In the basilica of Saint-Paul-Serge, a very beautiful Gothic choir built on the site of an interesting early Christian cemetery. A notable curiosity of the town is the Maison des Trois-Nourrices (1558), with opulently sculpted caryatids flanking its windows.

1 Choir of the cathedral of Saint-Just, 14th c. 2 Palais des Archevêques, 10th-14th c. 3 Maison des Trois-Nourrices, 1558, detail. 4 Titian (1477-1576): Portrait of a man in armour, Musée Municipal.

NIMES 5

NIMES *Gard*. J 16.

One of the most beautiful and harmonious gardens in France is the Jardin de la Fontaine at Nîmes. It was laid out in the 18th century on terraces around the ancient Spring of Nemausus, flanked by the Temple of Diana. The ruin dates from the 1st c. B.C. and curiously enough is tunnel-vaulted, but it is completely eclipsed by the splendour of the city's other Roman monuments. Nîmes was a city of considerable importance during the reign of the emperor Augustus and the impressive arena (beautiful both from the ground and when seen from the air), the rectangular temple known as the Maison Carrée (the only intact Roman temple to have survived) and the Tour Magne have remained as witnesses to the city's Roman splendour.

During the Wars of Religion, while Beaucaire became a Catholic stronghold, Nîmes went over to Calvinism, remaining faithful to the new creed in spite of edicts and persecutions. This Protestant heritage has had great influence on the city which has a long tradition of learning and culture.

5 Head, Gaulish sculpture, Musée Lapidaire. 6 Temple of Diana, 1st c. B.C. 7 La Tour Magne, 1st c. B.C. 8 Maison Carrée, 1st c. B.C. 9 Aerial view of the arena, 1st c. B.C. 10 Jardin de la Fontaine, 18th c.

NARBONNE 1

NARBONNE 2

NARBONNE 4

NARBONNE 3

NIMES 8

NIMES 9

NIMES 6

NIMES 10

NIMES 7

487

PERPIGNAN 5

PERPIGNAN *Pyrénées-Orientales.* H 19.

Perpignan has been French only since the Treaty of the Pyrenees in 1659 and in the 13th century was the capital of the kings of Majorca. It has kept all its Catalan charm to the present day and the old palace has survived, around its handsome square tower. The Castillet, a small defensive fortress in red brick, dates from the 14th century as does the Loge de Mer, a kind of town palace which was prettily altered in the Renaissance. Several sculptures by Maillol who went to school in the town may be seen in the streets. The most interesting churches are: the cathedral of Saint-Jean, a fine Gothic basilica with a single nave and fine Catalan altars of the 17th century, and the Romanesque church of Saint-Jean-le-Vieux beside the cathedral. Inside the cathedral, the popular wood carving of the Devôt Christ (a Christ on the Cross) a rather mannered work of German provenance dating from 1307. By the pendentive of the south portal, a very beautiful Christ in Majesty of 1219.

1 Le Castillet, 14th c. 2 La Loge de Mer, 14th-16th c., and Venus by Maillol (1861-1954). 3 Le Devôt Christ, Chapelle du Christ, 1307. 4 Christ in Majesty, church of Saint-Jean-le-Vieux, 1219. 5 The martyrdom of Saint Vincent, school of Valencia, late 14th c., Musée des Beaux-Arts.

PÉZENAS *Hérault.* I 17.

It was in this town that Molière wrote his famous play "Les Precieuses Ridicules". Now a small and sleepy town, Pézenas was once an important capital and the seat of the States General of the Languedoc, but it has survived unchanged since the 18th century. As in Aix-en-Provence (q.v.), the streets are lined with *hôtels* of the 16th-17th and 18th centuries, with their doorways, balconies and old staircases still intact. The houses were never restored and are all still inhabited so that Pézenas has escaped the fate of becoming a museum-city. Nonetheless, the local authorities have discreetly numbered the houses for the benefit of visitors. Maison des Consuls, with a fine 17th-century façade and a Renaissance staircase; old houses in the Cours Jean-Jaurès; former 14th-century ghetto still enclosed by gateways; the house of Jacques Cœur, whom business had brought from Bourges (q.v.) at one time; hôtel Malibran, with a superb late 17th-century staircase; hôtel d'Alfonce with a pretty gallery and curious staircase in the second courtyard, now rather unfortunately encumbered.

6 Maison des Consuls, façade of the 17th c. 7 Hôtel Malibran, staircase, late 17th c. 8 Hôtel d'Alfonce, courtyard and loggia, 17th c.

PONT-DU-GARD 11

PLANÈS *Pyrénées-Orientales.* H 19.

The little church of the village is an archaeological curiosity because of its quite exceptional trefoil shape (q.v. Chapelle de Peyrolles, Bouches-du-Rhône). It has been thought to be a former mosque or a chapel symbolising the Trinity but the truth has yet to be found. It was built in the Romanesque period.

9 The church and bell-tower, 11th-12th c. 10 Ground-plan of the church.

PONT-DU-GARD *Gard.* J 16.

The famous aqueduct of Gard dates from the late 1st century B.C. It was built by Agrippa, Augustus' son-in-law, who had made a canal to bring water from Uzès to Nîmes and who needed to bridge the river Gardon. The aqueduct is built in three tiers of arches, in gold-coloured stone, 150 feet high and 900 feet long, and stands in a fittingly beautiful landscape.

11 Pont du Gard, late 1st c. B.C.

PERPIGNAN I

PERPIGNAN 2

PERPIGNAN 4

PERPIGNAN 3

PÉZENAS 8

PLANÈS 10

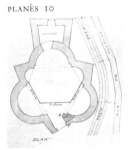

PLANÈS 9

PÉZENAS 7

PÉZENAS 6

LE PUY-EN-VELAY 4

LE PUY-EN-VELAY *Haute-Loire*. I 13.

The Romanesque architect of Le Puy-en-Velay made the most of the strange landscape with its bristling volcanic peaks, for he built Saint-Michel d'Aiguilhe on one, and the cathedral with its pointed Limousin-style spire on another. The façade of the cathedral is chequered in its decoration like an Arab embroidery and is now believed to have undergone important alterations in the 17th century. Nonetheless it is thoroughly Romanesque in spirit. The nave of the church is covered by six cupolas resting on squinches and shows a strong Moslem influence, as in the frequent use of polyfoil arches and the carving of some capitals. Immense fresco with a representation of Saint Michel — the largest of its kind for the period — in the north tribune above the transept. As in the façade, mosaic-type stone work is found in the cloister. Heavy columns in rather sinister black volcanic stone with fine capitals. In the Chapelle des Morts, famous fresco of the *Liberal Arts* (15th c.) behind a curtain (viewed on request). Saint-Michel d'Aiguilhe is only reached after a long and steep climb but is well worth the effort for it is a masterpiece of Romanesque architecture and the finest building in Le Puy, especially for its trefoil portal and lintel carved with sirens. Inside, frescoes and simple Romanesque capitals.

The lace-makers and souvenir sellers by the church doorway have been there ever since the times of the pilgrimage to Compostella.

In the Musée Crozatier, a famous painting in deplorable condition: the *Virgin with a mantle*, an anonymous French work of the early 15th-century, similar in theme to the painting by Enguerrand Quarton. Very eclectic museum with exhibits illustrating the history of Velay from prehistoric times to the Romanesque period. Also, beautiful scale models of machinery.

I View of the town. **2** Façade of the cathedral, 12th c. **3** Cloister, 12th c. **4** Romanesque railing in the cloister, 12th c. **5** Fresco, Saint Michael, height 18 feet, 12th c. **6** Trefoil portal of Saint-Michel d'Aiguilhe, 11th c. **7** Interior of Saint-Michel d'Aiguilhe, 11th c.

MUSÉE CROZATIER

8 Virgin with the Mantle, French school, c. 1480. **9** Mathieu Le Nain (1607-1677): Portrait of a man.

RIEUX-MINERVOIS 10   RIEUX-MINERVOIS 11   RIEUX-MINERVOIS 12

RIEUX-MINERVOIS *Aude*. H 17.

Curious Romanesque church with rounded choir and nave, and richly carved capitals, some foliated, others with fantastic animal subjects.

10 View of the church, 12th c. **11-12** Capitals of the church, 12th c.

LE PUY-EN-VELAY 3

LE PUY-EN-VELAY 2

LE PUY-EN-VELAY 5

LE PUY-EN-VELAY 6

LE PUY-EN-VELAY 9

LE PUY-EN-VELAY 7

LE PUY-EN-VELAY I

LE PUY-EN-VELAY 8

491

SAINT-ANDRÉ-DE-SORÈDE *Pyrénées-Orientales*. H 19.

The lintel in the church of Saint-André is almost identical to that of Saint-Genis (q.v.) and may be unhesitatingly attributed to the same Catalan artist and dated 1020. Both lintels show Mozarabic influence which was particularly strong in the Roussillon during the 11th century, when the mosque at Cordoba served as a model for Christian architecture.

1 Centre part of lintel in the portal of the church of Saint-André, early 11th c.

SAINT-GENIS-DES-FONTAINES *Pyrénées-Orientales*. H 19.

The lintel in the portal of the church of Saint-Genis is dated "the 24th year of the reign of Robert II" i.e. 1020. It is, therefore, one of the earliest examples of Romanesque art in the Roussillon. In style, it is very much inspired by a Cordovan ivory carving showing the Christ surrounded by ten apostles and inscribed in an arch which is as Mozarabic in spirit as the bordering of the lintel.

2 Lintel of the portal of Saint-Genis, 1020.

SAINT-GILLES-DU-GARD *Gard*. J 16.

The region is rich in Greco-Roman remains and it is not, therefore, so very surprising to find monumental sculpture of classical inspiration such as the wide façade of Saint-Gilles, similar to that of Saint-Trophime (q.v.) in Arles — the two masterpieces of Romanesque art of the Languedoc. Although somewhat deteriorated, the twelve statues of the apostles flanking the portals are of majestic beauty. Much of the Cluniac abbey church was destroyed during the wars of religion and only the centre portal dates from the original foundation. The decoration of the façade dates from the 13th century and is devoted to scenes from the life of Christ. Crypt with flattened pointed arches and a spiral staircase — amazing for its period — of great interest.

3 Façade of the church of Saint-Gilles, 12th-13th c. 4 Statue of an apostle, 12th c. 5 Detail of the base of the façade, 12th-13th c.

SAINT-GUILHEM-LE-DÉSERT *Hérault*. I 16.

The small abbey stands almost lost in a wild rocky landscape. Part of the cloister is now in America, in the famous Cloisters Museum, in New York, but the Romanesque church has remained. Beautiful apse with narrow pilasters. In the porch, one of the earliest known examples of groin-vaulting. In the nave, an antique sarcophagus containing remains of the sisters of Saint Guilhem, a faithful friend of Charlemagne and founder of the monastery.

6 View of the church, 12th c. 7 Apse, 12th c.

ST-MARTIN-DU-CANIGOU 8

SAINT-MARTIN-DU-CANIGOU *Pyrénées-Orientales*. H 19.

The abbey was rebuilt stone by stone at the beginning of the present century but dates from the early 11th century. All that remains of the original building is the pre-Romanesque nave and a few beautiful capitals in the cloister. The site is highly impressive and has remained unchanged throughout the centuries.

8 View of the abbey buildings, 11th-12th c., rebuilt.

SAINT-MARTIN-DE-FENOLLAR (at Maureillas) *Pyr.-Or.* H 18.

The most important Romanesque frescoes in the Roussillon may be seen in the small chapel (only 45 feet in length). Unfortunately mutilated (a window has been pierced in their centre), they are still in good condition and clearly belong to the Catalan school. Warm browns and yellows, slightly heightened with blue and green; strong, vigorous drawing; the expression of the oval-shaped faces is strikingly intense.

9 Fresco in the chapel of "La Mahut", Nativity, 12th c.

ST-GENIS-DES-FONTAINES 2

ST-ANDRÉ-DE-SORÈDE 1

ST-GILLES-DU-GARD 4

ST-GUILHEM-LE-DÉSERT 6

ST-GUILHEM-LE-DÉSERT 7

ST-GILLES-DU-GARD 5

ST-GILLES-DU-GARD 3

ST-MARTIN-DE-FENOLLAR 9

SAINT-MICHEL-DE-CUXA *Pyrénées-Orientales*. H 19.

Almost half of the pink marble cloister of the abbey church of Saint-Michel is now in the Cloisters, a curious museum of medieval European art in the out-skirts of New York, belonging to the Metropolitan Museum of Art. The other half has also been dispersed but has recently been reconstituted. Capitals almost identical to those in other abbeys of the Roussillon (q.v. Serrabone, Saint-Martin-du-Canigou). It would seem that the somewhat unimaginative repetition of animal and monster subjects in the sculpture of the region was due to a number of artists who were trained at Saint-Michel. Abbey church with horse-shoe arches inspired by those at Cordoba, and crenellated bell-tower with four tiers of arcades in the Lombard style. The Romanesque doorway leading from the church into the cloister is decorated with interesting animal motifs.

1 Tower of the abbey church, 11th c. 2 The cloister, 12th c.

SAINT-PAPOUL *Aude*. G 17.

It would seem impossible to still "discover" a cathedral in France yet this is the case at the almost abandoned village of Saint-Papoul, for the church was the see of a bishop and a Benedictine abbey from the 14th to the 18th century. Rather banal Romanesque apse supported by columns with archaic capitals. Sculpted corbels and cable-moulded string-coursing. 14th-century cloister still in the Romanesque style, somewhat neglected and overgrown by weeds but full of charm.

3 Tower and apse of the "cathedral" of Saint-Papoul, 11th and 14th c. 4 Romanesque cloister, 14th c.

SALSES *Pyrénées-Orientales*. H 18.

The fortress of Salses was admirably designed to withstand artillery and is surrounded by a fine brick-and-stone wall more than thirty feet thick. The fortress was originally built by Dom Sancho of Castile in 1497 and was restored by Vauban.

SALSES 5

5 Fortress of Salses, 15th c., restored.

SERRABONE *Pyrénées-Orientales*. H 19.

The sculpted pink marble tribune in the priory church of Serrabone is a masterpiece of the art of the Roussillon. The fantastic style of the decoration seems to have been inspired by Byzantine manuscripts and Sassanian textiles: the griffons, masks and monsters of the capitals are completely oriental in spirit, and resemble those at Saint-Michel-de-Cuxa (q.v.). The gallery along the south side of the church also has fine capitals. Very archaic groin-vaulting of the tribune. The bas-relief decoration of the corner-stones recalls the style of Byzantine book-binding.

THINES 8

6 Tribune of the church, pink marble, 12th c. 7 Capital in the tribune, 12th c.

THINES *Ardèche*. I 14.

The semi-circular apse of the church of this almost deserted village is richly decorated with polychrome brickwork and narrow pilasters, as at Cruas (q.v.). The lintel of the south portal and the single nave are also polychrome and as beautiful as the exterior.

8 Apse of the church, 12th c.

ST-MICHEL-DE-CUXA 1

ST-MICHEL-DE-CUXA 2

ST-PAPOUL 3

ST-PAPOUL 4

SERRABONE 6

SERRABONE 7

495

TOULOUSE *Haute-Garonne.* G 17.

In population and artistic importance, Toulouse ranks fourth among the cities of France. Its treasures are many but they are often concealed by forbidding walls or lie in obscure side-streets (churches, Renaissance *hôtels*, various museums). First among the most important buildings is the basilica of Saint-Sernin, the masterpiece of Romanesque architecture in the south of France. It was consecrated in 1096 by Pope Urban II and dedicated to the martyr-bishop of Toulouse, Saint Saturnin. It is the largest Romanesque church to be built on the plan of a Latin cross, being 432 feet in length by 240 feet wide. The nave and double aisles are carried by columns decorated with five hundred capitals, and were destined to accomodate pilgrims on their way to Saint James of Compostella. Apse with massed cupolas at the base of the Romanesque and Gothic tower, built in local brick and stone — rare for this region. The crypt contains an oustanding collection of relics; the ambulatory has some of the oldest examples of Languedoc sculpture of the 11th century: seven bas-reliefs in marble from the quarry of Saint-Béat, in a style inspired by Byzantine ivory carvings. The hermetic, beardless Christ is particularly striking. The Porte Miégeville bears the scene of the Ascension and is the first example of a Romanesque attempt at composition on a large scale. The artist was still unable to resolve the problem posed by the frame of the tympanum and the style is antique.

Toulouse is also rich in Gothic art: the church of the Jacobins, a citadel of orthodoxy in the Middle Ages (Toulouse was in the centre of the region of the Albigensian heresy) was built in the late 13th century. Remarkable and original double nave, brick walls 75 feet high, flying-buttresses and pulpit set against the wall for safety, as in monastic refectories. The cathedral of Saint-Étienne has suffered from continual restorations which were responsible for its crooked façade but its single nave is an example of the early Gothic style, being an early 13th-century, prototype of the style of the Languedoc. Much of the prosperity of the bourgeois of Toulouse in the 16th century, was due to the cultivation of woad, used for dyeing textiles. They left visible signs of their wealth which should be seen from the tower of the hôtel Assézat, built by Nicolas Bachelier: the old quarters are bristling with towers, rather like San Gimignano in Italy, which were proudly erected by the city councillors or *capitouls* after their nomination. From the street little can be seen of the *hôtels*, and the visitor should go into the magnificent court-yards, all of the 16th century and mostly built by Nicolas Bachelier. Nearly all are built in brick with stone decoration, except for the hôtel de Pierre (de Clary) which owes its name to its façade, entirely in sculpted stone. The hôtel Assézat has an Italianate courtyard with Doric, Ionic and Corinthian orders superimposed in the storeys. The style is more Nordic than Mediterranean and has been compared with that of the Cour Carrée in the Louvre.

The courtyard of the hôtel Bernuy (now a *lycée*) is in the transitional Gothic-Renaissance style, and is due to Louis Privat. The François I-style hôtel de Beringuier-Maynier has the most beautiful windows of any building in Toulouse.

Basilica of Saint-Sernin. 1 Apse and tower, 12th c. 2 Nave, 12th c. 3 Christ in Majesty, bas-relief, marble of Saint-Béat, in the ambulatory, late 11th c. 4 Porte Miégeville, early 12th c.

5 Double-nave of the church of the Jacobins, 13th c. 6 Palm-vaulting in the choir of the Jacobins, 13th c. 7 Interior of the cathedral of Saint-Étienne, 13th c. 8 Tower of the hôtel de Bernuy, 16th c.

8

1

2

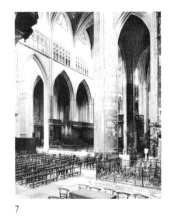

7

4

3

5

6

The museums of Toulouse are as rich and varied as the *hôtels:* most important is the Musée des Augustins which contains vestiges of medieval sculpture from all the demolished buildings of the city. Of the former monastic buildings, all of high quality, the small cloister, the chapter house and the large cloister with paired columns and 15th-century trefoil arches still survive. The collections include Gallo-Roman antiquities, figures of saints from the Chapelle de Rieux, sibyls from Saint-Sernin, works by Nicolas Tournier, leader of the 17th-century Toulousain school of painting, and paintings by Rubens, Delacroix, and Corot. The Musée Saint-Raymond is unique in France for its collection of Roman busts and marbles, ceramics and antique coins. In the Musée Paul Dupuy, minor arts from the 17th century to the present day, mostly regional.

6

I Courtyard of the hôtel Beringuier-Maynier, 1527. 2 Porch of the hôtel de Jean Ulmo, 16th c. 3 Portal of the hôtel de Pierre, by Nicolas Bachelier, 16th c. 4 Courtyard of the hôtel d'Assézat, 1557. 5 Courtyard of the hôtel de Bernuy, 16th c.

MUSÉE DES AUGUSTINS

6 Cloister and tower of the monastery, 14th c. 7-8-9 Capitals in the Cloître de la Daurade, 11th c. 10 Statue of a saint from the Chapelle de Rieux, 14th c. 11 P. P. Rubens (1577-1640): Christ on the Cross.

UZÈS 12

UZÈS 13

UZÈS *Gard.* J 16.

The Tour Fenestrelle owes its name to its five tiers of arcades. The 150 foot-high tower belongs to a former Romanesque cathedral, since destroyed. The arcading and scalloped decoration is characteristic of the town as may be seen from the main buildings: the courtyard of the bishop's palace (17th c.), Tour de l'Horloge (12th c.), hôtel de Castille (18th c.), the Town Hall and the church of Saint-Étienne (1778). Château du Duché, with fortified walls and 11th-century square keep, and a delightful Renaissance courtyard attributed to Philibert de l'Orme.

12 Tour Fenestrelle, 12th c. 13 Courtyard of the Château du Duché, 16th c.

1

4

5

10

2

3

8

7

9

11

VIGNOGOUL 1

VILLENEUVE 3

VILLENEUVE 2

VIVIERS-SUR-RHONE 5

VIGNOGOUL *Hérault.* I 17.

Former Cistercian abbey of which only the church remains. The style is well-developed though early Gothic; highly original apse with gabled windows opening in each bay of the eight-part pointed vault.

1 Apse of the abbey church, c. 1250.

VILLENEUVE-LÈS-AVIGNON *Gard.* J 16.

The golden effect produced by the town of Villeneuve when viewed from Avignon is rendered better by the painting *Villeneuve-lès-Avignon, the Fort Saint-André* (until recently, attributed to Corot) than by any photograph.

The tower of Philip the Handsome was built between 1293 and 1307 on "French territory" facing the domain of the Counts of Provence, and was raised higher in the 14th century when Avignon became the city of the Popes. The Fort Saint-André was built in the second half of the 14th century. Within its walls is the Charterhouse, with 14th-century frescoes in its chapel.

The Hospice contains one of the masterpieces of French 15th century painting: the *Coronation of the Virgin* by Enguerrand Quarton. The no less famous *Pietà* (now in the Louvre) also came from here and an ancient copy may be seen in the Hospice next to a *Virgin and Child*, a 16th-century ivory.

2 Attributed to Corot: Villeneuve-lès-Avignon, the Fort Saint-André, Musée de Reims. 3 Tower of Philip the Handsome (Tour de Philippe le Bel), late 13th c. 4 Enguerrand Quarton (15th c.): Coronation of the Virgin, 1454.

VILLENEUVE 4

VIVIERS-SUR-RHONE *Ardèche.* J 14.

The upper town, huddled on a rock, has kept many of its old houses around the cathedral Saint-Vincent, the most famous being the Renaissance Maison des Chevaliers, decorated with a sculpted frieze representing various scenes of a tournament. In the cathedral, interesting tapestries.

5 Maison des Chevaliers, c. 1550.

XIV

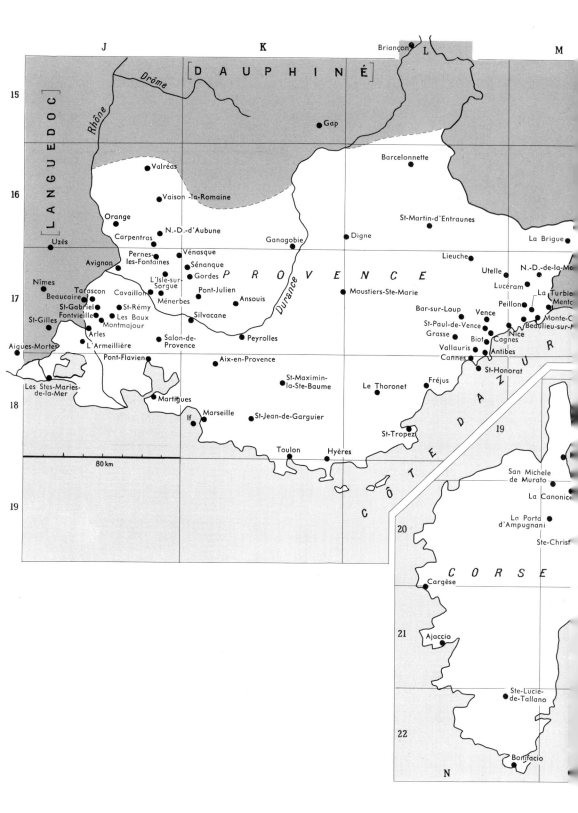

J   K   Briançon   L   M

[D A U P H I N É]

15   Drôme

Rhône

Gap

LANGUEDOC

16   Valréas

Vaison -la-Romaine   Barcelonnette

Orange   St-Martin-d'Entraunes

N.-D.-d'Aubune   La Brigue

Carpentras   Ganagobie   Digne

Uzès   Vénasque   Lieuche

Pernes-les-Fontaines   P R O V E N C E   Utelle   N.-D.-de-la-Me

Avignon   Sénanque   Lucéram

L'Isle-sur-Sorgue   Gordes   La Turbie

Nîmes   Pont-Julien   Ansouis   Peillon   Mente

17   Beaucaire   Tarascon   Cavaillon   Moustiers-Ste-Marie   Bar-sur-Loup   Vence   Monte-C

St-Gabriel   St-Rémy   Ménerbes   St-Paul-de-Vence   Beaulieu-sur-

St-Gilles   Fontvieille   Les Baux   Silvacane   Grasse   Biot   Cagnes   Nice

Montmajour   Vallauris   Antibes

Arles   Salon-de-Provence   Peyrolles   Cannes

Aigues-Mortes   L'Armeillière   St-Honorat

Pont-Flavien   Aix-en-Provence

Les Stes-Maries-de-la-Mer   St-Maximin-la-Ste-Baume   Le Thoronet   Fréjus   19

18   Martigues

80 km   If   Marseille   St-Jean-de-Garguier   St-Tropez   San Michele de Murato

Toulon   Hyères   La Canonic

C Ô T E   D' A Z U R   La Porta d'Ampugnani

19   Ste-Christ

20   C O R S E

Cargèse

21   Ajaccio

Ste-Lucie-de-Tallano

22   Bonifacio

N

PICASSO (BORN 1881), FAUN, OIL ON PAPER, 1946, MUSÉE D'ANTIBES
(Marianne Greenwood)

15TH-CENTURY WALL PAINTINGS, CHAPELLE SAINT-SEBASTIEN,
ROUBION *(Loïc-Jahan)*

The fact that Marseille had once been an ancient Greek colony might have predisposed Provence in favour of the purest of Mediterranean cultures. There are more Roman monuments in Provence than anywhere else in France. The province is equally rich in Romanesque art and a refined civilisation, such as that Petrarch knew at the Palace of the Popes, made Avignon the melting-pot for the arts of Italy and Flanders. The spirit of Provençal civilisation still lingers in the city of Aix, the capital, a city of fountains still haunted by the presence of Cézanne.

In Corsica, the tourist can still discover little churches and lonely cemeteries and convents that might have come straight from some Italian provinces — no less charming than the island's famous coves and creeks.

505

8

AIX-EN-PROVENCE *Bouches-du-Rhône.* K 18.

Famed for its fountains and plane-trees, its cultural traditions and its university, its noble dwellings and quiet squares, Aix-en-Provence is one of the most beautiful and artistically rich towns in France. Its history begins in the years 123-102 B.C. when it was known as Aquae Sextae and remains of the Roman town have been excavated on the plateau of Entremond, some 2 ¼ miles to the north-east of the present town. In the 15th century the " good king René" (Duke of Anjou, Count of Provence, King of Jerusalem and Sicily, etc.) held his court there, dying at the age of 72 in 1480. The cathedral Saint-Sauveur is partly Romanesque (1175), with a 14th-century tower and a Flamboyant façade dating from 1525. The Baptistery (5th c.) has been restored and its dome was added in the late 14th century. The small Romanesque cloister adjoins the church. In the nave, the great tryptych of the *Burning Bush* (height 10 feet), Nicolas Froment's masterpiece (1475); in the absidial chapel, the *Legend of Saint Mitre* of about the same date and probably by the same hand.

The church of Sainte-Marie-Madeleine was rebuilt in the early 18th-century and contains the famous tryptych which gave its name to its artist, the Master of the Annunciation of Aix, but only the centre panel, the *Annunciation*, is original (1443), the wings being copies with the originals in Brussels, Rotterdam and the Louvre.

12

The Musée Granet is rich in paintings, including a self-portrait by Rembrandt (c. 1660), Ingres' *Jupiter and Thetis* (famous for her neck) (1811), a series of French 18th-century portraits, a room devoted to Marius Granet (born in Aix 1815-1849) and his friends, some water-colours, and a charcoal self-portrait by Cézanne.

The Musée des Tapisseries in the Archbishop's palace (rebuilt in 1648 by cardinal Grimaldi) contains two precious series of Beauvais tapestries: six *Grotesques* after J.-L. Berain, and nine scenes from the *Story of Don Quixote* after Natoire (18th c.).

The rich Bibliothèque Méjanes is to be seen in the Town Hall (built between 1562 and 1658); in the hôtel Boyer d'Éguilles (late 17th c.), the Museum d'Histoire Naturelle; Musée du Vieil-Aix in the Hôtel d'Estienne de Saint-Jean with a façade attributed to Pierre Puget; the Post Office in the former Corn Market with a remarkable pediment by Chastel (1760); the Pavillon Vendôme (1665-1669) has a doorway flanked by fine caryatids.

13

Among the many fine fountains in the town are the Fontaine d'Albertas, in a square full of 17th-century *hôtels*, the Fontaine d'Argent, the Fontaine des Quatre-Dauphins, and the Fontaine Chaude in the Cours Mirabeau which runs with mineral water. Relics of the life of Cézanne who lived at Aix (1839-1906) are kept in his studio of the Chemin des Lauves which has been transformed into a museum. The Jas de Bouffan, where he lived, Gardanne, Le Tholonet, and the Montagne Sainte-Victoire have remained unchanged since his day.

I Façade of the cathedral Saint-Sauveur, 1525. 2 Leaf of the portal, a prophet, 16th c. 3 Cloister of the cathedral, 12th c. 4 Nicolas Froment (15th c.): centre panel of the tryptych of the Burning Bush, 1475. 5 Nicolas Froment (?): detail from the Miracle of Saint Mitre, Jacques de la Roque and his sons. 6 The Master of the Annunciation of Aix: The Annunciation, church of Sainte-Madeleine, 1443. 7 Pavillon Vendôme, 1669. 8 Pipe on the Fontaine d'Argent. 9 Fontaine des Quatre-Dauphins.

MUSÉE GRANET

10 Rembrandt (1606-1669): Self-portrait. II Ingres (1780-1867): Jupiter and Thetis, 1811. 12 Cézanne (1839-1906): Self-portrait. 13 Cézanne: The Montagne Sainte-Victoire, Tokyo, Ishibashi Coll.

MUSÉE DES TAPISSERIES

14 Bérain (17th c.): Musicians and female dancers.

MUSÉE ARCHÉOLOGIQUE

15 Trophy of four death-masks, Gallo-Roman period.

15

1

2

4

3

5

6

9

14

7

10

11

507

ANSOUIS 1

ANSOUIS *Vaucluse.* K 17.

Partly medieval, partly classical château five-storeys high, over-looking superb trimmed yew trees. Very fine façade with two rows of windows with interesting pediments. In the interior, original wood and plaster decorations of the 17th-18th centuries.

1 Façade and terrace, Renaissance period.

ANTIBES *Alpes-Maritimes.* L 17.

Famous for its Picasso museum. In 1946 after living in the château Grimaldi, Picasso made a gift of all the works he had created during his stay: paintings, ceramics, drawings, tapestries, sculptures and lithographs. The collection is unique of its kind and is the main attraction of the museum which also contains other modern works.

2 Pablo Picasso (born 1881): La Joie de vivre, Musée Grimaldi.
3 Nicolas de Staël (1914-1955): Le Fort d'Antibes, 1955, private coll. Paris.

ARLES *Bouches-du-Rhône.* J 17.

Every stone of this old city which was once a Roman port seems to radiate a serene, melancholy beauty. Arles later became the capital of the Camargue region but in the time of the Romans it was here that Julius Caesar had his galleys built. The Roman theatre could hold seven thousand spectators and its arena was the largest in the province (450 feet in diameter), with cells in its foundations to contain the wild beasts that were used for the circus games. The necropolis was the largest in Europe and extended alongside a shady road. The cathedral of Saint-Trophime was built in the Middle Ages over the relics of the first Provençal apostle, of the same name, and stood at the intersection of the roads to Rome and to Compostella. In the 17th century, Jules Hardouin-Mansart the architect of Versailles, directed the building of the Town Hall· which is famous for its flat vault, without supports. In more recent times, Frédéric Mistral drew attention to the original art of the province after it had shaken off its long-lasting classical traditions, by buying the hôtel de Castellane-Laval in 1907 with his Nobel Prize, and transforming it into a museum (Musée Arlaten) for collections of traditional Provençal art. To understand Arles the visitor should know something of its history. Roman, Romanesque and Provençal in turn, the beautiful city owes its unity to the quality of the light, the colouring and the charm of the landscape.

ARLES 11

ARLES 12

There is no more melancholy walk than that of the Aliscamps, in the necropolis between the ruined tombs to the little ruined church of Saint-Honorat. No cloister in France has more poetic charm than that of Saint-Trophime. The church has a porch in the form of a triumphal arch and is decorated like a reliquary with its magnificent sculptures of hieratic figures which might have come straight from some Roman sarcophagus. The museums of pagan and Christian art contain the finest examples of Hellenistic, Roman and early Christian sarcophagi with portraits of grave-faced personages with expressions, which may be found in Provence up to the present day and in Van Gogh's paintings when he used local models for his incomparable portraits of *La Berceuse* and the *Facteur Roulin*.

4 Aerial view of the theatre and arena. 5 The alley of the Aliscamps, and church of Saint-Honorat. 6 Portal of the cathedral Saint-Trophime, 12th c. 7 Jamb of the portal of Saint-Trophime, Saint John the Baptist and Saint Peter, 12th c. 8 Cloister of Saint-Trophime, 12th c. 9 Pagan sarcophagus, Gallo-Roman period, Musée Lapidaire Païen. 10 Sarcophagus of the Miracles of Christ, Musée Lapidaire d'Art Chrétien. 11 Simon Vouet (1590-1649): Self-portrait, Musée Réattu. 12 Vincent Van Gogh (1853-1890): Vincent's house, 1888, V.-W. Van Gogh Coll., Laren.

ANTIBES 3

ANTIBES 2

ARLES 4

ARLES 6

ARLES 5

ARLES 7

ARLES 8

ARLES 9

ARLES 10

509

L'ARMEILLIÈRE 1

L'ARMEILLIÈRE *Bouches-du-Rhône*. J 17.

Provençal classic architecture was directly inspired from Italy as may be seen by the façade of the château of L'Armeillière in the Camargue, built in the Henri IV style in 1606 by A.-P. de Sabatier. The windows are interestingly decorated in various styles.

1 Façade of the château, 1606.

AVIGNON 2

AVIGNON *Vaucluse*. J 17.

The part of Avignon which is enclosed behind the 14th-century ramparts has survived as an authentic medieval town, with its famous Palace of the Popes and its fine Renaissance houses of later date. The Pont Saint-Bénezet now only has four of its arches but is famous the world over as the *Pont d'Avignon* of the French popular song. A particularly striking view of the Palace may be obtained either from the Ile de Barthelasse or the walls of Villeneuve. It was the residence of the Popes from 1309 until 1379. The town of Avignon was acquired by the Counts of Provence in 1348 and was not really a French town until 1791. The imposing Palace still dominates the town although the level of the ground has risen around it and the moats have been filled in. The austere Palais Vieux was built during the pontificate of Benedict XII between 1334 and 1352 by the architects Pierre Poisson and Jean de Loubières; the Palais Nouveau, built under Clement VI from 1359 to 1370 is more richly decorated; in the interior, impressive rooms, some of the most beautiful frescoes in the Sienese-Gothic style of the 14th-century in the Tour de la Garde-Robe, showing the preeminence of the Avignon school of painters which lasted until the 15th century.

Of the churches, the cathedral Notre-Dame-des-Doms is the most important for its tunnel-vaulted nave (1180), its octagonal lantern crowning the cupola, and the Romanesque porch with triangular pediment and Corinthian columns, typical of the Provençal school of Romanesque architecture which was strongly influenced by Greco-Roman art. In the great Gothic church of Saint-Didier, the frescoes of a chapel which had been walled up are now restored. Paintings on three registers: a Descent from the Cross, the Annunciation, and a group of angels, attributed to Italian artists of the late 14th century working on the orders of Cardeni, a Florentine living in Avignon.

2 Pont Saint-Bénezet, 12th-13th c. 3 Cathedral of Notre-Dame-des-Doms, 1159. 4 The Palace of the Popes, 14th-15th c. 5 Courtyard of the Palace. 6 The Great Audience Chamber, 15th c. 7 Fresco in the Tour de la Garde-Robe: the Vivarium, 15th c. 8 Palais Cardinal, 17th c. 9 View of the Cardini chapel, in the church of Saint-Didier, frescoes of the 15th c. 10 Chapel of the Black Penitents, 17th c.

AVIGNON 10

510

AVIGNON 3

AVIGNON 4

AVIGNON 5

AVIGNON 6

AVIGNON 7

AVIGNON 8

AVIGNON 9

Also the chapel of Notre-Dame-du-Spasme, with Christ carrying the Cross by Francesco Laurana (1478), an Italian medallist and sculptor who had been called to the court of King René.

The Musée Calvet (a 18th-c. *hôtel*) contains an important series of panel paintings of the 15th-century school of Avignon as well as French works from the 17th century to the present day, and a fine room of ironwork. Lapidary museum with Greek and Gallo-Roman sculptures.

MUSÉE CALVET

1 Saint-Michael slaying the dragon, school of Avignon, 15th c. 2 The Fountain of Life, school of Avignon, 15th c. 3 David (1748-1835): The Death of Joseph Bara. 4 Chassériau (1819-1856): Sleeping Nymph. 5 Soutine (1894-1943): the Idiot.

MUSÉE LAPIDAIRE

6 So-called Vachères Warrior, Gallo-Roman period. 7 Celtic warrior.

BAR-SUR-LOUP *Alpes-Maritimes*. L 17.

In the church of this picturesque little Provençal village, two paintings on wood showing the two main tendencies in Renaissance *Niçois* painting: an Italianising style inspired by the Bréa, and the popular, realistic style of the fresco-painters.

8 Danse Macabre, *Niçois* school, 15th c.

LES BAUX 10

LES BAUX *Bouches-du-Rhône*. J 17.

The Wagnerian ruins of Les Baux are now filled with souvenir stalls during the day although they take on a tragic splendour at sunset. The village itself is rich in Renaissance houses, with monumental chimneys towering above the ruins and the main street leads up to the dismantled but still impressive fortress. From the 10th century up to the 14th the Lords of Baux had considerable power and rivalled the Counts of Provence. In the 16th century, Queen Jeanne, baroness of Les Baux, built a little oratory in a ravishing Renaissance style in the ravine of La Fontaine, where it may still be seen in good state. At the foot of the rocky spur of Les Baux, the dazzlingly white limestone quarries form a fascinating labyrinth.

9 General view of the village and fortress of Les Baux. 10 Queen Jeanne's Lodge, 1581. 11 The quarries.

AVIGNON 2

AVIGNON I

AVIGNON 3

AVIGNON 4

AVIGNON 7

AVIGNON 6

AVIGNON 5

LES BAUX II

LES BAUX 9

513

BEAULIEU-SUR-MER I

LA BRIGUE 4

BEAULIEU-SUR-MER *Alpes-Maritimes.* M 17.

The Villa Kerylos was built in a unique attempt to reconstruct an ancient Greek villa by the scholar Theodore Reinach who left it to the Institut de France at his death. The architecture, furnishings and decoration were reconstituted after the most reliable texts and examples of the period and are a perfect evocation of a long-vanished civilisation.

I Villa Kerylos, early 20th c.

BIOT *Alpes-Maritimes.* L 17.

Museum containing the works of Fernand Léger who lived and worked in Biot, containing some four hundred canvases, two hundred and fifty drawings and about a hundred ceramics, all by Léger.

2 Musée Fernand Léger. **3** Fernand Léger (1881-1955): The Builders.

LA BRIGUE *Alpes-Maritimes.* M 16.

When he left his native Piemonte the preacher-painter Jean Canavesi came to the little town of La Brigue above Nice and decorated several chapels with frescoes in a brutal, anecdotic and sometimes horrifying style, probably more convincing than that of his sermons.

4 Jean Canavesi (15th-16th c.): Hell, detail of the frescoes of the Passion in the chapel of Notre-Dame-des-Fontaines, 1492.

CAGNES *Alpes-Maritimes.* L 17.

When Auguste Renoir was almost crippled by rheumatism, but still went on painting despite his sufferings, he lived at Cagnes from 1903 until his death. In 1907 he built the house "les Collettes". The little town consists of a village perched up on the mountain side, and a port. The former fortress is now a museum of modern art.

5 Auguste Renoir (1841-1919): The Post Office at Cagnes, private coll. Paris.

CARPENTRAS *Vaucluse.* J 16.

Carpentras is one of the three towns of the Comtat (County) of Venaissin (the other two being Cavaillon and l'Isle-sur-Sorgue) where the Jewish community enjoyed a privileged status under the protection of the Popes of Avignon, from the Middle Ages until the Revolution. The synagogue was reconstructed in 1743 but remains as a precious witness to the town's Hebrew cult. Fine classical façade of the Hôtel-Dieu (inside, a beautiful pharmacy); church of Saint-Siffrein with nave in pure southern Gothic style although it was the work of a Breton architect, Colin Thomas de Dinan, with Romanesque elements such as the famous frieze of the nave decorated with motifs of flowers and garlands held by winged geniuses in an imitation of a ancient Roman motif. Remains of a Roman triumphal arch (in the courtyard of the former Bishop's palace) with relief of Gaulish warriors wearing animal skins and chained to a tree. In the museum, a very beautiful French primitive painting of the 15th century: *The Encounter at the Golden Gate* or *Saint Anne and Saint Joachim*.

6 Remains of a Roman triumphal arch, in the courtyard of the former bishops' palace, Gallo-Roman period. **7** Nave of the cathedral of Saint-Siffrein, 15th c. **8** Façade of the Hôtel-Dieu, by d'Allemand, 1760. **9** Interior of the synagogue, 18th c. **10** Encounter at the Golden Gate, French school, 15th c. **11** Ex-voto, 18th c., Musée Duplessis.

BIOT 3

BIOT 2

CARPENTRAS 6

CAGNES 5

CARPENTRAS 9

CARPENTRAS 7

CARPENTRAS 8

CARPENTRAS 10

CARPENTRAS 11

CAVAILLON *Vaucluse*. J 17.

Busy little market town with Romanesque cathedral of Saint-Veran. Curious five-sided apse. Also in the town, a very beautiful synagogue with interior decorated in stucco, wrought iron and woodwork in the finest and most exuberant 18th-century Italian style.

1 Interior of the synagogue, 1774.

DIGNE *Basses-Alpes*. L 16.

The architecture of the single nave cathedral is of a total simplicity for its thick ceiling-beams and semi-circular windows are its only decoration. Lombard style portal flanked by columnar statues of two lions, symbols of the devil who menaced the faithful at the church door — an ancient theme which was taken over by local folklore.

2 Main portal of the cathedral Notre-Dame-du-Bourg, 13th c.

FONTVIEILLE *Bouches-du-Rhône*. J 17.

It was in the windmill overlooking the village that Alphonse Daudet pretended he had written his *Lettres de mon moulin*. He had in reality lived in the château of Ambray and written the book in Paris but any pretext is good for a tourist attraction and the mill is now a museum.

3 Daudet's windmill.

FONTVIEILLE 3

FRÉJUS *Var*. L 18.

Fréjus was a very important Roman naval base and has a remarkable number of monuments to offer the visitor, including the amphitheatre, built at the time of Caesar — the oldest in France. The theatre with its wooden tiers has been largely used as a quarry. Cathedral with pretty 13th-century tower, and cloister with colonnettes of marble on two storeys, the first with pointed arches, the second with semicircular arches and with a vault painted in the 14th-century. The choir-stalls date from 1441; doors of the cathedral of 1550. The cupola of the baptistery is a pure relic of the 5th century, and is the town's main archaeological curiosity.

4 The arena, Gallo-Roman period. 5 The cloister, 13th c.

GANAGOBIE (at Peyruis) *Basses-Alpes*. K 16.

Ancient Benedictine priory. The scalloped decoration of the Romanesque portal shows direct Mozarabic influences. The 12th-century mosaics are now being restored. Cloister with large flattened arches and cylindrically vaulted galleries; columns with foliated capitals — a rarity in Provence.

6 Portal of the priory church, 12th c. 7 Cloister, 12th c.

GORDES *Vaucluse*. K 17.

The old town of Gordes and the surrounding region was discovered by the artist André Lhote between the wars and thanks to him and his friends the many fine old houses have been saved from ruin and tastefully restored. The Town Hall is a former Renaissance château of great impressiveness, built by Bertrand de Simiane in 1525. The surrounding countryside is punctuated by "bories" — small stone shelters of pyramidal form.

8 View of Gordes. 9 A "borie".

CAVAILLON 1

DIGNE 2

FRÉJUS 4

FRÉJUS 5

GANAGOBIE 7

GORDES 8

GANAGOBIE 6

GORDES 9

517

GRASSE 1

GRASSE *Alpes-Maritimes*. L 17.

A museum devoted to Fragonard (born in Grasse in 1732) and Provençal art has been installed in a beautiful 18th-century dwelling, the hôtel de Cabris or Trianon de Grasse, built for Mirabeau's daughter. Some dozen paintings by Fragonard may be seen in their appropriate setting as well as various drawings and relics. The Niçois painter Louis Bréa is well represented by a retable in the south aisle of the cathedral which is an early Gothic structure (late 12th c.) that was completed in the 18th century.

1 Jean-Honoré Fragonard (1732-1806): Self-portrait, c. 1750.
2 Louis Bréa (late 15th c.): altar of Saint Honorat.

IF (Château d') *Bouches-du-Rhône*. K 18.

IF 3

The rocky isle was fortified in the 15th century to serve as a forward defence for the port of Marseilles and has also been used as a state-prison. It has become famous to millions of readers of Alexandre Dumas' *Count of Monte-Cristo*.

3 Aerial view of the island and the castle.

L'ISLE-SUR-SORGUE *Vaucluse*. J 17.

The talent and the innate good taste of the inhabitants of the Venaissin county is well evident in the very beautiful church which was mostly built between 1650 and 1672 in a Gothic style by La Valfenière. Fine pointed vaults, lavish decoration: woodwork, marble, stucco, paintings and statues worthy of Puget all in the best Baroque tradition.

4 Nave of the church, 17th c. 5 Detail of the decoration, 17th c.

LIEUCHE *Alpes-Maritimes*. L 17.

From Toulon to the Italian frontier many chapels contain retables attributed to one member or another of the Bréa family. They are all characterised by a similar serenity and gravity — one might almost say monotony — of style, but despite their static and conventional composition, they are often moving and the technique is excellent.

6 Altar of the Annunciation, attributed to Louis Bréa, 1499.

LUCÉRAM *Alpes-Maritimes*. M 17.

During the Renaissance period the County of Nice decorated all its chapels with frescoes (*see* Roubion colour plate) and retables executed by the painters of the school of the Bréas, or else by more modest fresco-painters whose style may be sometimes odd or even debatable but always spontaneous. Lucéram possesses two such chapels with an oustanding choice of retables by the Bréas and 15th-century frescoes in the Bon-Cœur chapel, a mile from the little town. The 13th-century walls still survive.

7 Louis Bréa (late 15th c.): Retable in the chapel of Sainte-Marguerite, 1500. 8 The Nativity, fresco in the chapel Notre-Dame-du-Bon-Cœur, 15th c.

GRASSE 2

L'ISLE-SUR-SORGUE 4

LIEUCHE 6

L'ISLE-SUR-SORGUE 5

LUCÉRAM 7

LUCÉRAM 8

MARSEILLE *Bouches-du-Rhône.* K 18.

Marseille is one of the liveliest sea-ports in the world but it has no pretensions to being an art-city. Its main buildings and monuments are: the fortified church of Saint-Victor with crenellated towers, the former cathedral of La Major, a Romanesque building in pink stone; the hôtel de Cabre, 1535; the Town Hall by Gaspard Puget, brother of the Marseillais Pierre Puget, 1673; the pretty, still inhabited ruins of the chapel of La Vieille-Charité, also by Puget (elegant apse). Recent excavations in the Old Port have brought to light vestiges of the original city of Massilia, founded by the Phoenicians in 600 B.C. The 19th century was less discreet and has left the Roman-Byzantine style basilica of Notre-Dame-de-la-Garde, by Esperandieu, as a symbol of the port's colourful life. The 20th century has given Marseille Le Corbusier's famous Radiant City.

Marseille has eight museums with collections ranging from antique sculpture (Château Borely) to painting (Musée des Beaux-Arts) and there are also museums of naval history, Provençal folk-lore and the decorative arts.

Daumier and Monticelli were two of the city's most famous sons.

MARTIGUES 9

1 Basilica of Saint-Victor, 11th-12th c. 2 Desnoyer (born 1894): the transporting bridge at Marseille, Musée d'Art Moderne, Paris. 3 The Radiant City, by Le Corbusier, 1952. 4 The Hermes of Roquepertuse, Gallo-Roman period, archaeological museum. 5 Puvis de Chavannes (1824-1898): Massilia, fresco in the Town Hall.

MUSÉE DES BEAUX-ARTS

6 Françoise Duparc (1726-1778): The Milk-maid. 7 Daumier (born at Marseille, 1808-1879): Jean Harlé the Elder. 8 Monticelli (born at Marseille, 1824-1886): Large scene with figures, Musée Cantini.

MÉNERBES 10

MARTIGUES *Bouches-du-Rhône.* J 18.

Small and picturesque village that attracted many artists, particularly Ziem (a small museum has been devoted to his work). The chapel of the Annunciade is an excellent example of the Baroque style.

9 Interior of the chapel of the Annunciade, 17th c.

MÉNERBES *Vaucluse.* J 17.

MENTON 11

Ménerbes faces Gordes and Oppède and is similar in appearance to a shipwrecked boat, huddled behind its walls, the prow being the Castelet, a former fortress, where the painter Nicolas de Staël lived. In the 14th-century church a fine retable. In the streets, jutting balconies and mullioned windows opening into fine vaulted rooms in the old houses.

10 View of the village.

MENTON *Alpes-Maritimes.* M 17.

A music festival is held every year in front of the church of Saint-Michel which might be a pure Sicilian church for it is as Italian as it is Baroque. The church faces a pretty parvis decorated with patterns of black and white pebbles.

11 Parvis of the church of Saint-Michel.

MARSEILLE 1

MARSEILLE 5

MARSEILLE 2

MARSEILLE 4

MARSEILLE 3

MARSEILLE 7

MARSEILLE 8

MARSEILLE 6

MONTMAJOUR *Bouches-du-Rhône.* J 17.

The abbey was founded in the 10th century and the buildings that have survived date from different periods. The oldest in date is the pre-Romanesque chapel of Saint-Peter with a single nave, and a completely vaulted horse-shoe apse. From the second period, the 12th century, date the abbey church and the Sainte-Croix chapel. The church is built over a crypt in the rocky, irregular soil. The ground plan of the chapel is trefoil like that of the baptistery of Vénasque (q.v.) and the chapel is crowned by a lantern tower. The cloister was begun in the same period but has been altered on various occasions.

Typically Provençal flattened arches supported by thick pillars; some 12th-century capitals have survived in the northern gallery. The keep or tower of the abbey served as a defence for the abbey since the 14th century.

1 Keep and church, 12th and 14th c. 2 Nave of the chapel of Saint-Pierre, 10th c. 3 Sainte-Croix chapel, 12th c. 4 Gallery of the cloister, 12th c., altered.

MOUSTIERS-SAINTE-MARIE 5

MOUSTIERS-SAINTE-MARIE *Basses-Alpes.* K 17.

A picturesque road winds through gorges (shut, by a legendary chain) to the little town of Moustiers built in glowing, golden stone. In the centre, church of a former Romanesque monastery. The town was famous in the 17th and 18th centuries for its important faïence manufacture. Pretty chapel of Notre-Dame-de-Beauvoir overlooking the town.

5 Tower of the church, 12th c.

NICE *Alpes-Maritimes.* M 17.

The enormous town of Nice was first famous in about 1830 when it became popular with the English as a sea-side resort, and contains little of artistic interest. Its only artistic importance was due to the Bréas family who were born in Nice in the 15th and 16th centuries. They were Italianising painters who left many fine retables with gold and landscape backgrounds in chapels throughout the region. In the church in the Cimiez quarter, an early work by the eldest of the Bréas.

6 Louis Bréa (late 15th c.): Pietà, 1475, church of Cimiez. 7 Henri Matisse (1869-1954): Still-life with pomegranates, Musée Masséna.

NOTRE-DAME D'AUBUNE (at Beaumes-de-Venise) *Vaucluse.* J 16.

Pretty church with a square tower like that of Saint-Trophime at Arles (q.v.), with high Romanesque bays separated by fluted pilasters. It is one of many examples of Provençal Romanesque art influenced by Roman art.

8 Tower and apse of the chapel, 12th c.

NOTRE-DAME-DE-LA-MENOUR *Alpes-Maritimes.* M 17.

In the beautiful and somewhat severe site of the Provençal Alps, an Italianate chapel with a flat façade surmounted by a pediment, at the top of a stair-way lined by a low wall, like a jewel lost in the wilderness.

9 The chapel, 17th c.

MONTMAJOUR 1

MONTMAJOUR 2

MONTMAJOUR 3

MONTMAJOUR 4

NICE 7

NICE 6

N.-D.-DE-LA-MENOUR 9

N.-D.-D'AUBUNE 8

ORANGE *Vaucluse.* J. 16.

Two exceptional monuments have survived to attest to the former grandeur of the Roman city of Orange: the triumphal arch with three bays flanked by Corinthian columns — the finest arch built to commemorate the foundation of a city in the whole of France, and the theatre, whose semi-circular tiers could hold 40,000 spectators. The outer wall was built in the time of Hadrian, is 350 feet long, and 15 feet thick, and is built of stone blocks without any mortar being used in the construction.

1 The theatre, late 1st c. B.C. 2 The arch of triumph, 49 B.C.

PEILLON *Alpes-Maritimes.* M 17.

The paintings in the chapel of this curious "eagle's nest" village have been recent identified and are now attributed to Jean Canavesi, the preacher and fresco-painter from La Brigue.

3 Interior of the chapel of the White Penitents. 4 Jean Canavesi: detail of the frescoes, the Scourging of Christ, late 15th c.

PERNES-LES-FONTAINES *Vaucluse.* J 17.

Pernes was the former capital of the Venaissin County and owes its nick-name to the number and variety of its noisy fountains. But the main interest of the town (apart from the machicolated Porte de Villeneuve, 1550) lies in the frescoes in the Tour Ferrande: they are late 13th-century and the oldest to have survived in Provence. They are inspired by miniature paintings of the time of Saint-Louis and represent scenes of fighting horsemen, Pope Clement IV and Charles I of Anjou.

5 Fountain, 18th c. 6-7 Frescoes in the Tour Ferrande, late 13th c.

PONT-FLAVIEN 9

PEYROLLES *Bouches-du-Rhône.* K 17.

Like that of Planès, the little chapel Saint-Sépulcre is built on a trefoil plan and is an example of archaic Romanesque style surviving in the 14th century.

8 Saint-Sépulcre chapel, 14th c.

PONT-FLAVIEN (at Saint-Chamas) *Bouches-du-Rhône.* J 18.

Before building the Aurelian Way over the river Touloubre, the Romans first built an audacious bridge with a single arch, decorated at each end by a portico with fluted pilasters.

9 Pont Flavien, 1st c. A.D.

PONT-JULIEN (at Bonnieux) *Vaucluse.* K 17.

The Domitian Way crossed the torrent of the Coulon over a hump-backed bridge 220 feet long, with arches pierced by holes to allow the water to flow through them.

10 Pont Julien, 1st c. A.D.

PONT-JULIEN 10

SAINT-GABRIEL (near Tarascon) *Bouches-du-Rhône.* J 17.

The decorative audacity of the façade of the beautiful chapel is Romanesque in its inspiration, but tempered by the charm of the Provençal style. The tympana are purely Romanesque and even archaic in style, and represent Daniel in the lion's den, the Annunciation, the Visitation, etc.

11 Façade of the chapel of Saint-Gabriel, 12th c.

PEILLON 3

ORANGE 2

ORANGE 1

PEILLON 4

PERNES-LES-FONTAINES 7

PERNES-LES-FONTAINES 6

PEYROLLES 8

ST-GABRIEL 11

PERNES-LES-FONTAINES 5

525

ST-JEAN-CAP-FERRAT 3

ST-PAUL-DE-VENCE 11

SAINT-PAUL-DE-VENCE 12

SAINT-HONORAT (Lerins islands) *Alpes-Maritimes*. L 18.

Despite ruthless, successive restorations, the keep of the isle of Saint-Honorat still survives as a witness to the days when monks took refuge in it from pirates. It was built in the 11th century and is was crowned by machicolation in the 14th century. The conventual buildings include a charming little Gothic cloister with hexagonal marble pillars. The much restored chapel of the Trinity was built on a trefoil plan in the Carolingian period according to some rather optimistic authorities.

1 The keep, 11th-14th c., restored. **2** Apse of the chapel of La Sainte-Trinité, 9th c.

SAINT-JEAN-CAP-FERRAT *Alpes-Maritimes*. K 18.

The villa Ile-de-France was a former private residence of a rich art collector and is now open to the public. Paintings ranging from the Gothic period to the Impressionists, objects, furniture all bear witness to a refined and eclectic taste.

3 Patio of the villa "Ile-de-France": late 19th c., furnishings.

SAINT-JEAN-DE-GARGUIER *Bouches-du-Rhône*. K 18.

Numerous chapels and a few museums in the region contain ex-votos, examples of a popular, naive, and spontaneous art intended to show thanks for divine favours received. For the specialist, the main collections are to be found in the museums of Carpentras and Vieux-Martigues, the churches of Notre-Dame-de-la-Garde and Saint-Marcel at Marseille, the church of Saintes-Maries-de-la-Mer and Notre-Dame-de-Laghet.

4-5-6 Ex-votos in the chapel of the château, 17th c.

SAINT-MARTIN-D'ENTRAUNES *Alpes-Maritimes*. L 16.

The fine retable of the church is the work of the nephew of Louis Bréa, the Niçois painter, and represents the Madonna of the Rosary. The style is more mannered and graceful than that of his uncle, and the composition is interesting.

7 François Bréa (16th c.): Retable of the Rosary, 1555.

SAINT-MAXIMIN-LA-SAINTE-BAUME *Var*. K 18.

The enormous basilica of Sainte-Madeleine comes as a surprise, when seen towering over the flat surrounding landscape, but its size was due to the number of pilgrims who came to worship by the relics of the saint. The relics were later stolen by Vézelay which also acquired the basilica's pilgrims. It was built in a simple Gothic style. The interior is almost entirely 17th-century. Rich and varied decoration: 100 feet-high nave, choir-screen in carved wood, fine main altar, organ-casing, etc. Most interesting of all, a magnificent retable by a Venetian of Flemish descent.

8 The basilica of Sainte-Madeleine, 13th-15th c. **9** Retable of the Passion of Christ, by François Ronzen, 16th c.

SAINT-PAUL-DE-VENCE *Alpes-Maritimes*. L 17.

We should forget the showy celebrity of the site to admire the beautiful 16th-century walls overlooking the fields of orange trees, and the Gothic church with its rich collection of 16th and 17th-century paintings (in the sacristy, several pieces of 14th and 15th c. gold-and-silver-work). Most interesting of all, is the recent Marguerite and Aimé Maeght Foundation perched up on a hill-side facing Saint-Paul. The architect José Luis Sert used pink-brown brick, the stone of the hill-side and reinforced concrete for the two "impluvium" in the form of raised wings which have become the symbol for the Foundation. It is a museum, exhibition gallery, cultural centre and hostel for artists, including a chapel, sited in the middle of a beautiful park. Works by many of the finest artists of the Maeght gallery in Paris are exhibited: Braque, Giacometti, Chagall, Mirò, Tal Coat, Ubac and Kandinsky, etc. This veritable museum of the 20th century is both a human and a scientific conception of outstanding interest.

10 The fountain, 1850. **11** The Maeght Foundation, 1964. **12** Giacometti room.

ST-HONORAT 2

ST-HONORAT I

ST-JEAN-DE-GARGUIER 4

ST-JEAN-DE-GARGUIER 5

ST-JEAN-DE-GARGUIER 6

ST-PAUL-DE-VENCE 10

ST-MARTIN-D'ENTRAUNES 7

ST-MAXIMIN-LA-STE-BAUME 9

ST-MAXIMIN-LA-STE-BAUME 8

527

SAINT-RÉMY-DE-PROVENCE *Bouches-du-Rhône.* J 17.

The elegance of ancient Attica and all the charm of the Aegean is to be found among the remains at Glanum — the most important archaeological site in France. It was a Gallo-Grecian city founded in the 2nd century B.C., and it was built with a skill and grace that owed nothing to Gaul except its stone. The remaining monuments are in a rather decadent Hellenistic style. The triumphal arch has one bay flanked by Corinthian columns and bas-reliefs (Gaulish prisoners in chains) and is carved with great refinement. The elegant mausoleum of the Giulii has survived intact and is a cenotaph that was raised in honour of Augustus' grandsons. The base is decorated with lively bas-reliefs depicting warlike scenes from the Trojan legend and mythology. The house of the Antes has kept its impluvium and colonnaded peristyle and is similar to any Pompeian or Delian villa (fine mosaics). Also to be visited are the hôtel Mistral de Mondragon, a fine Renaissance period dwelling, in Saint-Rémy itself, and the cloister of the hospital Saint-Paul-de-Mausole where Van Gogh stayed in 1889-1890.

ST-RÉMY-DE-PROVENCE 5

1 Triumphal arch and mausoleum of the Giulii, 1st c. B.C., Glanum. 2 Bas-relief on the base of the mausoleum, 1st c. B.C. 3 House of the Antes, Hellenistic period 1st c. B.C. 4 Cloister of Saint-Paul-de-Mausole, 12th c. 5 Vincent Van Gogh (1853-1890): the Hospital fountain, 1889, encre-de-Chine drawing, V.-W. Van Gogh coll., Laren.

ST-TROPEZ 6

SAINT-TROPEZ *Var.* L 18.

From Easter to October the visitor may be sure of finding both silence and solitude inside the Chapelle de l'Annonciade — now a museum but the only place left where the art-lover can escape the holiday crowds. For Saint-Tropez was first discovered as a resort before the last war by Colette, Dunoyer de Segonzac, Signac and others, and then in recent years by film-stars, gossip-writers and the crowds at large. The former port was rebuilt exactly as it had once been but its churches, narrow winding streets, and green stone window-frames have survived the years, and the little town still has a quiet charm early in the morning. For the serious-minded tourist the museum will be the main attraction with its fine collection of important modern French works, offered by a discriminating collector.

6 Rue Gambetta, doorway 17th c.

MUSÉE DE L'ANNONCIADE *(Gramont Coll.)*

7 Vuillard (1868-1940): Under the lamp. 8 Bonnard (1867-1947): The Pink road. 9 Matisse (1869-1954): the Gypsy. 10 Derain (1880-1954): Sunlight effects on the sea. 11 Braque (1882-1963): View of l'Estaque.

LES STES-MARIES-DE-LA-MER 12

LES SAINTES-MARIES-DE-LA-MER *Bouches-du-Rhône.* J 18.

As blind as Albi cathedral and the church at Rudelle, the Romanesque church was fortified in the 13th century. It has become a symbol for the Gypsies and their traditions and contains the remains of their saints, Marie Jacobe, Salome, and Sara. Numerous ex-votos.

12 Apse of the fortified church, 13th-15th c.

ST-RÉMY-DE-PROVENCE 1

ST-RÉMY-DE-PROVENCE 2

ST-RÉMY-DE-PROVENCE 4

ST-RÉMY-DE-PROVENCE 3

ST-TROPEZ 7

ST-TROPEZ 10

ST-TROPEZ 9

ST-TROPEZ 8

ST-TROPEZ 11

SALON-DE-PROVENCE *Bouches-du-Rhône.* J 17.

Salon was the birthplace of Nostradamus and is now an important industrial centre and the site of a flying school. Overlooking the old town, the château of the archbishops of Arles. The church of Saint-Laurent is a good example of the Provençal Gothic style.

1 The Château de l'Emperi, 13th and 15th c.

SÉNANQUE *Vaucluse.* K 17.

Sénanque is one of the three Cistercian abbeys still active in Provence and lies at the bottom of a scented, sun-scorched valley on a bed of rock. Apart from the modern monastery buildings, a very beautiful old dormitory with a pointed barrel vault, and a church with an austerely beautiful Cistercian nave and cloister have survived.

2 Nave of the abbey church, 12th c. **3** The scriptorium, 12th c.

SILVACANE (at La Roque-d'Anthéron) *Vaucluse.* K 17.

In this beautiful site a Cistercian monastery was founded in the 11th century. Large and powerful nave built in plain but beautiful stone without the slightest hint of any superfluous decoration that might distract from meditation and prayer.

4 Nave and aisle of the abbey church, 12th c., restored.

TARASCON *Bouches-du-Rhône.* J 17.

Tarascon is separated from Beaucaire by the rapid waters of the Rhône and was one of the residences of King René who built the fortress that has still survived intact. Its four towers are set at right angles and rise 125 feet high. It is one of the most beautiful examples of a medieval castle in France.

5 King René's château.

LE THORONET *Var.* L 18.

TOULON 10

The purest Cistercian abbey in Provence. It stands calm and serene in a lovely site in a shady valley far from the noise and bustle of the red bauxite quarries of the province. Its great church is bare of all decoration and inexorably focuses attention on the main altar. On the north side a few steps lead to the dormitory lit by arched window-lights opening onto the roof of the cloister. The cloister has several levels and is of an astonishing harmony of design. Two galleries are sloping, the other two are flat, lit alternately by semi-circular twin bays surmounted by oculi as at Fontfroide (q.v.). At one end of the cloister, the sole surviving medieval monks' "lavabo" in France; it has kept its covering of stone tiles, which once covered all the abbey buildings. The whole cloister is a pure masterpiece: the visitor should follow the footsteps of the monks along its galleries and look out to see the pointed spire of the church or else simply sit on one of the narrow benches and give himself up to meditation. It is a place to linger in.

6 Abbey church, 12th c. **7** Monks' "lavabo" 12th c. **8** Gallery of the cloister, 12th c. **9** Chapter house, 12th c.

TOULON *Var.* K 18.

Apart from the beauty of the modern port with its great battleships and its swarming activity, Toulon can show the visitor a remarkable work by Pierre Puget: the two caryatids symbolising Strength and Weariness supporting the balcony of the Town Hall.

10 Pierre Puget (1622-1694): caryatids of the Town Hall, 1653.

SALON-DE-PROVENCE 1

SÉNANQUE 2

SÉNANQUE 3

SILVACANE 4

TARASCON 5

LE THORONET 6

LE THORONET 9

LE THORONET 7

LE THORONET 8

531

LA TURBIE I

LA TURBIE *Alpes-Maritimes.* M 17.

Roman monument commemorating a victory over the Ligurians and raised to the glory of Augustus. Its stonework has been split in two but it is still as majestic as ever.

1 Augustus' trophy, 5 B.C.

UTELLE *Alpes-Maritimes.* L 17.

The anonymous retable in the north aisle of the church of Saint-Véran is the most beautiful in the county of Nice and has for subject an Annunciation of moving simplicity. It has a naively-painted landscape for background instead of the customary gilt ground.

2 Retable of the Annunciation, church of Saint-Véran, 16th c.

VAISON-LA-ROMAINE *Vaucluse.* J 16.

Despite its name, Vaison-la-Romaine is the least important Roman city in France to-day. Excavations have revealed typical dwellings of the time but not a single masterpiece. The theatre was used as a quarry for too long, and the ruins are not picturesque enough to merit much attention. But the partly Merovingian cathedral has a fine antique nave. Rather too carefully restored cloister. Another historical curiosity is the chapel of Saint-Quenin (12th c.) with triangular apse and Corinthian decoration.

3 Portico of Pompey, Gallo-Roman period. **4** Cloister of the cathedral, 13th c.

VALLAURIS *Alpes-Maritimes.* L 17.

Picasso made the town's fortune by associating his name with it, stimulating its ceramic manufacture and, especially, by decorating its chapel with his beautiful fresco: *War and Peace.*

5 Pablo Picasso (born 1881): ceramic dish. **6** Picasso: man with a sheep, bronze. **7** Picasso: War and Peace, fresco in the chapel of the château, 1959.

VALRÉAS 8

VALRÉAS *Vaucluse.* J 16.

Somewhat composite-style church. Only the Romanesque south portal is interesting. 18th-century Town Hall with a fine façade facing the town square and superb plane-trees along the line of the former ramparts.

8 South portal of the church, 12th c.

VÉNASQUE *Vaucluse.* J 17.

The Merovingian period baptistery is a curious building built on a radiating ground-plan with four minor apses with semi-dome vaulting. The piers of the vaults spring from columns with archaic-styled capitals.

9 Minor apse of the baptistery, 7th c.

VENCE *Alpes-Maritimes.* L 17.

The Dominican chapel was built in 1950 and attracted many modern art-lovers. The whole of its decoration (walls covered with painted ceramic tiles), stained-glass windows and ornaments are the work of Henri Matisse. In the old town, pretty fountain and Gothic cathedral (choir-stalls by Jacques Bellot, 1459).

10 Henri Matisse (1869-1954): Saint-Dominique, ceramic tiles, 6 feet high, chapel of the Rosary. **11** Interior of the chapel.

VAISON-LA-ROMAINE 4

VAISON-LA-ROMAINE 3

UTELLE 2

VALLAURIS 7

VALLAURIS 6

VALLAURIS 5

VÉNASQUE 9

VENCE 10

VENCE 11

533

AJACCIO N 21.

The island of Corsica would appear even more Italian were it not the birth-place of Napoleon (August 15). The soberly furnished Bonaparte family house is still filled with historical memories. The Palais Fesch, the former dwelling of a cardinal — Napoleon's uncle — is now a fine museum of Italian painting. Very beautiful courtyard.

1 Napoleon's birthplace, lithograph, Bibliothèque Nationale, Paris. 2 Cosimo Tura (1429-1495): Virgin and Child, Musée Fesch.

BONIFACIO N 22.

The little town of Bonifacio rises high above its sheltered port on towering, impregnable cliffs. Church of Sainte-Marie-Majeure in the Geonoan style with a fine 13th-century tower. The contemporary church of Saint-Dominique was built by the Templars.

3 The fortress of Bonifacio.

LA CANONICA (near Casamozza) O 20.

The church is the prototype and masterpiece of several Romanesque churches in the style of Pisa which were built on the island in the early 12th century.

4 Apse of the church, 1119.

CARGESE N 21.

A Greek speaking town. A Greek colony first came to the town in 1676 and in 1774 it became a definitively Greek settlement.

5 Apse and tower of the Greek church, facing the Roman catholic church.

LA PORTA-D'AMPUGNANI O 20.

Pretty Italian Baroque church; standing beside it, a campanile somewhat excessively decorated with pilasters and volutes.

6 The church, 17th c.

SAN MICHELE-DE-MURATO O 20.

Romanesque church, rather Lombard in style with its bicolour brickwork and arcading.
It is one of the many delightful surprises awaiting the visitor to Corsica.

7 Apse of the church, 12th c.

SAINTE-CHRISTINE (near Crevione) N 22.

The little chapel is whitewashed every year and has the peculiarity of being built with a twin apse decorated with mural paintings.

8 Apse of the chapel, 15th c.

SAINTE-LUCIE-DE-TALLANO O 20.

In the convent church, two superb late 15th-century Italian retables by the Master of Castelsardo.

9 Conventual building with narrow pilasters.

AJACCIO I

AJACCIO 2

LA CANONICA 4

SAN MICHELE-DE-MURATO 7

CARGÈSE 5

LA PORTA-D'AMPUGNANI 6

STE-CHRISTINE 8

535

ANALYTICAL INDEX

GOTHIC ART (12th-15th c.)

CLASSICAL ART (16th-18th c.)

MODERN ART (19th-20th c.)

INDEX OF NAMES

INDEX OF PLACE NAMES

SOURCES OF ILLUSTRATIONS

Photographs not listed are by courtesy of JEAN ROUBIER

SOURCES OF ILLUSTRATIONS

Photographs not listed are by courtesy of JEAN ROUBIER

COMPOSITION, PHOTOGRAVURE AND OFFSET
BY IMPRIMERIE DÉCHAUX
COLOUR PLATES PRINTED BY LES IMPRIMERIES DE BOBIGNY
FROM BLOCKS MADE BY BUSSIÈRE ARTS GRAPHIQUES
PAPER PRINTOPAAK VAN GELDER
BINDING BY DHUIÈGE